Encyclopaedia of Indian Theatre - 2

MAJOR SANSKRIT DRAMATISTS

Encyclopaedia of Indian Theatre - Series

1. Bhasa

2. Major Sanskrit Dramatists

3. Kalidasa (Press)

Encyclopaedia of Indian Theatre - 2

MAJOR SANSKRIT DRAMATISTS

Biswajit Sinha

Raj Publications
Delhi - 110009 (INDIA)

2011

ISBN 81-86208-18-6 (Series)
ISBN 81-86208-21-6

Published by : Mrs. Poonam Goel
Raj Publications
R-115/2, Model Town - III,
Delhi - 110009
Tel. : 7466486
E-mail : rajpub@now-india.net.in

Laser Typesetting by : Aarati Computers, Delhi-110 009

Printed at : Chawla Offset Printers, Delhi-110 052

PRINTED IN INDIA

In

Fond Memory of My Sister
Deepali Bose

Contents

Preface

Of late, India's Kutiyattam Sanskrit theatre, the only surviving tradition has been recognised by the UNESCO as one of the masterpieces of the oral and intangible heritage of humanity". This proclamation is the first of its kind. UNESCO has defined the Oral and intangible heritage as "The totality of tradition—based creations of a cultural community, expressed by a group of individuals and recognized as reflecting the expectations of a community in so far as they reflect its cultural and social identity; its standards and values are transmitted orally, by imitation or by other means. Its form are, among others, language, literature, music, dance, games, mythology, rituals, customs,handicrafts, architecture and other arts. In addition to these examples, account will also be taken of traditional forms of communication and information".

Through this proclamation, UNESCO has hoped that it would raise awareness about the importance of safeguarding intangible heritage.

As Indian, we should be proud that this land had once witnessed the prolificacy of a prolong old classical theatrical tradition, dictated for thousand years by a single manual called '*Natyasastra*'. In those days dramatic arts reached its heights for the delineation of wide varieties of characters, incidents and finer human emotions.

Ours is a multilingual country having different ethnic groups with their own myriad dialects, rituals, customs, habits, art forms and traditions. But no one takes a serious count of those oral traditions, valuable vestiges of our unique folk forms and styles, supported by the people that took shape under different social, political, religious and cultural millieu. Some unveiled, some still hidden and many lost.

Alongwith *natyadharmi* and *lokdharmi*, started the journey in the modern phase with the influx and assimilation of western ideas and styles. Indian dramatists doing all sorts of experimentations and creative excercises, ever since the advent of new technologies and multimedia. The era of fusion is trying to set new trends, where drama meets music, dance, painting, poetry and other idioms. A bird's eye view of the India's theatrical practices or a condensed history is easy to present. But for an exhaustive documentation of a tradition that dates back to the days of 'Veda', becomes an up hill task. But one ought to safeguard, restore, revive, document and disseminate this precious treatrical heritage. Today there is a real need for an encyclopaedia or similar reference tool to understand Indian Theatre in its depth and breadth. Though eventful, but in the last fifty years, no Akademies, Cultural organisations, or Drama Schools have given any serious considerations in this direction.

The corpus is huge and to prepare a single reference volume in the realm exhaustively and meticulously is impossible especially when the work is to be undertaken single- handedly and nor the product of any collaborative work.

Realizing the magnitude of the efforts and materials that involve, instead of bringing out an all encompassing volume, under the series '*Encyclopaedia of Indian Theatre*' came out the first volume on '*Bhasa*' — the first regular dramatist of ancient Indian. Thus, all the initial volumes (each an independent one) are biographical in nature.

Series Two deals with some great masters of Sanskrit drama like Asvaghosa, Bhatta-narayana, Bhavabhuti, Bodhayana, Dhananjaya, Harshadeva, Jayadeva, Krishna Misra, Murari, Rupa Goswami, Saktibhadra, Sudraka and Visakhadatta.

In the present volume, attempts has been made to supply all pertinent informations about this handpicked Sanskrit playwrights in the form of a comprehensive information package furnishing the date, time, legends and life of the dramatists.

An acquantance and insight into their works is offered by providing synopsis, list of dramatis personae, time-analysis, plot and critical views on each plays.

To Drama Students and Art Historian is handed a painstaking chronicle of various productions of Sanskrit plays commencing from 19th century up to the end of the last millenium, enacted in India and abroad in original as well as various vernaculars of the world supplemented by rare and invaluable photographic reproductions of various productions, costumes, translators and directors of the plays.

To enhance the scope, an enumeration of bio-critical notices and studies in the form of select bibliography is also presented for each individual author.The work can be called an innovative reference tool combining the unique features of two traditional reference sources. The encyclopaedia and the biographical dictionary.

Series Three is a definite guide to Kalidasa.

I hope the theatre buffs enjoy browsing the present volume as much I have enjoyed in writing it.

Biswajit Sinha

1

Aśvaghosa

Buddhist philosopher and teacher, Aśvaghosa gained prominence as a poet and playwright only in recent times. It is unfortunate that this dramatic genius life was allowoed to lapse into total oblivion until the discovery of fragments of manuscripts on palm - leaf at Turfan by Luders.

Aśvaghosa was a contemporary of king Kanishka (A.D. 78 - 106) or according to Chinese tradition, his preceptor.

His magnum opus 'Buddha - Carita' doest not contain any information about him, not even his name. However, in his second celebrated work '*Saundarānanda*', some information regarding him is furnished in the 18th or the last Sarga which states :-

"*Saundarānande Mahākāvye Ajñāvyākaraṇo Nāmàṣṭādaśaḥ Sargah. Āryasuvarṇāksīputrasya* Sāketakasya *Bhikṣorācārybhadantāśvaghoṣasya Mahākāvermahāvādināḥ* Kṛtiriyan. Hence we may deduce some idea about the author and his personality. He was an Ārya (a noble and a revered person); 'Survarṇākṣīputra' (son of Suvarṇākṣi, the golden eyed); 'Sāketaka' (an inhabitant of Sāketa or Ayodhya); 'Bhikṣu' (a mendicant or a Buddhist monk); "Ācarya" (a spiritual teacher); 'Bhadanta' (a great and a revered person or a Buddhist monk); "Mahakavi (a great poet) and Mahāvādin (an eloquent speaker, an exponent of great things or truths, a sound logician, an expert debatoréx).

The legend goes like this that he proved his worth by making the horses listen to his lectures, leaving aside the fodder and thus, was named as 'Aśvaghosa'.

He is the earliest Buddhist poet, dramatist and philosopher to use Sanskrit and the authorship of *Buddhacarita*, *Saudarānanda*, and *Śāriputra - prakaraṇa* is attributed to Aśvaghosa of the 1st or 2nd century A.D. Some are of the opinion that these works were by three different authors.

Interestingly Chinese and Tibetan legends speak of six Aśvaghosas. The name 'Aśvaghoṣa' might have been adopted by different writers at various periods.

He was a Brahmaṇa by birth, a Śaiva by faith, but was very critical of the rigid caste - system of established Brahmanism as revealed in his writings and thus, embraced Buddhism. He engaged himself in the propagation of new faith and soon elevated to the rank of a teacher of Buddhist doctrine.

According to Tibetan tradition Aśvaghoṣa was a prominent figure in the fourth Buddhist Council convened by the Emperior Kaniṣka. Infact Aśvaghoṣa is said to have helped in organising this (council). He became very popular for his ability in explaining the intricate points of Mahāyana Buddhism.

Hsuan - Tsang (7th century) refers to him as a Pusa (Bodhisattva). He must have belonged to some such orthodox Hinayana school which was gradually melting into the Mahayana, the Mahasanghika school. He developed a deep reverence for Lord Buddha (Mahayana Buddhabhakti), but never worship him as God, but at the sametime his doctrinal stands on the frontier of the Hinayana school.

Though one cannot say when the first actual play was written in India. But the earliest dramatic pieces that have been handed down to us is of Aśvaghoṣa '*Sariputra - prakaraṇa*' that go back to Kuṣaṇa period of C. 100 A.D. and later found at Turfan in Central Asia.

Prof. M.M. Ghose thinks that the date of the Nāṭyaśāstra is the Ist century B.C. and to be in saferside, Aśvaghosa who was a poet in the court of Kaniṣka (circa 58 B.C. to 120 A.D.) was well acquinted with the dramatic rules laid down by Bharata.

Aśvaghosa has made a niche for himself in the field of dramatic art for his admirable style and taste in rendering into drama purely religious and didactic themes. His *'Sārīputra - prakarana'*, also known as *'Sāradvatī-putra-prakaraṇa'* is the oldest extant Sanskrit drama that follows the norms laiddown in the *Nāṭ yaśaśtra* for the composition of drama and amongst his plays, this prakaraṇa in nine acts that depicts the incidents that led up to the conversion of the young Maudgalyayana and Sarīpuṭra by the Buddha.

In all two known textual traditions of this drama has been handed down to us. First is the Kushana era MS which is known up till now as the oldest Indian MS written originalaly in India during the reign of Kanishka and Huvishka and imported later on into Central Asia. MS was unearthed by the third Royal Prussian Turfan Expendition Party at Qyzil near Kuca in Chinese Turkestan. These fragments originally formed parts of several smooth Talipat palm leaves written in a script that is very similar to that of the dated North Indian inscriptions of the time of the Northern Kshatrapas and Kushanas. The MS appears to have been a palimpsest because these are numerous letter - forms of the early Central Asian Brahmi of the Turfan reviser of the late Kushana epoch.

Second is also a palimsest and appears to have been written originally in the late Kushan epoch and the textual tradition is represented by the fragments of a Central Asian palm - leaf MS which was written in Central Asia in the earliest type of Central Asian Brahmi. The synopsis of the drama is as follows :

Sārīpuṭraprakaraṇa

The story of this Prakarana goes like this the Sāriputra had an interview with Asvajit, then he discussed the question of the claims of the Buddha to be a teacher with his friend, the Vidusaka, who raised the objection that a Brahmin like his master should not accept the teaching of Buddha who is a Kshatriya; Sāriputra repels the objection by reminding his friend that if the medicine cures the sick, it does not matter if it is given by one of lower cause as does water one in thirst.

Maudgalyayana greets Sāripatra inquiring of him the cause of his glad outlook and learns his reasons. The two go to Buddha who receives them and a fortells to them that they will be the greatest of his disciples in knowledge and magic power. Play closes with philosophic dialogue between Sāripuṭra and the Buddha, which includes a solemic against the belief in the existence of a permanent self; it glorifies his two new disciples by the Buddha himself and finally formal benediction, as usual .

In the same manuscript of '*Sārīpuṭraprakaraṇa*', there are portions of two other dramas. But the titles are missing and are incomplete like Krishna Miśra's *Prabodhacandrodaya*, one of them is an allegorical drama that depicts various virtues as characters such as Buddhi (Wisdom / Intelligence), Kirti (Fame), Dhriti

(Firmness/ Putence) etc. While the Buddha with a halo around him, also takes part. The plot is, therefore, religious that glorifies Buddha.

The second play could have been a full fledged Prakaraṇa like the Mṛcchakaṭ ika, that revolved around the story of Somadatta and a courtesan Magadhavati with the Vidushaka named Kumudagandha, a maid - servant and a roughe (Dusta) as principal dramatis personae. Analogous to other plays, it could also be a story of conversion to Buddhism and therefore, religious in intent but has much that is amorous.

The plays are ascribed to him on the ground that each of these are contained in the single manuscript and having the appearance of his writings, as all the plays are deeply concerned with Buddhist philosophy.

The *Rastrapalanataka* is ascribed to Aśvaghosa by some scholars and the existance of which is known to us only from some direct and indirect references embodied in Buddhistic, Brahmanistic and Jinistic works portrayed the conversion of Rashtrapala of some royal or aristocratic family. This story of Rashtrapala's indomitable urge for renunciation and faith in religion had universal appeal became very popular to both the Hinayana and Mahayana schools of Buddhism, but finally found its place in the Jinistic canon. The Nataka is however, not known to have any Chinese or Tibetan translation. Some references to Rashtrapala natak are given below.

(1) Fu fa tsang yin yuan chuan is the earliest known reference and is a Sutra or Record (chuan) on The Nidana or cause of transmitting the Dharmapitaka of the Chinse Tripitaka. This work is th third Chinese translation in verse done in 472 by Ki-Kia-Ye in assistance with T'an-yao of the Pe-wei or Northern Wei dynasty (386 - 534). The author of the Sanskrit original which is now lost (but existed when the Cheg - yuan catalogue was compiled (785- 804)) is not known. In the Chinese rendering, however, there is an elaborate account of Aśvaghosa. It is mentioned that he was a musician - preacher in company with an opera party in Hoa-che (Pataliputra) and composed a melodrama entitled 'Lo -tch'a-ho-to (*Rashtrapalanataka*) for converting the citizens to Buddhism, and the nirveda (renunciation) theme of the drama. The enactment of this highly successful drama resulted in the renunciation of five hundred Kshatriya princes of Pataliputra. The king fearing that his subjects might leave the kingdom and take to religion, he had to ban the play.

(2) The second reference to the drama is found in a 6th century teatise entitled *Vadanyaya* on the Nigrahasthana of Buddhistic logic by Dharmakirti.

(3) Third reference is traceable in the '*Nyayamanjari granthibhanga*' of Chakradhara on Jayantabhatta's *Nyayamanjari* (900) in the form of quotation from the prastavana.

(4) In the '*Nyayavinishchayavivarana*' of Vadirajasuri, a protege of the Western Chalukya king Jayasimha II (1018 - 12) the reference to the drama can be found, on Akalankabhatta's '*Nyayavinishchaya*' in the form of the selfsame citation from the prastavana.

(5) An allusion to the drama can be found in the *Pimdanijjutti* (Pindaniryukti): which is ascribed to Bhadrabahusvamin. An altered form of the same story can be noticed in its Jinistic version where the author of the Rashtrapalanataka is mentioned as 'Asadabhui' (Ashadhabhuti).

Nothing can be said fully about his plays as full stories are not available to us, yet each plays show power and dramatic merits. The Sanskrit of these scattered manuscripts contain negligiable errors. He employs standard Sanskrit with few irregularities. There are three varities of Prākrits being used, somewhat like old Māgadhī old Ardha Māgadhī and old Śaurasenī.

As regards his literary style, 'Bharati' is the Vritti dramatic style in the '*Śarīpuṭraprakarana*'. His language is simple in diction and clarity is evident in his writings, but in few places, he employs certain words which later became obsolete in their peculiar nuances, but still direct in its appeal to the common populace.

His use of the Quietistic sentiment in the prakarana is remarkable as the plot aims at the glorification of Buddhistic faith. Buddhist in its approach and out look, the concluding benedictory verse is also altered to suit the Buddhistic atmosphere.

Aśvaghosa was fully conversant with the dramatic arts and had more than one models before him.

What type of a Sūtradhāra was used by Aśvaghosa is not known to us owing to the missing of the first portion of the drama.

S.C. Bhatt has rightly pointed out that the character of the 'Vidushaka' is an important point of affinity with the dramatic theory, although, here a character of this kind is somewhat disjointed. The use of Sanskrit by the principal characters including the Buddha himself, is another point of great interest as it shows that the classical Sanskrit drama was a widely prevalent form in Ashvaghosa's time roughly the 1st century B.C.

T.G. Mainkar observed that though available in the fragments, but his three plays suggest the existence of dramatic conventions, as found in the Nāṭ yaśāstra of Bharata, and seem to set the pattern for the classical drama of later times such as :

(i) Division into Acts,

(ii) The Presence of Viduṣhaka;

(iii) Change of Language from Sanskrit to Prakrit;

(iv) Use of Prose and Verse; and

(v) The use of the different metres known to classical poetry.

Other striking elements in his plays are:

----- Hero of the play is a dhiraśānta type Brāhmaṇa.

----- No of Acts corrresponds to the No. prescribed for such a type of Pranarana.

----- Follows Bharata's dictum in the free use of any Rasa.

----- The plot is invented that its genesis lies in the Mahāvagya.

His mastery in the realm of drama must go unchallanged. In his prakaraṇa, we find no serious deviations from dramatic practices prescribed by Bharata. Biswanath Bhattacharya feels that his work was not appreciated by the later critics, perhaps due to his conversion into Buddhism and not the ignorance of the Śāstra. His works gradually lost its hold in Indian mind.

Besides dramas, his other literary output comprises of mahakavyas such as

I. *Buddha - Carita*; and

II. *Saundarānanda*.

These two works are considered to be absolutely genuine. *Buddha - Carita* is his first and the best work, but the Sanskrit text of this precious ornate epic is not complete. Written in 28 contos in true epic style, the mahakavya provides us the whole biography of Lord Buddha thas starts with his birth and closing in his death and the division of his relics.

The second poetic and philosophical mahakavya is '*Saundarānanda*' that deals with the conversion of Buddha's reluctant half - brother, Nanda, immersed in his love for his beloved Sundarī to Buddhism. Thus, the epic culls out a specific episode from Budha's life by elaborating it in 18 sargas or cantos.

His other noteworthy works are :-

(III) *Mahāyānaśraddhotpāda :* It discusses the early Mahāyana views.

(IV) *Vajra - sūchi :* In this work, he attacks the caste system.

(V) *Gaṇḍīstotragātha :* It proves his metrical skill and his profound knowledge of music.

Aśvaghosa's contribution to Sanskrit literature is unique. He created a new genre of ornate Kavyas that was used as vehicle for popularising the Buddha's teachings.

His great scholarship, philosophical mind, gift for poetry and sense of piety made him very popular. He was highly praised by Hsuan - Tsang, Hwui Li and I - tsing.

His epic poems and plays were well received by the Buddhistis of both the sects of India and Greater India. His "*Buddhacarita*" is said to have been widely read in the Malay Archipelago (Sumatra, Java and the adjoining islands).

In the words of Roma Chaudhuri "Aśvaghosa was a versatile genius. - a monk and a missionary, a philosopher and a theologician, a grammarian and a linguist, a rhetorician and a metrician, a musician and an instrumentalist a Hinayanaist and a Mahāyānist, a scholar and a devotee, a poet and a dramatist. As a matter of fact, he was a perfect emblem of the grand and glorious eternal idea of Samanvaya or harmony".

'Sārīpuṭraprakaṇa in Performances'

There are ample evidence to prove that '*Sariputraprakarana*' of Asvāghosa used to be enacted in the Buddhist monastries of Mathura. Fa-hsien said : "Actors were hired to perform a play in which Sariputra who was originally Brahmin goes to Buddha to ask for ordination. The lives of Maudgalyaputra and Kasyapa are also performed in this way (in Mathura)".

***Mahakavya 'Saundarananda' in Performance* (Adaptation)**

Lahron ke rajahamsa (swan of the Waves, a Hindi play in three acts written by Mohan Rakesh is based on Ashvaghosha's 'Saundaranand'. Here the playwright tries to explore the restlessness and inner conflict of man in search of his own path of his salvation. The prince of Kapilavastu and the step - brother of Gautama Buddha is the main character who suffers spiritual agony in his attraction towards Buddha's teachings on the one hand and his love for his beautiful wife 'Sundari' on the other. Sundari's confidence in the powers of her tremendous physical attraction is shattered and her ego deflated when finally Nand appears as a clean - shaven sadhu. In her direct conflict with Nanda, Sundari fails to win him over. Nanda who has embraced the philosophy of Buddhist renunciation but stands as a forlorn man in utter confusion. The intension of Rakesh in delineating our predicament by means of a historical theme is to suggest that the tension is rooted not in time but in human nature. This play attempts to shake off the excessive sentimentalism of his earlier play 'Ashad ka ek din'. A critic observes that inspite of the seriousness and relevance of the theme and a very sensitive and imaginative build-up of the first two acts, the play fritters, itself away in the third. The main conflict becomes weak and the form of the play loses itm charity and unity.

In the year 1966 - 67, Repertory of the National School of Drama presented '*Lehron ke Rajhans*' under the direction of Om Shivpuri and sets by E. Alkaji. In the opening year there were ten shows of this plays in Hindi.

A scene from 'Lehron ke Rajhans'; directed by Om Shivpuri for the NSD.

Om Shivpuri and Savita Bajaj in 'Lehron ke Rajhans'

The cast of 'Lehron ke Rajhans' is as follows :

On Stage

Nand	Om Shivpuri
Sundari	Sudha Sharma
Alka	Shobhana Butani / Savita Bajaj
Shyamang	Virendra Sharma
Shuetang	Ram Gopal Bajaj
Anand	Mohan Maharishi
Metrey	Kavi Ratan Sharma
Niharika	Shyama Jain
Shashank	Nand Arora
Shefalika	Naima Khan

Beej Gupta	Sushil Chowdhury
Mandakini	Indrani Majumdar
Mandarak	Mahesh Chandra
Naagdaas	A. Raghavan

Off Stage

Stage Management	Nand Arora, Susheel Chowdhary
Set designed by	E. Alkazi
(constructed by)	Tarseem Lal, Dalip Chand
Costumes	Roshen Alkazi
(assisted by)	Usha Sathe, Uttara Baokar
Music	Panchanan Pathak
Technical assistant	Govind Prasad
Lighting	G.N. Dasgupta
assisted by	S. Ramanujam, B.L. Chopra
Make-up	Indu Bhushan Ghose
Properties	Dev Mohapatra
(assisted by)	G.V. Thakar, A. Raghavan
Front of House	Kamlakar Sontakke, Raksha Shroff, Surekha Varma, Mukund Naik.

To commemorate 20th death anniversary of Mohan Rakesh, the National School of Drama Repertory Company organised 'Mohan Rakesh Natya Samaroha' which opened with a performance of *Ashadh ka ek din* on 2rd December 1992 and concluded with Kirti Jain's production of '*Lehron ke Rajhans*' Shri Bhaskar Chandravarkar scored the music. Shri Ashok Sagar Bhagat designed the lights while Dolly Ahluwalia designed the costumes for these play. Shri M.K. Raina designed the sets for *Lehron ke Rajhans*. The festival created a lot of interest among the theatre lovers of Delhi with the halls running to full houses forcing the school to arrange matinee performances. The schedule of performances are as follows : - 19, 20 Dec. 1992 and 4 to 10, 21 - 31 January, 1993.

A Scene from the play Lehron ki Rajhans Directed by Kirti Jain

National School of Drama's Repertory company's visit to Mauritius was one of the major events of the year 1993. It took part in the 4th International Hindi Sammelan that was held during the months of November - December. The company was invited to perform Mohan Rakesh's Ashadh ka ek din, *Lehron ke Rajhans* and *Adhe Adhure*. The three - play festival opened with *Lehron ke Rajhans* on 6 December followed by a repeat performance of it on 7 December 1993.

The synopsis of the play is an follows.

Act - I

Sundari, the wife of Prince Nand, the brother of Buddha, has made elaborate arrangements for Kamotsav - a celebration of Love and Desire. A large number of guests are expected. The next morning, Devi Yashodhara, the wife of Buddha, is to be ordained a Bhikshuni.

Sundari is informed by Maitreya, their friend, that all the guests have expressed their inability to attend the function. This unexpected turn of events shocks and annoys Sundari.

Act - II

The next day Sundari, while apologizing to Nand for her behaviour pleads with him to forget the unpleasant episode. What follows is a delicately crafted love-scene in which she persuades Nand to spend the day with her. Just as Nand, while helping with her toilete, anoints her forehead with a motif, they are interrupted by Alka, Sundari's maid. Alka informs them that Gautam Buddha himself had visited their mansion for 'Bhiksha' but had to return empty handed. On hearing this Nand seeks her consent to leave her promising to return and complete the motif after having apologised to his brother.

Act - III

Despite his promise Nand fails to return. Sundari is full of misapprehension. Finally, returns but with his head shaven. Sundari, fearing that he has become a Bhikshu, breaks down. Nand on his part is disillusioned both with Buddha who has shaved his head against his wishes and by Sundari's reaction.

He leaves home to find other solutions to his questions.

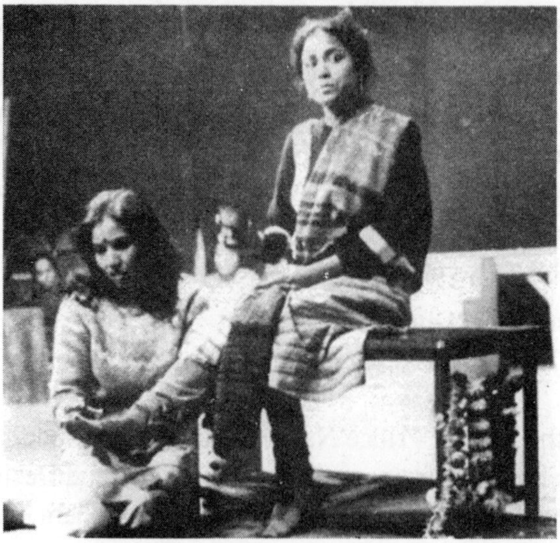

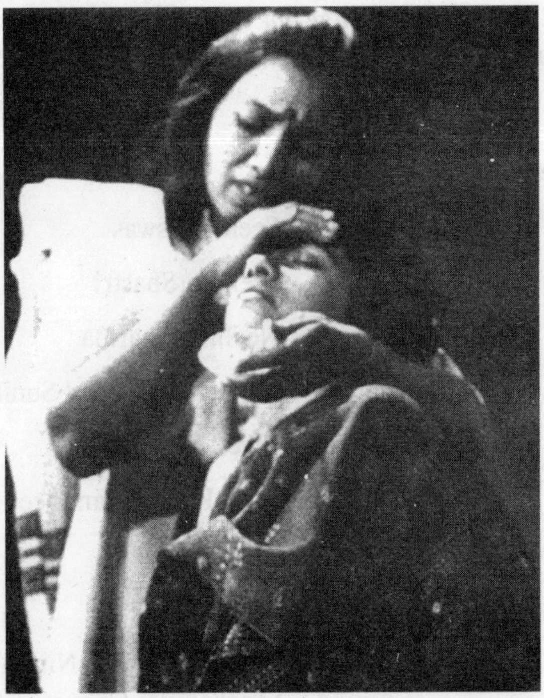

Kirti Jain, the director of the play admits that she read '*Saundaranand*' of Ashvaghosh and was so fascinated by the delicate imagery and sensuality in its description of their love and sorrow at separation that she decided to use some of these verses (translated by Kedarnath Singh) to heighten the conflicts of the characters in the play and provide another dimension to the relationship. In her own words :

The play remains very relevant because it not only deals with the question of choice between the worldly and unworldly, material and the spiritual, through the complex dynamics of a man woman relationship but essentially with the search of every man for his own identity, for the meaning of his existence. Since it is question that transcends time and historicity we decided to place it in a historical formalistic setting. We tried to create a space which is a metaphor by itself and also a space where the character live out their experiences. The entire play is very 'real' at one level and very metaphorical at another.

We tried to play with this duality in the overall design of the production - whether it be the music, or the set design or the way the characters move on stage. This was indeed a major challenge for all of us as a team. Our attempt is to explore the meaning of the text at a many levels as possible.

The cast included :-

Sundari	...	Seema Biswas
Nand	...	Jitendra Shastri
Alka	...	Neelima Sharma
Shyamang	...	Rohitashva Gaur / Sunil Singh
Shwetang	...	Vivek Mishra
Maitreya	...	Amit Ranjan Banerjee
Niharika	...	Premlata
Bhikshu Anand	...	Abhijit Lahiri
Others	...	Hemant Pandey, Nirmal Das, Uma Vaish, Sanghamitra Chatterji, Anju Jaitley, Kanika Dang, Mahendra Mewati
Chorus	...	B. Ratna, Nutan Surya, Alka Badola, Abhijit Lahiri, Sitaram Panchal, Govind Pandey.
Musician	...	Om Prakash, Pradeep Datta, Partho Bandyopadhyay
Set Design	...	M.K. Raina.
Light Design	...	Ashok Sagar Bhagat.
Music	...	Bhaskar Chandravarkar.
Costume Design	...	Dolly Ahluwalia
Direction	...	Kirti Jain.

The Birth Anniversary of Adya Rangacharya's 'Sriranga' was celebrated by Karnataka Nataka Rangayana by organising a theatre festival in 1993. Mohan Rakesh's Lehron ke Rajhans was presented on the occasion, the play was translated by Siddalingapattanashetty and directed by P. Gangadharaswamy.

WORKS : A BIBLIOGRAPHY

Text

Buddha - carita / by Asvaghosa; ed. by E.B. Cowell .- Oxford : [s.n.], 1893.

Buddha - carita / by Aśvaghosa; ed. by E.H. Johnston .- Calcutta : [s.n.], 1935.

Buddhacarita / by Aśvaghosa. *In* Zwei Zentralasiatische Fragmente des Buddhacarita. - Leipzig : Abhandlungen der Sāchsischen Akademie der Wissenschaftem, 1953.

Buddha - carita / by Aśvaghosa; ed. by F. Weller .- Berlin [s.n.], 1953.

Friedrich Weller (1889-1980)

Friedrich Weller was born on 22.7.1889, the only son of a master craftsman in Markneukirchen. Saxony. He served in the army in War I. On his return he resumed his studies, and qualified for the teaching profession. He got the venia legendi, permission to read Sanskrit, Chinese, and history religions of Eastern Asia in 1922 with the thesis Der Chinesische Dharmasamgraha, mit einem Anhang ueber das

Lakkhanasuttanta des Dighanikaya, Leipzig, 1923. The young scholar worked as an aid in antiquarian bookshops to earn a livelihood.

In 1928, Weller was appointed an assistant professor. Ths helped him in getting appointed in the Sino - Indian Institute of the Harvard University in Peking. The director of that Institute was A. von Stael-Holstein. He had published the Kashyaparivarta in Sanskrit, Tibetan and Chinese in 1926. Weller was asked to determine the history of these texts and also of the Mongolian version (which he himself eventually edited in 1962). There followed the best three years of his life (1930-1933) as Weller later said.

In 1936, Weller became co-editor of "Journal for Oriental Literature" In 1938, he succeeded J. Hertel in the chair of Indology in Leipzig. The Indian Institute of Leipzig was bombed in 1943, it took years to re-establish it. Weller received a National Award by the government of the German Democratic Republic in 1955 and a citation in 1975 on occasion of his 65th and 85th birth anniversaries. Weller resigned after 35 years of teaching in 1957. The last 20 years of his life were marked by failing health. He died on 19.11.1980. In his will he turned over his library and the money of the two state-awards to the Saxon Academy of Sciences, Leipzig of which he had been a member since 1943. Friedrich Weller studied Buddhist literature in every language that it has been written. Weller established new methods of analysis and criticism of such texts. His work culminated in a new view of the history of Buddhism.

Friedrich Weller achieved renown through his editing and translation of the Buddhacharitamahakavyanama, Ashvaghosa : Das Laben des Budha, tibetisch und deutsch, 2 volumes, Leipzig, 1926 and 1928. Whereas the Sanskrit text of the Buddhacharita had only 17 cantos of which 13 are old, the Tibetan and Chinese texts had 28 cantos. The hope of discovering references to the era of Ashvaghosha lay at the root of his editorial endeavour. He expected to contribute to the dating of Buddhist councils and king Kanishka's rule (on which depended the early history of Buddhism and Indian chronology in general). Weller found that the Tibetan text could not be considered a correct version of Ashvaghosha's original work. In an essay Schauplatz und Handlung im Buddhacarita, ("scene and plot in the Buddhacharita"), "Journal of the German Oriental Society" 1939, Weller stated that in the first canto the two traditions of events concerning the Buddha's birth are confused in a manner which hardly can be attributed to the eminent writer Ashvaghosha. He explained that the apparent disorder of those scenes could be understood if canto I were considered to be a description of a series of paintings or sculptures representing the events.

Buddhacarita / by Aśvaghosa; ed. by Ramchandra Das Sastri. - Varanasi : Chowkhamba Vidya Bhavan, 1983.

217 p.; 18 cm.

Buddhacarita / by Aśvaghosa; ed. with a Hindi translation by Sūryanārāyaṇ Caudharī. - Purnea : [s.n.], 1942 - 44.

2 Vols.; 18 cm.

Includes index.

Text of cantos 1 to 14 and Hindi translation of cantos 1 to 28; The work was first edited by E.V. Cowell from Oxford in 1893; translated by him in English appeared in "Sacred books of the East" (Vol. 46).

Buddhacarita / by Aśvaghosa; ed. with an English prose translation from the Sanskrit supplemented by a Tibetan version, introd. and notes by E.H. Johnston. - Lahore : University of Punjab, 1935 - 36.

2 Vols.; 26 cm. — Punjab University Oriental Publications; 31 - 32.

Contents : Vol. 1 : Text in Devanāgarī script.

Vol. 2 : English translation & notes.

Buddhacarita / by Aśvaghosa; ed. with notes by Dattātraya Śāstrī Nigūḍkar. - Bombay : Oriental Publishing Co., 1912.

xxiv, [267] p.: facsim, plate; 22 cm.

Includes introd., notes and English translation by K.M. Joglekar and index.

Buddhacarita / by Aśvaghosa; ed. tr. into English by Johnston .- Calcutta : Punjab University Oriental Publications, 1935 - 36.

-------. *Acta Orientalia,* 1937.

Buddhacarita / by Aśvaghosa; tr. into English by E.H. Johnston. - Delhi : Motilal Banarsidass, 1984.

165, 230, 130 p.; 22 cm.

Buddhacarita = The life of Buddha / by Aśvaghosa; ed. with English tr., notes etc. by Irina Schotsman .- Varanasi : Central Institute of Higher Tibetan Studies, 1995.

xii, 308 p.

Translation

Bengali

Buddhacarita / by Ashvaghosha; tr. by Rathindranath Thakur .- Calcutta : Vishvabharati, 1945.

86 p.; 16 cm.

English

Buddhacarita / by Aśvaghosa; tr. into English by E.H. Johnston - Delhi : Motilal Banarsidass, 1984.

165; 230, 22 cm.

Buddhacarita / by Aśvaghosa; ed. by Ramchandra Das Sastri .- Varanasi : Chowkhamba Vidya Bhavan, 1983.

217 p.; 18 cm.

Buddhacarita or Acts of the Buddha / by Aśvaghosa; ed. by E.H. Johnston .- Lahore : Punjab University, 1935 - 36.

2 Vols.; 25 cm. (Punjab University Oriental Publications; 31 - 32).

Contents : *Vol. 1* : Sanskrit text.

Vol. 2 : English translation, introduction and notes.

Buddhacarita = The life of Buddha / by Asvaghosa; ed. with English tr., notes etc. by Irina Schotsman .- Varanasi : Central Institute of Higher Tibetan Studies, 1995.

xii, 308 p.

Hindi

Buddhacarita / by Aśvaghosa; tr. by Sūryanārāyaṇ Caudharī .- Kathautiya, Purnea: The translator, 1942 - 44.

2 Vols.; 18 cm.

Includes index.

Also contains Sanskrit text.

Buddhacarita / by Aśvaghosa; tr. into Hindi prose by Suryanarayan Chaudhari .- Kathautiya : Samskrit Bhavan, 1954.

2 Vols.; 18 cm.

Buddhacarita / by Aśvaghosa; tr. by Suryanarayan Chaudhuri .- 2nd ed. - Kathautia, Bihar : Sanskrit Bhavan, 1953.

Tr. of Sarga 15 - 28.

Buddhacarita / by Ashvagosha; tr. by Suryanarayan Chaudhuri and Ramchandra Das. - Varanasi : Caukhamba Vidya Bhavan, 1962.

Tr. of Sarga 1 - 14.

Buddhacaritam (Vol.1) / by Ashvagosha; tr. by Ramchandra Das Sastri .- Varanasi : Caukhamba Vidyabhavan.

Buddhacarita / by Ashvagosha; tr. by Viṣṇudatta Sharma. - Meerut : Jnan Book Depot, 1969.

Malayalam

Buddhacarita / by Aśvaghoṣa; tr. by E.V. Rāman Nampūtiri .- Trivandrum : The translator, 1933.

112 p.; 19 cm.

Translation of cantos 1 and 2 only.

Buddhacaritam / by Asvaghosa; tr. into Malayalam by C.P. Kesavan Vaidyan .- Kottayam : N.B.S., 1971.

237 p.; 21 cm.

Polish

['Buddhacarita' and Saundarananda] / by Aśvaghoṣa; tr. into Polish by A. Gawronski .- Ossolineum : [s.n.], 1966.

Sariputraprakarana

Text

Sariputraprakarana / ed. by Heinrich Lueders. *Proceedings of the Berlin Academy*, 1911.

Heinrich Lueders (1869-1943)

Heinrich Lueders was born on 25.6.1869 in Luebeck. He studied German philology in Muenchen. Later he went ot Goettingen where he studied Indology. He went to England where he was librarian of the Indian Institute of Oxford University. He studied manuscripts in the India Office at London. In 1903, Lueders became professor at Rostock. Earlier, he qualified as university lecturer in 1898. He was a member, secretary, and later President of the Berlin Academy of Sciences. From 1909-1935, he held the chair of Indologyin Berl in University.

Heinrich Lueders worked on a critical edition of the Mahabharata and contributed many papes to "Epigraphia Indica". In later years he specialised in Buddhist Sanskrit texts from Central Asia and published fragments of the oldest extant Sanskrit drama. Ashvaghosha's Sariputraprakarana. In Berlin, Lueders concentrated on the Sanskrit texts brought to Germany from Central Asia by the four Turfan expeditions. He was assisted by his wife Else. Lueders, who deciphered and catalogued these manuscripts. Lueders discovered fragments of Sanskrit dramas. Among them was the Sariputraprakarana of Ashvaghosha which he published in "Proceedingsof the Berlin Academy", 1911.

Śāriputra / by Aśvaghoṣa; ed. by Lūeders. - Berlin " Sitzungs berichte der Kōniglich preussischen Akademic der Wissenschaften, 1911.

[Śarīputra] / by Aśvaghosa. *In* Bruchstūcke Buddhistischer Dramen : Kōniglich preussische Turfan - Expeditioness, Kleinere Sanskrit - Texte I, 1911 / by Lūeders. Reimer, Berlin; 1911.

Translations

Bengali

Sanskrita sahitya sambhar / ed. by Gaurinath Sastri & et al. [Vol. 11] .- Calcutta : Navpatra Prakashan, [197 -].

Includes Bengali rendering of Aśvaghosa's '*Sariputraprakarana*'

Saundarananda

Text

Saundarānanda / by Aśvaghoṣa; ed. with a Hindi translation by Sūryanārāyaṇ Caudharī. - Purnea : Sanskrit Bhavan, 1948.

xx, 287 p.; 19 cm.

Saundarananda / by Aśvaghosa .- Delhi : Motilal Banarsidass, 1986.

268 p.; 17.5 cm.

Saundarānanda / by Aśvaghoṣa; critically ed. with notes in English by E.H. Johnston .- London : Oxford University Press, 1928.

xiv, 171 p.; 24 cm. (Punjab University Oriental Publications)

Published for the University of Punjab.

Includes index.

Saundarananda / by Aśvaghoṣa; ed. & tr. by Johnston .- London : Oxfordf University Press, 1932.

Saundarananda / by Aśvaghosa; ed. & tr. into English by E.H. Johnston. - Delhi: Motilal Banarsidass, 1975.

123 p.; 22 cm.

Saundarananda / by Aśvaghosa; ed. by E.H. Johnston .- Lahore : [s.n.], 1928.

Saundarānanda / by Aśvaghosa; ed. by F. Weller. - Berlin : [s.n.], 1953.

Saundarānanda / by Aśvaghoṣa; ed. by Haraprasād Śāstrī .- Calcutta : Asiatic Society of Bengal, 1910.

xxiv, 138, [4] p.; 22 cm.

Includes append (Bibliotheca India New Series No. 1251).

Translation

Bengali

Sanskrita sahitya sambhar / ed. by Gaurinath Sastri & .. et al. [Vol. 9]. - Calcutta: Navpatra Prakashan, [197 -].

Includes Bengali rendering of 'Saundarananda' of Aśvaghosa.

English

Saundarananda / by Aśvaghosa; tr. by E.H. Johnston .- Delhi : Motilal Banarsidass, 1975.

123 p.; 22 cm.

Hindi

Saundarānanda / by Aśvaghoṣa; ed. with a Hindi translation by Sūryanārayaṇ Caudhurī .- Purnea : Sanskrit Bhavan, 1948.

xx, 287 p.; 19 cm.

Saudarananda / by Ashvagosha; tr. by Ramdin Pandeya. - Lucknow : Ganga Fine Art Press, 1928.

Saundarananda / by Asvaghosha; tr. into Kannada by Kadava Shanbhusharma. - Mangalore : Kannada Prapancha Prakashana, 1956.

129 p.; 18 cm.

BIO - CRITICAL NOTICES

Aggarwal, H.R. The Importance of tradition and Aśghoṣa in determining the date of Kālidāsa. *All India Oriental Conference* XVII; Pp. 257 - 260.

---------*Poona Orientalist* XIX; 1954; Pp. 12 - 16.

--------- A short history of Sanskrit literature .- 2nd rev. ed. - Delhi : Munshiram Manoharlal, 1963.

Contents : Asvaghosa. Pp. 86 - 93.

Aggarwal, Indubala. Influence of Dirghanikaya on Asvaghosa / by Indubala Agarwal.

Ph.D. thesis in Hindi, approved by Agra University in 1979.

Aggarwal, Veena. Comparative study of Asvaghosha and Kalidasa with special reference to their philosophy of life / by Veena Agarwal.

Ph.D. thesis in Hindi, approved by the Aligarh Muslim University in 1978.

Aufrecht, Theodor. Catalogus catalogorum .- Weisbaden : Franz Steiner Verlag Gmb. H., 1962.

2 Vols.; 26 cm.

Bagchi, P.C. The Rāṣṭrapālanāṭaka of Aśvaghoṣa. *In* Sardesai Commemoration volume .- Bombay [s.n.], 1938.

Noteworthy study on Aśvaghoṣa.

Banerji, Sures Chandra. A Companion to Sanskrit literature .- Delhi : Motilal Banarsidass, 1971. P. 17.

Bharadwaj, Mithilesh. Philosophical ideas in the poems of Asvaghosha / by Mithilesh Bharadwaj.

Ph.D. thesis in Hindi, approved by the Meerut University in 1982.

Bhartiya, Kanti Kishore. Sanskrit natakkar .- Uttar Pradesh : Prakashan Śakha, Suchana Vibhag, 1959.

(Hindi - Samiti granthamala; 25).

Contents : Aśvaghosa. Pp. 115-122.

Bhatt, S.C. Drama in ancient India .- New Delhi : Amrit Book Co., 1961. Pp. 70 - 71.

Bhattacharya, Biswanath. Ashvaghosa : a critical study .- Santiniketan : Visva - Bharati, 1976.

---------. Bhattacharya, Biswanath Asvaghosha : critical study of his authentic kavyas apocryphal works with special reference to his contribution to the classical Sanskrit literature and his doctrinal stand point as a Buddhist / by Biswanath Bhattacharya.

D. Litt thesis approved by the University of Calcutta in 1970.

---------. Asvaghosa : a critical study of his authentic Kavyas and the apocryphal works with special reference of his contributions to the classical Sanskrit literature and his doctrinal stand point as a Buddhist .- Santiniketan: Visva-Bharati, 1976.

li, 417 p.; 24.5 cm.

Bhattacharya, Biswanath. Asvaghosa : a critical study by Biswanath Bhattacharya: *Journal of Ganganath Jha Kendriya Sanskrit Vidyapeetha* July - Sept. 1977; Vol. 33, No. 3; Pp. 204 - 205.

Book Review

---------. *Journal of Karnatak University* (H); 1978; Vol. 22; Pp. 220 - 221.

---------. Sanskrit drama and dramaturgy. 2nd ed.- Delhi : Sharada Publishing House, 1994. Pp. 185 - 190.

---------. Bhattacharya Biswanath. 'Aśvaghoṣa : a critical study / by Biswanath Bhattacharya.

Vishveshvaranand Indological Journal / ed. by K.V. Sarma; March 1977; Vol. XV No. 1; Pp. 153 - 154.

Book review by K.V. Sarma.

---------. 'The Varjrasuci : an apocryphal work of Asvaghosa' / by Biswanath Bhattacharya. *Vishveshvaranand Indological Journal;* March 1966; Vol. 4, No. 1, Pp. 51 - 52.

Bhuyan, Sarojini. Buddhacharita as an epic / by Sarojini Bhuyan.

Ph.D. thesis approved by the University of Poona in 1986.

Chaudhuri, Roma. Aśvaghoṣa .- New Delhi : Sahitya Akademi, 1988.

51 p.; (Makers of Indian literature).

Chaudhari, Saraswathi. Imagery of Asvaghosa : critical and comparative study / by Saraswathi Chaudhari.

Ph.D. thesis approved by the Bhagalpur University in 1980.

Comparative Indian literature (Vol. 1) / ed. by K.M. George .- Trichur : Kerala Sahitya Akademi, 1984. P. 561.

Datta, Samir Kumar. Asvaghosha as a poet and a dramatist : critical study / by Samir Kumar Datta.

Ph.D. thesis approved by the Jadavpur University in 1972.

Dey, S.K. History of Sanskrit literature .- Calcutta : Calcutta University, 1947.

Dictionary of oriental literatures (Vol. II) : South and South - East Asia. - Delhi : Vikas Publishing, 1975.

Dwivedi, Jayashankar. Comparative study of the style, vocabulary, grammar and alamkaras of Kalidasa and Aswaghosha / by Jayashankar Dwivedi.

Ph.D. thesis in Sanskrit, approved by the Varanaseya Sanskrit Viswavidyalaya in 1966.

Encyclopaedia of Indian literature (Vol. 1) .- New Delhi : Sahitya Akademi, 1987, Pp. 249 - 252.

Garg, Ganga Ram. An encyclopaedia of Indian literature .- Delhi : Mittal Publishers, 1982, Pp. 28, 376.

Gawronski, A. Aśvaghoṣa .- Ossolineum : [s.n.], 1966.

Brief biographial sketch with Polish translations of extracts from Buddhacarita and Saundarananda.

Gurner, C.W. Aśvaghoṣa and the Rāmāyaṇa / by C.W. Gurner. *Journal and Proceedings of Asiatic Society of Bengal* (JASB New Series); 1927, Vol. 23, No. 3. Pp. 347 - 67.

Hakeda, Y.S. Buddhist hybrid Sanskrit words in Aśvaghoṣa's kāvyas. *Journal of American Oriental Society*, 1962; Vol. 82, No. 2.

Indian theatre : traditions of performance / ed. by Farley P. Richmond, Darius L. Swann and Phillip B. Zarrill .- Delhi : Motilal Banarsidass, 1993.

Joshi, D.G. 'The first dramatist in Sanskrit : Aśvaghoṣa or Bhāsa?' / by D.G. Joshi.

Paper presented at the *All India Oriental Conference* (22nd session) held at Gauhati, Assam in January 1965.

Keith, A. Berridale. The Sanskrit drama in its origin, development, theory and practice .- Oxford : OUP, 1924.

405 p.; 22 cm.

---------. Sanskrit - natak : udbhav aur vikas : siddhanta aur prayog / tr. into Hindi by Udaybhanu Singh .- Delhi : Motilal Banarsidass, 1965.

Krishnamachariar, M. and Srinivasachariar, M. History of classical Sanskrit literaṭure .- Delhi : Motilal Banarsidass, 1989. Pp. 598 - 599.

Krishnamoorthy, K. 'A New play by Asvaghosa' / by K. Krishnamoorthy. *Journal of Oriental Institute;* June 1962; Vol. 11, No. 4; Pp. 428 - 432.

Law, Bimala Charan. Aśvaghosa / by Bimala Charan Law. - Calcutta : Asiatic Society, 1946.

iv, 92 p.; 24 cm. (The Asiatic Society Monograph Series; 1).

Includes bibliography and index.

An attempt to build up a connected account of the life and labours of Aśvaghoṣa.

Lal, Ramesh Chandra. Evaluation of Asvaghosha's poetic art with special reference to Saundarananda / by Ramesh Chandra Lal.

Ph.D thesis approved by the Allahabad University in 1981.

Lūeders. Bruchstūcke Buddhistischer dramen.

Contents : Aśvaghosa Pp. 17 - 24.

Macdonell, A.A. India's past : a survey of her literatures, religions, languages and antiquities .- Varanasi : Motilal Banarsidass, 1956. Pp. 104 - 105.

Marasinghe, E.W. The Sanskrit theatre and stagecraft .- Delhi : Sri Satguru Publicatins, 1989 .- (Sri Garib Dass Oriental series; No. 78).

Masterpieces of Indian literature [Vol. 2] / ed. by K.M. George. - New Delhi : National Book Trust, 1997.

Contents : Buddhacharita of Asvaghosa. Pp. 1159 - 1162.

Merriam - Webster's Encyclopaedia of literature. - Springfield, Massachusetts : Merriam - Webster, Inc., 1995.

P. 80.

Mishra, Sudhakar. Philosophical study of the poems of Asvaghosha / by Sudhakar Mishra.

Ph.D. thesis in Hindi, approved by the Avadh University in 1984.

Nashin, Kishwar Jabin. Indian culture as depicted in the works of Asvaghosha / by Kishwar Jabin Nashin.

Ph.D. thesis approved by the Allabad University in 1979.

Nobel, Johannes.

Ashvaghosa / by Johannes Nobel, 1931.

A paper on Ashvaghosa by a German Indologist.

Pandey, Ram Kishore. Comparative study of Buddhacharita and Raghuvamsa / by Ramkishore Pandey.

Ph.D. thesis in Hindi, approved by the Kanpur University in 1976.

Parikh, J.T. Sanskrit comic characters.- Surat : Popular Book Depot, 1952.

Pass, A. Ashvaghosa Le Gesta del Buddha : Buddhacarita Cant. I - XIV. - Milano: [s.n.], 1979.

Gives a critical insights into the life and works.

Pass, Alessandro. 'Aśvaghosa : Le gesta del. Buddha by Alessandro Passi. *Vishveshvaranand Indological Journal, March - Sept. 1979,* Vol. XVII, Nos. I - II. P. 312.

Book review by K.V. Sharma of Italian tr. of 'Buddhacaritam'.

Puri, Prabha. Comparative study of the works of Kalidasa and Aswaghosha / by Prabha Puri.

Ph.D. thesis in Hindi, approved by the Kurukshetra University in 1969.

Roy, Ashim Kumar and Gidwani, N.N. A dictionary of Indology (Vol. 1) .- New Delhi : Oxford & IBH Publishing Co., 1983.

P. 143.

Ruben Walter. 'Aśvaghoṣa and the Rāmāyaṇa' / by Walter Ruben. - *Journal of Royal Asiatic Society;* Vol. 23. Pp. 347 - 67.

Sahitya Akademi - New Delhi : The National bibliograph of Indian literature. - New Delhi : The author, 1962 - 1990.

5 Vols.

Sethi, Atmaram. Anudit Hindi sahitya : vishishta granthasuchi / by Atmaram Sethi .- Gurgaon : Indian Documentation Service, 1981.

Contents : Sanskrit (Pp. 1 - 624).

Sharma, Lakshminarayan. Literary and cultural study of Buddhacharita / by Lakshminarayan Sharma.

Ph.D thesis in Hindi, approved by the Vikram University in 1983.

Sharma, Lekh Ram. Critical study of myths and legends refered to in Asvaghosha's works with special reference to Buddhacharita and Sundarananda / by Lekh Ram Sharma.

Ph.D. thesis approved by the Kurukshetra University in 1982.

Shekhar, I. Sanskrit drama : its origin and decline .- Leiden : E.J. Brill, 1960.

Contents : Aṣvaghoṣa, Pp. XXIII, 39, 75, 112, 113, 121, 127, 142, 143, 148, 155, 160, 175, 194.

Siegling, Wilhelm. A glossary to Ashvaghosa's Buddhacarita. 1985.

Includes an introduction by E. Waldschmidt.

Singh, Sukhbir. Critical study of Saundarananda / by Sukhbir Singh.

Ph.D. thesis in Hindi, approved by the Meerut University in 1973.

Sud, Suman. Karuna rasa : from the view point of Valmiki, Bhasa, Asvoghosa, Kalidasa and Bhavabhuti / by Suman Sud.

Ph.D. thesis in Hindi, appoved by the Kurukshetra University in 1969.

Tirtha : the treasury of Indian expressions / ed. by Vijaya Ghose. - New Delhi : CMC Ltd., 1992. P. 203.

Tiwari, Achyutananda. Asvaghosha, individual and poet : critical study / by Achyutananda Tiwari.

Ph.D. thesis in Hindi, approved by the Banaras Hindu University in 1974.

Tiwari, Bishambernath. Art and philosophy of Asvaghosha / by Bishmaber nath Tiwari.

Ph.D. thesis approved by the Agra University in 1960.

Varadpande, M.L. 'Religion and theatre / by M.L. Varad pande. *Sangeet Natak Akademi Journal;* July - Sept. & Oct. - Dec. 1979; Vols. 53 - 54. Pp. 5 - 13.

Verma, Tekram. Vocabularly of Asvaghosha / by Tekram Verma.

Ph.D. thesis in Hindi, approved by the Ravishankar University in 1984.

Vyas, Kripa Shankar. Critical study of personality and poetic genius of Asvaghosha / by Kripa Shankar Vyas.

Ph.D. thesis in Hindi, approved by the Saugar [H.S. Gaur] University in 1964.

Vyas, Rashmikant. Comparative study of the depiction of nature in the works of Kalidasa and Aswaghosha / by Rashmikant Vyas.

Ph.D. thesis approved by the Vikram University in 1979.

Wassiljew, W. Der Buddhismus.- St. Petersburg : [s.n.], 1860.

Includes a legendary biographical account of Aśvaghoṣa.

Winternitz, M. History of Indian literature (Vol. 3) / tr. from German into English by Subhadra Jha. - Delhi : Motilal Banarsidass, 1985.

Yadav, Rajdeva. Critical study of the Buddhistic philosophy in the works of Asvaghosha / by Rajdeva Yadav.

Ph.D. thesis in Hindi, approved by the Kashi Vidya Peeth in 1982.

2

Bhaṭṭa Nārāyaṇa

Bhatta Narayana in all probablity lived before the eight century, but his date cannot be fixed with certainty. Some scholars holds the view that he belongs to six century, however there is very little information about him or his date.

Grill supposes this dramatist to have lived in the 6th or 7th century and Prof. Max Mueller provides a mere suggestion that he might be a contemporary and friend of Bana perhaps identical with Bhadra Narayana of Harshacharita from an examination of the works which quote from the *Venisamhara*.

Mr. Cunningham argues that the Sena Dynasty reigned in Bengal between 650 - 1108 A.D. A'disura is also shown to be a contemporary of Ansu Varma, king of Nepal, whose date is known as comprising the years 637 - 541 A.D. A'disura, the first king of the Sena Dynasty must have been lived in the 7th century. And as the migration of the Kanouja Brahmanas took place in his reign, the date of the composition of the *Venisamhara* of Bhaṭṭa Nārāyana fall in the latter half of the 7th or the first quarter of the 8th century.

Historians, however, unanimously hold the view that the playwright belonged either to the latter half of the 7th or the beginning of the 8th century as contemporaneous of Bhavabhuti or a little later. The style of *Venisamhara* reveals that the dramatist followed in the foot step of Bhavabhuti.

His date, as above view is supported by ample documentary evidences and Bhatta Narayana's work was profusely quoted by scholars in diverse fields.

Anandvardhana, the author of *Dhvanyaloka* who flourished under Avantivarman of Kashmir (855 - 884 A.D.) cited from *Venisamhara*. Vamana who lived about the middle of the 8th century in his *Alankara Sutra Vritti* quotes from the work. The *Dasharupaka* belonging to the middle of the 10th century, lays *Venisamhara* under contribution for illustration.

Saraswati Kanthabharana (the work that can be placed later than 1070 A.D.) by Bhojadeva quotes from *Venisamhara*.

Mammata, the author of *Kavyaprakasa*, whose date is fixed somewhere between 1150 - 1250 A.D. also quoted copiously.

Though thee are references to the *Pañcarātra* doctrines in his famous Sanskrit drama and one can find some criticism of the Cārvākas, but this does not provide any further information about Bhaṭṭanārāyana, the author of '*Veṇīsaṃhāra*'. *Avantisundarikatha* ascribed to Dandin refers to him as the author of three works. Tradition also makes him first a student of the famous Buddhist philosopher, Dharmakirti and then his opponent and joint author of *Rupavatara*.

It is said that Bhaṭṭa Nārāyaṇa was one of the five Brahmins invited by King Ādiśura to Bengal. He probably migrated from Kānyakubja or Kanoja to Bengal in about 800 A.D. joined the court of king Ādiśura. He was the leader of or the chief among these five Brahmanas who belonged to the Gauda sect and was a great devotee of Lord Vishnu and very probably belonged to the Advaita School of philosophy. This ancient playwright was of the Śāṇḍilya gotra and was surnamed Mṛgarāja, the only information that he gave about himself in the prologue to his play.

This honorary title 'Mṛgarāja' was added to his name and Ādiśura had rewarded him for his spiritual services by granting five villages the number of these villages increased later and Bhaṭṭa Nārāyaṇa became thte founder of a dynasty of kings.

The noble laureate Rabindranath Tagore is a decendent of Bhaṭṭa Nārāyaṇa and tradition assigns to the dramatist the position of the first ancestor of the celebrated Tagore family.

An enthralling and very popular play in Sanskrit, '*Venisamhara*' or 'Binding of the braid of hair' by Bhaṭṭa Nārāyaṇa is the story of the fulfilment of Bhimasena's vow to tie the loose tresses of Draupadi as indicated in the title of the play itself.

In his preface to '*Bhatta Naraya: makers of Indian literature*,' Asoke Chatterjee Sastri writes ... Bhattanarayana has shown his complete command of the Mahabharata. Practically the entire war of eighteen day of this great epic has been covered by Bhaṭṭanārāyaṇa. But that war episode of the Mahabharat has been dramatised with necessary additions, omissions and alterations to suit the purpose of the dramatist". He further adds that "From a serious study of this work, it is evident that Bhatta was quite conversant with the fundamental doctrines of the Samkhya, Vedanta and Yoga systems of Indian. Phbilosophy Apart from his complete command of the Mahabharata, he was well acquainted with history, the Puranas and also the Bhagavata and the like.... As regards his knowledge of grammar, he seems to have violated the injunctions of Panini in some cases".

The popularity of this play in India is primarity due to its partiality for the cult of Kṛṣṇa. But the unnecessary prose narrations mar the progress of the plot. The atmosphere of war and the fury of revenge is maintained throughout the play, as the theme that Bhattanarayana chose offered enough scope for dpicting such scenes of savagery, horror, blood - spilling, death and terror.

Henry W. Wells in his '*The classical drama of India*' wrote ... Many pages of the Indian epic are, indeed, far removed from meditations such as the Bhagvad Gita. Some will seem to modern readers more like the saga mythology of Scandinavia or to resemble the early and relatively savage mythology of pre-Homeric Greece. This violent, primitive, and brutal action at times transfers itself into impressive drama. *Venisamhara*, by Bhatta Nārāyana, possess these qualities. To be successful produced it must, accordingly be played in a very different manner from any style required by other plays... it is a moving story, firmly of a piece, full of pain, trouble, tragedy and despair. Though possessing little of the grace of luminosity found in the works of the more famous Sanskrit dramatists, it comes close to expression which the violent West has long known and knows only too well today. It may remind us of the song of Roland, or even of stark dramas based on heroic incidents of the latest war. Potentially, atleast, the play has by no means passed out of the repertory of world drama'.

Venisamhara offers us a variety of sentiments such as anger, disgust, laughter, pathos, even shringara. But the dominating remains the 'Heroism' or the 'Vira rasa'.

Bhaṭṭa Nārāyaṇa would be also reckoned as a successful playwright so far as the characterizations is concerned. Impetuous Bhimasena, jealous Karna, frustrated Aśvathāman, obstinate Duryodhana, spirited Draupadi and meek Bhānumati are excellently portrayed. To a considerable extent, Bhaṭṭa Narayan's 'Karna' and 'Duryodhana' moves us emotionally too.

Though his play is not that great, but he is revered for his masterly poetic style. His style belongs to Gauḍa type. The prose and the verses are full of vigour and power, but hinders the rapid movement of action.

It is said that like Harsha's '*Ratnavati*', the '*Venisamhara*' is favoured by Sanskrit scholars to illustrate the rules of dramaturgy. He follows the precepts of dramaturgy and skilfully built the play by employing all the tricks for stage effect.

Though *Venisamhara* seems to be the sole work of Bhattanarayana, but with the latest researches on oriental literature it is discovered that in the *Subhasitasamgrah* (*Collection* of Good Verses) is ascribed to him. It is also said that Bhatta might be the author of the purva - prithika (first part) of *Dasukumracaritam*. In one index of a manuscript of the '*Dasakumara Caritam* (copied by one Harisarma) it is written that apart from *Venisamhara*, he composed another drama entitled '*Janakiharana*'. The authorship of the above - writings is, however, debatable.

VEṆĪSAṀHĀRA

Synopsis

The drama shows how Bhima fulfills his pledge by drinking the blood from the chest of Duḥsāsana and breaks the thighs of Duryodhana, both of whom were responsible for the molestation of Draupadi in the royal court of Kurus. His pledge was that Draupadi shall not tie her hair into a braid until Bhima Kills Duḥśāsana who had pulled her by hair and breaks the thighs of Duryodhana who had insulted her with the order to shampoo his legs.

Based on Mahabharata story, this Nāṭaka in six acts begins with the Pāṇḍavas's resolution of war with the Kurus and frustrated negotiations for a amicable settlement, then goes through various war episodes and finally ends up with the killing of Duryodhana by Bhima and his tying up (samhara) the loose hair (veni) of Draupadi with his hands dripping with the blood of slain Kauravas.

Dramatic Personae

Males

Yudhisthira	-	The eldest Pāndava.
Bhimasena	-	The younger brother of Yudhisthira and the principal personage in the play.

Arjuna, Nakul and Sahadeva	-	The remaining three younger Pāndava princes.
Krishna	-	Friend and ally of the Pāndavas.
Dhritarastra	-	The Father of the Kaurava princes and uncle of the Pāndavas.
Duryodhana	-	The eldest son of the above and rival of Yudhisthira.
Karna	-	The friend of Duryodhana and his principal ally.
Kripa	-	The former preceptor of the Kuru Princes.
Ashvathaman	-	The warlike son of Drona and nephew of Kripa.
Sanjaya	-	Dhritarashtra's charioteer.
Sundaraka	-	An attendant on Karna.
Jayandhar	-	Chamberlain of the Pāndavas.
Vinayandhar	-	Chamberlain of the Kauravas.
Charvak	-	A Rākshasa in the disguise of a Muni, a friend of Duryodhana.
Rakshasa	-	Rudhirapriya, a male goblin.
Charioteers, chamberlains etc.		

Females

Draupadi	-	The wife of the Pāndavas.
Bhanumati	-	The wife of Duryodhana.
Gandhari	-	The mother of the Kauravas.
Duḥshala	-	Wife of Jayadratha and sister of the Kauravas.
Rakshasi	-	Wife of Rudhirpriya.

Female attendants on Draupadi, Bhanumati, the mother of Jayadratha, etc.

Plot :-

The broad outline of the play is given below :-

Prelude : After the recital of the benedictory stanzas and the announcement of the drama, the 'Sutradhara brings to the notice the audience about Krishna is being sent as an envoy who would act as a mediator between the Kauravas and the Pandavas and hopefully the impending war could be averted and subsequently peace be effected not only to the benefit of the contending parties but of the whole world.

Act One :-

Unfortunately Bhima overhears this and enters in an angry mood, followed by Sahadeva, cursing the Sūtradhara for his audacity to exposes such a wish.

He blames Sahadeva and his other brothers for having tamely put up with the insults heaped upon them by the Kauravas from time to time. He furthers tells that even if Krishna were to succeed in effecting peace he is determined to break it.

Bhima them moves towards Draupadi's mansion and await the arrival of the latter. Bhima cannot resist his anger when he finds Draupadi with her hair hanging loose and her eyes streaming with tears. Bhima enquires the cause of her grief and is told by her attendant that Duryodhana's wife has just passed a sarcastic comment on her dishevelled hair and the proposal of the Pandavas to be content with the grant of five villages.

Bhima now vows to kill Duryodhana and consoles her by saying that she will soon tie up her hair with his hand wet with Duryodhana's blood.

Message comes that Krishna has failed in his venture and has returned unsuccessfully in making peace. Bhima and Sahadeva willingly obeys the summons, take leave of Draupadi to take part in the ensuing war. The war drum is row beaten and all chiefs are asked to prepare for the battle.

Act Two :-

The effect of the revengeful pride of Bhima and also threat of war and an atmosphere of hatred that builds up in the first act dilutes in this act. It opens with the emergence of Kanchukin who announces the deaths of Bhisma, Abhimanyu and others.

In Act two, a frivolous love episode between Duryodhana and his queen is offered. Duryodhana's wife, Bhānumatī relates an ominous dream to her friend and an attendant. The dream goes like this : a Mungoose has slain a hundred serpents symbolizing all the Kaurava brothers. Their conversations is overheard by Duryodhana who at first becomes suspicious of betrayal, on hearing the name of 'Nakula' mentioned by her., but his doubts gets clear when he hears the story till its end. He appears before his wife to enjoy her sweet company and ask her to remove the fears from her mind. In the meanwhile, due to a hurricane, they takes shelter in a neighbouring wooden house. Jayadrath's mother appears alongwith her daughter-in-law to inform Duryodhana of Arjuna's pledge to kill her son before the sunset or failing which he would himself sacrifice his life in the flames. Duryodhana laughts at her fears and advice her to rejoice at Arjuna's certain death and mount his chariot for the battle.

Third Act :-

It shows the horror of the battle field with Drona's death at the hands of Dhrishṭadyumna while sitting in meditation when he cast off his arms, deceived by the false news of his son's death. This leads to a well - crafted scene of altercation between Ashvathama (torn between sorrow and fury) and Karna (unsympathetic and sneering). Asvathāma puts blame on Duryodhana of partiality and decide not to fight anymore while the latter continues to be in command.

Kripa (The former preceptor of the Kuru princes) tries to assuage his misery, promises to have him installed the general of the forces and takes him to Duryodhana. In the meantime Karna misrepresents to Duryodhana Drona's action and poisons his ears against the preceptor and his son. Kripa and Ashvathaman enter and are received with due respect and Duryodhana consoles Ashvathaman about his father's death. Now Kripa offers his proposal to make Ashvathama the general of the forces, but learns that the generalship has already been promised to Karna.

Act Four :-

In this act, Duryodhana is shown wounded, but on his way to recovery. He hears the news of Duḥśāsana's death from his charioteer. Thre is a tedious account of Karṇa's son 'Vṛsasena' and other losses. While Duryodhana was mourning his brother's loss, Sundaraka, an attendant on Karṇa hands over to him a leaf on which Karṇa has written a message with an arrow deeped in his own blood. Duryodhana prepares himself for the battle to rescue his friend who has resolved to die. But he is prevented by the arrival of his aged parents, Dhṛtarāshṭra and Gāndhārī, and Sañjaya.

Act Five :-

Dhṛtarashtra and Gāndhārī urges Duryodhana in vain to make peace, but he refuses to do so. On hearing the Karṇa's death, broken hearted Duryodhana proceeds to the battle field, unaided. Arjuna and Bhima emerges and thus, the act brings them in the vicinity of the battle field, where Duryodhana's parents have come to visit him. Bhim insists on their saluting with insults their aged uncle, Duryodhana reproves them, but Arjuna insists that it is just retribution for the acquiescene of the aged king in Draupadi's ill treatment. However, Yudhisthirā's messengers takes them away who orders the fight to cease for the day.

Now Aśvathaman appears to avenge the death of Duhsāsana and to turn the tide of fortune against the Pandavas. Duryodhana receives him cold by which makes him to depart in disgust.

Dhṛtarashtra sends Sanjaya after him to pursuade him to overlook his son's conduct. Duryodhana mount his chariot while his parents seeks Salya's tent.

Act Six :-

On hearing Bhima's pledge to kill him, Duryodhana tries to hide himself in a pool. But he is discovered. Krishna sends word to Yudhisthira to order public rejoicings. The fight continues till Duryodhana is defeated and slained at the hand of Bhima. This act brings the utter confusion of Yudhisthira and Draupadi, presented in all absurdity, as a demon Charvaka who conveys the false news of Bhimā's death to them. Deeply shocked by the news (from this demon, a friend of Duryodhana in disguise as Muni), Draupadi and Yudhisthira decides to put an end to their life by entering the funeral pyre.

At this juncture, appears Bhima who breaks the news of Duryodhana's death and thereby, the fraud is discovered.

At the close of the scene Bhima arranges Draupadi's hair and also to tie it up. Arjuna and Krishna enter and congratulate Yudhisthira on his victory and tell that the demon Charvaka who has caused so much distraction would meet his fate at the hand of Nakula.

The play ends in conforming with traditional norms by offering an happy ending and terminates with usual *Bharata Vakya*.

Veṇīsaṁhāra in Performances

In the adjunct of the well known cultural forum named 'Vidyotsahini Sabha' founded in 1855 by eminent writers, scholars, philanthropists, rich landlords and art patrons Shri Kaliprasanna Sinha, an aristocratic theatre was established in this Jorasanko area of North Calcutta.

Vidyotsahini Theatre which was opened in 1857 staged Bhattanarayan's famous play '*Venisamhara*' in Bengali. The Bengal rendering of Ramnarayan. Tarkaratna was staged in the presence of a distinguished audiences comprising of both Indians and Europeans. Wearing jewellery worth lakhs of rupees, Kaliprasanna Babu himself appeared in the role of Bhanumati and the 'Karna' was played by Mohendra Mukherjee. Play was a great success owing to good acting by the trained actors under able guidianship and direction of Babu Kaliprasanna Simha who had indepth knowledge of the classical traditon. Three is a dispute regarding the premier of this play. On 9 April 1857, 'Bidyotsahini Theatre' of Kaliprasanna Sinha staged '*Benisamhara*', mention Manmathnath Ghosh, the biographer of Kaliprasanna.

But journal '*Samvad Prabhakar*' gives another date of the performance. It stated in its 15th April 1857 issue that. At the residence of Babu Kaliprasanna, on 11 April, Saturday, 1857, the play '*Benisamhara*' was enacted in the residence of Sir Kaliprasanna Sinha. Dramatis personae included Kshetramohan Sinha, Manmohan Sinha, Mahendranath Mukhopadhyay (Karna), Manimohan Sarkar. In the play the actor who played Bhanumati (wife of Duryodhana) stood out for his excellent performance and the crowd hailed him with joy.

Natyacharya Radhamadhav Kar has mentioned that at the invitation of Saradacharan Mitra, in the residence of Ray Ramaprasad Mitra Bahadur, '*Benisamhar*' was staged in 1869. The stage was supplied by an amateur theatre group from Shibpur. Maheshchandra Nyayratna selected the cast for the show that was witnessed by Shri Dinbandhu Mitra, the author of '*Nilpardan*', that created history in the realm of Indian theatre.

In the modern era, the enactment of Sanskrit play in their original form is not much in vogue. From the very begining the efforts to revive the Indian theatre was made through the adaptation of classical dramas in various Indian languages and that further enlivened by their stage productions to reach out to wider audiences instead of a few learned Sanskrit scholars. It does not mean that the classical master pieces are not being played in Sanskrit. In 1869, the students of the Government College performed *Veṇī - saṁhāra* in Sanskrit.

In Poona, a prose performance of '*Venisamhara*' in Sanskrit was produced in the year 1871.

'*Satrusamhar*', a Bengali production of Bhattanarayana's '*Venīsaṃhara*' was performed on 12 December 1874 at Great National Theatre, Calcutta. The play was rendered by Harulal Ray.

'*Hindi Natakojjivaka Samajam*' was founded by Vaddadi Subbarayudu, a well known Telugu playwright at Rajahmundry in 1884. The group produced his own translation of '*Vēṇī samhāram*' in Telugu. Vaddadi was a great actor who earned his repute as an actor in the roles of Dharmaraja and Aswathama.

Venisamhara of Bhattanaraya was rendered into Oriya version by Harihar Rath in six acts. Published in 1896, the play was staged and dedicated to the Ramchandra Bhanja.

In November 1926, the fourth Oriental Conference was held at Allahabad where in '*Veṇīsaṁhāra*' was performed in Sanskrit, and major roles seemed to have been monopolised by family members of Dr. Ganganath Jha.

At the invitation of the Maharajadhiraja of Darbhanga, the 'Fourteenth Session of the All India Oriental Conference' was held at Darbhanga from 15th to 18th October 1948. In this conference, 'Veṇisaṁhara' was enacted in Sanskrit.

On October 15, 1948, only the third act was produced at the All India Oriental Conference; Darbhanga. The act depicts the heroic quarrel between prince Karna and Ashwathaman who has just heard of the news of the death of his father 'Dronacharya'. The cast comprised of:-

Cast

Rākshasa	...	Shri Madannath Jha.
Karna	...	Shri Chetannath Jha.
Sūta	...	Sri Madannath Jha.
Ashvathāmā	...	Shri Krsnaballabha Jha.
Duryodhana	...	Shri Virendra Jha.
Krpāchārya	...	Shri Buddhikara Jha.
Rakśasī	...	Shri Brahmandasiṁha Jha.

Actors in the Drama 'Veni - Samhara' produced at the All - India Oriental Conference, Dabhanga in 1948.

The *Veṇīsaṁhāra* of Bhaṭṭanārāyana was staged in Sanskrit at the Sixteenth Session of the 'All India Oriental Conference' which was held under the auspices of the Lucknow University in the early fiftees.

Another production of *Veṇīsaṃhāra* of Bhaṭṭanarayana in Sanskrit was by the Madras Sanskrita Academy. The Late S. Satyamurti gave a brilliant performance as 'Aśvathaman'.

DRAMATIC WORKS : A BIBLIOGRAPHY

Text

Venisamhara / ed. by K. Tarkacarya .- Calcutta, 1958.

Veṅisaṃhāram of Nārāyaṇa Bhaṭṭa is a drama in six acts on the Mahābhārata episode of the satisfaction of Bhīma's revenge celebrated by the killing of the Kaurava chiefs, then with blood - stained hands the binding up braid of Draupadī, which she had sworn to leave untied until the wrong done to her was avenged.

Venisamhara / by Bhaṭṭa Nārāyaṇa; ed. by M.R. Kale. - Delhi : Motilal Banarsidass, 1977.

Text with English translation, notes, introduction etc.

Also published in 1989.

Venisamhara / by Bhattanarayana .- Delhi : Motilal Banarsidass, 1980.

Text with English tr. by M.R. Kale.

Venisamhara / ed. by S. Shastri .- Meerut : [s.n.], 1960.

Venisamhara with the commentary of Jagaddhara / ed. by K.P. Parab .- 3rd ed. - Bombay, 1913.

Venisamharam : with the commentary by Jagaddhara / by Bhaṭṭanārāyaṇa; ed. by Kasinatha Panduranga Paraba .- Varanasi : Chaukhamba Orientalia, 1987.

11, 216 p.; 22 cm.

Venisamharam : with the commentary by Jagaddhara / by Bhaṭṭanārayana; ed. by Narayana Rama Acarya .- Delhi : Sri Shakti Publications, 1986.

211 p.; 22 cm.

Veṇīsaṃhāram / by Nārāyaṇa Bhaṭṭa; ed. by J. Grill .- Leipzig : [s.n.], 1871.

Veṇīsaṃhāram / by Nārāyaṇa Bhaṭṭa; ed. with an introd., English translation and critical notes by G.V. Devasthalī .- Bombay : Booksellers Publishing Co., 1953.

xvi, 396 p.; 21 cm.

Includes appendices & index.

Veṇīsaṃhāram / by Nārāyaṇa Bhaṭṭa; ed. with an introd., English translation and notes by M.R. Kāḷe & S.R. Dharādhar .- Bombay : Śāradā Krīḍan Press, 1910.

[384] p.; 21 cm.

Includes appendices and index.

Text includes Jagaddhara's commentary.

Veṇīsaṃhāram / by Nārāyaṇa Bhaṭṭa; ed. by K.P. Parab and K.R. Madgavkar .- Bombay : Nirnaya Sagar Press, 1898.

Veṇīsaṃhāram / by Nārāyaṇa Bhaṭṭa; ed. with a commentary 'Bālabodhinī' by Appā Śāstrī Rāśīvaḍekar. - Poona : Āryabhūṣaṇ Press, 1909 - 10.

[918] p.; 21 cm.

Includes notes in English by K.N. Dravid.

Veṇīsaṃhāram / by Nārāyaṇa Bhaṭṭa; ed. with an introd., English translation, notes and appendices by A.B. Gajendragaḍkar .- Poona : The editor, 1922 - 23.

3 Vols.; 22 cm.

Venisaṃhara - natakam / by Bhaṭṭa Nārāyaṇa; ed. with 'Kamalesvari' Sanskrit - Hindi comm. by Balagovinda Jha. - Varanasi : Krishnadas Academy, 1984.

52, 410 p.; 18.5 cm.

Venisamhara / by Bhattanarayana. - Delhi : Butala & Co., 1986.

223 p.

Nirnaya Sagar ed. reprinted.

Translations

Bengali

Sanskrita sahitya sambhar / ed. by Gaurinath Sastri & ... et al. [Vol. 4] .- Calcutta: Navpatra Prakashan, [197 -].

Includes Bengali rendering of 'Venisamhara' of Bhattanarayana by Jagadish Tarkatirtha.

Veṇīsaṃhāra / by Bhaṭṭa Narayana; tr. into Bengali by Jyotirindranath Thakur. - 1901.

Shatrusamhara = [Venisamhara] / by Bhattanarayana; tr. into Bengali by Harlal Ray, 1874.

Veṇisamhara / by Bhaṭṭa Naryana; tr. into Bengali by Kedarnath Sharma .- 1870 [1277].

Includes commentary.

This lucid translation was chosen as college text book.

Venisamhara / by Bhattanarayana; tr. into Bengali by Muktaram Sharma, 1855.

Bimukta venibandhan = [Venisamhara] / by Bhattanarayana; tr. into Bengali by Nagendranath Ghosh, 1886.

Veṇīsaṃhara / by Bhaṭṭa Narayana; tr. into Bengali by Ramnarayan Tarkaratna. - 1856.

This is the first rendering of the play in Bengali.

Veṇisaṃhara. *In* Sanskrit sahityer anubad - dhara / by Sabitri De Calcutta : Chinmay Majumdar, [1983].

Contents : Venisamhar (Pp. 168 - 172).

English

Binding of the braid of hair / by Bhattanarayana; tr. into English by Sourindra Mohan Tagore of 'Veni-samhara .- Calcutta : [s.n.], 1880.

Venisamhara of Bhatta Narayana / by Bhatta Narayana; ed. by M.R. Kale .- Delhi: Motilal Banarsidass.

Text with English translation, notes, introduction etc.

Venisamharam / by Bhattanarayana; English tr. by C. Sankararama Sastri.- 2nd ed. - Madras : [s.n.], 1961.

Veṇisaṃhāram / by Nārāyaṇa Bhaṭṭa; ed. with an introd.; English tr. & notes by M.R. Kale and S.R. Dharadhar .- Bombay : Shāradā Krīdan Press, 1910.

[384] p.; 21 cm.

Includes appendices and index.
Play contains Jagaddhara's commentary.

Hindi

Veṇisaṃhāra / by Bhaṭṭanārāyaṇa .- Mirzapur : [s.n.], 1973.

Veṇīsaṃhāra / by Bhaṭṭanārāyaṇa .- Lahore : Sahitya Bhawan, 1924.

Venisamhara / by Bhattanarayana; tr. into Hindi by Ambikadatt Vyas. [19th cent.].

Veṇīsaṃhāra / by Bhaṭṭanārayaṇa; ed. with Sanskrit text and Hindi tr. by Gaurīnāth Pāṭhak. - Banaras : Śāradā Saṁskṛt Granthamālā, 1940.

vi, 446 p.; 18.5 cm.

Venisamhara - / by Bhaṭṭanarayana; ed. with 'Kamalesvari' Sanskrit - Hindi comm. by Balagovinda Jha. - Varanasi : Krishnadas Academy, 1984.

52, 410 p.; 18.5 cm.

Venīsaṃhāra / by Bhaṭṭanārāyaṇa; tr. by Ādityaṇārāyaṇa Pāndeya. - Varanasi : Caukhamba, 1969.

Veṇīsaṃhāra / by Bhaṭṭanārāyaṇa; tr. by Guruprasad Śāstrī .- Varanasi : Bhargava Bhusan Press, 1938.

Veṇīsaṃhāra / by Bhaṭṭanārāyaṇa; tr. by Jvālāprasād .- Bombay : Venkateśvar Press, [n.d.].

Venisamhara / by Bhattanarayana tr. into Hindi by Jvalaprasad Miśra. 1887.

Veṇīsaṃhāra / by Bhaṭṭanārāyana; tr. by Mahāvira Prasād Dvivedī .- Lucknow : [s.n.], 1943.

Veṇīsaṃhāra / by Bhaṭṭanārāyaṇa; tr. by Rāmdev Jhā .- Varanasi : Caukhamba Sanskrit Series, 1953.

Veṇīsaṃhāra / by Bhaṭṭanārayana; tr. by V.D. Śāstrī .- Roorkee : Kavyamala, Devlok, 1932.

Veṇī saṁhāra / by Bhaṭṭanārāyaṇa; tr. from Sanskrit by Aśok Kauśik .- New Delhi: Diamond Pocket Books, 1991.

159 p.; 18 cm.

Hindi rendering of the classical play.

Veṇīsaṃhāra / by Bhaṭṭanārāyaṇa; tr. into Hindi by Hardayālsiṃha .- Allahabad : Indian Press, 1939.

Kannada

Vēṇīsaṃhāra / by Nārāyaṇa Bhaṭṭa; tr. by Dhōṇḍo Narasiṃha Muḷabāgal .- 2nd ed. - Dharwar : The translator, 1914.

vi, 143 p.; 18 cm.

Vēṇīsaṃhāra / by Nārāyaṇa Bhaṭṭa; tr. by Jayarāyācārya .- 2nd ed. - Mysore : G.T.A. Press, 1907.

viii, 140 p.; 21 cm.

First published in 1896.

Malyalam

Vēṇīsaṃhāram / by Nārāyaṇa Bhaṭṭa; tr. by Pantaḷam Kēraḷa Varma Tampurān. - Trivandrum : S.R. Book Depot., 1939.

127 p.; 23 cm.

Marathi

Vēṇīsaṃhāra / by Bhaṭṭa Narayana; tr. into Marathi by Parshuramtatya Godbole.

Vēṇīsaṃhāra : sār va vicār / by Nārāyaṇabhaṭṭa; tr. with a commentary by Mahadev Vyaṅkaṭeś Lele .- Bombay : Vividha. jnanavistar, [n.d.]

96 p.; 24 cm.

Contains an abridged rendering into Marathi with occasional comments.

Nepali

Veni Samhar / by Bhattanarayana; tr. into Nepali by Harinarayan Upadhyay.

Oriya

Venisamhara / by Bhattanarayana; tr. into Oriya by Harihar Rath. 1896.

Venīsamhara / by Bhattanarayana; tr. into Oriya by Mṛtyunjaya Rath, 1920.

Telugu

Venisamhara natakamu / by Bhattanarayana; tr. into Telugu by Vaddadi Subbaraya Kavi .- Rajahmundy : The translator, 1928.

94 p.; 20 cm.

Bhīmapratijña / by Nārāyaṇa Bhatta; tr. by B. Venkaṭanāñcārayya. - Guntur : Bikāri Simha, 1935.

106 p.; 18 cm.

Telugu translation of original Sanskrit drama 'Veṇīsaṃhāram'.

Vēṇīsaṃhāramu / by Nārāyaṇa Bhaṭṭa; introd., by Divākarla Vēṅkaṭāvadhāni; tr. by Bulusu Vēṅkaṭēśvarulu.- Kakinada : The translator, 1951.

xii, 124 p.; 18 cm.

Vēṇīsaṃhāramu / by Nārāyaṇa Bhaṭṭa; tr. by Koḍāli Satyanārāyaṇarāvu. - Rajahmundry : Śrī Sītārāmā Book Depot., 1926.

vi, 95 p.; 21 cm.

Vēṇīsaṃhāra nāṭakamu / by Nārāyaṇa Bhatta; tr. by Śrīpāda Kṛṣṇamūrtiśāstri.- Rajahmundry : [s.n.], 1907.

iv, 96 p.; 18 cm.

Vēṇīsaṃhāramu / by Nārāyaṇa Bhaṭṭa; tr. by Vaḍḍādi Subbārāyuḍu .- Rajahmundry: Karrā Accayya & Sons, 1924.

x, 99 p.; 21 cm.

BIO - CRITICAL NOTICES

Adya Rangacharya. Drama in Sanskrit literature. - 2nd ed. Bombay : Popular Prakashan, 1967. Pp. 44, 48, 62, 91.

Aggarwal, H.R. A short history of Sanskrit literature. - 2nd rev. ed. - Delhi : Munshiram Manoharlal, 1963.

Contents :

(Bhattanarayana, P. 182).

Aggarwal, Shail.

Critical study of Venisamhara in the light of Dasarupaka / by Shail Agarwal.

Ph.D. thesis approved by the Banaras Hindu University in 1987.

Aufrecht, Theodor. Catalogus catalogorum. - Weisbaden : Franz Steiner Verlag Gmb. H., 1962.

2 Vols.; 26 cm.

Bandyopadhyay, Sureshchandra. Sanskrit sahityer itihas .- Calcutta : The Dacca Students Library, [1970 ?]

Bhartiya, Kanti Kishore. Sanskrit natakkar .- Uttar Pradesh : Prakashan Shakha, Suchana Vibhag, 1959.

(Hindi - Samiti granthamala; 25).

Contents : Bhattanarayana. Pp. 169 - 183.

Bhat, G.K. Sanskrit drama : problems and perspectives .- Delhi : Ajanta Publications, 1985. Pp. 50, 68, 175, 236.

Bhatt, S.C. Drama is ancient India. - Delhi : New Delhi : Amrit Book Co., 1961. p. 90 - 91.

Bhattacharya, Bimanchandra. Sanskrit sahityer ruprekha. - 5th ed. - Calcutta : Vidyodaya Library Pvt. Ltd., 1972.

Bhattacharya, Biswanath. Sanskrit drama and dramaturgy. - Delhi : Sharada Publishing House, 1994. Pp. 241 - 252.

Bhattacharya, Hillol.

Tragedy : ek bicchinnatar itihas *Syas Natya Patra* - 16; 1999.

Comparative Indian literature (Vol. 1) / ed. by K.M. George .- Trichur : Kerala Sahitya Akademi, 1984. P. 567.

The cultural heritages of India [Vol. V] / ed. by Sumit Kumar Chatterji .- rev. ed. - Calcutta : The Ramakrishna Mission Institute of Culture, 1978.

P. 241, 251 - 252.

Dange, Sadashiv A & Dange, Sindhu S. Critiques on Sanskrit dramas. - 2nd rev. ed. - New Delhi : Aryan Books International, 1994.

Dasgupta, S.N. and De, S.K. History of Sanskrit literature .- Calcutta, 1947.

Deep Shikha. Comparative study of the dramas of Bhasa based on the Mahabharata and Veni samhara of Bhattanarayana from the angle of skills of dramatics / by Deep Shikha.

Ph.D. thesis in Hindi, approved by the Meerut University in 1986.

Deshpande, R.R. Interpretation of Veṇīsaṁhāra. *All India Oriental Conference* VI; P. 43 - *Conference* XVII (Summary); P. 30.

Dictionary of oriental literatures (Vol. II) : South and South - East Asia. - Delhi : Vikas Publishing, 1975.

Dubey, R.P. 'Hero of the Venisamhara' / by R.P. Dubey. *Prajna;* March 1967; Vol. 12, No. 2; Pp. 185 - 190.

Encyclopaedia of Indian literature .- New Delhi : Sahitya Akademi, 1987.

Pp. 477, 1105, 4537.

Faijunnesha Begum. Venisamharam : a study / by Faijunnesha Begum.

Ph.D. thesis approved by the Burdwan University in 1987.

Gajendragadkar, A.B. The Venisamhara : a critical study.

Garg, Ganga Ram. An encyclopaedia of Indian literature .- Delhi : Mittal Publishers, 1982. Pp. 49, 483 - 484.

Jain, Shanti. Venisamhara : a critical study / by Shanti Jain.

Ph.D. thesis approved by the Magadh University in 1969.

Keith, A. Berriedale. The Sanskrit drama in its origin, development, theory and practice .- Oxford : OUP, 1924.

405 p.; 22 cm.

Keith, A. Berriedale Sanskrit - natak : udbhav aur vikas : siddhanta aur prayog / tr. into Hindi by Udaybhanu Singh. - Delhi : Motilal Banarsidass, 1965.

Konow, S. Das Indische drama .- Berlin, 1920.

Lēvi, Sylvain. The theatre of India / tr. from the French by Naryan Mukherji .- Calcutta : Writers Workshop, 1978.

2 Vols.

Contents : Bhatta Narayan. Pp. (I) 201 - 203, 241; II (101).

Venisamhāra. Pp. (I) 34, 134, 140; (II) 101 - 103.

Macdonell, A.A. India's past : a survey of her literatures, religious, languages and antiquities .- Varanasi : Motilal Banarsidass, 1956. P. 114.

Masterpieces of Indian literature (Vol. 3) / ed. by K.M. George .- New Delhi : National Book Trust, 1997.

P. 1968 - 69.

Misra, Thakkana. Bhattanarayanakṛta Venisamhara - nataka : samalocanatmaka adhyayana .- Agra : Shabdasri Prakashan, [1991].

x, 276 p.

Mishra, Thakkana. Venisamhara : a critical study / by Thakken Mishra.

Ph.D. thesis in Hindi, approved by the Agra University in 1968.

Panda, P.K. Contribution of Orissa to Sanskrit . - Delhi : Pratibha Prakashan, 1987.

Contents : Veṇisamhāram. Pp. 88 - 89.

Pandey and Vyasa. Sanskrit sahitya ki ruprekha. 1948.

Pathak, M.C. Sanskrit nāṭaka men atiprākṛta tattva. - Jaipur : Devanagar Prakshan, [n.d.].

18, 468 p.

Roy, Ashim Kumar & Gidwani, N.N. A Dictionary of indology (Vol. 1) .- New Delhi : Oxford & IBH Publishing Co., 1983. P. 214.

Sahitya Akademi - New Delhi. The National bibliography of Indian literature. - New Delhi : The author, 1962 - 1990.

5 Vols.

Sastri, Gaurinath. Sanskrit sahityer itihas. - Calcutta : Sarasvata Library, 1969 ? [Aśvin 1376].

Sethi, Atmaram. Anudit Hindi sahitya : vishishta grantha suchi / by Atmaram Sethi .- Gurgaon : Indian Documentation Service, 1981.

Contents : Sanskrit (Pp. 1 - 624).

Shekhar, I. Sanskrit drama : its origin and decline .- Leiden : E.J. Brill, 1960. Pp. 142, 148, 162, 171, 173, 179, 181.

Tewari, Shashi. 'Venisaṃhar mein karun ras kī yojna' / by Shashi Tewari. *In* Treatment of pathos in Sanskrit dramas / ed. by Pushpendra Kumar.- Delhi: Nag publishers, 1981. Pp. 33 - 44.

Tope, T.K. Bhaṭṭa Nārāyaṇa and Bhavabhūti. *All India Oriental Conference* (Summary); P. 194.

Vedavyasa. Sanskrita sahitya ka itihas. - Lahore, 1920.

Wells, Henry W. The Classical drama of India. - Bombay : Asia Publishing House, 1963. P. 26.

Winternitz, M. History of Indian literature (Vol. 3) / tr. from German into English by Subhadra Jha. - Delhi : Motilal Banarsidass, 1985.

3

Bhavabhūti

The literary historians are fortunate enough that Bhavabhuti unlike many a classical writers, has given us atleast some informations about himself and his family in the prologues of his three plays.

In the prologue of 'Mālatimādhava', the author has given us much information about himself and his ancestors. Similar statements appear in the other two plays of Bhavabhūti viz. The Mahāvīracarita and the Uttararāmacharita. In the colophons of several acts of these dramas or atleast at the end, the name of Bhavabhūti is mentioned as their author. But in the colophon of the sixth act of a Ms. of the Mālatīmādhava, about 500 years old, which Shankar Pandurang Pandit obtained from, we come to know that from Vidarbha he had shifted to Ujjayini where, before Mahākala, his dramas were staged. Bhavabhuti, thus, tells us significantly about himself, his ancestry, his learning, his teacher and his writings. Known for his Rama plays to which he gave an altogether new garb, this superb dramatist did not earn recognition from his contemporaries. Though Bhavabhuti's indebtedness to Kalidasa is manifest in many places of his magnum opus, Uttararāmacarita, but it is to be admitted that he is the best among the successors of Kalidasa. He was the master of pathos.

According to Kalhana's Rajatarangini, he was the court-poet of Yasovarman, king of Kanyakubja, who was defeated by Muktapida Lalitāaditya of Kashmir sometime after A.D. 736. From Gaudavaho it appears that Bhavabhuti did not see the downfall of his patron. Vāmana (8th century A.D.) in his Kāvyā laṁkārasutravṛtti, quotes verses from Bhavabhūti. A verse of Mahāvīracarita is cited as an example of Gauḍī style. Similarly he has quoted a verse from Uttararāmacarita as an instance of Rūpaka.

Rājaśekhara (880 - 920 A.D.) in his Kāvyamīmāṁsā quotes verses from the Mālatīmadhava of Bhavabhūti. In his Bālarāmāyana, he calls himself an incarnation of Bhavabhūti. It is clear that he must have lived prior to 800 A.D. and it can be proved by his verses being quoted in the works on poetics like Daśarūpaka (10th century A.D.), Aucityavīcaracarca and Suvṛttatilaka of Ksemendra (11th century A.D.), Kāvyaprakāśa (12th century A.D.) and anthologies like Śārṅgadharupaddhati, Kavīndravacanasamuccaya, Saduktikaruāmṛta. Prof. Kane places his literary activities between A.D. 700 and 730. He must have lived in the later half of the 7th century and in the beginning of the 8th century A.D.

Tradition made Bhavabhuti and Kalidasa, two of the nine gems of court of Vikramaditya. It is believed that Kalidasa was already recognised gem in the court of Vikramaditya, there came to him one day a Brahmana poet, and begged him to use his infuence in getting him the royal patronage. This poet was none other than Bhavabhuti. Bhavabhuti started reciting his Uttararamacarita while Kalidasa who was playing a kind of chess caled 'Sara' was half listening. When he finished, Kalidasa praised his work and agreed upon to use his influence for him if he drops a bindu in the last line of one of his verses. Bhavabhuti accepted the suggestion and eventually there had been one more addition of gems in the court of Vikramaditya.

According to another legend, once a dispute arose at Amaravati, the abode of the gods, about the relative merits of the two great Sanskrit dramatists, Kalidasa and Bhavabhuti. One group held Kalidasa to be superior to Bhavabhuti, while another section of the gods held different stand. When the dispute could not be settled between the two, they agreed to refer it to the arbitration of Saraswati, the goddess of learning. With the scale of justice in her hands, each section placed its arguments and counter arguments, and the scales tilted continually, as the debate progressed, sometimes in favour of one and sometimes in favour of the other. When the matter could not be resolved by arguments, the goddess took a pearl out of her earring and placed it in the pass favouring Kalidasa, to decide the matter in his favour and against Bhavabhuti. One may object to the goddess's partiality, but there is near unanimity that Bhavabhuti ranks the highest among Sanskrit dramatist after Kalidasa.

Born in a Brahmana family of Kasyapa gotra at Padmapura in Vidharbha (Berar), Bhavabhuti was the son of Nilakantha and Jatukarni. He bore the appelation

Srikantha and the surname Udumbara. He was also a Somayajin.

According to some commentators Srikantha was his real name and later when he became popular as Bhavabhuti on the basis of his literary, allegorical and fascinating use of this particulars word : *Sambapunatu Bhavabhutipabitramurtin*. His grand father Bhatta Gopala had performed the Vajapeya sacrifice while Jnananidhi was the name of his guru. Brought up in a family of pious Brahmana ancestors, Bhavabhuti believed in the Purvamimamsa cult of sacrifices with heaven as its goal, and in the daily observance of five worship by the house holders. He belived in the efficacy of Tapas and performance of vows like Paraka, santapana.

For centuries he has fascinated his readers with his exceptional poetic talent and command over the Sanskrit language.

Bhavabhuti's authorship of three plays namely Matimadhavam, Mahaviracaritam, and Uttararamacharitam are beyond any doubt and debate. He is second only to Bhasa in choosing the life of Rama for dramatisation. His two natakas on the life of Rama, the great hero of the first Indian epic are the Mahaviracarita and the other Uttararamacarita. The significant phases of Rama's life till his coronation at Ayodhya is depicted in the first play covering the six kandas of the Ramayana, while the second nataka deals, as the title itself suggest, Rama's life after that period, the Uttara-Rama-Carita or the later fortunes of Rama is excellent for its exhibition of pathos as the main sentiment. Interestingly in the opinion of Indian dramaturgy, the erotic or the heroic rasa alone should dominate in a play. It goes without saying that this play stands unsurpassed in terms of the intensity of Karuna rasa. The play produces a tender and sympathetic impression upon the mind of the reader and the spectator who is moved to tears to hear or witness the lamentations of Rama, Sita, Janaka and other dignitied personages suffering at the hands of cruel destiny. This is one of the most exquisite creations in the Indian dramatic literary art.

In the realm of prakarana, he is given second position and placed next to Sudraka, but has given no chance to others to supersede him in 'Malatimadhava' which depicts the love story of Malati, daughter of a minister of the country, and Madhava, a young scholar studying in the city of Ujjaini.

M.V. Lele of Indore noticed for the first time Umbekācharya mentioned as the author of the play. Umbeka was described as one who has obtained his literary power through the favour of the illustrious Kumārilasvāmin. In the colophon of the third act in the same manuscript the play was stated to have been penned by a pupil of Kumārila. On the basis of these two remarks, S.P. Pandit felt out Bhavabhūti and Umbeka were identical and that Bhavabhūti was a pupil of the great Mīmāṁsaka Kumārila. Dr. R.G. Bhandarkar in the preface of his edition of the Mālatimādhava stated that this view did not conflict chronologically with any knownf act, but as Bhavabhuti no where mention Kumārila as his teacher and do not makes mention of Mīmāṁsā as his subject of study, he felt suspicious about the statements.

On the evidence of the Rājataraṅgiṇi and other text, it is established that Bhavabhuti flourished in the first quarter of the eighth century A.D. He can not, therefore, be identified with Umbeka who flourished half a century later.

Besides, in other manuscripts of his works, Bhavabhūti do not mention Umbeka as his another name and Umbeka also nowhere tells us that he was also known as Bhavabhūti. The name Umbeka, as Prof. V.V. Mirashi, points out appears to be Dravidian, but the names of Bhavabhūti's ancestors viz Mahākavi, Gopāla and Nīlakaṇṭha are of Sanskritic origin like those of the Brahmanas mentioned in the copper-plate in Vidarbha. Bhavabhūti flourished in a different age and was a different person from the Mimāṁsaka Umbeka.

In his plays, Bhavabhuti styles himself Pada-vākya-pramāṇajña, which show that he has mastered the Vyākaraṇa, Mīmāṁsa and Nyāya.

He was highly proficient in Vedānta and Vedas, the Upanishads, dramaturgy, political sciences and erotics.

He used a large number of Alaṁkāras in his plays and is fully conversant with Rhetorics. In Mālatimādhava, he employed the longest Daṇḍaka metre (54 letters in a quarter) with great effect in describing goddess Cāmuṇḍā. He uses a large number of metres and well-versed in the science of Prosody.

While commenting on this play Prof. Keith said "The plot, however interesting, is extremely badly knit together; the action is dependent to an absurd degree on accident; Mālatī twice on the verge of death is twice saved by mere chance. Moreover, the characters live apart from all contact with real life; they are in a city like the characters of the Mṛcchakaṭika, but seem to exist in a world of their own in which the escape of tigers and the abduction of maidens with murderous intent cause no surprise. There is little individuality in hero or heroine, though the shy modesty of the latter contrasts with the boldness of Madayantikā, who flings herself at Makaranda's head. A friend of Mādhava, Kalahaṁsa, is asserted later to be a Vita, but has nothing characteristic, and probably the assertion is without ground".

The characters in the play excells in emotional outbursts and the capacity of the poet to give them suitable expression accounts for the appeal of the play.

Mālatīmādhava contains all constituents of the Śṛṅgāra rasa. In this prakaraṇa also he employs Karuṇa rasa successfully but he never loses sight of Śṛṅgāra. Peculiarly there is no other rasa to be seen in the play but the Vipralambhaśṛṅgārā and Bībhatsa.

His prose is flat, but versification is highly charming and Kālīdāsian in effect.

The Mālatīmadhava has the same metres as the Uttararāmacarita plus the Narkuṭaka and a Daṇḍaka of six short syllables and sixteen amphimacers; here the Vasantatilaka takes first place (49), Śārdūlavikrīḍita (32), Sikharini (21), and Hariṇī (12). The Mālinī (21) and Mandākrāntā (15) take on greater importance, while the sloka is negligible (14). His employment of 8 Āryas shows the changed character of Bhavabhūtī's versification from that of Kālidāsa.

It can be mentioned here that there is an epitome of Mālaṭīmāḍhava in verse called Ṛjulaghvī by Maiṭhila-śarman and commentaries on it by Ḍharānanḍa, Jagaḍḍhara, Tṛpurāri, (Mānānka, Rāghavabhatta, Nārāyaṇa, Prākṛṭacārya, J. Viḍyāsāgara, Pūrṇasarasvaṭī and Kunjavihāri).

Mahāvīracarita appears to be his first play that has been greatly influenced by the Arthaśāstra (science of wealth). In Mahāvīracarita, the playwright has given a political colouring to the conflict between Rama and Ravana who all the whihle works through his minister Mālyavat. Bhavabhuti has tried his best to build up a new glamorous character of the hero and has achieved success. In the play Rāma is an ideal personage. His character is moderate, righteous, heroic and protective.

He kills the monkey commander Bāli, who came to fight with him on Rāvaṇa's initiative. Whatever seems improper, objectionable and adverse in Rāma, is only due to Rāvaṇa's evil character.

In the beginning of the play, the poet states that in Mahāvīracarita, the heroic sentiment is delineated in its latent and manifest aspects through the medium of extraordinary characters. He gives logic for the employment of vīra as the main sentiment of his play. He admits, as he is fond of vīra and adbhuta sentiments, therefore he has composed the story of Rama, the subduer of those going against religion. The work contains the descriptions of the uprooting of the sorrow of the three worlds and is full of descripion of valour and patience and is wonderful.

In metre the Mahāviracarita shows a free use of the śloka, as is inevitable in an epic play; it is found 129 times; the Śārdūlavikrīḍita (75), Vasantatilaka (39),

Śikhariṇī (31), and Sragdharā (28) are the other chief metres; the Upajāti, Mandākrāntā, and Mālinī are not rare, but the Āryā (3) and Gīti (1) are almost gone, and there are only sporadic Aupacchandasika, Puṣpitāgrā, Pṛthvī, Praharṣini, Rathoddhatā, Vaṅśasthā, Śālinī, and Hariṇi.

A critic observes that his prose is void of charm and is too much laboured, bristles with difficult words and long compounds whereas his verses are comparatively easy and bright. The dialogue of the characters fails to bringout the characteristic traits of them. All the characters, from a maid-servant to Rāma, speak more or less in the same manner. Such as stiff and rigid language is a great impediment on the way of appreciating the play.

According to Keith, the Mahāvīracarita lacks the novelty of the Mālatīmādhava, but Bhavabhūti's effort to give some unity to the plot is commendable, though it is unsuccessful. The fatal error, of course, is the narration of events in long speeches in lieu of action.

Thus, so for his style is concerned, his main draw back is over-elaboration. The excess of reduntant verses can be felt throughout the length and breadth of the play. He never miss a single chance to display his power of versification. This want of restraint is visible in the quarrel scenes between Rāma and Paraśurāma. Biswanath Bhattacharya comments that nothing but playwrights love of words has made the quarrel linger through almost three full acts though the victory over Paraśurāma is not at all the main issue of the play, neither it is so much related with the killing of Rāvaṇa. The prolongation of this bandying appears the more inordinate in the background of the actual fight of Rāma with Rāvaṇa which hasbeen executed in a single Act. Strangely enough, the arch-enemy of Rāma is not granted even as much chance to show his valour as is granted to Vālin. Such a treatment makes Rāvaṇa appear very weak and thereby renders the victory of Rāma over him almost trifling. Though the purpose of the playwright is to present Rāma as a Mahāvīra, he fails apparently in doing so.

Though the play can not be considered to belong to the highest class, but nevertheless it can not be shunted to the background. For his poetic excellence and in presenting a Nāṭaka of Vīra-rasa Mahaviracarita is an useful addition in the field of Sanskrit dramatic literature.

There is a commentary on the play by Vīrarāghava.

His main work 'Uttararāmacarita' is regarded as a serious rival, to the 'Abhijñānaśākunṭala' of 'Kalidasa for the first place in Sanskrit dramatic literature.

In this play, he has successfuly made a known story, a great story of conjugal love. The love depicted in this play has been rendered sublime and pure by means of the sacrifice done by both the parties. In the selection of conjugal love for dramatic representation Bhavabhūti strikes an absolutely new path. Biswanath Bhattacharya writes : None before him attempted to depict a married and, so, common place love affair effectively in a drama. Though in the Nāṭakas of Kālidāsa, Śūdraka, etc. we see the married wives of the heroes yet it is not conjugal love which becomes the object of dramatisation and glorification. But Bhavabhuti is singularly successful in depicting the conjugal love of Rāma and Sītā as an object of ardent appreciation and charm. His poetic genius and exuberant imagination impart an exquisite rainbow - hue and a rare depth of sentiment to the love of this couple. The romantic sentiment finds a full play in the drama in the background of deep pathos.

Keith feels that the Uttararāmacarita reaches no higher level as a drama; he has a period of twelve years to cover, as he had fourteen in the Mahāvīracarita, and to produce effective unity would be hard for any author; Bhavabhūti has made no serious effort to this end; he has contended himself with imagining a series of striking pictures.

A critic has righty observed that Bhavabhūti has usually chosen nature's elemental scenes. He is a habitual witnessing only the pristine form of nature where the birds are warbling in ardent passion, hilly rivulets are flowing swiftly, and being echoed by the falling ripe of fruit of black berries (Uttara. 2.10). Unlike Kālidasa he could never see the humanized form of nature.

His Rāma and Sītā have been humanised and they share the joys and sorrows of life like ordinary human being. His Sītā is an embodiment of womanly love and self-abregation. She faces the repeated trials in a remarkable way.

The play deals with the later history of Rama in an entirely new, experimental fashion and and not merely an adaptation of popular mythology. A creative genius, the novely of his play reside not only in its certain obvious departures from Valmiki, but more centrally, as some critic puts it, it is an aesthetic departure : mood rather than event, psychology rather than action, sentiment rather than character, consititute Bhavabhuti's main focus, and determine the style of his dramatic organisation. One critic argues that few seem to have appreciated the fact that Bhavabhuti makes use of magical, pastoral, and dream like situations in the play in order to establish in the mind of the spectator a particular mood or state without which the nature of its poetic vision and the quality of its dramatic experience can not be realised. According to A.P. Singh if a comparative analysis of the treatment of the story in Valmiki, Kalidasa and Bhavabhuti goes to show that, of the three, Bhavabhuti's is the most tender and sensitive rendering. He makes his reader to experience certain human emotions with deep inwardness, and to sensitise his perception of a moral - aesthetic complex at the emotional, not intellectual, level. He does not dramatises a political theme and is free of a 'problem-play orientation and to keeps his audience not to indulge in debate or conflict. But with clarity he presents a complex, intriguing moral question in all its ramifications.

Whether this is conjugal love of Rama and Sita; filial love of Janaka, Kausalya, Ram, Sita, Mother Earth, Ganga; Comraderie (Vasanti), a kind of neighbourly fondness (Tamasa, Murala); brotherly love (Lakshmana); feudal devotion (Durmukha, Sumantra and the Chamberlaine); and saintly kindliness with a touch of the filial (Valmiki), Vasistha, Arundhati, Dr Pati observes that the dramatist has successfuly delineates Karuna rasa through every conceivable perspectives and can be witnessed in all the seven acts of the play.

The Uttararāmacarita has the same metres as the Mahāvīracarita, but omits Sragdharā; it adds the Drutavilambita and Mañjubhāṣinī; the occurances of the śloka are (89), the Śikhariṇī is second (30), Vasantatilaka third (26), and Śārdūlavikrīḍita fourth (25).

While commenting on the best of Bhavabhuti plays, the Uttararāmacarita, C. Panduranga Bhatta says His all - empracing attitude to nature, deepest perception of life and situation unveiling of the truth and hard realities intermingled with lofty ideals of our tradition, the dashing personality along with his revolutionary ideas, haunting pathos, and above all his poetic brilliance are enough to rank him as one of the best poets in Sanskrit literature.

He is more a dramatic poet than a dramatists. T.G. Mainkar opines that his lacks the restraint and innate sense of economy so necessary for a true dramatist. The outstanding quality of Bhavabhuti is his high level of seriousness which only great idealists possess. Humour is altogether absent in his plays and he does not introduce the Vidushaka in any of them. It appears that his plays, because of their heavy diction and undramatic dialogue, were not popular theatre pieces.

There are commentaries on the play by Vīrarāghava, Āṭmarāma, Lakṣ manasūri, A. Borooah, J. Viḍyāsāgara, Abhirāma, Premacanḍra Tarkavāgīśa, Bhotajiśāstrin, Ṭārākumāracakravarṭin, Rāmacanḍra, B.S. Ghate, Ghanaśyāma, Lakṣmīkumāra Tāṭācārya, Rāghāvācārya, Pūrṇasarasvaṭī, and Nārāyaṇabhatta, and one anonymous.

S.K. Dey writes : Bhavabhūti praises himself for his 'mastery of speech' and claims merit for felicity and richness of expression as well as depth of meaning'; and the praise he claims for himself is fully deserved. The qualities in which he excels are his power of vivid and often rugged description, the nobility and earnestness of his conception, a genuine emotional tone, and a love for all that is deep and poignant as well as grand and awe-inspiring in life and nature. Contrasted with Kālidāsa, he lacks grace and polish and a fastidious technical finish.

S.V. Dixit tells us that the plays of Bhavabhuti are heavy for the stage. The scenes having supernatural elements are found in large numbers in the plays such as the appearance of missiles and Śiva's bow, flying of demons, the cemetery scenes, weird rites and Kapalakundala's miraculous power of flying in the air, aerial kidnapping, the enactment of the play within play, Sītā in invisible form, the characters in the forms of rivers and the earth, the use of aerial car etc. All these makes the play difficult to be staged.

Besides, one can find in the Mālatimādhava, a description of Mālatī's love torment in a passage covering six pages by Lavaṅgikā. Besides unwanted lengthy wordy war in Mahāvīracarita. Again the prolong description of the cemetery in the Act V of Mālatīmādhava.

Many verses and phrases are found repeated in the plays and even the same verse are spoken by different characters. He has expressed his frustration very clearly in his Mālatīmādhava. Nevertheless he cherished high hopes for wide popularity in days to come.

From Citsukhācārya's Tattvapradīpikā, it can be said that Bhavabhūtī might have penned some Nāṭikās and Prabandhas. We find a number of verses ascribed to him, but not found in his three dramas, but are available in various anthologies.

Malatimadhava

Synopsis

Composed in the tradition of Aśvaghoṣa's Sārīputra Prakaraṇ, Bhavabhuti's Mālati - Mādhava is a Prakaraṇa in ten acts that centres round a love - affair of the young hero Mādhava and the heroine, Mālatī, both of whom belong to a non-princely families.

Mālati is the daughter of Bhūrivasu, the minister of Ujjayin and Mādhava, the son of Devarāta, the chief minister of the state of Vīderbha or Berar.

Bhūrivasu, minister of the king of Padmāvati however, had once asked his old companion, now turned nun, Kāmandakī to arrange a marriage between his daughter Malati and Mādhava, son of his old friend Devarāta. He sends his son to Pandmāvati with the hope that Bhūrivasu would remember a compact of their students days to marry their children to each other.

Mālati is nursed by a Buddhist nun called Kāmandakī at Ujjayin Mādhava is sent there as it was customary in those days for students to attend the school of the Buddhist to learn logic. They fall in love with each other. The king presses minister of Ujjayin to marry Mālati in marriage for a favourite of his own called Nandana, the queen's brother.

Inspite of oppositions and obstacles, love of this young students Madhava and Mālati, therfore, had a happy finale through strange vicissitudes and the skiful intervention of Kāmandakī and thwart the king's plan.

Makaranda is dressed as a girl is sent as the heronine to the wedding of Nandana; while the Madhava and Malati is taken to a Shiva temple for a secret marriage. A tiger dashes through the city that frightens the people and Makaranda rescues the life of Madayantika and both falls in love. Malati is kidnapped by Kapalakundala, disciple of Aghoracharya, to a mountain temple to be offered as a victim. There begins hero's pursuit. Unable to bear eachother's separation, they attempt at suicide. Madhava decides to offer his flesh to ghost. He hears a cry and rushes to the temple, slays the priest and saves Malati. He breaks the good news, saves Bhurivasu and Kamandaki from committing suicide.

The play has thus two love stories, one between Mālatī and Mādhava and in the sub plot we find the love affair of Makaranda, a trusted friend of Mādhava and Madayantika, the beautiful sister of Nandana.

Dramatic Personae

Mādhava	...	Devarāta's son
Makaranda	...	Mādhava's friend
Kalahamsaka	...	Mādhava's servant, in love with Mandarīkā
Mālatī	...	Bhūrivasu's daughter
Lavangikā	...	Mālatī's foster-sister
Madayantikā	...	Nandana's sister and friend of Mālatī.

Kāmandakī	...	Buddhist mendicant nun, friend of both Bhūrivasu and Devarāta
Avalokitā	...	Chief pupil of Kāmandakī
Buddharakshitā	...	Pupil of Kamandakī and friend of Madayantikā.
Mandārikā	...	Servant girl of the convent, sweetheart of Kalahamsaka.
Aghoraghaṇṭa	...	A Śaivite adept and worshipper of Karāla (a form of the Fierce Goddess)
Kapālakuṇḍalā	...	Aghoraghaṇṭa's pupil.
Saudāmanī	...	Former pupil of Kāmandakī, now a Śaivite adept.

Porteress and Two maid servants (of Bhūrivasu's household).

Man	...	(official in Nandana's household).

Characters not appearing on stage are :-

The King	...	Ruler of Padmāvatī
Bhūrivasu	...	A Minister of the King
Devarāta	...	Minister to the King of the southern state of Vidarbha.
Nandana	...	Minister and intimate friend of the King.

Plot :-

Act One : Bhūrivasu, minister at Padmāvatī and Devarāta, minister to the king of Vidarbha had once made a vow in the presence of an old friend, now turned nun, Kāmandakī to marry their children to each other. Now Bhūrivasu has a daughter named 'Mālatī' and Devarāta, a son called 'Mādhava'. To remind Bhūrivasu of the compact, Devarāta sends his son to the Buddhist school at Padmāvati to learn Ānvīkṣikā.

Kāmandakī extends her hand to bringout the union of Mādhava and Mālatī. She makes such an arrangement by which Mādhava would pass by Mālatī's mansion often and hopefully, one day she would see the handsome youth and fall in love at the first sight.

But the major obstacle in their union is the desire of the king of Padmavatī that Mālatī should be married to his boon companion Nandana. Kāmandakī realizes that she would have to act cautiously and only a secret marriage of the young people is the remedy. Saṁayāsinī decides to arrange the meeting of the two and their marriage. She instructs her attendant Avalokitā to arrange to send Mādhava to the Madana-garden so that at the Madana-festival, he might come in contact with Mālatī. Another attendant of Kāmandakī, Buddharaṣkitā is deputed to work on the mind of Nandana's sister 'Madayantikā', so that the latter may fall in love with Mādhava's friend called Makaranda.

Mandārika is commissioned to hand over the portrait of Mādhava drawn by Mālatī to Mādhava, at the instance of Mālatī's foster-sister Lavaṅgikā. Interestingly this Mandarika is also loved by Kalahaṁsaka, a follower of Mādhava.

As planned, Mādhava meets Mālati in the Madana-garden. Lavaṅgika not only tactfully takes away the Bakula-garland from Mādhava (which he was wearing), but also expresses Mālatī's love through a speech. When Mādhava tells all these incidents to Makaranda, Kalahaṁsaka appears with the portrait of Mālatī. Mādhava is deeply in love with Mālatī's and starts drawing her portrait by his side.

Act Two :-

On her return from Madana-garden Lavaṅgikī relates her interview with Mādhava to Mālatī. In the meanwhile, the king of Padmāvatī asks Bhūrivasu for the hand of Mālatī on behalf of his favourite Nandana. In reply, the minister tells that his Majesty has full power over his daughter.

After seeing the Bakula-garland and her own portrait drawn by Mādhava, Malati is convinced of his love for her, but as she has a very high sense of honour and thinks highly of her duty to her father, she refuses to a stolen marriage that would bring disgrace on her parents. Kāmandakī makes all efforts to appease Mālatī and even goes to narrate the course of conduct followed by Śakuntalā, Urvasī and Vāsavadattā in analogous situations. Kāmandakī, however, succeeds partially in her noble venture.

Act Three :-

Due to Buddharakṣītā's efforts, Lovely and vivacious Madayantika gradually takes interest in Makaranda. In the Kusumākara garden, Kāmandakī arranges a meeting of the lovers Mādhava and Mālatī. The latter is instigated to collect flowers with her own hands for the worship of Śiva on the Kṛṣṇacaturdaśī day. In Kusumākara garden, he overhear the conversation between Mālatī, Lavaṅgikā and Kāmandaki. In reply to Kāmandakī's description of the lovelorn condition of Mādhava, Lavaṅgikā vividly expresses how Mālatī is languishing because of love. In the temple of Siva, when the loves are to meet, a cry is heard and it is reported that a tiger has escaped from the cage and approaching Madayantikā who is in danger of death. Mādhava discloses himself and they all moves hurriedly only to find that Madayantikā has been rescued by Makaranda badly wounded in the attempt, Makaranda becomes unconsious.

Act Four :-

Madhava also faints away after seeing his friend in a swoon. They comes to know that king resolves on the mating of Mālatī and Nandana. Madayantikā rejoices at hearing the news that Mālatī would be her brother's wife. The nun Kāmandakī tries to console Mādhava by stating that Bhūrivasu had not given his consent to the king's choice and what the minister told to the king was that the latter had full power over his daughter - meant the king may give away his own daughter, not, Bhūrivasu's daughter 'Mālati'. Broken hearted and fully despaired of success through Kāmandakī's help alone Mādhava resolves upon being a vendor of human flesh in the cemetery and returns to the city with Makaranada.

Act Five :-

The priest Aghoraghaṇṭa completes his Mantrasādhana and his acolyte Kapālakuṇḍalā travels through the air to Padmāvatī in search of beautiful maiden to offer in sacrifice to the goddess Cāmuṇḍā. She spots Mādhava in the cemetery and recognises him. Mādhava wishes to offer human flesh to the spirits, but they vanishes. Suddenly he hears cries from a nearby temple of Karālā and rushes in time to save Mālatī from the clutches of Aghoraghaṇṭa and Kapālakuṇḍalā and fights with Aghoraghaṇṭa. At this moment enters soldiers deputed by Kāmandakī to besiege the temple.

Act Six :-

Aghoraghaṇṭa is slain by Mādhava, but spares the life of Kapālakuṇḍala. The latter swears revenge. The marriage of Nandana and Mālati is to be held and according to custom, before the marriage, Mālatī goes to offer prayer to city-deity alongwith Lavaṅgīkā and Kāmandakī. By a clever stratagem of Kāmandakī, Mādhava meets Mālatī at the temple. A special bridal dress was sent to Mālatī by the king for the ceremony. As directd by Kāmandaki, both Mādhava and Makaranda hides themselves as soon as Malatī enters the inner sanctuary with Lavaṅgika. Mālatī reveals her intense feeling for Mādhava before Lavaṅgika and requests her to put an end to her life and falls at her feet. Mādhava quickly changes places with Lavaṅgikā. Mālati requests Lavaṅgika (ie, Mādhava) to always remember her lover Mādhava and to put the Bakula-garland round her neck, that had sustained her so far. When Mālatī touches Mādhava's body, she becomes highly embarrased. Mādhava also confesses his deep longing for Mālatī. At this juncture, emerges Kāmandakī and cheerfully plans a secret marriage. She also directs Makaranda to put on the bridal dress and accordingly is led home as a bride. Both Mādhava and Mālatī flee to Kāmandakī's abode.

Act Seven :-

In this act we see that Nandana's marriage is over and Makaranda has been successful in playing the part of Mālatī. When Nandana makes an advance, he is repulsed by his bride, feels dejected and finally leaves the apartment. Madayantikā comes with Buddharakṣitā to rebuke her sister-in-law. Makaranda pretends to be asleep. Lavaṅgikā puts the blame upon Nandana, while Madayantika in defence, states that the reported love of Mālatī for Mādhava has driven his brother to abuse the bride. As the conversation progresses, at one point, Madayantikā discloses her love for Makaranda and is prevailed upon by Lavaṅgikā and Buddharakṣitā to be ready even for a Gāndharva-marriage. When Madayantikā is about to leave, she finds her lover masquerade as Mālati and elopes to rejoin their friends Mālatī and Mādhava who have taken refuge at Kāmandakī's abode.

Act Eight :-

After marriage, Mādhava and Mālatī are passing their happiest moments. When they were enjoying the moon-light appears Madayantikā, Buddharakṣitā, Lavaṅgikā and Kalahaṁsaka. They breaks the news that Makaranda is engaged in an encounter with the city Police. The escapees are succoured by Mādhava who rush on with Kalahaṁsaka to assist Makaranda. Mālati directs Lavaṅgika to follow Mādhava and request him to be cautious and also, deputes Buddharakṣitā and Avalokitā to inform Kāmandakī of the happenings. In this tumult Mālatī is taken away by Kapālakuṇḍalā to Śrīparvata to be offered as a victim to the deity. Now arrives Mādhava and Makaranda after a successful fight with the Police. Not finding Mālatī there they assume that she must have gone to see Kāmandakī and thus proceeds towards her above.

Act Nine :-

This act focuses on the grief-stricken Mādhava who with his friend

Makaranda is looking for his beloved Mālatī. He addresses the surrounding animals, clouds etc. for news about her and eventually faints aways. Seeing his friend in misery, Makaranda decides to end his life by throwing himself into the river Pāṭ alāvatī. At this moment arrives Saudāminī, a pupil of Kāmandakī, with the Bakula-garland as the token of recognition to inform Mādhava about Mālatī's whereabouts. She informs that Mālatī is safe. When Mādhava comes to his senses, she tells him that Mālatī had been stolen away by Kapālakuṃḍala, but rescued by her. All of a sudden this Kāpālikā of good nature flies up and carries Mādhava with her. Makaranda who is left alone, now goes to Kāmandakī to narrate the whole incidents.

Act Ten :-

A scene of lamentation begins with Kāmandakī, Lavaṅgikā and Madayantikā. They decide to commit suicide by throwing themselves down from a hill adjoining the river 'Madhumati'. For the same purpose, Bhūrivasu is also going to Suvarṇabindu. At the end of the play, Saudāminī returns with the lovers and prevents them from the suicidal acts. She bows down to Kāmandakī and produces a letter from the king that approves the marriage and thus ends the prakarana.

Mahaviracarita

Synopsis

Perhaps playwright's first play, 'Mahāvīra-carīta' or 'the life of the Great Hero' dramatizes the Rama story in seven acts. Based primarily on the subject matter of the six Kāṇḍas of the epic Ramayana, the play begins with the visit of Rama to the hermitage of Viśvamitra and ends with his return to Ayodhya in the aerial car. As the very hame suggests, Bhavabhuti tries to show Rāma as a great warrior who rescues his wife Sītā from the grasp of Rāvana, (the ten-headed monster), the king of Lanka. In exhibiting Rāma's strength, the entire play is permeated by Vīra-rasa (The sentiment of heroism). While narrating the incidents from the epic, the dramatist makes many alternations and thus, reshape the original story such as Ravaṇa being shown as a suitor of Sītā, vying with Rāma (The presentation of Ravaṇa as a rival of Rāma from the very begining of the play); Ravana's minister Mālyavat's plot to pitch Paraśurāma against Rāma and to send Sūrpaṇakhā in disguise as Mantharā to workout the exile of Rāma and also, the presentation of Vālin as an ally of Rāvaṇa.

Plot :-

Act One :-

At his hermitage on the Kauśāmbī river, sage Visvāmitra wanted to perform a sacrifice, but to get rid of Rākṣasas he goes to seek Daśaratha's help and returns back with Rāma and Lakṣmaṇa to aid him. Janaka, the king of Mithilā is also engaged in a sacrifice; so he deputes his brother Kuśadhvaja, alongwith his daughter Sītā and Urmila, his brother's daughter to attend Viśvāmitra's sacrifice. Seeing Rāma, Kuśadhvaja thought that only Rāma would be an ideal match for Sītā. However, Janaka has already proclaimed that he would offer Sītā's hand to one who wouid break the bow of Śiva. But Kuśadhavaja felt that Rāma might not be able to do so. In this act, Ahalya is being freed from her curse by Rāma.

An envoy from Rāvana comes in the meantime to demand Sītā's hand in marriage for Rāvaṇa. This messenger had first gone to Janaka who advised him to see Kuśadhvaja at Viśvāmitra's sacrifice. Viśvāmitra told the envoy that the matter rests with Janaka. The demon Tāḍakā makes her appearance and is defeated by Rāma. After Tāḍakā's death, Viśvāmitra presents the celestial weapons (Jṛmbhaka missiles) to Rāma and summon's Śīva's bow by the Yogic power and Rāma succeeds in breaking the bow in the presence of Rāvana's messenger who departs in rage. Viśvāmitra arranges for the marriage of Rāma with Sītā of Lakṣmaṇa, Bharata and Śatrughana, with the three daughters of Kuśadhvaja, - Urmila, Māṇḍavī and Śrutakīrti. Dasāratha is invited to Mithilā where the ceremonies will be held after the yajña is over. The demons, Subāhu and Mārīca emerges, but are killed by Rāma.

Act Two :-

Rāvaṇa's minister Mālyavat hears from the messenger about the happenings at Viśvāmitra's Siddhāśrama and Śūrpaṇakha breaks the news about the marriages of Rāma and his brothers and also about the gift of Indra's bow to Rāma by Agastya. Mālyavat plots Śūrpaṇakha how to make good the defeat sustained and when comes a letter from Paraśurāma where he expresses his concern with the findings of molestation of the sages in the Daṇḍakāranya by the Rākṣasas. Both Mālyavat and Surpaṇakha gets an opportunity to incite Paraśurāma to avenge the breaking of Siva's bow. The former, therefore, goes to Mahendradvipa, the abode of Parasurāma and instigate him to attack Rāma.

After arriving at Mithila, Paraśurāma insults Rāma. Though he admires the latter, but as he had vowed to make the earth bereft of Kṣatriyas, decides to kill

Rama and thus, demands a conflict. But king Janaka and his purohit Śatānanda tries in vain to avoid the struggle.

Rāma is called by the mother-in-law for the Kaṅkanamocana ceremony.

Act Three :-

In this act also the exchange of insults continues. Vasistha and Viśvāmitra makes all efforts to avoid as struggle between the youth and Paraśurama. But both of them fails. Daśaratha also fails to appease him and is ready to fight with the savage Brahmin. At this moment, Rāma appears and vows to control Paraśurama.

Act Four :-

This act unfolds Paraśurama's defeat at the hand of Rāma and the former salutes with respect the victor. But Mālyavat does not give up and makes another plot by which Śūrpaṇakhā will assume the form of Mantharā, the maid to Kaikeyi and make Kaikeyi, the king Dasaratha's favourite wife for the two boons promised to her by the king-by one boon, Bharata will be crowned as king and by the second, Rāma will have to be in exile in the forest for fourteen years. This would definately destroy the concord of the royal family.

Rāma is at Mithilā with his father-in-law when Śūrpaṇakha in disguise as Manthara emerges with an alleged letter from Kaikeyi asking for the boons. In the meantime, Bharata and his uncle Yudhājit have asked Dasaratha to crown Rāma forthwith; Dasaratha gives his consent, but Rāma intervenes and is adamant to go into exile into the forest alongwith Sītā and Lakṣmaṇa, and Bharata remains at Nandigrāma to look after the kingdom in the name of Rāma who has given his golden footwear (*pādukās*) to Bharata.

Act Five :-

Rāma's doings in the forst in known to us through the conversations between the aged vultures Jaṭayu and Sampāti. The latter bids Jaṭāyu to take care of Rāma. Meanwhile Rāvaṇa carries off Sītā. Jaṭāyu is killed in her defence and thus fared on his duty. Rāma and Lakṣmana meet dying Jatāyu who informs them about Sītā's capture. They move towards Kiṣkindhā. On the way Virādha is killed. Rāma and Lakṣmaṇa wander in mourning and meet Vibhīṣaṇa, brother of Rāvana, banished from Laṅkā. Vibhīṣaṇa expresses his willingness to meet them at Ṛṣ yamukha where also are the jewels dropped by Sītā in her despair. Mālyavant, however, persuades Vālis to forbid their entry. Vālin is wounded and enjoins brother Sugrīva to become their ally. Sugrīva lend his aid to Rāma's search for Sītā. Vālin throws himself from a precipice and dies.

Act Six :-

Mālyavant's all plan fails and now he hears about burning of Laṅka by Hanūmant. Ravana arrives, doting on Sītā; Mandodari is harsly dispelled by Rāvana, when the former informs him of the advance of the enemy. An envoy of Rāma named 'Aṅgada' arrives at Laṅkā; but Rāvana treats him with contempt and messenger escapes Ravana prepares for the fight. Indra places his war-chariot at the disposal of Rāma. Both Indra and Citraratha who, as divine watch Rāma in his fight with Rāvaṇa. Rāvaṇa performs feats of valour, but Hanumant revives with ambrosia Rāma and his fellows. But finally Rāvaṇa dies beside his son Meghanāda, a gallant warrior.

Act Seven :-

In the last act, Vibhīṣaṇa is crowned as the Ruler of Laṅkā. The cities Laṅkā and Alakā, represented by their deities, exchange condolences. Sītā successfully emerges from the fire-ordeal and proves her chastity and is being congratulated by the gods and others. An aerial journey begans and carries Rāma, Laksmana, Sīta, Sugrīva and Vibhīsana towards Ayodhya. Hanumant breaks the news of Rāma's imminent arrivals. Bharata with his army proceeds to welcome Rāma. They are greeted by Vasiṣtha, Arundhati and Dasaratha's widows. Arundhati consoles Kaikeyī and assures her that she was absolutely innocent and in no way held responsible for Rāma's misfortune, as it was all the evil design of Śurpaṇakhā in the form of Kaikeyī's maid. The play closes with the arrival of sage Viśvāmitra with his pupils, when he crowns Rāma

'Uttararāmacharita'

Synopsis

This is Bhavabhuti's third play based on the seven Kāṇḍa of the Rāmāyana in which Sītā's chastity is questioned and she is separated from Rāma for a time, to be reunited after many trials. The play begins with the arrival of the victorious Rāma to Ayodhya and closes with the reunion of Rāma and Sītā in the hermitage of sage Vālmiki. In between a series of incidents occurs.

To fulfil his duty towards his people, Rama abandons Sita because of her long stay in Lanka. The common people were away from the fire ordeal of Sita who refused to be convinced and started uncharitable remarks on Rāma's acceptance of Sita. Sita goes to dwell in the forest of Daṇḍadaka, where she lived earlier with her husband. Rama sends her away under the pretext of satisfying her desire to re-visit the forest.

To perform another kindly duty, Rama comes to Janasthana to kill sudra ascetic Shambuka.

In the Daṇḍakāranya, he beholds his deserted hermitage and reminiscises the best moment shared with his wife. He meets Vasanti who is deeply hurt by the desertion of Sita and accuses Rama who cares more for his kingly duty and personal glory than for Sita.

Rama weeps bitterly for his faultless wife, curses and accuses the public for his misery. He breaks down and faints. Invisible Sita a witness to Ramā's profound love for his wife and silent suffering.

Fortunately Sita is alive and resumed by Bhagirathi from her attempt to commit suicide. Sita and her twin sons, Kusa and Lava are under the custody of Valmiki. Bhagirathi asks her to go to Panchavati to worship the Sun-god to grant her the power to be invisible to mortal eyes.

Rama admits before Vasanti that he abandoned Sita only to satisfy his subjects, but has not taken another wife to perform Ashvamedha Yajna. He had, instead, installed Sita's image cast in gold.

Sita comes to know about Rāma's deep love for her and his terrible suffering. She forgets humiliation and injustice meted out to her and mentally reconciled to her husband.

In Valmiki's hermitage, the royal mothers, sage Vasistha, Arundhati and Janaka have arrived to be present at the sacrifice at the hermitage of Ṛsyaśṛṅga.

The Ashvamedha horse wanders towards the ashrama and is kept captive by the sons of Sita that leads to a terrible fight between Lava and Chandraketu in command of the horse-guards.

Rama who returns from Panchavati stops the fight. Astonishad by the stark resemblance Kusha and Lava bears to Sita that Rāma is convinced that they are none other than his sons and feels that Sita must be alive.

The truth is unfolded in the garbhanataka when the divinities proclaim the purity of Sita. The people of Ayodhya feels guilty and bow down to her and acclaim the queen. Arundhati hands over Sita to Rāma.

Bhavabhuti ignores the tragic end in the Ramayana and in conforming with classical dramatic norms that does not countenance a tragic end, he draws the curtain wth a happy union.

Dramatis Personae

Rama	Saudhataki, a hermit
Sita	Janaka
Chamberlain	Arundhati
Ashtavakra	Kaushalya
Lakshmana	Attendant
Attendant	Lava
Durmukha	Soldier
Atreyi, an ascetic	Chandraketu
Vasanti, Forest Goddess	Sumantra
Sambuka	Kusha
Tamasa	Prithvi
Murala	Bhagirathi
Bhandayana, a hermit	Voices, Spirits of the Air, etc.

Plot :-

Act One :-

The scene takes place at, Rama's palace. At Ayodhya coronation of Rama is over and Janaka and the other invitee's have departed. The Queen-mothers, Vasiṣṭha and Arundhatī goes to attend the twelve-year sacrifice of Ṛṣyaśṛnga, Rāma's brother-in-law. Sitā enceinte is sad as all the relatives have left Ayodhya. Rāma is consoling her. The people of Ayodhya still question Sītā's chastity, as they are not satisfied with the Fire-ordeal of Sītā in Lankā. Meanwhile, news is brought by Aṣṭāvakra from the hermitage of Ṛṣyaśṛṅga to Rāma. Vasiṣṭha bids Rama to meet every wish of his wife, but being the king he must first of all comfort his subjects. Even Queen-mothers want Rāma to fulfil the pregnancy - longing of Sītā without any hesitation. To appease the citizen of Ayodhya, Rāma is willing to abandon even his beloved Sītā. After Aṣṭāvakra's departure, Lakṣmaṇa urges. Rāma to look at the paintings that depicts the scenes of their wanderings up to the purification of Sītā by fire. So they enter the gallery and browses the art works, a review of past events in Rāma's life such as Jṛmbhaka missiles always in attendance on Rāma; the marriage - ceremonies at Mithilā; Rāma's encounter with Paraśurama; Mantharā episode; Rāma's meeting with the Niṣāda-chief 'Guha' in Śṛṅgavera city (The Ingudī tree episode); the Bhāgīrathī river where Rāma prays her to look upon Sītā as her daughter-in-law; the Vata - tree called Śyāma that reminds Rāma of those days he had passed happily in the region; his fight with the demon Virādha; their entry into the southern forest; the Prasravaṇa hill; at Pañcavaṭī, the Śūrpaṇakha episode; Sītā's abduction in Janasthāna; the slaying of Jaṭāyu; the Citrakūṭa region and the headless demon Danu; the hermitage of Mataṅga; the Śabarī, Śramaṇā;the lake Pampā. Hanūmat and while looking at the picture that shows Mālyavat mountain, Rāma breaks down heavily on recalling the events following Sītā's abduction.

As Sītā's has become exhausted, Lakṣmana keeps the paintings aside. Sītā feels like visiting again the forest. Rāma gives words to let her go to the groves on the banks of the Bhāgīrathī. Rāma instructs Lakṣmaṇa to get the chariot ready. The latter goes out and Sītā falls asleep; using Rāma's hand as a pillow.

Now, the Brahmin Durmukha breaks the news that the people of Ayodhyā doubt Sītā's purity. Rāma resolve to abandon Sītā forever, thereby saving the solar race from defamation. Some ascetics living on the Yamunā enter to request Rāma to save them from the demon Lavaṇa Rāma deputes Śatrughna to attack Lavaṇa and leaves Sita who is asleep.

Finding Sītā in deep sleep, he leaves her with broken heart. When Sītā awakes, Durmukha escorts her to the chariot to take her to the Bhāgirathī regions.

Act Two :-

In this act, we learn from the conversation of an ascetic Ātreyī to the sylvan deity 'Vāsanti' that twelve years have elapsed since Sītā was abandoned.

The sage Vālmiki has composed the Rama story and now accepted two wonderful twins Kuśa and Lava as his pupils and teaching them the art of archery. We also find that Rāma is organising the Aśvamedha sacrifice with Sītā's golden image as his consort. She also tells us that a brahmin had lost his son prematurely because of Śambūka who was practising penance in an unauthorised manner and the Brāhmin seeks the help of Rāma. The latter rushes in his aerial car to punish him and thus, he is expected to arrive in the Daṇḍaka forest at any moment. Thus, enters Rāma with sword in his hand to slain Sambūka and kills him. Purified by this death Śambūka emerges in spirit form and brings a news from the sage Agastya and his wife Lopāmudrā to pay a visit to their hermitage.

Act Three :-

This act shows two rivers Tamasā and Muralā converse and we learn that Sītā would have killed herself but saved by river Gaṅga and entrusted her two sons, born in her sorrow, to Vālmiki to bring them up. Now Rāma is about to arrive in the Daṇḍaka forest. The sight of its surroundings where Rāma had lived with Sītā during the exile might affect Rāma severly. The river Ganga has arranged to bring Sitā in the Daṇḍaka (to enable her to be convinced of Rāma's true feelings for her) under the pretext of performing some rites on the occasion of the twelfth - anniversary of Sītā's twins. Unseen by mortals, Sīta appears in an invisible form and under Tamasā's care, revisits the region and while wandering, she finds her pet elephant which she had reared up years ago is attacked by an older elephant. Hearing the cry for help from Vāsantī, Rāma rushes to the spot only to find the younger one triumphant. This reminds Sītā of her two lads who might have grownup sufficiently as twelve years have lapsed. At the sight of the scene of their early love, both faints. After recovery, Sītā revives Rāma by her tender touch which Rāma recognises too well. After recovery, Vāsantī expresses her anger over the ill treatment meted out to innocent Sītā.

But invisible Sītā stops her and unseen by Rāmā, Sīta hears from his own lips that in the Aśvamedha sacrifice, he has kept Sītā's golden image as his consort and had not remarried. Convinced Sītā departs, leaving Rāma fainting.

The act ends with Rāma's return to Ayodhyā.

Act Four :-

The act takes place at Vālmīki's hermitage, where Kausalyā, Rāma's mother meets Janaka, retired from kingly duties. Here Vasiṣtha, Arundhati also go to stay at hermitage. None of them go to Ayodhyā from which Sītā had been ill treated and expelled. While they were in conversation, the merry noises of the children of the hermitage interrupts them. On questioned, they come to know that one of them is Lava, who has a brother Kusha and who has heard of Rāma from Vālmīki's work. The boys bear a great resemblance to Rāma and Sītā. The party approaches Vālmiki to tell them details about the boys. They are told that all would be unfolded when time comes. Rāma's Aśvamedha horse now arrives, guarded by soldiers. Lava decides to oppose the proclamation by the guardians of the horse, challenging any one to capture it. Lava is not ready to submit and captures the horse.

Act Five :-

Lava confronts with the guardians of the sacrificial horse and employs the

Jṛmbhaka missile. After rendering them motionless, he meets Candraketu, who guards the horse for Rama. They admires each other and are not willing to fight. Sumanta, Candraketu's charioteer notices striking resemblance between Rāma and Lava. The latter explains his reasons for capturing the horse and states that being an ideal kṣatriya, he can not bear the derogatory remarks of the guardians and to utter surprise of Candraketu, Lava is intolerant to even Rāma's prowess. Lava boldly replies that prowess was not the monopoly of any one and the less one speaks of Rāma's prowess, the better and then he goes to reminds them to weak points in Rāma's carrier such as the killing of Tāḍakā, who was a woman; while fighting with Khara, took three steps backwards; the unjust slaying of Vālin etc.

Candraketu can not bear the taunts and prepares to fight with him.

Act Six :-

Th duel between Lava and Candraketu and the magic weapons they use is described by a Vidyādhara and his wife, flying in the air. Their furious long fight is put to an end by Rāma who admires Lava's bravery and on questioning, he finds that magic missiles came to him spontaneously. Now appears Kusa from hermit-age. Rama is surprised at the resemblance between himself and the twins and admires the youth. He hears details about them. Rama wonders whether they are his own sons or not. He realizes that Sīta was abandoned in the same forest-region; the Jṛmbhaka missiles were at their command; the two brothers resembled him and Sītā and his heart thrills at their sight; their age was in consonance with the fact that pregnant Sītā was banished twelve years ago and finally Rāma himself had suspected that Sītā would give birth to twins etc. Both Kuśa and Lava recite Vālmīkī's poems from the Rāmāyaṇa dealing with the Rāmā love for Sītā.

Rama becomes sad and at this juncture arrives Janaka and Kausalya. Both of them faint away at the sight of Rāma who looks pallid.

Act Seven :-

At the invitation of Vālmikī, the people of Ayodhyā, representatives of gods, Asuras and other heavenly being watches a dramatic piece composed by Vālmikī and performed by the Apsaras. They enact all the incidents subsequent to the desertion of Sītā.

It shows how the terrible sufferings of Sītā who casts herself in the Bhāgīrathī and reappear as Pṛthvi, the earth goddess takes her. She gives birth to twin-boys and both Pṛthvi and Ganga carries a new-born infant and later keeps the boys sunder Vālmiki's custody. They feel themselve sacred owing to their association with innocent Sītā. The drama ends with Sītā's disppearance into the earth while witnessing the drama, Rāma faints; but Vālmīki stages a miracle. Suddenly Sītā emerges from the waters; Bhāgīrathī and Pṛthvi hand her over to Arundhati who blames the citizen of Ayodhyā for Sītā's misfortune. The citizen gives a full - throated approval to Sītā's restoration. Sītā goes to her husband and brings him back to his senses. Vālmīki presents to them Rāma's sons, Kusa and Lava.

Dramas in Performance

R.D. Karmarkar has rightly commented that if Kalidasa is called the Shakespeare (or Goethe) of India, Bhavabhuti can with greater justification be called the Milton of India asserting eternal providence end justifying the ways of god of men. Dr. R.G. Harshe in his work *'Observations on the life and works of Bhavabhuti'* informs us that "all the dramas of Bhavabhuti were staged at the annual festival of Kalapriyanatha of Ujjaini. It seems that the representations had commenced early in the morning, after the customary oblations to the Dawn and had continued all day long with a long interval to enable the audience to take the mid - day meal. In the Introduction to Mahaviracharita and Malati - Madhava, the dramatist tells us that all these plays were staged by the same dramatic company and this seems confirmed by the fact that the scenic apparatus remains almost the same for all the plays.

The actor who staged the dramas of Bhavabhuti were his intimate friends and taking into consideration the interest that they took for them, they must have taken much pains for their representations. We learn from the dialogue between the sutradhara and the actor in Malati - Madhava that each one had to learn by heart his role and that he had many rehearsals before the public representation. All the actors did not dress at the sametime but they were ready at the desired moment. The most important role, that of Kamandaki, was played by the sutradhara and that of her disciple, Avalokita, by the actor in question. It would be wrong to conclude there from that all the roles of women were played by men. It is necessary to pointout in this precise case that Kamandaki and her two disciples, Avalokita and Buddharaksita, were Buddhist nuns and it was quite impossible to get the heads shaved in the case of true women, it was essential to have men for those roles in this drama. It is possible that they might had women for the other roles of women.

Malatimadhava in performance :-

In 19th century, the Bengali translation of Malatimadhav was staged in Bangarangalay, Pathariaghata.

At the residence of Gopinath Tagore, 'Malatimadhava' was staged and in the premier show the cast included :

Malati ... Kshetra Sen

Madhava ... Jadu Chatterjee

Makarand ... Mohandranath Mukhopadhyay

In its repeat show in the palace - garden, there was major changes in the cast. 'Madhava' was played by Mohendranath Mukhopadhyay. 'Aghorghantayogi' was Hari Bandyopadhyay. But Kshetra Sen remained 'Malati'. The play was witnessed by Viceroy Lord North brook. Mahendranath in his reminiscences wrote : *After the successful production of 'Malaltimadhava', His Highness Lord Northbrook expressed his desire to meet the hero of the play. Not only Maharaja himself, but Sir Michael Madhusudan Dutt also warned him that he must greet him with the word 'My Lord' and never hail him with 'Sir' But when that exciting moment came, perplexingly Mohandrababu did the same blunder. Viceroy enquired "Were you the hero when I came to his residence? Mohendrababu in choaked voice said "Yes Sir". Maharaja at once rectified his clumsy mistake and said "Yes, my Lord; there were two heroes, he was one of them. Mohendrababu, the hero of 'Malatimadhava' became very upset after this encounter."*

The play was enacted in Sanskrit in 1972 in Poona and the audience appreciated its fine musical scores.

Malatimadhava was enacted in Bengali by Oriental Theatre (House of Babu Krishchandra Deb) at Calcutta on 15 February 1873, and Bengali rendering was by Ramnarayan Tarkaratna.

Bhavabhuti's 'Malatimadhava, the same Bengali rendering of Ramnarayan Tarkaratna was performed by Bengali Theatre on 21 March 1874.

'Malati and Madhava' was staged in English by the Union of East and West at the Wigmore Hall in the month of October 1921. This old play has been described as "The Sanskrit Romeo and Juliet", but though it tells the usual Sanskrit love story with a happy ending. The Daily Chronicle writes that it has, however, quite a clever double plot of two lover affairs, with young love triumphant in each case against eldering rivalry, and with one of the young men masquerading as a bride to save his lady from unwelcome nupitals. "Malati and Madhava" is especially interesting in view of its incidental contrasts between Buddhism and Hinduism, and its sidelights upon the question of human sacrifice. Miss Mary Summer played Malti, the heroine, with her Oldvic comrade, Mr Ernest Milton, for lover.

As to the acting, Miss Mary Summer did excellently as Malati. She achieved a depth of sincerity equalled by nobody else, and her make-up was really convincing. In most of the cast the effect of Indian clothes was to make the actresses look startlingly and uncompromisingly English Mr Ernest Milton acted strenuously as Madhava (Romeo), and Mr. Wilfred Fletcher did well as his friend.

This classic was presented in Kathak style in 1958 for the first time at Talkatora Theatre on the occasion of National Dance Seminar arranged by Sangeet Natak Akademi and it was presented by Shri Ram Bharatiya Kala Kendra and Kathak Kendra. Choreographed by Lacchu Maharaj and Birju Maharaj and music was composed by Senior Dagar Brothers and Nirmala Joshi. Costumes and Set was design by Naina Devi. This attempt marked the beginning of a full fledged dance - dramas in Kathak technique in the capital.

Bhavabhuti's 'Malati - Madhava' in dance - drama (1958) Birju Maharaj and Kumudini Lakhia.

Another praise worthy presentation of 'Malatimadhava' in Sanskrit was by 'Samskrita Ranga' which came into being in 1958 in Madras.

Again in January 1959, at the Annual Conference of the Music Academy, Madras, Bharatiya Kala Kendra's Kathak ballet group under the direction of Birju Maharaj presented this dance drama on the occasion. It was for the first time that the North Indian Programme of music and dance was included in its annual Conference that created the rousing enthusiasm among South Indian audiences.

In 1972 Bharatiya Kala Kendra, New Delhi (a training centre for dance and music) had produced the Sanskrit classic 'Malatimadhava' in the Kathak style. Extreme freedom of movement, gesture and mime with senscious groopings and compositions by talented dancers eathralled sthe audience of the time.

On 8 February 1995, theatre group 'Dost' presented Bhavabhuti's 'Malatimadhava' in Hindi at Gwalior. It was directed by Alok Chatterjee (NSD Alumni of 1987).

Uttaramacharitam in pérformance :-

In 1826, for the first time the newspaper *'Samachar Chandrika'* in its editorial section voiced for an indigenous theatre on the English model and subsequently another newspaper *'Samachar Darpan'* in its 17th september.

1831 Issue reported that a committee was set up for the inception of a theatre by the natives. Amongst its eminent members, the name of Prasanna Kumar Tagore deserve special mention as he came formed to form *'Hindu Theatre'* in his garden house at Narkeldanga which opened to public on 28 December 1831.

Sushil Kumar Mukherji rightly points out that this was the first theatre established by a Bengali housed in the Bengali quarter of the city for a Bengali audience. However, the inaugural play chosen by the Hindu Theatre was not a Bengali play. But alongwith Shakespear's Julias caesar (Act V), First Act of Bhavabhuti's 'Uttararamacaritam' in English was staged. The rendering was by H.H. Wilson. A review of the performance appeared in *'Samachar Darpan'* in its 7th January 1832 issue.

Calcutta Monthy Journal mentions that in the month of January 1832 [Paus 1238], The English version of 'Uttararamacharita' was staged at the instance of Prasanna Kumar Tagore. *Hindu Reformer* states that the play was performed in Sudor Bagan. The English rendering was done by H. H. Wilson, the President of Sanskrit College, Calcutta.

In English version, many eminent persons such as Prof. Ramchandra Mitra and Gangacharan Sen and students from the wellknown Sanskrit College and Hindu college. H.H. Wilson took charge of the stage designing and to train the whole cast. *'Journal Asiatique'* writes that only few portions from the play was enacted. It was performed in Shudor garden - palace at Beleghata. The distinguished audience comprised of Raja Radhakanta Deb, Chief Justice of Supreme Court and Colonel Young.

Vijayarama Gajapati Maharaja founded the *'Jagannadha Vilasini Sabha'* at Vizainagaram in 1874. His successor Ananda Gajapati Maharajah patronised it and took keen interest in its cultural activities. The association was popularly known as *'Butchi Sastri Company'* as its actor-manager Ganti Butchi Sastri was behind the success of this theatrical organisation. The organisation was also called the 'Sanskrit Academy' as it performed only Sanskrit play like Bhavabhuti's Uttararamacharita.

Dramatic Association called *'Andhra Bhāshābhimānī Samājam'* was formed on 31st April 1899 to enact the plays of Venkataraya Sastry. The eminent Telugu Scholars like Sri Poondla Ramakrishnayya, Gunapati Yenadi Reddi and a host of others associated themselves with this organisation. The Samajam felt that Vedam Venkataraya Sastry was the dramatist and the other Telugu playwrights were nowhere. The group attracted enlightened graduates, poets, writers and many of the old students of Sri Sastry who happened to settle down at Nellore. Sri Sastry was made the President of the Samajam and under his direction it started enacting his in Telugu rendering of Sanskrit classics. The Samajam functioned upto 1925. The last performance of the Samajam was the translation of Harsha's Ratnavali (Published in 1921) enacted on the night of the Silver Jubilee Day in 1925. He also translated Vikramorvasiya of Kalidasa (published in 1921) and was wonderfully produced on the stage in 1922 several times. Three dramas Ratnavali, Vikramorvasiya and Malavikagnimitra (published in 1919) were translatea by the persuation of Sri D. Venkatarama Reddi of Kavali for whose satisfaction even Uttararacaritam (published in 1920) was enacted with success. Only his play Malavikagnimitra was never staged.

Shri Vedam Venkataraya Sastry (21/12/1853 - 18/6/1929), was a dominant figure in the Telugu literary field for over a half a century beginning from the last quarter of the nineteenth century and ending with the first of the twentieth. This literary giant, became a byword for Sanskrit and in 1886, he was appointed as Sanskrit Pandit at the Madras Christian College where he served till 1910.

An important factor in the life of Sri Venkataraya Sastry was his dramatic activity as a literary past time. He was not only a playwright but a stage director as well. In the eighties of the 19th century it was his practice to see that every year his students at college enacted the Sanskrit Drama prescribed for that year. Thus he saw Abhijñana Śākuntala, Uttararamacarita, Nagananda, Priyadarsika and the like enacted year after year.

He successfully got enacted Bhavabhuti's Uttararāmacarita nataka which was considered by many of the western way of thought as unsuited for the stage. It was such a grand success with Sastry's trained students doing it so perfectly, that the Madras public called it as 'ati-Śākuntalam' i.e., even better than Śākuntalā of Kālidāsa in creating the rasa or feeling among the audience.

Even outside the educational limits, associations of Sanskrit lovers enacted these dramas and the reputed advocate and Sanskrit scholar, the late Sri T.S. Narayana Sastry of Madras, used to act as Sri Rāma in Uttararamacharita under the direction of Venkataraya Sastri.

In modern times, Bhavabhuti's masterpiece 'Uttararamacharita' was produced by Habib Tanvir in Hindi in his usual simple lokadharmi style which was appreciated both by the critics and the general masses alike. At Kalidasa festival in Ujjain, Habib Tanvir presented his 'Uttararāmacharitam'.

Uttararamacarita of Bhavabhuti was staged in Sanskrit, titled 'Pratimottara' together with Bhasa's Pratimanataka in the year 1985 by the M.P. Natak Lok Kala Academy, Ujjain under the direction of Prabhat Kumar Bhattacharya.

Performances of plays is a vital part of training to the students in the National School of Drama. Student productions are directed by the faculty members or by invited directors from all over the country as well as abroad under the Cultural Exchange Programmes of the Governement of India. Students performance in the productions are assessed by external examiners and members of the Faculty. During the year 1991-92, the students of NSD presented Bhavabhuti's Uttara Ramacharita under the direction of Shri Prasanna in November 1991.

Kavita Nagpal commented that there is no one in Delhi who can match Mohan Upreti when it comes to theatre music. Upreti bent his talent to provide music for Prasanna's Hindi version of Bhavabhuti's 12th Century Sanskrit classic, Uttara Rama Charita. Prasanna's directorial effort with the second year students of the NSD was a lustrous sample of what an empathetic director can do with a text and its portrayers. Uttararamacharita was a meritorious production and displayed a flawless marriage of word, music, design besides reminding us of the fact that much of what goes about in the name of modernism in the West today was a part of Indian tradition centuries ago. Prasanna's framing highlighted the inherent alienation effect in the drama about Rama's life after the banishment of Sita.

A Scene from Uttara Rama Charita Directed by Prasanna (1991)

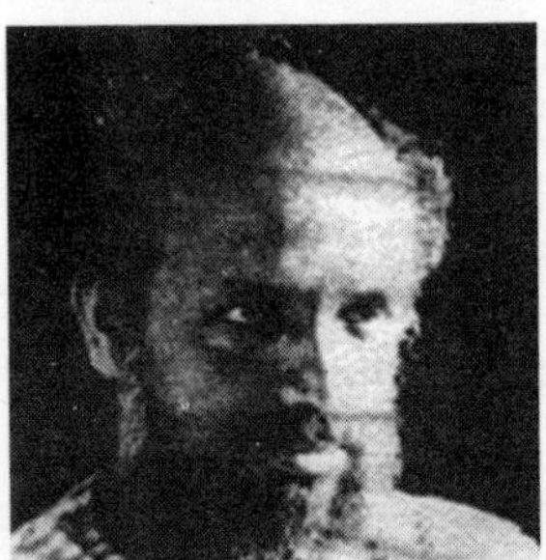

Prasanna

B.V. Karanth; remembered for his Hindi adaptation of Uttararamacharita'

From 21 July to 2 August 1992 third year students performed Uttararamacharitam in Nahan and Shimla. Again on an invitation from Kalidas Academy Ujjain, the students participated in the Kalidas Samaroh. On 7 November 1992, they presented the play 'Uttara Rama Charita'. Today, the theatre music cassettee of 'Uttara Rama Charita' is available at the NSD Book Shop, Bhawalpur House, Bhagawandas Road, New Delhi.

Sītātyāgaḥ is a Sanskrit radio play that follow the incident of the exile of Sītā as given in the Uttararamacarita and the Raghuvansa by and large. A part of this work by K.T. Pandurangi is from Bhavabhuti's magnum opus from which lines and stanzas have been and reproduced profusely by the adaptor. The very fact that it was successfully broadcast from the Bangalore station of the All India Radio.

Costume design of Uttararamacarita

Rāma

[Adapted from a figure of a prince in Ajanta Cave No. 17. Also from Dr. Motichandra, p. 187, Fig. 298. His crown — kirīṭa — (conical) slightly triangular in shape, Cave No. 17, Ajanta pl. xxvi 28 Harringham]

Sītā

[Visualised from a painting in Ajanta Cave No. 17. Also from Dr. Motichandra, p. 225, Fig. 410. Hairstyle of one long plait of a Virahiṇī nāyikā]

Vāsantī

[Approximated from Śālabhanjikā figurines in 6th century A.D. Assam. Her hairstyle adapted from Ajanta Cave No. 17, Harringham, pl. xxx (27)]

Tamasā

[Adapted from C. Sivaramamurti's "Some aspects of Indian culture" friezes of river goddess, p. 16 (Fig. 5 and 6) also p. 30 (Fig. 22). And various reliefs of river goddesses at Ellora - Kailas temple (8th century A.D.)]

BIBLIOGRAPHY

PRINCIPAL WORKS

Malati - Madhava

Text

Malatimadhava / edited by Christian Lassen. — Bonn. [19the century]

First Act only.

Christian Lassen (1800-1876)

Christian Lassen, a Norwegian by birth, settled in Germany and continued A.W. Von Schlegel's Indological studies in Bonn. He was born on 22.10.1800 in Bergen, Norway. A full professor in Bonn, this great scholar who edited the first act of Bhavabhuti's Malatimadhava died on 8.5.1876 in Bonn.

[Malatimadhava] Bhavabhuti granthavali / by Bhavabhuti; ed & tr. into Hindi by Ram Pratap Tripathi .- Allahabad : Lokbharati Prakashan, 1973.

58, 597 p.; 22 cm.

Includes Sanskrit text of 'Malatimadhava'.

Malatimadhava : with the commentary of Jagaddhara / ed. with a literal English tr. by M.R. Kale .- Delhi : Motilal Banarsidass, 1983.

[455] p.; 21.5 cm.

Mālatīmādhava / ed. with a commentary 'Bhāvamanoharā' by Haridās Siddhāntavāgīś Bhaṭṭācārya .- Nakipur, Khulna : The editor, 1914.

v, 536 p.; 18 cm.

Ten acts play on the love of Mādhava and Malati with the commentary of Jagaddhara.

Mālatīmādhava / ed. with a commentary 'Tattvabodhini' and a Bengali translation by Kuñjavihārī Tarkasiddhānta Bhaṭṭācārya .- Calcutta : Śastra - Pracār Press, 1920.

ix, 484 p.; 21 cm.

Mālatīmādhava / ed. with a literal English translation, notes and introd. by M.R. Kāḷe .- Bombay : Oriental Publishing Co., 1908.

vi, 353 p.; 22 cm.

Play includes the commentary of Jagaddhara.

Mālatīmādhava / ed. with notes by Rāmkṛṣṇa Gopāl Bhaṇḍārkar .- 2nd ed. - Bombay : Govt. of Bombay, 1905.

xxii, [558] p.; 22 cm. - (Bombay Sanskrit Series; 15)

First published in 1876.

Mālatīmādhava .- Trivandrum : University of Travancore, 1953.

xlix, 655 p.; 24 cm.- (Trivandrum Sanskrit Series; 170).

Includes indexes.

Contains the commentary 'Rasamañjari' of Pūrṇasarasvatī and introd. by K.S. Mahādeva Śāstrī.

Malatimadhava / by Bhavabhuti; critically ed. by Michael Coulson; rev. by Roderick Senclair. - Delhi : OUP, 1989.

lxi, 280 p.; 22.5 cm.

In Roman script.

Includes notes in English.

Malatimadhava / by Bhavabhuti; ed. by Mangeśa Ramakrishna Telang; rev. by Vasudeva Lakshmana Panaśikar. 6thed . Bombay : Nirnaya Sagar Press, 1936.

124, 3 p.; 22 cm.

Malatimadhavam / by Bhavabhuti; ed. by V.A. Ramasvami Śastri; with Purnasarasvati's comm. 'Rasamanjari' .- Trivandrum : University of Travancore, 1953.

47, 655 p.; 24 cm.

Malatimadhava / by Bhavabhuti; ed. with Sanskrit - Hindi comm. 'Chandrakala' by Śesharaja Śarma .- Varanasi : Chowkhamba Sanskrit Series office, 1954.

16, 475 p.; 18 cm.

Mālatīmādhava with the commentaries of Tripurāri and Jagaddhara / ed. by M.R. Telaṅga and W.L. Paṇaśīkar-Bombay : NSP, 1905.

Translations

Assamese

Malati - Madhava / by Bhavabhuti; tr. into Assumese by Dandinath Kalita .- Tezpur : The author, 1951.

180 p.; 18 cm.

Bengali

Malatimadhava / by Bhavabhuti; tr. into Bengali by an anonymous .- 1898 [1305].

In Prose translation.

Malatimadhava / by Bhavabhuti; tr. into Bengali by Kaliprasanna Ghosal. - 1858 [Samvat 1915].

Malatimadhava / by Bhavabhuti; tr. into Bengali by Kaliprasanna Sinha. - 1858 [Shakabda 1780].

Kaliprasanna Sinha, translated Malatimadhava in 1858.

Malatimadhava / tr. into Bengali by Jyotirindranath Tagore. 1900 (1307)

Jyotirindranath Tagore (1849-1925); translated 'Uttararamacharitam', & 'Malatimadhava' and Mahaviracharitam into Bengali.

Malatimadhava / by Bhavabhuti; tr. into Bengali by Loharam Shiroratna. - 1860.

Malatimadhava / by Bhavabhuti; tr. into Bengali by Nagendranath Bandyopadhyay. - 1870.

Malatimadhava / by Bhavabhuti; tr. into Bengali by Ramnarayan Tarkaranta .- 1867.

Sanskrita Sahitya Sambhar / ed. by Gaurinath Sastri & et. al [Vol. 17] .- Calcutta: Navpatra Prakashan, [1978-].

Includes Bengali rendering of 'Malatimadhava' of Bhavabhuti.

Dutch

[Mālatīmādhava] / tr. into Dutch by P.A.S. van Limburg Brouwer. - 1871.

English

Bhavabhuti's Malatimadhava : with the commentary of Jagaddhara; ed. with a literal English tr. by M.R. Kale. - Delhi : Motilal Banarsidass, 1983.

[455] p.; 21.5 cm.

[Mālatimādhavam] Malati and Madhava / tr. from the original Sanskrit by H.H. Wilson .- Calcutta : Society for the Resuscitation of Indian Literature, 1901.

x, 133p.; 15 cm.

Select specimens of the theatre of the Hindus (Vol. 2) / tr. into English by Horace Hayman Wilson. - 3rd ed. - New Delhi : Asian Educational Services, 1984.

Includes 'Malatimadhava' of Bhavabhuti.

Three Sanskrit plays / tr. into English by Michael Coulson .- London : Penguin Books, 1881.

430 p.; 19 cm.

Includes Bhavabhuti's 'Malatimadhava'.

French

Mālatimādhava / by Bhavabhuti; tr. into French by G. Strehly.- Paris : Leroux, 1885.

German

[Mālatīmādhava] / tr. into German by L. Fritze. - Leipzig : [s.n.], 1883.

Gujarati

Mālati Mādhav / tr. by Maṇilāl ubhāi Dvivedi. - Nadiad : The translator, 1912.

xvi, 152 p.; 21.5 cm.

Natyakathao / ed. by Jivanlal Amarshi Mehta. - Ahmedabad : The editor, 1927.

viii, 104 p.; 16 cm.

Includes Gujarati tr. of Bhavabhuti's writings.

Hindi

Bhavabhuti granthavali / by Bhavabhuti; ed. & tr. into Hindi by Ram Pratap Tripathi. - Allahabad ; Lokbharati Prakashan, 1973.

58, 597 p.; 22 cm.

Includes Hindi tr. of 'Malatimadhava'.

Mālati - Mādhav / tr. by Satyanārāyaṇ Śarmā. - 3rd ed. - Agra : Sahitya Ratna Bhaṇḍār, 1927.

ii, 167 p.; 18.5 cm.

First published in 1918.

Malatimadhava / by Bhavabhuti; tr. into Hindi by Sītaram 1898.

Mālatīmādhava / by Bhavabhūti, tr. by Sītārāma Lālā rev. ed. - Kanpur : Girjākishor, 1955.

Mālatīmādhava / by Bhavabhuti; tr. by Vishṇu Prabhākar .- New Delhi : Sasta Sahitya Mandal, [n.d.]

Mālatīmādhava / by Bhavabhuti; tr. by Śeṣrāj Śarmā. - Varanasi : Caukhamba Prakashan, 1971.

Malatimadhava / by Bhavabhuti; tr. into Brajbhasa [Hindi] by Somnath Mathur alias 'Shashinath' 1752.

Translated version appeared under the title *'Madhav Vinod'*.

Malatimadhava / by Bhavabhuti; tr. into Hindi by Shaligram 1881.

Malayalam

Mālatimādhava / tr. by Koṭṭārattil Śaṅkuṇṇi .- 2nd ed. - Kottayam : M.S. Book Depot, 1939.

191 p.; 19 cm.

Mālatimādhava / tr. by T.C. Bhāskaran Mūsatu .- Palghat : Prabhat Press, 1932.

100 p.; 19 cm.

Marathi

Mālatīmādhava : sār va vicār / tr. with a commentary by Mahādev Vyaṅkateś Lele .- Bombay : Vividhajñānavistār, 1900.

iv, 84 p.; 24 cm.

An abridged rendering with comments.

(Adaptation)

Islampūrkar, Vāman Śāstrī. Praṇayīmadhav / by Vāman Śāstrī Islampūrkar .- Bombay : Vāsudev Moreśvar Potdār, 1889.

xii, 272 p.; 18 cm.

Novel based on Bhavabhuti's famous Sanskrit play 'Mālatīmādhava'.

Nepali

Malati - madhava / by Bhavabhuti; tr. into Nepali by Sambhuprasad Dhuṅgel, 1969.

Oriya

Malatimadhava / by Bhavabhuti; tr. into Oriya by Mṛtyunjaya Rath. 1916/1917.

Tamil

Mālatīmādhava / tr. by K. Appāturai Piḷḷai .- Madras : Poṇṇi Publications, 1952.

ii, 56 p.; 18 cm.

An abridged rendering in Tamil.

Telugu

Mālatīmādhavamu / tr. by Janamañci Veṅkaṭarāmayya .- Madras : [s.n.], 1903.

xii, 108 p.; 18 cm.

Mālatīmādhaviyamu / tr. by Dāsu Śrīrāmulu; pref. by Pāḍi Vēṅkaṭnārāyaṇamūrti .- [s.l.] : [s.n.], 1900.

ix, 99 p.; 21 cm.

(Adaptation)

Sūryanārāyaṇaśāstri, Mallādi. Bhavabhūtinaṭakamulā vacanamu. - Madras : Vāviḷḷa Rāmasvāmi Śāstrulu & Sons, 1915.

ii, 118 p.; 17.5 cm.

Stories from Bhavabhuti's dramas.

Mahaviracaritam

Text

Bhavabhuti granthavali / by Bhavabhti; ed. & tr. into Hindi by Ram Pratap Tripathi .- Allahabad : Lokbharati Prakashan, 1973.

58, 597 p.; 22 cm.

Includes Sanskrit text of 'Mahaviracarita'.

Mahāvīracarita / by Bhavabhūti; ed. and tr. by John Pickford .- London : [s.n.], 1871.

Mahaviracharita / by Bhavabhuti; ed. by Anudoram Borooah .- 2nd ed. - Gauhati: Government of Assam, Publication Board, 1969.

[220] p.; 24 cm.

Mahāvīracarita / by Bhavabhūti; ed. by Jivananda. - Calcutta : [s.n.], [n.d.]

142 p.

Mahāvīracarita / by Bhavabhuti; ed. by T.R. Ratnam Aiyar and Parab .- Bombay: Nirṇayasāgar Press, 1910.

Includes commentary 'Bhāvapradyotini' of Vīrarāghava.

Mahāvīra - carita / by Bhavabhuti; ed. with introd. & notes by Todar Mall. - Lahore : University of the Panjab, 1928.

liv, 352 p.; 25 cm.

Includes indexes and appendices.

Work that deals with the earlier part of the story of Rama was revised.

Mahāvīracarita / by Bhavabhūti; ed. with notes by Sridhara Ganesha Joshi, 1887.

187, 28 p.

Translations

Bengali

Sanskrita Sahitya Sambhar / ed. by Gaurinath Sastri & ṭ et. al. [Vol. 13]. - Calcutta : Navpatra Prakashan, [197-].

Includes Bengali rendering of 'Mahaviracarita' of Bhavabhuti.

English

Mahāvīra - caritam / tr. into English prose by John Pickford .- London : [s.n.], 1871.

The first English rendering of the drama.

. **Gujarati**

Natyakathao / ed. by Jivanlal Amarshi Mehta .- Ahmedabad : the editor, 1927.

vii, 104 p.; 16 cm.

Includes Gujarati tr. of Bhavabhuti's writings.

Hindi

Bhavabhuti granthavali / by Bhavabhuti; & ed. & tr. into Hindi by Ram Pratap Tripathi .- Allahabad : Lokbharati Prakshan, 1973.

58, 597 p.; 22 cm.

Includes Hindi tr. of 'Mahaviracarita'.

Mahaviracarita / by Bhavabhuti; tr. into Hindi by Baldevprasad Mīśra. [19th cent.]

Mahāvīracarita / by Bhavabhuti; commentary by Rāmcandra Mīśra. - Varanasi : Caukhamba Vidyabhavan, 1955.

Mahaviracarita / by Bhavabhuti; tr. into Hindi by Sītaram 1899.

Mahāvīracarita / by Bhavabhūti; tr. by Sītārāma Lālā rev. ed. - Kanpur : Girjakishor, 1954.

Malayalam

Mahāvīracarita / by Bhavabhūti, tr. into Malayalam by Parameswaran Pillai.

Marathi

Mahāvīracarita : sār va vicār / tr. by Mahādev Vyaṅkaṭeś Lele .- Bombay : Vividhajñānavistār, 1901.

iv, 87 p.; 24 cm.

An abridgred translation with occasional comments.

Telugu

Mahāvīracaritra / tr. by Dāsu Śrīrāmulu [Srirama Dasu Kavi.] - [s.l.] : [s.n.], 1902.

183 p.; 16 cm.

Tr. of 'Mahāvīracarita', Sanskrit drama in seven acts.

Mahāvīracaritramu / tr. by Mallādi Sūryanārāyaṇa Śāstri .- Eluru : P.V. Śarma & Co., 1948.

iv, 120 p.; 21 cm.

Tr. of Mahāvīracarita.

(Adaptation)

Sūryanārāyaṇaśāstri, Mallādi. Bhavabhūtināṭakamula vacanamu .- Madras : Vāviḷḷa Rāmasvāmi Śāstrulu & Sons, 1915.

ii, 118 p.; 17.5 cm.

Stories from Bhavabhuti's dramas.

Uttararāmacarita

Text

Bhavabhuti granthavali / by Bhavabhuti ed. & tr. into Hindi by Ram Pratap Tripathi .- Allahabad : Lok Bharati Prakashan, 1973.

58, 597 p.; 22 cm.

Includes Sanskrit text of 'Uttararamacarita'.

Rāma's later history, or Uttararāmacarita / critically ed. in original Sanskrit and Prakrit with introd., English translation & notes by Śrīpāda Kṛṣṇa Belvalkar .- Cambridge (Mass.) : Harvard University Press, 1915.

3 Vols., 26 cm. - (Harvard University Series; 21-23).

Play in seven acts that depicts the later part of the story of Rāma.

Uttararāmacarita / by Bhavabhuti Calcutta : [s.n.], 1831.

Uttararāmacarita / by Bhavabhūti .- Madras : [s.n.], 1882.

Also contains the comm. of Ramachandra Budhendra.

Uttararāmacarita .- Tanjore : [s.n.], [n.d.].

Includes the commentary of Laksmana Suri.

Title page missing.

Uttararāmacarita / by Bhavabhuti; ed. & tr. into Hindi with notes by T. Jha. - Allahabad : [s.n.], 1961.

Uttararāmacarita / by Bhavabhuti; ed. by B.S. Ghate with English translation by V.S. Paṭavardhan .- Nagpur : [s.n.], 1895.

Uttararāmacarita / by Bhavabhūti; ed. by C.H. Tawney .- Calcutta : [s.n.], 1871.

Uttararāmacarita / by Bhavabhuti; ed. by C. Shankara Rama Sastri .- Madras : Balamanorama Press, 1932.

Uttararāmacarita / by Bhavabhūti; ed. by Carulata Sompat Kumara Tatarya .- [s.l.] : [s.n.], [n.d.].

336 p.

In Telugu script.

Title page missing.

Includes the commentary 'Kalā'.

Uttararāmacarita / by Bhavabhūti; ed. by Isvara Chandra Vidyasagara .- Calcutta: [s.n.], 1872.

Uttararāmacarita / by Bhavabhūti; ed. by M.R. Kale .- Delhi : Motilal Banarsidass, 1908.

Text with English translation, notes, appendices etc. with the commentary of Vīrarāghava, the famous commentator on the play. The introduction gives the personal history of Bhavabhūti, his date and a critical review of his work.

Uttararāmacarita / by Bhavabhūti; ed. by Nellore Sajjaya Tirurmala Tatacharya .- Mysore : Cakravarti Iyengar, Vidya Tarangini Press, 1891.

227 p.

In Telugu script.

Text contains commentary Bhāvatalasparśinī of Vīrarāghava.

Uttararāmacarita / by Bhavabhuti; ed. by P.V. Kāṇe .- Bombay : Nirṇayasāgar Press, 1915.

xxii, [346] p.; 21 cm.

Sanskrit play with Ghanaśyāma's commentary 'Sañjīvana' and an English rendering by C.N. Jośī.

Uttararāmacarita / by Bhavabhūti; ed. by P.V. Kane .- Bombay : [s.n.], 1921.

Includes the commentary of Ghanaśyāma and notes.

-. 4th rev. ed. - Delhi : Motilal Banarsidass, 1962.

Uttararāmacarita / by Bhavabhuti; ed. by Premacandra Tarkavāgīśa at the request of E.B. Cowell. - Calcutta : [s.n.], 1862.

Uttararāmacarita / by Bhavabhūti; ed. by Ratnam Aiyar and Parab .- Bombay : Nirṇayasagara Press, 1899.

Text contains the commentary of Vīrarāghava.

-. 2nd ed. - Bombay : Nirṇayasagara Press, 1906.

174 p.

--------. / by Bhavabhūti; ed. by K.N. Jogalekar .- 5th ed. - Bombay : Nirṇayasagara Press, 1915.

178 p.

Uttararāmacarita / by Bhavabhuti; ed. by R.A. Pandeya and R.N. Mishra .- Varanasi: University Publication, 1977.

Uttararāmacarita / by Bhavabhuti; ed. by R.G. Bhāṇḍārkar .- Bombay : [s.n.], 1905. - 2nd ed. - (Bombay Sanskrit series).

Uttararāmacarita / by Bhavabhūti; ed. by S.K. Belvalkar .- Cambridge (Mass.) : Cambridge University Press, 1915.

Uttararāmacarita / by Bhavabhūti; ed. by S.K. Belvalkar .- Poona : Oriental Book Supplying Agency, 1921.

107 p.

Uttararāmacarita / by Bhavabhuti; ed. by T.R. Ratnam Ayyar and K.P. Parab with the commentary of Vīrarāghava. - Bombay : NSP, 1899.

Uttararāmacarita / by Bhavabhuti; ed. by V.M. Gopālakṛṣṇamācārya, T.I. Raghunāthācarya and A.K. Rāmānujācārya .- Madras : Ānanda Press, 1906.

xiv, 336, [6] p.; 21 cm.

Contains a commentary 'Kalā' by Addaṅgi Kumāra Tātācārya.

In Telugu script.

Uttararāmacarita / by Bhavabhuti; ed. with a comm. by Jivananda .- Calcutta : [s.n.], 1881.

266 p.

Uttararāmacarita / by Bhavabhuti; ed. with a commentary 'Mitabhāṣiṇī', English tr., critical notes & introd. by Śāradārañjan Rāy .- Calcutta : Kohinur Printing Works, 1924.

[584] p.; 18 cm.

Uttararāmacarita / by Bhavabhuti; ed. with a commentary 'Sarvārthabodhinī' and a Bengali translation by Haridās Siddhānta vāgīś Bhaṭṭacārya .- 2nd ed. - Nakpur, Khulna : The editor, 1921.

xvi, 445, [112] p.; 21 cm.

Uttararāmacarita / by Bhavabhuti; ed. with a Sanskrit commentary and Bengali translation by Gurunāth Bhaṭṭācārya Vidyānidhi .- Calcutta : Jānakīnath Kāvyatīrṭha, 1915.

xlviii, 412, [92] p.; 21 cm.

Indlues index.

Uttararāmacarita / by Bhavabhuti; ed. with an English translation, notes; vocabulary and introd. by Vināyak Sadāśiv Paṭvardhan .- 2nd ed. - Bombay : Indu Prakāś Press, 1909.

iv, [323] p.; 21 cm.

Also contain Bhaṭṭajī Śāstrī Gokhale's commentary 'Bhāvabhūtārthabodhika'.

Uttararāmacarita / by Bhavabhuti; ed. with commentary, notes & tr. by P.V. Kane & C.N. Joshi .- Delhi : Motilal Banarsidass, 1962.

xliv, 157, 271 p.; 22 cm.

English rendering by C.N. Joshi.

Uttararāmacarita / by Bhavabhuti; ed. with commentary of Ramachandra Budhendra .- Madras : [s.n.], 1882.

Uttararāmacarita / by Bhavabhuti; ed. with notes by Srinivasa Govinda Bhanape .- Bombay : Tattvaviveka Press, 1893 [S 1815].

118, 110 p.

Uttararāmacarita [with the commentary of Vīrarāghavācārya].- Madras : V. Rāmasvāmi Śāstrulu, 1940.

240 p.; 20 cm.

In Telugu script.

Uttararamacarita [with Sanskrit - Hindi commentaries by Anandasvarupa] / ed. by Janardanasastri Pandey.- Delhi : Motilal Banarsidass, 1986.

[600] p.; 18.5 cm.

Uttararamacarita / by Bhavabhuti; ed. with a commentary by Brahmananda Śukla .- Meerut : Sahitya Bhandar, 1963.

32, 544 p.; 22 cm.

Uttararamacarita / by Bhavabhuti; ed. with commentary, notes etc. by P.V. Kane & C.N. Joshi; English tr. by C.N. Joshi .- Delhi : Motilal Banarsidass, 1962.

xliv, 157, 271 p.; 22 cm.

Uttararamacarita / by Bhavabhuti; ed. by Śripada Krishna Belavalkar .- Cambridge (Mass.) : Harvard University, 1922.

107 p.; 26 cm.

First published in 1916.

(Adaptation)

Majalgaonkar, Achyat Tatya Bobade. Sītātyāgah. *In* Kālidāsīyoparūpakāṇāṁ samuccayaḥ .- Darbhanga : Kameshwar Singh Sanskrit University, 1963. Pp 105-107

A dramatic adaptation of the Sītātyāga as depicted both by Kālīdāsa and Bhavabhūti.

A small play with just three scenes.

Pandurangi, K.T. Sītātyāgaḥ.- Bangalore.

It is a Radio play in Manuscript having three small scenes called the Dhvanitaraṅgas that depict the scene of the exile of Sītā. Based Uttararamacharitam & Raghuvaṁsa by and large a part of this work is from the Uttararamacaritam from which likes and stanzas have been reproduced profusely.

Translations

Bengali

Uttararamacharita / by Bhavabhuti; tr. into Bengali by Jyotirindranath Thakur. - 1900.

Uttararamacharita / by Kalidasa; tr. into Bengali by Nṛsiṃha Mukhopadhyay .- 1873.

Includes commentary.

Uttararāmacarita / ed. with a Sanskrit commentary and Bengali translation by Gurunāth Bhaṭṭācārya Vidyānidhi .- Calcutta : Jānakināth Kāvyatirtha, 1915.

xlviii, 412, 92 p.; 21 cm.

Includes index.

A drama in seven acts on the later life of Rama.

Sanskrita Sahitya Sambhar / ed. by Gaurinath Sastri & et. al. [Vol. 6] .- Calcutta: Navpatra Prakashan, [197-].

Includes Bhavabhuti's 'Uttararamacarita'.

(Adaptation)

Sītar banabas / by Ishvarchandra Vidyasagar. - 1860.

This play was inspired from Bhavabhuti's 'Uttararamacharita'. The first two parts are the translation of the first act of the classic.

English

Bhavabhuti's Uttararamacharitam / tr. by G.K. Bhat 2nd ed. - Surat : Popular Publishing House, 1965.

Rama's later history or Uttar - Rama - Charita / critically ed. in the original Sanskrit and Prakrit with an introduction and English translation and notes and variants by Shripad Krishna Belvalkar .- Cambridge (Mass.). Harvard University Press, 1915.

3 Vols.; 25.5 cm. - (Harvard Oriental Series / ed. by Charles Rockwell Lanman; 21, 22, 23).

Sanskrit plays from epic sources / tr. into English verse by Henry W. Wells .- Baroda : Maharaja Sayajirao University, 1968.

xi, 258 p.; 22.5 cm.

Includes *Uttararamacharita* by Bhavabhuti.

Specimens of the theatre of the Hindus / tr. into English by Horace Hayman Wilson. - 3rd ed. - New Delhi : Asian Educational Services, 1984.

Includes *Uttararamacarita* of Bhavabhuti.

Six Sanskrit plays / ed. & tr. by Henry W. Wells .- London : Asia Publishing House, 1964.

xxxi, 487 p. : plates; 21 cm.

Includes "*Uttara Ramacarita*" of Bhavabhuti.

Uttararamacarita / by Bhavabhuti; ed. by G.K. Bhat .- Surat : Popular Book Store, 1953.

ix, 193 p.

Uttararāmacarita / by Bhavabhuti; tr. into English by C.H. Tawney .- Calcutta : [s.n.], 1871.

Also published in 1875.

Uttararāmacarita sikāri Kacēri, 1937.

viii, 150 p.; plate: 18.5 cm.

Uttararamacharita / by Bhavabhuti; tr. into Gujarati by Manilal Nabhubhai Dvivedi [19th cent.].

The translation was ranked as an excellent translation for many years.

Uttararamacarita / by Bhavabhūti; tr. by Padmāvati Dēśai .- Ahmedabad : The translator, 1949.

lxvi, 202 p.; 18.5 cm.

Uttararamacarita / by Bhavabhūti; tr. by Umāśaṅkar Jēthālāl Jośi .- Ahmedabad : Jivan Sāhitya Mandir, 1950.

lxxxviii, 328 p.; 18.5 cm.

Translations of original verses in same metre : with a running Gujarati commentary Bhāvārthabōdhini and a critical introduction

Hindi

Uttararamacarita / by Bhavabhūti; .- Bombay : [s.n.], 1887.

Uttararamacarita / by Bhavabhūti; .- Hoshiarpur : Sahitya Prakashan, 1958.

Uttararamacarita / by Bhavabhūti; tr. into Hindi by Baldevprasad Miśra. [19th cent.].

Uttararamacarita / by Bhavabhūti; commentary by Tariṇīś Jhā .- Allahabad : Rāmnārāyaṇ Lāl Benīprasād, 1961.

Bhavabhuti granthavali / by Bhavabhuti ed. & tr. into Hindi by Ram Pratap Tripathi .- Allahabad : Lokbharati Prakashan, 1973.

58, 597 p.; 22 cm.

Includes Hindi tr. of 'Uttararamacarita'.

Uttararāmacarita / by Bhavabhūti; tr. by Devdatta Śāstrī and Raghunandanprasāda Śuklā .- Varanasi : Sanskrit Pustakalay, 1930.

Uttararāmacarita / by Bhavabhūti; tr. by Devdatta Tivarī .- Calcutta : Jñān Ratnākar Press, 1874.

Uttararāmacarita / by Bhavabhūti; tr. by Hardayālsiṃha .- New Delhi : Sasta Sahitya Mandal, 1954.

Uttararāmacarita / by Bhavabhūti; tr. by Harimangal Miśra .- Allahabad : Grihalakshmi Karyalay, 1921.

Uttararāmacarita / by Bhavabhūti; tr. by Indra. - Delhi : Rajpal & Sons, 1957.

Uttararāmacarita / by Bhavabhūti; tr. by Kṛṣṇacandra .- Varanasi : Caukhamba Vidyabhavan, 1916.

Uttararāmacarita / by Bhavabhūti; tr. by Satyanārāyaṇa 'Kaviratna' .- Agra : Bharatī Bhandar, 1915.

Uttararāmacarita / by Bhavabhuti; tr. by Satyanārāyaṇ Śarmā .- 5th ed. - Agra :

Ratnāsram, 1934.

xxxii, 146, 13 p.; 18.5 cm.

Includes appendices.

First published in 1913.

Uttararāmacarita / by Bhavabhūti; tr. into Hindi by Kaviratna Satyanarayana Sharma .- Agra : Bharti Bhawan, 1970.

Prose and verse.

Uttararamcharita / by Bhavabhuti; tr. by Satyanarayan Kaviratna .- New Delhi : Rajkamal Prakashan, 1986.

179 p.; 18 cm.

Uttararāmacarita / by Bhavabhūti; tr. by Thakurdatta Miśra .- Allahabad : Kitab Mahal, 1956.

Uttararāmacarita / by Bhavabhūti; tr. into Hindi by Anandasvarup; ed. by Janardan Pandey .- Delhi : Motilal Banarsidas, 1963.

Uttararāmacarita / by Bhavabhūti; tr. into Hindi by Ramdas Rāy .- Ranchi : Pandit Gauri Shankar Sharma, 1928.

Prose and verse.

Uttararāmacarita / by Bhavabhūti; tr. into Hindi by Rāmdās Rāya .- Gazipur : Ashokashram , 1935.

Uttararāmacarita / by Bhavabhūti; tr. by Śeṣrāj Śarmā Regmī and Kantanāth Śāstrī Telang .- 4th ed. - Varanasi : Caukhamba Vidyabhavan, 1952.

Uttararamacarita / by Bhavabhūti; tr. into Hindi by Satyanarayana Kaviratna .- New Delhi : Raj Kamal Prakashan, 1998.

179 p.

First published in 1986.

Uttararamacarita / by Bhavabhūti; tr. into Hindi by Sītaram, 1897.

Uttararāmacarita / by Bhavabhuti; tr. into Hindi by Sītārām Lāl. rev ed. - Allahabad : Indian Press, 1954.

Uttararamacarita / by Bhavabhūti; tr. into Hindi by Vishwanāth Dubey, 1896.

Kannada

Kannada Uttararamacharite / by Bhavabhuti; tr. into Kannada by K. Krishna Murti .- Mysore : Sharada Mandira, 1974.

154 p.; 18 cm.

Nāṭakāmṛta - bindugalu / by Kālidāsa and others; tr. into Kannada by L. Basavaraju .- Mysore : Gaurishankar Book Depot, 1958.

Contains some portions of 'Pratimanatakam' & 'Uttararāmacarita' of Bhababhūti.

Uttararāmacarita / by Bhavabhūti; tr. into Kannada by Basavappa Sastri .- Mysore : GTA Press, 1911.

(Karnataka Granthamale; No. 55).

Prose and verse; some verses set to music.

Uttararāmacarita / by Bhavabhūti; tr. into Kannada by C.Hanumante Gauda. *Karṇātaka Kavi caritre* 3; 1974.

Uttararāmacarita / by Bhavabhūti; tr. into Kannada by C.P. Krishna Kumar .- Mysore : Vagdevi Pustakagalu, 1983.

Prose and verse.

Uttararāmacarita / by Bhavabhūti; tr. Kannada by Dhondo Narasimha Mulabagila .- Dharwad : Karnataka Vidyavardhaka Sangha, 1892.

2nd ed. published in 1924.

Prose and verse.

Uttararāmacarita / by Bhavabhūti; tr. into Kannada by Galaganatha (V.T. Kulakarni).

Uttararāmacarita / by Bhavabhūti; tr. by K.A. Kotrappa .- Mayakonda (Chitradurga): [s.n.], 1966.

Uttararāmacarita / by Bhavabhūti; tr. into Kannada by K. Krishnamoorthy. 2nd ed. - Mysore : Sharada Mandira, 1956.

Prose and verse.

Uttararāmacarita / by Bhavabhūti; tr. into Kannada by K. Krishnamoorthy and B.R. Modak .- Dharwad.

Contains text in Devanāgarī script on opposite pages.

Uttararāmacarita / by Bhavabhūti; tr. into Kannada by Moleyaru Shankaranarayana Bhatta .- Bela (Kasaragodu) : M. Subraya Bhatta, 1952.

Uttararāmacarita / tr. by Mōḷeyāra Śaṅkaranārāyaṇa Bhaṭṭa .- Mangalore : M. Subraya Bhaṭṭa, 1952.

xxxii, 138, 6 p.; 18 cm.

Includes index.

Uttararāmacaritra / tr. by Dhōṇḍo Narasiṃha Muḷabagal .- 2nd ed. - Dharwar : Karṇāṭaka Vidyāvardhaka Saṅgha, 1924.

ix, 132 p.; 18 cm.

First published in 1392.

Uttararāmāyaṇada kathācitra / by Bhavabhuti; tr. by N.S. Virappa.- Bangalore : S.S.N. Book Depot, 1947.

iv, 86 p.; 18 cm.

Maithili

Uttararāmacarita / by Bhavabhūti; tr. into Maithili by Munshi Raghunandan Das. - Kashi : Mithilamoda Karyalaya, 1912.

In two parts.

--------. Patna : Maithili Academy, 1984.

125 p.

Uttararāmacarita / by Bhavabhuti; tr. into Maithili by Rajkumar Miśra .- Pandaul: The author, 1954.

ii, 126 p.; 18 cm.

Uttararāmacarita / by Bhavabhūti; tr. into Maithili by Raja Kumar Misra .- Pandaul: Madhubani : [s.n.], 1984.

126 p.

Malayalam

Uttararāmacarita / by Bhavabhūti; tr. by Chanbattil Chattukutty Mannadiar .- [s.l.]: [s.n.], 1892.

Uttararāmacarita / tr. by Campattil Cāttukuṭṭi Mannāṭiyār .- 3rd ed. - Trichur : B.V. Book Depot, 1943.

148 p.; 23 cm.

This is one of the first of its kind, is written in chaste Malayalam and is a pleasant contrast to the Sanskrit - ridden work of Kerala Verma.

Uttararamacarita / by Bhavabhūti; tr. into Malayalam by Champattil Chattukkuṭṭi Mannaṭiyar .- Trichur : Vidyavinodini Press, 1947?

12, 162 p.; 18 cm.

Introduction by K.V.M.

Uttararāmacarita / by Bhavabhūti; tr. into Malayalam by C.P. Achyutha Menon.

Manipuri

Uttararām carit / tr. from Sanskrit original by Aribam Gokul Śarma .- Imphal : The translator, 1968.

137 p.; 18 cm.

Marathi

Śri Uttararāmacarita : sār va vicār / tr. with a commentary by Mahādev Vyaṅkaṭeś Lele .- Bombay : Vividhajñānavistār, 1902.

iv, 87 p.; 24 cm.

An abridged rendering in Marathi with occasional comments.

Uttararāmacarita / by Bhavabhūti; tr. into Marathi by D.M. Hatwalane .- Pune : Deshmukh Prakashan, 1965.

Uttararāmacarita / by Bhavabhūti; tr. into Marathi by P.B. Godbole .- Bombay : L.M. Disaza Printing Press, 1859.

(Adaptation)

Behere, Nārāyaṇ Keśav. Sitā-vanavās athavā Rāmāyanantil viṣamkāṇḍa / by Nārāyan Keśav Behere. - Nagpur : The author, 1936.

127 p.; 18 cm.

Mythological story based on Bhavabhūti's Uttararāmacarita and other works.

Islāmpūrkar, Vāman Śāstri Karuṇrāghav / by Vāman Śāstrī Islāmpūrkar .- Bombay : Vāsudev Moreśvar Potdār, 1889.

xviii, 244 p.; 18 cm.

Novel based on Bhavabhuti's 'Uttararāmacarita'.

Nepali

Uttararāmacaritabhāvānuvād / tr. by Kālidās Parājulī .- Varanasi : The translator, 1934.

28, 142 p.; 18 cm.

A free rendering of the Bhavabhuti's 'Uttararāmacaritanātaka' from Sanskrit.

Oriya

Uttararamacharita / by Bhavabhuti; translated into Oriya by Harihar Rath. [Late nineteenth century]

Uttararamacharita / by Bhavabhuti; tr. into Oriya by Kavi Madhusudan Rao, 1907/ 1908.

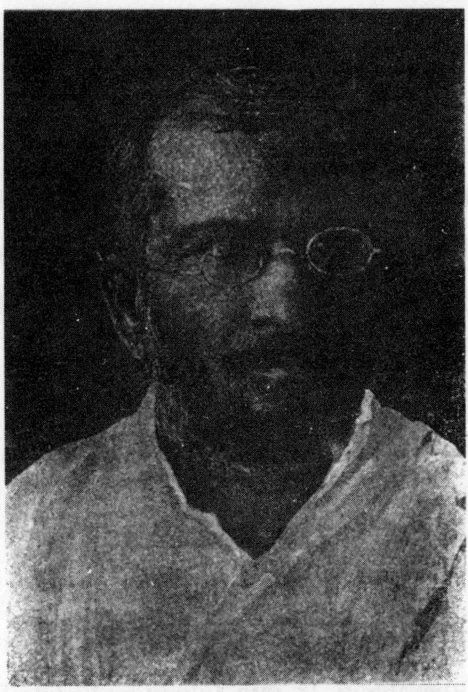

Madhusudan Rao

Tamil

Uttararāmacarita / tr. by K. Santānam .- 2nd ed. - Madras : Alliance Co., 1949.

viii, 123 p.; 18 cm.

First published in 1940.

Telugu

Andhrīkṛtōttararāmacaritramu / tr. by Mantripragaḍa Bhujaṅgarāvu .- Eluru : The translator, 1918.

ix, 109 p. : plate; 22 cm.

Tr. of 'Uttararāmacarita'.

Uttararāghavamu / tr. by Balijēpalli Lakṣmīkāntamu .- 3rd ed. - Guntur : The translator, 1930.

iv, 116 p.; 18 cm.

Tr. of 'Uttararāmacarita'.

Uttararamacharita / by Bhavabhuti .- Vijayawada : Vinod Publications, 1956.

33 p.; 17.5 cm.

Uttararāmacarita / by Bhavabhūti; tr. into Telugu by Dasu Kavi Srirama.

Uttararāmacarita / by Bhavabhūti; tr. into Telugu by Dwivedi Brahmananda Sastry.

Uttararāmacarita / by Bhavabhūti; tr. into Telugu by Janamanchi Venkata Ramiah.

Uttararamacarita / by Bhavabhuti; tr. into Telugu by Jayanti Ramayya .- Muktesvaram: the translator, 1931.

159 p.; 21.5 cm.

Uttararāmacarita / by Bhavabhūti; tr. into Telugu by Korade Ramchandra Sastry.

Uttararamacarita / by Bhavabhuti; tr. into Telugu by Rayaprolu Subbarao .- Tirupati: the translator, 1959.

136 p.; 21 cm.

Uttararāmacarita / by Bhavabhūti; tr. into Telugu by Vavilala Vasudeva Sastry.

Uttararāmacarita / by Bhavabhūti; tr. into Telugu by Vedula Brahmananda Sastry.

Uttararamacharita / by Bhavabhuti; ed. by Nelaturi Ramadasayyangar.- Hyderabad:

Andhra Pradesh Sahitya Akademi, 1970.

389 p.; 21 cm.

Uttararāmacaritam / tr. by Vēṅkaṭarāmakṛṣṇakavuḷu .- Kakinada : the translators, 1913.

iv, 85 p.; 18 cm.

Contains four acts.

Uttararāmacaritramu / tr. with an introd. by Vēdamu Vēṅkaṭarāyaśāstri .- Madras: The translator, 1920.

lxxii, 98 p.; 23 cm.

Uttararāmacaritranāṭakamu / tr. by Mallādi Sūryanārāyaṇaśāstri .- Rajahmundry : Callā Jagannatham, 1929.

96 p.; 22 cm.

Tr. of 'Uttararāmacarita'.

(Adaptations)

Anonymous. Sītā - vanavāsam.

Telugu play based on Uttara - Rāma - carita of Bhavabhūti, with innovations. Here Śurpaṇakhā creates the split; finally she confesses and Sītā is accepted back.

Pandurangi, K.P. Sītātyāga .- [s.l.] : [s.n.], 1959.

A play based on the theme of Vālmīki, Kālidāsa and Bhavabhuti.

Mentioned in the 'Bibliography of stageable plays in Indian languages / ed. by C.C. Mehta' (Vol. 1, 1963).

Sūryanārāyaṇaśāstri, Mallādi. Bhavabhūtināṭakamulā vacanamu. - Madras : Vāviḷḷa Rāmasvāmi Śāstrulu & Sons, 1915.

ii, 118 p.; 17.5 cm.

Stories from Bhavabhūti's dramas.

BIO - CRITICAL NOTICES

Acharya, Nandiswar Prasad. Evolution of the dramas of Bhavabhuti from the view point of Aucitya theory of Acarya Ksmendra / by Nandiswar Prasad Acharya.

Ph.D. thesis approved by the Meerut University in 1980.

Acharya, P.B. Tragicomedies of Shakespeare, Kalidasa and Bhavabhuti .- New Delhi : Meherchand Lachhmandas, 1978.

264 p.; 22 cm.

Comparative study.

Adya Rangacharya. Drama in Sanskrit literature .- Bombay : Popular Prakashan, 1967.

Pp. 13, 16, 39, 44, 58, 61, 70, 72, 78, 91, 167-190, 193, 194.

Aggarwal, H.R. A short history of Sanskrit literature. - 2nd rev. ed. - Delhi : Munshiram Manoharlal, 1963.

Contents : (Bhavabhuti P. 182-)

Anjali. Self expression in the characters of Bhavabhuti / by Anjali.

Ph.D. thesis in Hindi approved by the Gurukul Kangri University in 1981.

Arya, Nirmal. Critical study of Bhavabhuti and his dramas / by Nirmal Arya.

Ph.D. thesis in Hindi, approved by the Banaras Hindu University in 1961.

Aufrecht, Theodor. Catalogus Catalogorum .- Weisbaden : Franz Stener Verlag Gmb. H, 1962.

2 Vols.; 26 cm.

Bālakṛṣṇamūrti, Paṅganāmāmula. Kāḷidāsa Bhavabhūti Kathalu / by Paṅganāmamula Bālakṛṣṇamūrti .- Vijayawada : Kavitilaka Granthamala, 1947.

iv, 88 p.; 18.5 cm.

Stories in Telugu from the plays of Kālidāsa and Bhavabhūti.

Bandopadhyaya, Sureshchandra. Sanskrit sahityer itihas .- Calcutta : The Dacca

Students Library, [1970?].

In Bengali.

Banerji, Sures Chandra. A Companion to Sanskrit literature .- Delhi : Motilal Banarsidass, 1971.

Baumgartner, Alexander. [Critical study of Uttararamacharita].

Alexander Baumgartner (1841-1910.)

Alexander Baumgartner was born on 27.7.1841 in St. Gallen, Switzerland. He was an able editor and an erudite Sanskrit scholar who discussed works like Bhavabhuti's Uttararamacharita and Mahaviracharita. He died on 5.9.1910 in Luxembourg.

Bharadwaj, G.D.

Studies in the commentary of Jagaddhara on the dramas of Bhavabhuti.

Ph.D. thesis approved by the Aligarh Muslim University in 1980.

Bhartiya, Kanti Kishore. Sanskrit natakkar. - Uttar Pradesh : Prakashan Sakha, Suchana Vibhag, 1959.

(Hindi - Samiti granthamala; 25).

Contents : Bhavabhuti. Pp. 135 - 141.

Bhartiya, Shashi Kiran. Critical study of the social and cultural conditions described in the dramas of Bhavabhuti.

Ph.D. thesis in Hindi approved by the Agra University in 1975.

Bhat, G.K. Sanskrit drama : problems and perspectives. - Delhi : Ajanta Publications, 1985.

Bhat, G.K. Bhavabhūti - New Delhi : Sahitya Akademi, 1979.

3rd ed. published in 1980.

Bhat, G.K. Sanskrit drama : a perspective on theory and practice - Dharwar : Karnatak University, 1975.

Silver Jubilee Publication of Karnatak University.

Bhat, G.K. Sanskrita natyasristi .- Pune : Continental Prakashan, 1964.

Bhat, G.K. Tragedy and Sanskrit drama .- Bombay : Popular Prakashan, 1974.

Bhatt, S.C. Drama in ancient India .- New Delhi : Amrit Book Co., 1961.

Bhattacharya, Barundev. Sanskrit dramatic practice : Bhavabhuti / by Barandev Bhattacharya.

Ph.D. thesis in Bengali approved by the Rabindra Bharati University in 1986.

Bhattacharya, Bimanchandra. Sanskrit sahityer ruprekha. - 5th ed. - Calcutta : Vidyodaya Library Pvt. Ltd., 1972.

Bhattacharya, Biswanath. Sanskrit drama and dramaturgy. - Delhi : Sharada Publishing House, 1994.

Bhattacharya, Hillol. Tragedy : ek bicchhinnatar itihas . - *Syas Natya Patra* - 16; 1999.

'Bhaṭṭa Nārāyaṇa and Bhavabhuti' / by T.K. Tope *All India Oreintal Conference XV* (Summary); P. 194.

'Bhavabhuti' / by S.K. De *Indian Historical Quarterly;* June 1943; 19 (2); Pp. 101-118.

Bhavabhuti. A critical edication of the Malatimadhava / by Bhavabhuti; tr. by Michael

Coulson, rev. by Roderick Sinclair. - Delhi : Oxford University Press, 1989.

Introduction deals with the study of the play.

Bhavabhuti : a revaluation / by Nanda Kishore Mishra *All India Oriental Conference* XV (Summary); P. 54.

'Bhavabhūti and Arthaśāstra' / by V. Raghavan. *Walter Ruben Felicitation Vol.* (Berlin); 1968.

'Bhavabhuti and his contemporary detractors' / by G.C. Jhala, *JOI* (Baroda); March - June 1965; Vol. XIV, Nos. 3-4. Pp. 448-463.

'Bhavabhūti and Mīmāṃsā' / by V.A.R. Sastri. *In* A. Chettiar Commemoration Volume, Anamalainagar, 1941.

'Bhavabhuti and Umbeka' / by V.V. Mirashi. *All India Oriental Conference Proceedings;* 1957; Vol. 2, 19th session.

'Bhavabhuti and Umbeka' / by V.V. Mirashi *Indian Historical Quarterly,* March 1958; Vol. 34, No. 1; Pp. 29-39.

'Bhavabhuti and the Veda' / by V. Raghavan. *JASB* (New Series); 1956-57, Vols. 31-32.

(Śrāddha - Śatābdi Special Volume)

Published June 1959; Pp. 218-221.

'Bhavabhuti' / by R.D. Karmakar' *Annals of the Bhandarkar Oriental Research Institute;* 1962; Vol. XLIII.

Pp. 166-167.

Book review by V.M. Bedekar.

'Bhavabhuti / by V.V. Mirashi' *Visveshvasranand Indological Journal / ed. by K.V. Sarma;* Sept. 1976; Vol. XIV, No. II. Pp. 328-330.

Book review by Jagnnath Agrawal.

'Bhavabhuti by V.V. Mirashi' / by T.S. Parthasarathy. *Triveni;* 1976, Vol. 44.

Book review.

Bhavabhuti : his mind and art / by Hari Ram Mishra *All India Oriental Conference XVII* (Summary); Pp. 38-40.

-----. *Maharaja's College Magazine* (Chhatarpur, M.P.) July 1954.

'Bhavabhuti's concept of love' / by R.R. Ambardekar. *Indian Literature;* 1978, Vol. XXI 3; Pp. 78-87.

'Bhavabhūti's quotations from the Rāmāyaṇa' / by R.G. Bhandarkar. *Indian Antiquary* 2, Pp. 123-124.

'Birth place of Bhavabhuti' / by V.V. Mirashi *Indian Historical Quarterly;* June 1935; Vol. 11, No. 2; Pp. 287-299.

Borooah, Anunddoram. Bhavabhuti and his place in Sanskrit literature. - Calcutta: [s.n.], 1878.

Borooah, Anundoram. Bhavabhuti and his place in Sanskrit literature. - Gauhati : Publication Board, 1971.

72 p.; 28 cm.

The Cambridge guide to Asian theatre / ed. by James R. Brandon. - Cambridge : Cambridge University Press, 1993.

The Cambridge guide to world theatre / ed. by Martin Banham. - Cambridge : Cambridge University Press, 1988.

Chandramouli, Jaya. Commentaries on Uttara Ramacharita / by Jaya Chandramouli.

Ph.D. thesis approved by the University of Bombay in 1977.

'Critical fallacies as regards Uttararāmacarita' / by R.M. Joshi *All India Oriental Conference VI.* xiv.

The Cultural heritages of India [Vol. V] / ed. by Suniti Kumar Chatterji. - rev. ed. - Calcutta : The Ramakrishna Mission Institute of Culture, 1978,

P. 243-

Dalal, Minakshi L. Conflict in Sanskrit drama .- Bombay : Samaiya Publications Pvt. Ltd., 1973.

Contents : Bhavabhuti . Pp. 220-236, 247-254.

Dange, Sadashiv A & Dange, Sindhu S. Critiques on Sanskrit dramas. - 2nd rev. ed. - New Delhi : Aryan Books International, 1994.

Das, Sarbeshwar. The comic and romantic in Sanskrit dramas with special reference to Bhāsa, Kālidāsa, Harṣa and Bhavabhūti. *Summary of Papers: All India Oriental Conference* (Bhuvaneshwar); 1959; Vol. XX .

Dasgupta & Dey. History of India literature : classical period. - Calcutta : University of Calcutta, 1947.

De, Sabitri. Sanskrit Sahityer anubad - dhara. - Calcutta : Chinmay Majumdar, [1983].

Contents :

On Malatimadhava (Pp. 144-157).

On Uttararamacharita (Pp. 161-167).

De, Sushil Kumar. Aspect of Sanskrit literature. - Calcutta : Firma KLM, 1959.

'The Denouncement and its dramatic propriety in Abhijnanasakuntala, Uttararamacarita and Mṛcchakatika' / by P.B. Acharya.

Sanskrit Ranga (Annual Number); Vol. 6; Pp. 38-58.

Deo, Surendra. A comparative study of the dramas of Kalidasa and Bhavabhuti / by Surendra Deo.

Ph.D. thesis approved by the Agra University in 1963.

Dictionary of oriental literatures (Vol. II) : South and South - East Asia. - Delhi : Vikas Publishing, 1975.

Dixit, S.V. Bhavabhuti : his life and literature / by S.V. Dixit . - Tilakwadi, Belgaum : [s.n.], 1958.

Dixit, Sushma. Comparative estimation of parallelism in the incidents and characters of Valmiki, Kalidasa and Bhavabhuti / by Sushma Dixit.

Ph.D. thesis in Hindi approved by the Kurukshetra University in 1972.

'The Dramatic problem of Uttararāmacarita' / by G.L. Bhat. *Bharatiya* Vidya - 30; 1970. Pp. 10-20.

Dubey, Manju. Critical study of Bhavabhuti's Mahaviracharita / by Manju Dubey.

Ph.D. thesis approved by the Aligarh Muslim University in 1978.

Dwivedi, Shiv Balak. Dhvani in the dramas of Bhavabhuti / by Shiv Balak Dwivedi.

Ph.D. thesis approved by the Kanpur University in 1984.

Encyclopaedia of Indian literature .- New Delhi : Sahitya Akademi, 1987 - 1994.

Pp. 491-492, 1103, 1104, 1108, 1109, 1206, 2434, 2558, 3570, 4445, 4660, 4661.

Frazer, R.W. A Literary history of India. - London : T. Fisher Unwin, 1898. Pp. 288-93.

Gairola, Vachaspati. Sanskrit sahitya ka itihas. - Varanasi : Chaukhamba Vidyabhavan, 1960.

Garg, Ganga Ram. An Encyclopaedia of Indian literature. - Delhi : Mittal Publishers, 1982.

Pp. 51, 227-228, 231-32, 458-59.

Gaur, Saroj. Comparative and psychological study of Bhavabhuti and his works / by Saroj Gaur.

Ph.D. thesis approved by the Kanpur University in 1983.

Gera, Vimla. Mind and art of Bhavabhuti .- Delhi : Meharchand Lachhmandas, 1973.

xv, 292 p.; 22 cm.

Gera, Vimala. Mind and art of Bhavabhuti / by Vimala Gera.

Ph.D. thesis approved by the University of Delhi in 1971.

Ghosh, Suparna. Comparative study of the dramas based on Ramacarita : the Pratimanatakam of Bhasa and the Mahaviracharitam of Bhavabhuti / by Suparna Ghosh.

Ph.D. thesis approved by the Patna University in 1979.

Glimpses of Sanskrit literature / ed. by A.N.D. Haksar. - New Delhi : Indian Council for Cultural Relations, 1995.

Contents : Bhavabhuti. Pp. 22-23, 108, 118-21, 133.

Goswami, Usha. Psychological study of the characters of the dramas of Bhavabhuti / by Usha Goswami.

Ph.D. thesis approved by the Rajasthan University in 1982.

Gupta, Rama. Critical estimate of Bhavabhuti and his works / by Rama Gupta.

Ph.D. thesis approved by the University of Calcutta in 1978.

Hajela, Pushpa. Treatment of nature in Sanskrit drama from Bhasa to Bhavabhuti / by Pushpa Hajela.

Ph.D. thesis approved by the Aligarh Muslim University in 1961.

Hari Singh. Study of the dramas of Bhavabhuti : philosophical and cultural scene / by Hari Singh.

Ph.D. thesis approved by the Punjab University in 1987.

Harshe, R.G. Observations on the life and works of Bhavabhuti / tr. from the French by Jang Bahadur Khanna. - Delhi : Meharchand Lachhamandas, 1974.

vii, 103 p.; 22 cm.

Originally published in 1938.

Harshe, R.G. Observations on the life and works of Bhavabhuti (French); Editions Littēraires de France, 1938.

Hiriyanna, M. Sanskrit studies. - Mysore : Kavyalaya, 1954. P. 39 ff.

Includes essay 'Uttararamacarita'.

Inamdar, V.M. Uttara Rama Charita : a preface. - Dharwar : Mrs. Inamdar, 1957.

Jagirdar, R.V. Drama in Sanskrit Literature. - Bombay : Popular Book Depot, 1947.

Jain, Nemichandra. Indian Theatre : tradition, continuity and change. - New Delhi : Vikas Publishing House, 1992.

Jha, Deva Kant. Critical and comparative study of Abhijnanasakuntalam and Uttararacharitam / by Deva Kant Jha.

Ph.D. thesis approved by the Magadh University in 1970.

Jha, Satyanarayan. Critical analysis of the Uttara Ramacarita / by Satyanarayan Jha.

Ph.D. thesis approved by the K.S. Darbhanga University in 1976.

Jha, Vinodananda. Critical study of Bhavabhuti as a dramatist / by Vinodananda Jha.

Ph.D. thesis approved by the K.S. Darbhanga University in 1979.

Karmarkar, R.D. Bhavabhuti . - Dharwar : Karnatak University, 1963.

Karmakar, R.D. Bhavabhuti .- Dharwar : Karnatak University, 1971.

121 p.; 21.5 cm.

Katar, Usha Kiran. Comparative study of the depiction of 'Love' in the works of Bhavabhuti and Harsha / by Usha Kiran Katar.

Ph.D. thesis in Hindi, approved by the Rohilkhand University in 1983.

Keith, A. Berriedale. The Sanskrit drama in its origin, development, theory and practice. Oxford : OUP, 1924.

405 p.; 22 cm.

Keith, A. Berriedale. Sanskrit - Natak : udbhav aur vikas : siddhanta aur prayog / tr. into Hindi by Udaybhanu Singh. - Delhi : Motilal Banarasidass, 1965.

Khanna, Kund. Critique of the language of Bhavabhuti / by Kund Khanna.

Ph.D. thesis approved by the Ravishankar University in 1982.

Krishnamachariar, M and Srinivasachariar. History of classical Sanskrit literature. - Delhi : Motilal Banarasidass, 1989.

Pp. 615-623.

Kumāratātācārya, A. Bhavabhūti - bhāratī. Madras.

'Kundamālā and Uttararāmacarita' / by K.A. Subramanya Iyer *7th All India Oriental Conference;* Pp. 91-97.

Lēvi, Sylvain. The theatre of India / tr. from the French by Narayan Mukherji. - Calcutta : Writers Workshop, 1978.

Contents : Bhavabhūti (Vol.I) 8, 30, 133, 182, 184, 188-193, 196-201, 239, 240, 253, 272-74; (Vol.II) 11, 13, 22, 28, 30, 55, 66, 68, 75, 87, 118.

Uttararāmacarita Pp. (Vol. I) 2, 196-201, 240, 253, 272; (Vol. II) 22, 45, 57, 66, 95, 118.

Macdonell, A.A. India's past : a survey of her literatures, religions, languages and antiquities. - Varanasi : Motilal Banarasidass, 1956.

'Mahaviracharita of Bhavabhuti' *Journal of University of Gauhati;* 1969; Vol. 20, No. 1, Pp. 129-135

Book Review.

Marasinghe, E.W. The Sanskrit theatre and stagecraft. - Delhi : Sri Satguru Publications, 1989. - (Sri Garib Dass Oriental Series; No. 78).

Masterpieces of Indian literature [Vol. 2]. - New Delhi : Natinal Book Trust, 1997.

Contents : Uttararamacharita - Bhavabhuti. Pp. 1227-1229.

Maya, Rama. Emotions and their correlative values in the dramas of Bhavabhuti / by Rama Maya.

Ph.D. thesis approved by the Aligarh Muslim University in 1967.

McGraw - Hill encyclopaedia of world drama (Vol. 3) / ed. by Stanley Hochman. - 2nd ed. - New York : McGraw - Hill, Inc., 1984.

Merriam - Webster's Encyclopaedia of literature. - Spring field, Massachusetts : Merriam - Webster, Inc., 1995.

P. 136.

Mirashi, Vasudev Vishnu. Bhavabhuti / by Vasudev Vishnu Mirashi; tr. into Hindi by Keshav Rao Musalgamkar. - Bombay : Popular Prakashan, 1972.

424 p.; 22 cm.

Mirashi, Vasudev Vishnu. Bhavabhuti .- Bombay : Popular Prakashan, 1968.

397 p.; 22 cm.

In Marathi.

Mirashi, V.V. Bhavabhūti .- Delhi : Motilal Banarsidass, 1974.

7, 412 p.

Critical study on the classical dramatist in English.

'Old Sanskrit Romance', *The Daily Chronicle;* 24 October 1921; P. 8, Column 4.

Review of the drama Malati and Madhava of Bhavabhuti in English by the Union of East & West.

Pandey, Prakash Madhao Rao. Literary aspects of Bhavabhuti / by Prakash Madhao Rao Pandey.

Ph.D. thesis approved by the Nagpur University in 1978.

Pandey, Radhakant. Comparative study of Kundamala of Dinnaga and Uttararamacharita of Bhavabhuti / by Radhakant Pandey.

Ph.D. thesis approved by the Kanpur University in 1974.

Pathak, H.S. Comparative study of Kalidasa and Bhavabhuti / by H.S. Pathak.

Ph.D. thesis in Hindi, approved by the Ravishankar University in 1983.

Pathak, M.C. Sanskrit nāṭaka men atiprākṛta tattva. - Jaipur : Devanagar Prakasha, [n.d.].

18, 468 p.

Pathak, Madan Mohan. Concept of love in the dramas of Bhavabhuti / by Madan Mohan Pathak.

Ph.D. thesis approved by the K.S. Darbhanga University in 1974.

Pati, Madhusudan. Sanskrit drama : essays in revaluation / by Madhusudan Pati . - Delhi : Amar Prakashan [1991].

Contents ; 'Uttararāmacharitam : dramatic design and moral perspective. Pp. 47-66.

'The Portrayal of Rāma in Sanskrit plays' / by Manjula Sahadev. *Quarterly Journal of National Centre for Performing Arts;* 1982, Vol. II, No. 1. Pp. 14-24.

Premlal. Dramas of Bhavabhuti : a critical study / by Premlal.

Ph.D. thesis in Hindi, approved by the Himachal Pradesh University in 1981.

Principal sentiment in the Uttara Ramacharita' / by Ramesh Betai. *Journal of Gujarat Research Society;* Oct. 1970; Vol. 32, No. 4; Pp. 202-212.

-----. *Sri Venkateswara University Oriental, Journal*; Jan. - Dec. 1970; Vol. 13, No. 1-2, Pp. 51-64.

Raghavan, V. Bhavabhuti and Arthaśāstra. *New Indology : Festschrift Walter Ruben* Zum 70 Geburtstag. - Berlin : Akademic - Verlag, 1971.

Raghavan, V. The Social play in Sanskrit. - Bangalore : The Indian Institute of Culture, 1952.

(Transaction; No. 11).

Raghavan, V. Some old lost Rama plays. - Annamalainagar : Annamalai University, 1961.

Rai, Ganga Sagar. Mahakavi Bhavabhuti / by Ganga Sagar Rai. - Varanasi : Chowkhamba Vidyabhavan, 1965.

Raja, C. Kunhan. Survey of Sanskrit literature. - Bombay : Bharatiya Vidya Bhavan, 1962.

'Rama in the works of Kāidāsa and Bhavabhūti' / by Vidya Niwas Misra : *Cultural Forum,* 1967; Vol. 9, No. 4. Pp. 57-60.

Ramabhadur. Comparative study of Pratimanatakam and Mahaviracharitam / by Ramabhadur.

Ph.D. thesis in Hindi, approved by the Rohilkhand University in 1982.

Rao, T.S. Bhavabhuti and his masterly genius. - Poona.

Ray, Ashim Kumar & Gidwani, N.N. A Dictionary of Indology (Vol. 1). - New Delhi : Oxford & IBH Publishing Co., 1983.

Contents : Bhavabhuti. P. 217.

Ray, Dvijendra Lal. Dvijendra granthāvalī / by Dvijendralāl Rāy .- Calcutta : Basumatī Sāhitya Mandir, [n.d.].

3 Vols.; 25 cm.

Vol. 1 contains literary appreciation of Kālidas and Bhavabhūti.

Ray, Dvijendralal. Kālidāsa aur Bhavabhūti. - Bombay : Hindi Grantharatnakar Karyalay, 1921.

Studies on two classical Sanskrit poets and playwrights.

Ray, Dvijendralal. Kalidas aur Bhavabhuti / by Dvijendralal Ray; tr. into Hindi by Rupnarayan Pandey. - Bombay : Hindi Granth Ratnakar, 1956.

Rāy, Dvijendralāl. Kālidāsanum Bhavabhūtiyum / by Dvijendralal Rāy; tr. by A.K. Śāstri; introd. by P.K. Nārāyana Piḷḷa. - Trivandrum : The translator, 1928.

208 p.; 23 cm.

Original title in Bengali 'Kālidās o Bhavabhuti.

Ray, Gangasagar. Mahakavi Bhavabhuti. - Varanasi : Chowkhamba Prakashan, 1965.

Ray, Gangasagar. Mahakavi Bhavabhuti. - Dharwar : Chowkhamba Prakashan, 1963.

Sahitya Akademi - New Delhi. The National bibliography of Indian literature. - New Delhi : The author, 1962 - 1990.

5 Vols.

Sankalia, H.D. 'Kundmālā and Uttara-rāma carita'. *St. Xavier's* College Magazine 22; 1929-30; Pp. 63-76 & Journal of Oriental Institute, 15; 1966, Pp. 322-34.

Critical studies.

Sastri, Gaurinath. Sanskrit sahityer itihas. - Calcutta : Sarasvata Library, 1969? [Aśvin 1376].

In Bengali.

Satishchandra Vidyabhushan. Bhavabhūti / by Satīśacandra Vidyābhūṣaṇa; tr. into Hindi by Jvālādatta Śarmā. - Lucknow : Ganga Pustakamala Karyalay, 1924.

Sethi, Atmaram. Anudit Hindisahitya : vishishta grantha-suchi / by Atmaram Sethi. - Gurgaon : Indian Documentation Service, 1981.

Contents : Sanskrit (Pp. 1-624).

Sharma, Asha. Comparative study of Mahaviracharita of Bhavabhuti and Anargharaghava of Murari / by Asha Sharma.

Ph.D. thesis in Hindi, approved by the Kanpur University in 1979.

Sharma, Braj Vallabha. Bhavabhuti ke natak .- Bhopal : Madhya Pradesh Hindi Granth Akademi, 1973.

363 p.; 21.5 cm.

Sharma, Brajavallabh. Systematic study of the dramas of Bhavabhuti / by Brajavallabh Sharma.

Ph.D. thesis approved by the Vikram University in 1969.

Sharma, Raka. Natyalankaras in the dramas of Bhavabhuti / by Raka Sharma.

Ph.D. thesis approved by the Aligarh Muslim University in 1982.

Sharma, Braj Vallabh. Bhavabhuti ke natak / by Braj Vallabh Sharma. - Bhopal : Madhya Pradesh Hindi Grantha Academy, 1973.

Shastri, Dvijendranath. Sanskritasahityavimarsha. - Meerut : Bharati Prakashan, 1956.

Shekhar, I. Sanskrit drama : its origin and decline .- Leiden : E.J. Brill, 1960.

Pp. xxiv, xxvi, 64, 70, 86, 121, 133, 135, 138, 143-145, 148, 155, 156, 162, 163, 171, 173, 181-189, 191, 193, 194.

Singh, Ayodhya Prasad. Bhavabhuti aur unki natyakala. 2nd ed. - Delhi : Motilal Banarsidas, 1988.

19, 376 p.; 22.5 cm.

First published in 1969.

Singh, Prabhat. Evaluation of Canons of Sanskrit dramaturgy in Sanskrit dramas with special reference to the dramas of Kalidasa and Bhavabhuti / by Prabhat Singh.

Ph.D. thesis approved by the Punjab University in 1985.

'Sītā in Sanskrit plays' / by V. Gulab Davane. *Journal of Bombay University* 46 (1977). Pp. 18-26.

'The Social play in Sanskrit' / by V. Raghavan. *The Journal* of the BHU; 1937-38; Vol. II. Pp. 23-54, 307.

'Some points of text and interpretation in the Malati-Madhava / by Michael Coulson.

Samskrita Ranga (Annual Number); 1972; Vol. 6; Pp. 70-76.

Sreekantaiya, T.N. Imagination in Indian poetics and other literary studies. - Mysore: Geetha Book House, 1980.

Srivastava, Indira. Examination of the dramas of Bhavabhuti from the angle of Natya Sastra.

Ph.D. thesis in Hindi, approved by the H.S. Gaur University in 1985.

Sud, Suman. Karuna rasa : from the view point of Valmiki, Bhasa, Asvaghosa, Kalidasa and Bhavabhuti / by Suman Sud.

Ph.D. thesis in Hindi, approved by the Kurukshetra University in 1969.

Tirtha : the treasury of Indian expressions / ed. by Vijaya Ghose. - New Delhi : CMC Ltd., 1992.

Pp. 132, 203.

'Tragicomic suffering in Sakuntala, Uttararamacarita; Cymbeline and the Winter's tale' / by Aniya Dev. *Journal of Comparative Literature* (Jadavpur), 1968, Vol. 8; Pp. 50-84.

Treatment of pathos in Sanskrit drama / ed. by Pushpendra Kumar. - Delhi : Nag Publishers, 1981.

'The treatment of the supernatural and the wonderful in Sanskrit dramas' / by Mukunda Madhava Sharma. *Proceedings and Transactions of the All - India* Oriental Conference; (23rd session) at Aligarh in Oct. 1966. - Poona: BORI, 1969.

Pp. 290-298.

Upadhyaya, Baldev. Sanskrit sahitya ka itihas. - Kashi : Sharda Mandir, 1945.

In Hindi.

'Uttararāmacarita' / by M. Hiriyanna. *Mysore University Magazine,* 1917.

'Uttararāmacarita : a poet's reply to his critics' / by K.S. Shukla. *18th All India Oriental Conference.*

'Uttararāmacarita as a play of reconciliation' / by G.K. Bhat. *All India Oriental Conference XVI* (Summary); Pp. 74-75.

[Uttararamacharita Drama de Bhavabhuti, Paris, Collection Emile Senart] / by Manomohan Ghosh. *Indian Historical Quarterly* Sept. 1936; Vol. 12, No. 3; Pp. 541-543.

Review of translated book by Nadine Stehoupak.

'The Uttara - Rāmacarita of Bhavabhūti : play or poem' / by K. Visvanathan. *Aryan Path* 1975; Vol. 46, No. 5.

'Uttararāmacaritam : a critique of Vālmīki' / by Harsh Kumar. *22nd All India Oriental Conference.*

'Uttara Rāmacarite Bhavabhutir viśiṣyate' / by R.D. Karmarkar. *Journal of Oriental Institute;* 1952, Vol. 1. Pp. 228-230.

Verma, Jaynarayan and Gupta, Pushpa. Sanskrit sahitya ka itihas. - Ghaziabad : Tarun Prakashan, 1991.

Venkataramayya, C.K. Bhavabhuti mahakavi .- Bangalore : Kannada Sahitya Parishat, 1977.

692 p.; 22.5 cm.

In Kannada.

Vyas, Bhola Shankar. Sanskrit kavi darsana / by Bhola Shankar Vyas. - Varanasi : Chowkhamba Vidyabhavan, 1955.

Warder, A.K. Indian kāvya literature (Vol. 4). - Delhi : Motilal Banarsidass, 1983.

Contents : Bhavabhūti. Pp. 271-372.

Wells, Henry W. The Classical drama of India. - Bombay : Asia Publishing House, 1963.

'Wigmore Hall : two Indian plays' *The Daily Telegraph;* 24 October 1921; P. 4, Column 5.

Review of the drama 'Malati and Madhava in English produced by the Union of East and West.

Winternitz, M. History of Indian literature (Vol. 3) / tr. from German into English by Subhadra Jha. - Delhi : Motilal Banarsidass, 1985.

'Women in Bhavabhūti's plays' / by Ratnamayi Devi Dikshit. *19th All India Oriental Conference*.

4

Bodhayana

Bodhāyana, an author of remarkable prahasana entitled 'Bhagavadajjukiyam' probably flourished between the begining of the christian era and the 4th century A.D.

It is interesting to note that the appearance of the titles 'Bhagavadajjuka' and 'Mattavilāsa' engraved in the rock in Mahendra's own inscription dated 610 A.D. at Mamandur, together with the statement in the Nirnaya Sagar Press edition of 1911 that the king Mahendra composed the plays 'Bhagavadajjuka and Mattavilāsa' ought to afford some evidence for Mahendra's authorship of the play. A quotation in it from Ṭaṭvasamāsa, one of the oldest and basic works on Sānkhya philosophy and a classification of dramas in an ancient mode amply attest its antiquity. The authorship has, therefore, been under question.

Of the three commentators of this play, one attributes it to Boḍhāyana, another to Bharata and a third leaves it anonymous. A poet Bodhāyaṇa is praised by Sukumāra in his Raghuviracariṭa, a play of the 12th century.

In the first edition of this text (Jayantamangalam, Kerala, 1925), the anonymous commentator attributes the authorship to Bodhayana Kavi.

'Bhagavadajjukiyam' is aptly called the 'Prahasanaratnam' and the title is befitting that centres on a recluse (Bhagavan) entering by Yogic powers the body of a courtesan (Ajjuka) called Vasantasena.

M. Krishnamachariar feels that this play was apparently intended by its author to bring into ridicule the doctrines of Buddhism - a method, among others, which the Brahmins employed to stem the rising tide of that religion.

This much acclaimed satirical play is about an intellectual sage (Sanyasi) and his, extremely materialistic pupil Sāṇḍilya. The dancer Vasantasena (pinning for her lover) is mistakenly killed by Yama (Lord of death). Śāndilya forces his guru to bring Vasantasena back to life. The only way the sage can do this, is to give the dancer his own life. Vasantasena comes alive as the sage dies. However, she loses her own identity and assumes that of the sage, thereby becoming unable, to recognise her own past (including her family and her lover). Yamaduta recognises his mistake and in a hurry, injects the soul of the dancer into the body of the Guru. Eventually Yamaduta reverses the souls and things fall back into place with all being well that ends well. According to critic Smita Nirula. "A case of mistakes identities, the story is reminiscent of our more familiar (and more recent) Hayavadhana by Girish Karnad.

Bhagavadajjukiyam occupies an unique position in the domain of Sanskrit prahasana or farce. This is a play having Mukha and Nirvahaṇa saṁdhis. Minakshi L. Dalal in her book entitled 'Conflict in Sanskrit drama' observes that like the Bhāsa plays, this prahasana allows introduction of death, etc. on the stage. The death of Vasantasena, the rapid effect of poison in her body, etc. create real suspense, which later takes a humorous turn. The conflict of personalities, as one personality having quite the opposite nature enters the body of the other, is ingenious, and make the drama interesting. The interchange of bodies, and the conflicts arising out of it are also clever and fill the situation with humour. In this farce, the main sentiment intended to be developed is the humorous one.

The best of all the prahasanas in Sanskrit literature is perhaps the Bhagavadajjukiyam of Bodhayana Kavi. A critic observed that the playwright does not depend entirely upon satire to tickle his audience and succeeds in creating humour of superior taste, but he is masterly in the treatment of the ludicrous and in the delineation of the characters. Not just the foolery of the characters that causes laughter, but it is caused as well by the comic situation. His style is simple, but not void of elegancy. Though the conversation between the teacher and his pupil is too lengthy at times, but yet readers finds it absorbing having comic relief. Theme is a courtesan without any vulgarity. A critic observed that although a comedy, 'Bhagvadajjukiyam' projects a profound idea, viz, the gaining of enlightenment by the arrogant guru. Like other Sanskrit plays, this play also reveals through its poetic expression the quality of life and thought prevalent in ancient India.

Bhagavadajjukiyam

Synopsis

A saint and his disciple come to a garden outside the city. In the same garden, arrives a courtesan to meet her beloved. Now enters the Yamdoot who by mistake takes away the life of this courtesan. The disciple sees the dead body and atonce gets attracted to her and thereby requests the saint to enliven her. The affectionate Guru after realizing his desperation obliges by putting his own life into the courtesan's body as a result of which 'Vasantasena' becomes alive with saint's soul in her. In the meantime, Yamadoota is abused by the Yama for the blunder. The former comes again to give the courtesan back her life. As 'Vasantasena' is already alive, confused Yamdoot puts Vasantsena's life to the Saint's body who at once wakes up and starts behaving like a woman.

The disciple gets completely disoriented with all these happenings. Atlast the Yamadoot intervenes. To get everything resolved and thus, finally everybody comes back to their original self.

Dramatis Personae

SUTRADHĀRA *Director,* the person responsible for the production, and the principal actor.

VIDŪṢAKA *Buffoon,* the comic companion of the Director.

PARIVRĀJAKA *Mendicant*, a wandering Hindu holy man. (This part is played by the Director).

ŚĀṆḌILYA, the Mendicant's disciple. (This part is played by the Buf foon).

GAṆIKĀ *Courtesan,* whose personal name is Vasantasēnā, but who is usually addressed as 'Ajjukā', a term of respect for courtesans.

Maid-Servant (CEṬI) named 'Madhukarikā' - one of Vasantasēnā's hand-maidens. 'Madhukarikā', means 'little honey-maker, i.e., 'little honey bee'.

YAMAPURUṢA *Yama's Agent,* Messenger of Yama, the Good of Death, who is responsible for taking the souls of the dead ofYama's realm.

MĀTA *Mother*, of Vasantasēnā.

RĀMILAKA, Vasantasēnā's lover.

VAIDYA *Doctor,* (This part may be taken by the actor who plays the Agent of Yama).

Plot :-

Bhagavadajjukiyam of Bodhayana is hailed as one of the masterpieces in the Prahasana tradition of classical plays. It commences with a discussion on Hindu dharma. Śāṇḍilya, a student is studying in a garden with his teacher, a Buddhist saint called 'Parivrajaka'. Previously the disciple got himself converted into many religious practices just to fill his appetite though had never been successful. Ajjuka, a courtesan alongwith her maid servent enters the garden and sits down under a tree to wait for her beloved. The student gets distracted by the sight of this courtesan inspite of the teacher's protest. The pupil is unwilling to study from the very begining. Now arrives the messenger of Yama who, as a snake bites the courtesan and takes her soul to the abode of Yama.

Again the student's attention is diverted to her (who is beaten by the serpent) and is drawn to her. Ignoring teacher's warning, he rushes towards Courtesan only to find her dead.

Meanwhile, the maid servant hastens to convey the news to the mother of the courtesan and leaves the dead body under the care of the student. To impress 'Śāṇḍilya', the ascetic employs his own yogic power and makes his soul enter the body of Ajjuka.

When the body of Ajjuka (with the saint's soul) is resurrected, she starts behaving like the Bhagavan and talk philosophy to the discomfort of the student. The mother and the lover reaches by this time along with a curer of snake - bites, whom the courtesan puts to shame, making him turn away. Everyone takes her to be mad.

In the meantime, the servents of Yama discover that by mistake they have taken the soul of Ajjuka and therefore, comes back to restore it in her body, but only to find that it is already been occupied by another. Eventually seeing the body of the saint Parivrājaka vacant they place her soul into his frame.

Irritated by Ajjuka's peculiar behaviour, Śāṇḍilya is forced to go back to his teacher, who only talks of love (as possessing the woman's soul). This makes the pupil and other beholders utterly confused by this strange happening. The conflict of misplaced souls, thus, offers tremendous scope for wit and humour. Finally the problem is solved when the Yamadoota realizes his mistake and a second messenger from Yama comes to rectify the previous errors. The trouble ends with the exchanges of souls that brings us to the end of the play.

Bhagavadajjukiyam in Performances

In modern times, at 'Star Theatre' of Calcutta, Bodhayana's satire 'Bhagavajjukiyam' was performed in Bengali under the title 'Mukti' on 1 January 1931. The play was translated into Bengali by Apareshchandra Mukhopadhyay.

This comedy of farce was performed in Sanskrit by Samskrita Ranga at the Museum Theatre, Madras in the year 1960. It was directed by V. Ranghavan. Painted stage setting such as the tree was reminiscent of European scenic tradition, but the simple placement of the figures on the open stage was in keeping with ancient Indian theatre practice.

The Priest and the Prostitute. Performed in Sanskrit by Samskrita Ranga at the Museum Theatre. Madras, 1960. Directed by V. Raghavan.

Bhagavadajjukiyam, an one-act comedy was produced by the National School of Drama in the same year (1960). The numerous painted stage settings representing gate, flowers, clouds, walls, seat and fence etc. reflected Western scenic traditions.

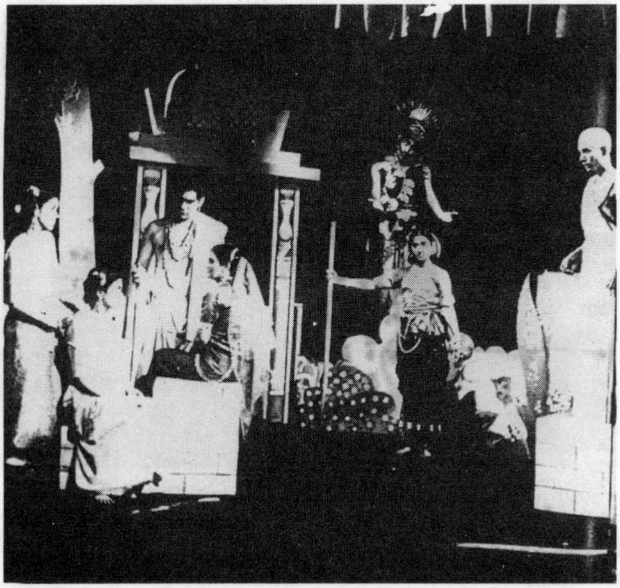

***The Priest and the Prostitute,* a one-act Sanskrit comedy. National School of Drama. New Delhi, 1960. The Messenger of Death stands over the Prostitute, while the Priest bashfully turns away from his gathered friends.**

On 14 April 1961, Bhagavadajjukiyam was staged' by the students of National School of Drama. Hindi version was translated by N.C. Jain and directed by D.N. Thakkar.

Shanta Gandhi directed 'Bhagavadajjukiyam' for the National School of Drama's 'School Production' in the year 1967-68. There were six shows in the opening year.

Nemi Chandra Jain's Hindi adaptation of Bodhayana's 'Bhagavadajjukiyam' was staged by the Srinagar Theatre workshop trainees under the direction of K.M. Sontakke and sponsored by the National School of Drama.s

The harlot turns yogi in the Malayalam version of Bhagavadajjukiyam, produced by Thiruvarang.

The Thiruvarang drama troupe was established in 1964. The troupe was actively engaged in the collection of folklore, legends, songs, vaytharis (bols) etc. from different parts of Kerala especially villages and tribal belt. Experimental stage productions were undertaken. One of the major objectives of the troupe was to revive our rich folk and classical stage traditions. In 1971, the troupe presented at the drama festival sponsored by the Kerala Sangeetha Nataka Akademi, a Malayalam version of the classical Sanskrit play. Bhagavadajjukiyam. This classical play was also presented at the All India History Congress sponsored by the Calicut University in 1977.

The troupe conducted a three day drama festival at Ernakulam sponsored by the Lions Club of Cochin East in March 1978. The play Bhagavadajjukiyam was staged at the open air auditorium of Rajendra Maidan at Ernakulam. For the sake of Ernakulam audience, the play was again presented on June 10, 1978 in connection with the Silver Jubilee celebrations of Bank of Baroda Employees Union. The cast of Thiruvarang production of 1976 was :

Sutradhara	-	Jagannathan S.
Vidushaka	-	S. Natarajan
Yogi	-	Nedumudy Venu
Sandilyan	-	Gopi
Yamaduta	-	Jagannathan
Vasanthasena	-	L.R. Rugmini
Madhukarika	-	Vasantha Gopala - Krishna (Leela Panikkar)
Parabhrithika	-	Lailamani
Vaidyan	-	G. Sivaraman Nair
Ramilakan	-	S.R. Gopalakrishnan
Amma	-	Sulochana
Light, Makeup	-	Gopi, Pujappura
Choreography	-	M. Parameswara Menon (Nattuvan)
Vadithram	-	R. Padmanabhan, Kavalam.
Direction	-	Kavalam Narayana Panikkar.

For Rang Shivir, Bhopal, Shri M.K. Raina directed 'Bhagavadajjukiyam' and was presented at the 'Kalidasa festival' in 1976.

On 30 March 1977, Bodhayana's 'Bhagavadajjukiyam' was staged by National School of Drama [School Production'] in Hindi. The play was directed by Amal Allana and the Hindi version was rendered by N.C. Jain. There were six shows in the opening year. The play was presented in stylised form employing 'Noh' as a base. But critic J.N. Kaushal feels that due to stylised use of the spoken word, dance and music, the play not only lost clarity, but spontaneity so essential for comedies.

The prominent dramatis personae were :-

Parivrajak	-	Anupam Kher
Shandilya	-	Anang Desai

Yamadoot	-	G.P. Namdeo
Vaidya	-	Satish Kaushik
Vasantasena	-	Anita Kanwar

Among the chorus Mridula Kaushik stood out for her sonorous voice and clear diction.

B.V. Karanth directed 'Bhagavadajjukiyam' for the National School of Drama, New Delhi and was presented at the Kalidasa Festival, Ujjain in 1979.

On 23rd & 24th July 1980, the adaptation of N.C. Jain was performed by Srinagar theatre workshop trainees under the direction of K.M. Sontakke.

Kerala Kala Mandalam presented 'Bhagavadajjukiyam' of Bodhayana in Kuḍiyattam style on 25 July 1985 at Sri Chitra Hindu Religious Library Auditorium during 'Kootiyattam Kalotsavam' organised by the Trivandrum Cultural Society.

Fringe Performances

In the year 1994, Repertory Company of the National School of Drama launched a new programme of 'Fringe Performances' that consist of among other activities, the play reading sessions of world classics as well as contemporary plays. The first set of presentations under the 'Fringe Performances' was the dramatic reading of two classics : Bodhayan's Bhagavadajjukiyam in Bharat Bhusan Aggarwal's Hindi translation and Bhasa's Urubhangam in N.C. Jain's Hindi translation from 21 to 23 October in Studio Theatre of the Repertory Company.

Theatre Fiasko is the main wing of the Drama Department of Joensuun Vapaaopisto, an adult education centre of Joensuu, a city in eastern Finland. The Repertoire of this Finn theatre troupe has been both Finish and international, classical and modern, serious philosophical drama and funny circus productions.

On 24 October 1995, Theatre Fiasko staged Bodhyana's 'Bhagavadajjukiyam' in Finish. It was presented by Asmita and Nipa. This originally written Sanskrit play went through one translation into HIndi by Nemi Chand Jain, only to be translated again into Finish by Pirkko Kurikka.

This hilarious comedy was directed joinly by Tuire Hindikka and Surya Mohan Kulshreshtha.

Scene from Theatre Fiasko's Bhagwadajjukiyam

The Saṁskrita Ranga of Madras has successfuly brought to the stage in original Sanskrit the unique 7th century prahasana 'Bhagavadajjukiya'.

Non - group of Delhi staged an adaptation of Bodhayan's Sanskrit classic by Hemant Mishra under the title 'Ek aur Bhagwadujjukiyam'. The play depicted the exploitation of the innocent masses by the politicians. Sanskrit classic, thus, had a pararell with the recent political crisis in the country; but a drama critic felt that the amalgamation of mythology and present day reality was a mishomer.

The paper 'Hindu' writes in its 6 August 1993 issue that Govardhan Panchal, the winner of the Gujarat Governments prestigious Omkar Thakur Award had unmatched zeal for Sanskrit theatre. Though actors for Sanskrit plays are scarce now a days and more so, the problem with ancient classics is that they demands artists who can sing, dance and act. Still under his able guidance, the Gurjara Sanskrit Rangam- an academy of Sanskrit drama and culture based in Ahmedabad, of which he was also the President had produced Bodhayana's great satire the 'Bhagavadajjukiyam'.

As a part of theatre training in the National School of Drama, every year, the students in the second year, are introduced to Sanskrit classics - as text, and in performance. The various training inputs like study and analysis of a few selected Sanskrit plays, principles of Natyashastra, Indian aesthetics, understanding of Sanskrit theatre architecture, stylised acting learning from witnessing traditional dance

/ theatre performances etc. cultiminate in a public performance of a Sanskrit play production by students under the guidance of a teacher / director. In 1995, the second year students presented 'Tridhara' : a performance of three Sanskrit plays - Kalidasa's Abhijñanashakuntalam in Sanskrit, Bodhayana's Bhagavadajjukiyam andVishakhadatta's Mudrarakshasa in Hindi under the direction of Rita Ganguly, a senior faculty member of NSD and a well known classical singer also trained in several classical dance traditions. Held from 17-22 November 1995, the five hour long performance in the specially erected Vikrisht Madhyam auditorium was aesthetically visualised and designed incorporating meticulously the various aspects of Sanskrit play production like stylised acting, music, spatial design etc. Thus, an effort was made for the first time to capture the spirit and ambience of Sanskrit stage through a detailed study and research of various texts like Vastushastra Shilpashastra and Manasara - shastra in consultations with scholars, architects, designers and technicians.

Scenes from National School of Drama's production 'Bhagavadajjukiyam' in Hindi, Directed by Rita Ganguly (1995).

On 5 March 1995, the Repertory Company of the National School of Drama performed Bhagavadajjukiyam for the participants of the National Theatre Workshop organised by Sangeed Natak Akademi in Delhi.

The Kutiyattam repertory contain Bodhayana's Bhagavadajjukiyam, first published by Anujan Asan of Cochin. Kūṭiyāṭṭam is believed to be about 2000 years old, but the literary evidences tells us that this theatric form dates back only to the ninth century when King Kulaśekhara alongwith with friend Tolan, modified it into its existing form. It is performed in Kūttampalam (ie, temple theatre). The repertoire comprises of the major play of Bhasa, Harsha, Śaktibhadra, Mahendravikramavarman, Kulaśekhara, Nīlakaṇṭha and also Bodhayana's 'Bhagavadajjuka'.

It is interesting to note that Bhagavadajjuka (The Hermit and the Harlot) takesthirty - five days to perform, from the introduction of the first character to the completion of the act.

On 27 March 1995, **Udayanavarnanam** from Bhagavadajjukiyam was performed by Kerala Kalamandalam, Cheruthuruthy in Kutiyattam Mahotsavam, organised by the Sangeet Natak Akademi, New Delhi. This prahasana was presented in Kutiyattam style which has a unique and an exalted place among the traditional forms of Indian Theatre. Believed to be our only surviving link with the ancient Sanskrit Theatre, Kutiyattam has been practised, preserved and developed over centuries by the Chakyars of Kerala.

***Udayanavarnam from Bhagavadajjukiyam : Girija and Sylaja, Kerala Kalamandalam;* performed in 1995 at the Kutiyattam Mahotsavam organised by Sangeet Natak Akademi, New Delhi**

Presented below an account of the text, text of performance, caste, Accompanists, make - up & costumes & the troupe :-

Text :- The story of *Bhagavadajjukiyam*, a Prahasana, as described earlier is derived from a hilarious situation created by a 'bhagavan' (yogin) transposing his soul into the body of an 'ajjuka' (prostitute) and vice versa. This transmigration is necessitated by the yogin's eagerness to impart spiritual knowledge to his disciple Sandilya. The play has been quite popular on the Kutiyattam stage, and a detailed Attaprakaram is available for the play.

Text of performance :- The heroine Vasantasena and the Chedi Parabhritika enter the flower garden and walk around. The heroine tells her friend "Oh! Parahudiye. This garden looks so beautiful. In the spring season, all the plants and trees blossom and the flowers spread fragrance by the touch of the gentle breeze. Everything has become more attractive and beautiful. One one side the flies reach to enjoy honey by sucking and taking it to their wives." The Chedi (friend) says, "Oh! Ajjuke, this lotus lake has turned more beautiful. The lake is full of lotus flowers and buds. The swans come fast to eat the stalk of lotus and part it with their wives. They play happily in the lake. Hence the water is moving and the breeze being touched by the waves becomes cold and due to the fragrance of the lotus flowers becomes more enjoyable. Then the heroine says, "Hearing the sound of the fountains of the lotus lake, the peacocks suspecting the sound as thunderbolt, start dancing".

[The sound of the Mizhavu to support the dance]

Heroine : *"Hanje parahudiya kahim kahim upavasamo?"* Hello, Parabhritike, where shall we sit in the garden?

Chedi : *"Ajju ee etassim kussumida sahayaradi iya mandide siya pattaye mu kutha yam uva visiya ekkam vathuyam gayadu Ajjuya."* Hello, Ajjuke, we shall sit on this granite pad under the Sahakari tree which is beautifully decorated by flowers and you sing a song.

Heroine : *'Evam hodu'.* Be so.

[Both sit on the granite pad and sing together]

Parabhrita madhukara nada jyaghosha

kama esha udyane

Tishtati sahakara saro muhyati

nunam manopi muneh

(In this garden the cuckoos flock together, eat the buds and tender leaves and are satisfied. The bees get intoxicated by drinking honey and sing beautifully at the dusk. The Lord of Love, Kamadeva is very happy and the garden is full on flowers. He thinks, let me go to encourage the minds of youngsters. He starts prepared with bow and arrow in his hands. The song of the bees and the cuckoos become the sound of the bow of Kamadeva. He waits on the branches of the mango tree. At this sight even the minds of the sages will be moved, no doubt.)

[The heroine and the friend exit]

Cast

Vasantasena (Heroine) : Shyalaja

Parabhritika (Chedi) : Girija

Accompanists

Mizhavu : P.V. Iswaranunni, A.N. Hariharan

Edakka : M. Narayanan Namboodiri

Make - up & Costumes

P.M. Rammohan, A.S. Rangan, M. Kunjan

Troupe

Kerala Kalamandalam, Cheruthuruthy.

The performance was recorded by the Sangeet Natak Akademi for its archives and is accessible for the art scholars.

In April 1995, R.S. Shekle conducted workshop for Gyan Bharti School children of Delhi and produced Bhagavadajjukiyam under the Extension Programme of the National School of Drama.

A Scene from Bhagavadajjukiyam directed by Rita Ganguly at Vikrisht Madhyam Prekshagriha in Bahawalpur House

On 20 January 1996, the 'Bhagavadajjukkiyam' of Bodhayana was choregraphed in Kuchipudi style by the celebrity Radha and Raja Reddy at Azad Bhavan Auditorium, New Delhi.

The dance drama was produced under the aegis of Natya Tarangini.

Bhagavadajjukiyam in 'Kuchipudi' style

Raja and Radha Reddy presented the ever popular Sanskrit satire. 'Bhagavadajjukiyam' in Kuchipudi idiom by adding the Poorvaragam and other ritual portions of the tradition. The Tagore Theatre of the Indian Council for Cultural Relations at Azad Bhawan had the rare experience of a highly satirical and humour drama in dance-ballet. Natya Taranam Troupe's production celebrated all the diverse elements that make for an enjoyable dance - drama - good principle dancers, an enthusiatic supporting corps, a taut script without unnecessary munderings, well - sung music and additional sound effects. At the heart of this production's success was Bodhayan's riproaring 'Hasya Rasa Bharita' text Bhagavadajjukiyam written nearly 2000 years ago.

The same production was pemiered at the Sangeet Natak Akademi Kuchipudi Festival in Hyderabad which was one one of the best works presented there.

Bhagavadajjukiyam in Kuchipudi idiom, presented Natya Taranam Troupe

'Rupantar Natya - Prashikshan Kendra' is a theatre training institue based in Gorakhpur of Uttar Pradesh. Under its one year Acting Course, Sanskrit play Bhagavadajjukiyam of Bodhyana was enacted in Hindi by the students under the able direction of Sri Akhilesh Khanna of National School of Drama. The classic was successly staged in the Auditorium of Gorakhpur University on 30 November and 27 & 30 December, 1997.

The same production found inclusion in the Fifth Bilingual (Bengali / Hindi) One Act Play Competition held at Durgabadi and organised by the group 'Mausumi' of Gorakhpur. It was presented on 26 December 1997.

In the month of May, 1998, 'Rupantar Theatre Training Centre' of Gorakhpur presented Bodhayana's 'Bhagavadajjukiyam' in monologue, played by Nagesh Chandra Mishra and was directed by Shri Shailesh Srivastava at their 'Dikshanta Samaroha'.

In the month of December 1998, a three day festival was organised by the Prithvi Theatre, Mumbai in association with Keli, a Mumbai - based organisation dedicated to promoting traditional and classical art forms. Kutiyattam, an 1,800 year old ancient Indian classical theatre in Sanskrit and part of the Festival, drew a packed house, an indication that Sanskrit theatre still has a future in this country. Two women artists, accompanied by three male and two female musicians, kept the audience enthralled for nearly two hours. Critic Mohammed Wajehuddin reports : *"Dancing to the beats of drum-like instruments, Kalamandalam Girija and Kalamandalam Shylaja reached the hearts of an awestruck audience. Through gestures and signs, without uttering a word, they told a story in Kutiyattam, a classical form of theatre from Kerala called Bhagavadajjukiyam by Bodhayana, a 6th century A.D. poet who belonged to the Baudhayana School of South India.*

It is a hilarious situation created by bhagavan (yogin) who transposes her soul into the body of an ajjuka (prostitute) and vice versa.

The play opens at a flower garden where heroine Vasanasena and Chedi Parabhiritika have come for a walk. The heroine tells her friend that the garden looks beautiful and in the spring, flowers blossom and spread the fragrance through breeze. She says that flies come and suck flowers, enjoy honey and take them to their wives.

To which Chedi replies that the lake is full of lotus. The swans come and bark at the stalk of lotus and also share it with their wives. They play in the lake. The water moves due to the waves and gentle breeze. The sight becomes enchanting.

Then the heroine says that the peacocks start dancing as they mistake the sound of fountains to be thunderbolt. The story becomes more interesting when the heroine asks her friend for a place to sit. They sit on a granite pad under a tree and sing a song.

The song in short goes like this. In this garden the cuckoos flock together, eat buds and are satisfied. The bees get intoxicated.

The lord of love, Kamadeva is happy. He prepares to leave so that he can encourage the young minds.

The song of bees and cuckoos become the sound of Kamadeva.

He waits on the branches of mango tree. The sight is so beautiful and even sages could be moved. And at this point the heroine and her friend exit.

Keli felicitated Padashree Ammannur Madhava Chakyar, an 84-year-old exponent of Kutiyattam, at Y.B. Chavan Auditorium. Pandit Jasraj presented a traditional golden bangle and royal cloth on behalf of Keli and Prithvi Theatre.

Madhava Chakyar has also been honoured with Kalidas Samman by the Government of Madhya Pradesh.

Mr. Ramchandran, secretary of Keli, says : "The festival is dedicated to the memory of Painkulam Rama Chakyar who broke conventions and brought this theatre form out of temples." He also trained three girls from outside the Nambiar community though he faced stiff resistance from his own community.

The three-day festival was spread over three venues - Y.B. Chavan Centre, Prithvi Theatre and Model English School, Dombivli (East)."

Padmashree Ammannur Madhava Chakyar (left) and Kalamandalam Girija and Kalamandalam Shylaja (right) presenting Kutiyattam Udyana Varnana at Prithvi Theatre.

DRAMATIC WORKS : A BIBLIOGRAPHY

Text

Bhagavadajjuka prahasana / by Bodhayana; ed. & tr. into English by Michael Lockwood & A. Vishnu Bhat .- Madras : C.L.S., 1978.

Bhagavadajjukam / by Bodhayana Kavi; ed. with critical notes and English introd. by P. Anujan Accan; preface by M. Winternitz. - Chendamangalam : Pāliyam MSS. Library, 1925.

xxvi, 98 p.; 21 cm.

Includes author's own commentary.

Bhagavadajjukīya Jayantamangalam, Kerala. - 1925.

Bhagavadajjukīyam / ed. by P. Anujan Achan. - Trichur : Mangalodayam Press, 1925.

Includes an anonymous commentary.

Bhagavadajjukīyam / ed. by P. Vetari. - Madras : [s.n.], 1925.

Metatheater and Sanskrit drama / ed. & tr. by Michael Lockwood and A. Vishnu Bhat. - New Delhi : Munshiram Manoharlal, 1995.

Includes the text and English tr. of 'Bhagavadajjuka'.

Bengali

Mukti / by Bodhayana; tr. into Bengali by Apareshchandra Mukhopadhyay. - Calcutta.

Original title in Sanskrit Bhagavajjukīyam.

Dogri

Bhagavadajjukiyam / by Bodhayana; tr. into Dogri by Namim Chetna.

English

Bhagavad ajjukam / by Bodhayana. *In* Three Sanskrit lighter delights / tr. into English by C.C. Mehta .- Baroda : M.S. University of Baroda, 1968.

Bhagavadajjukam / by Bodhayana; tr. into English by C. Minakshi. *South Indian Studies (Madras),* 1978; Vol. 1; Pp. 59-78.

Bhagavadajjuka prahasana : a philosophical farce / ed. & tr. into English by Michael

Lockwood and Vishnu Bhat. - Madras : Christian Literature Society, 1978.

xv, 126 p.; 22.5 cm.

This volume ascribes the work to Raja Mahendra Vikrama Verma Pallava.

Adapted and greatly altered version.

Bhagavadajjukam / by Bodhayana; ed. by A. Banerji Sastri. *Journal of the Bihar and Orissa Research Society;* March & June 1924, Vol. 10, Nos. 1 & 2.

Bhagavadajjukam / by Bodhayana; ed. by Veturi Prabhakara Sastri .- Madras : Vavilla Ramaswami Shastrulu, 1925.

'The Hermit and the harlot' / by Bodhayana; tr. of 'Bhagavadajjuka' into English by A.B. van Buitenen *Mahfil (The Journal of South Asian Literature);* 1971 [Fall - Winter]; Vol. 7, Nos. 3 & 4; Pp. 149-166 (East Langsing, Michigan).

Metatheatre and Sanskrit drama / ed. & tr. by Michael Lockwood and A. Vishnu Bhat. - New Delhi : Munshiram Manoharlal, 1995.

Gujarati

Mruchchhakatik ane Bhagavadajjukiya / com. & tr. by Sundaram [alias Tribhuvandas Purushottam Luhar. - 2nd ed. - Ahmedabad : Ravani Prakashangruh, 1959.

xiv, 150 p.; 18.5 cm.

Includes Bodhayana's farce in Gujarati translation.

Hindi

Prachin vyanga natak : Sanskrit ke teen vikhyat prahasano ka anuvad / comp. & tr. by Nemichandra Jain and Urmibhusan Gupta. - New Delhi : Vani Prakashan, 1998.

84 p.; 21 cm.

Latin

L'asceta transmutato in etera / by Bodhayana; tr. into Italian by F. Belloni - Filippi.

In Teatro Indiano / by M. Vallauri. - Milan : Nuova Accademia Editrice, 1959.

Reprint.

L'asceta transmutato in etera / by Bodhayana; tr. into Italian by F. Belloni - Filippi. - Lanciano : Carabba, 1931.

Tr. of 'Bhagavadajjukiyam.

Kannada

Bhagavadajjukiya mattu sulesanyasi / by Bodhayana Kavi; tr. into Kannada by K.V. Subbanna. - Sagara : Akshara Prakashan; 1977.

59 p.; 22 cm.

Malayalam

Bhagavadajjukam / by Bodhayana. *In* Vyāyoga and prahasana / tr. by by K.P. Narayana Pisharoty. - Trichur : The translator, 1972.

A Malayalam rendering.

Telugu

Bhagavadajjukamu / by Bōdhāyana Kavi; tr. by Veṭūri Prabhākaraśāstri. - Madras: The translator, 1920.

iv, 46 p.; 18 cm.

Farce, orginally in Sanskrit.

BIO-CRITICAL NOTICES

Appukuttan Nair, D. Kudiyattam : fantasy and poetry in drama.

Discusses of Bodhayana's Bhagavadajjukiya in Kutiyattam idiom and in particular, Shandilya's soliloque that, alone takes serval night to perform.

Aufrecht, Theodor. Catalogus catalogorum. - Weisbaden : Franz Steiner Verlag Gmb. H., 1962.

2 Vols.; 26 cm.

Bandopadhyay, Sureshchandra. Sanskrit sahityer itihas. - Calcutta : The Dacca Students Library, [1970?]

In Bengali.

'Bhagavadajjukeeyam'. *In* Trivandrum Cultural Society Souvenir, July 1985.

Synopsis of the play.

Bhattacharya, Ashokanath. Bhagavadajjukīyam : some new problems : summary - *All India Oriental Conference* IV; Vol. I, 1926 Vide the author's paper : Rupakas : how many are they? *Indian Historical Quarterly* Vol. II. Pp. 413-415.

Bhattacharya, Biswanath. Sanskrit drama and dramaturgy. - Delhi : Sharada Publishing House, 1994.

Pp. 375-377.

Comparative Indian literature (Vol. 1) / ed. by K.M. George .- Trichur : Kerala Sahitya Akademi, 1984.

P. 569.

Dalal, Minakshi L. Conflict in Sanskrit drama. - Bombay : Somaiya Publications, 1973. Pp. 271-272.

[Dance] *Delhi Times;* 19 January 1996.

On Bodhayana's Bhagavadajjukiyam production in the Kuchipudi idiom. Includes brief synopsis.

Encyclopaedia of Indian literature (Vol. 1). - New Delhi : Sahitya Akademi, 1987. P. 422.

Garg, Ganga Ram. An encyclopaedia of Indian literature. - Delhi : Mittal Publishers, 1982.

Pp. 41, 57.

Krishnamachariar, M. and Srinīvasachariar. History of classical Sanskrit literature. - Delhi : Motilal Banarsidass, 1989. Pp. 369-370.

'Humourous adaptation of Bodhayan's satire' *The Statesman;* 29 January, 1996.

Includes the plot of Bodhayan's satire 'Bhagvad Ajjukeeyam alongwith a critical appraisal of Natya Taranams Kuchipudi adaptation of the classical drama.

Kaushal, J.N. Last month in Delhi / by J.N. Kaushal. *Enact;* May - June 1977; No. 125-126.

On NSD's production of Bodhayan's 'Bhagvadajjukiam.

Keith, A. Berriedale. The Sanskrit drama in its origin, development, theory and practice. - Oxford OUP, 1924.

405 p.; 22 cm.

Keith,A. Berriedale. Sanskrit - natak : udbhav aur vikas : siddhanta aur prayog / tr. into Hindi by Udaybhan Singh.- Delhi : Motilal Banarsidass, 1965.

Mainkar, T.G. Studies in Sanskrit dramatic criticism. - Delhi : Motilal Banarsidass, 1971.

Mankad, D.R. Bharatavakya and the Bhagavadajjukam : miscellany *Indian Historical Quarterly* March 1931; Vol. 7, No. 1; Pp. 187-190.

Mankad, D.R. Types of Sanskrit drama. - Karachi : Urmi Prakashan Mandir, 1936.

Masterpieces of Indian literature [Vol. 2]. - New Delhi : National Book Trust, 1997.

Contents : 'Bhagavadajjukam - Bodhayana'. Pp. 1153-1154.

The National bibliography of Indian literature. - New Delhi : Sahitya Akademi, 1962-1990.

5 Vols.; 24.5 cm.

Sharma, Virbala. Sanskrit mein ekanki rupak. - Bhopal : Madhya Pradesh Hindi Granth Akademi, 1972.

Contents : Bodhayana Pp. 143-153.

'Three Sanskrit lighter delights : Bhagavad - Ajjukam, Matta Vilasa, Ubhayabhisarika' *Journal of M.S. University Baroda;* April 1970; Vol. 19, No. 1.

Book review of C.C. Mehta's translation.

-----.. Journal of Oriental Institute, Dec. 1970, Vol. 20, No. 2, Pp. 192-194.

5

Dhananjaya

Writer of one of the best teatises on dramatic literature, Dhananjaya flour ished in the latter half of tenth century. He describes himself as the son of Vishṇu who enjoyed the patronage of Vākapaṭīrāja II also known as Munja, Utpaladeva, Amoghavarsha, Prithvivallabha, or Shrivallabha, the ruler of Dharwar (Central India), the king of Mālwā who reigned in the last quarter of the 10th century (974-995 A.D.).

Some even identify him with Dhanika, author of the *Avaloka* commentary, while others opined that the two were brothers. Besides 'Avaloka', Dhanika also wrote poetry and gives his own illustrations of Dhananjaya's definitions.

Though Dhananjaya's date is unascertained, but it is suggested that Dhanika was living about the middle of the tenth century.

Daśarūpaka, the title of his book derives its name from the ten principal forms of drama as mentioned in the Nātyaśāstra which is followed closely by Dhananjaya.

Keith has rightly stated that "It was inevitable that the complicated and confused work of Bharata should be superseded for many purposes by something more accessible and easy to follow, and this need was supplied by the Daśarūpaka of Dhananjaya. The work is divided into four books that deals with

(i) Subject - matter and plot of the drama.

(ii) The hero, heroine and other characters, language of the drama.

(iii) The prologue and its varities and different kinds of drama.

(iv) Emotions and sentiments.

Besides introductory remarks, Book One lays down the fundamental definitions of natya, nritya and nritta; Pantomine and Dancing as accessories; Basis of classification of dramas; sub-divisions of the subject- matter and its treatment in a play; the elements of the plot; the five stages of Action and the five junctures; the Opening and its subdivisions; the Development and its subdivisions; the Pause and its subdivisions; The Conclusion and its subdivisions; Sixfold application of the subdivisions; Twofold treatment of the Subject - matter; The five kinds of Intermediate Scene; Asides, Confidential Remarks, and the like; Conclusion of the First book.

The Book Two defines the characteristics of the hero, the four types of Hero; The Hero as lover; Companions of the Hero; The opponent of the Hero; Qualities of the Hero; the three kinds of Heroine; The Hero's wife as Heroine; A maiden or another's wife as Heroine; A courtezan as Heroine; Calssification of Heroines according to their relations with the Hero; Messengers of the Heroine; The twenty natural graces of the Heroine; Assistants of the Hero when a king; Grouping of characters according to rank; The Gay style of Procedure; The Grandiose style of Procedure; The Horrific style of Procedure; other styles of Procedure. Employment of the Styles of Procedure; Lord characteristics of a drama; Language of the various characters; Prescribed modes of address; Conclusion of the Second Book.

Book Three furnishes sections on :- The Nāṭaka as the typical variety of drama; the beginning of a play; The Eloquent style; The introduction and its various forms; the subdivisions of the Vīthī; Use of these introductory elements; Selection of the Principal Subject; Adaptation of the story; Arrangement of the dramatic structure; Appropriate arrangement of the beginning; Characteristics of an Act; The sentiments and their uses; Actions not permitted on the stage; The contents of an Act; The number of Acts in the Nāṭaka; Description of the Prakaraṇa; Description of the Nāṭakā; Description of the Bhāṇa; The forms of Gentle Dance; Description of the Prahasana; Description of the Dima; Description of the Vyāyoga; Description of the Samavakāra; Descriptin of the Vīthī; Description of the Utsrṣṭkāṅka; Description of the Ihāmṛga; Conclusion of the Third Book.

Book Four comprises of chapters on Sentment and its production; Determinants and Consequents defined; A state defined; The Involuntary States; The thirty- three Transitory States; the Permanent States; Four fold character of the Sentiments; Sentiment defined; The Erotic Sentiment; Varieties of the Erotic Sentiment; Privation and its stages; Separation and its varieties; Union and its characteristics; The Heroic Sentiment; The Odious Sentiment; The Furious Sentiment; The Comic Sentiment; The Marvelous Sentiment; The Terrible Sentiment; The Pathetic Sentiment; Various matters ommitted in this work; Conclusion of the Fourth Book; Conclusion of the entire work.

The third chapter of the 'Daśarūpaka' thus describes the ten forms (daśarūpa) of drama which are Nāṭaka, Prakaraṇa, Bhāṇa, Vyāyoga, Samavakāra, Īhāmṛga, Aṅka (or Utsṛṣṭkāṅka), Ḍima, Vīthī and Prahasana.

Ramification of Drama	**Act**	**Rasa**	**Saṃdhī**
Aṅka	1	Karuṇa	2
Bhāṇa	1	Vīra or Śṛṅgāra	2
Dima	4	Dīpta Raudra	4
Ihāmṛga	4	Śṛṅgāra	3
Nāṭaka	5 - 10	Vīra or Śṛṅgāra	5
Nāṭikā	4	Śrṅgāra	5
Prahasana	1	Hāsya	2
Prakaraṇa	5 - 10	Vīra or Śrṇgāra	5
Samavakāra	3	Vīra	4
Vīthī	1	Śṛṅgāra	2
Vyāyoga	1	Dīpta Raudra	3

As shown earlier, the book contains section of Rasa in its fourth part. Though he does not treat the daṁkāras, but examines Rasa at length, noteworthy among which is Dhananjaya's refutation of suggestion (Vyanjana) and his leaning towards the theory of Bhattanayaka and Tatparya vritti. In this respect, another significant work in the field of dramaturgy called 'Bhavaprakashana' (or prakasha) of Sharadatanaya is guided by Dhananjaya's work.

Next to *Nāṭyaśastra*, the earliest available work on the theory of Sanskrit drama, the most outstanding work in the realm was the work of Dhananjaya's called the '*Dasarupaka*'. In the form of a brief manual, Dhananjaya provides the rules of dramatic composition actually laid down in the great compendium of Hindu dramatic science, i.e. the Bhārātīyanāṭyaśāstra. While commentity on *Nāya Śāstra*. George C.O. Haas said: This monumenal work, although regarded as authoritative and even ivnested by tradition with the character of semidivine revelation, was altogether too cumbersome for ordinary use and had the additional disadvantages of diffuse style and a somewhat unsystematic arranagement. From the point of view of the dramatist, particularly, it was unsatisfactory, since the purely dramaturgic portions were submerged, so to speak, in a mass of histrionic and general prescriptions. The author of the Dasārūpa accordingly aims, as he himself says, to restate the principles of dramaturgy in more concise and systematic form..."

He had great reverence for Bharata's norms. He followed him for terminology and definitions with slight variations. His deviation from Bharata's *Nāṭ yaśāstra* is regarded as insignificant and trival. But at the sametime, it can not be denied that Dhananjaya omits the greater part of the topics of Bharata's model.

It can be noted that the treatment of theatrical art and architecture as well as music, dance etc., belonging to performing arts genres are excluded in this work. He even gives a new division of types of Heroine. His classification of the types of Heroine is somewhat different from Bharata who recognizes four varies : divyā, nṛpapatnī, kulastrī, gaṇikā. While Dhananjaya provides three kinds of heroine (nāyikā) as shown in the diagram, numbers indicate the sixteen varieties:-

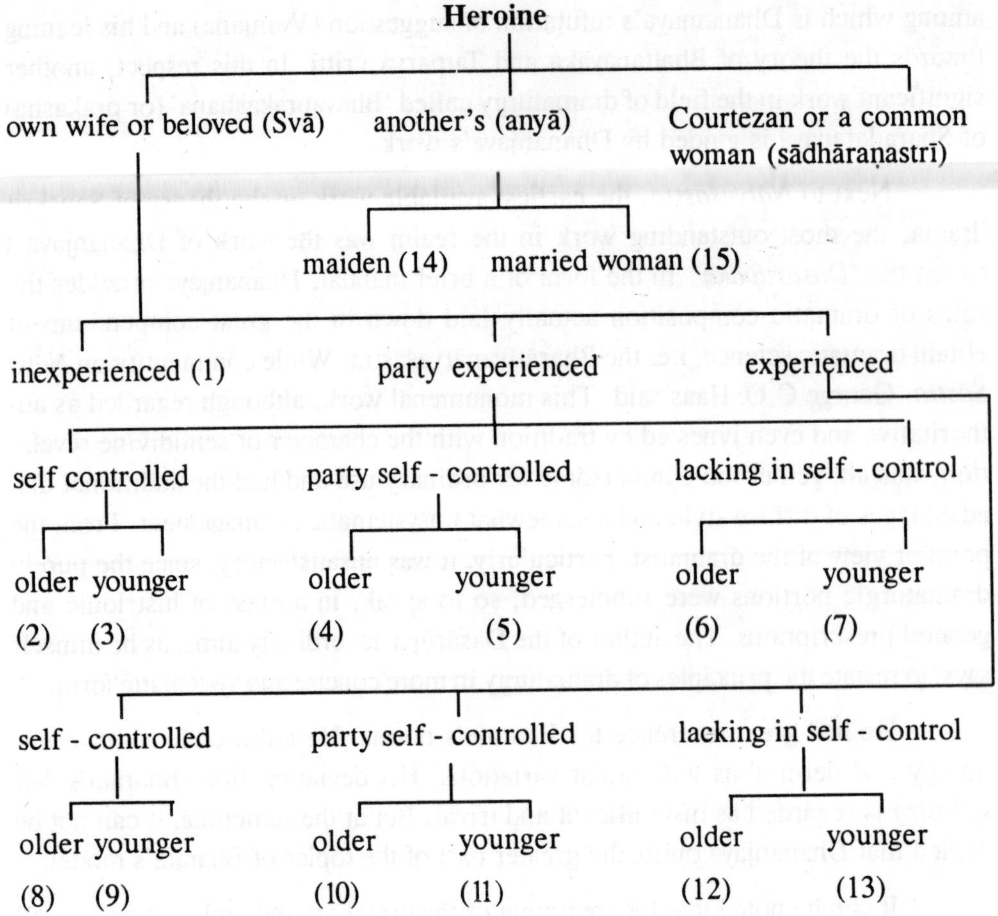

He gave a new distinction in his treatment of the Erotic Sentiment too. While quoting part of the definition of the nāṭika given in Bharata's work, Dhananjaya tries to modify it in the direction of greater latitude. As said earlier, the other variations between these two great works are however negligiable.

The Daśarupaka is metrical and is composed for the most part in the ordinary śloka meter but others meters have also been employed by Dhananjaya. Metres employed are ārya, sragdharā, indravajrā, vasantatilaka; upajati, śārdū lavikrīḍita.

As far as style is concerned, Daśarūpaka differs and having manifold merits than Bharata'a Nāṭyaśastra. Dhananjaya's work is highly condensed and avoids all formulaic 'padding' except where it is absolutely required by the meter. Bharata's work is on the other hand very diffuse, abounds in transitional and introductory formulas; and often uses stock phrases to fill incomplete lines.

Fitz - Edward Hall opined that "Although but moderate in antiquity, the 'Daśa rūpa' has long been the favourite authority, among the Hindus, for everything connected with the theatre; and it has not been superseded by any more modern performance of similar character. The only one with which I am acquianted is the *Nāṭya - pradīpa* of Sundara Miśra, author of the *Abhirāma - mani. The Nātya - pradipa* was written in Sāka 1535, answering to A.D. 1613. It is chiefly made up of selection from the Daśa - rūpa and its commentary, and from the *Sāhitya - darpana*. Further, the latter also refers to the Daśarūpa, criticizes some of its statements and above all bases its treatment of dramaturgy to a large extent on Dhananjaya's work and repeats verbation or with minor variations a large number of its sections.

His work has been copiously cited in many other rhetorical and dramaturgic treatises and in various commentaries on Hindu play. For example, in the *Pratāparudrīya'* one can find ten quotations from the Daśarūpa that speaks of the scope and importance of the Daśarūpa.

His work was commented upon by perhaps his younger brother Dhanika in his *Avaloka*. It is without this commentary, Daśrūpaka itself is incomplete.

Another noteworthy commentarty is *'Rūpaḍīpikā'* by Bahurupamisra who comments on the text and gloss of Ḍhananjaya and Ḍhanika, and thereby treats both as Ḍaśarūpa.

Mention could be made of commentaries by Nṛsimhabhatta by Ḍevapāṇi, by Kṣoṇīḍharamiśra, and by Kūravirāma.

DRAMATIC WORKS : A BIBLIOGRAPHY

Text

Dasarupaka / by Dhananjaya; ed. by Kāshīnāth Pāṇdurang Parab. - Bombay : Nirṇaya Sāgara Press, 1897.

The volume includes a detailed table of contents, a list of the works quoted in the commentary, and an index of all verses thus cited from other author with an indication of their source in many cases.

-----. Bombay : Nirṇayasāgar Press, 1917.

Dasarupaka / by Dhananjaya.

-----. Calcutta : Jīvānanda Vidyāsāgara, 1878.

A reprint of Hall's text.

Dasarupaka / by Dhananjaya; commentary 'Avaloka' by Dhanika and the sub-commentary 'Laghutika' by Bhattanṛsimha; ed. by T. Venkatacharya. - Madras : Adya Library and Research Centre, 1969.

lxxv, 343 p.

Dasarupaka / by Dhananjaya, the 'Dasarupavaloka' commentary by Dhanika; ed. with Eng. tr. by Caranatirtha. - Varanasi : Chowkhamba Sanskrit Series Office, 1969.

15, 132 p.; 22.5 cm.

Daśarūpaka / by Dhanañjaya; ed. by Fitzedward Hall. - Bibliotheca Indica, 1861-65.

Text contained the commentary of Dhanika, and is based on a collation of six manuscripts, five of them incomplete.

Daśarūpaka / by Dhanañjaya; ed. by Kāśīnāth Pāṇḍuraṅga Parab and Nārāyaṇ Rām Ācārya. - 5th ed. - Bombay : Nirṇayasāgar Press, 1941.

[160] p.; 22 cm.

Dāśarūpaka / by Dhanañjaya; ed. with an English tr., introd. and notes by George C.O. Haas. - New York : Columbia University Press, 1912.

xlv, 169 p.; 23 cm.

In Roman script.

Treatise on Hindu dramaturgy.

Daśarūpaka / by Dhanañjaya; ed. with an English tr. & notes by J.K. Śāstrī. - Gondal : Rasaśālā Auṣadhāśram, 1942.

iv, 112 p.; 24 cm.

Contains the commentary 'Avaloka' of Dhanika.

Daśarupaka / ed. by S. Sastri. - Bombay [s.n.], 1927.

[Dasarūpaka] In Bibliotheca Indica, N.S. Fasc 12, 24, 62 : Collection of oriental works [Vol. 36]. - Osnabrück : Biblio Verlag, 1980.

39, 241 p.; 21.5 cm.

Reprint of the edition, Calcutta 1861 - 1865.

Published under the patronage of the Hon. Court of Directors of the East India Company, and the Superintendence of the Asiatic Society of Bengal.

Vol. 36 Contains Dhananjaya's *Dasarupa.*

Translations

Bengali

Daśarupaka / by Dhananjaya, tr. into Bengali by Sourindra Mohan Tagore .- Calcutta.

Dasharupaka / by Dhananjaya; tr. with notes & comm. in Bengali by Bishnu Basu .- Calcutta : Theatre Research Institute, 1974.

154 p.; 18 cm.

English

Daśarūpa : a treatise on Hindu dramaturgy / by Dhanañjaya; tr. from the Sanskrit with the text an introd. and notes by George C.O. Haas. - New York : Columbia University Press, 1912.

xlv, 169 p.; 22 cm.

(Columbia University Indo - Iranian Series / ed. by A.V. Williams Jackson; 7)

Includes append. & index.

The Daśrūpa : a treatise on Hindu dramaturgy / by Dhananjaya; tr. into English with the text, introd. and notes by George C.O. Haas .- Delhi : Motilal Banarsidass, 1962.

xlv, 169 p.; 22.5 cm.

Includes indexes.

Dasarupaka / by Dhananjaya, the 'Dasarupavaloka' commentary by Dhanika; ed. with English tr. by Caranatirtha. - Varanasi : Chowkhamba Sanskrit Seires Office, 1969.

15, 132 p.; 22.5 cm.

Daśarūpaka / by Dhanajaya, ed. with Dhanikas commentary, notes, English tr. etc. by J.K. Shastri.

Kannada

Dasharupaka / by Dhananjaya; tr. into Kannada by K.V. Subbanna. - Sagar : Akshara Prakashan, [n.d.].

lxii, 360 p.; 22 cm.

Maithili

Maithili Daśarūpak / by Dhanañjaya; tr. by Devakānta Jhā. - Patna : Maithili Akademī, 1979.

xx, 322 p.; 21 cm.

Telugu

Āndhra Daśarūpakamu / by Dhanañjaya; tr. by Mallādi Sūryanārāyaṇaśāstri. - Eluru : Rama & Co., [n.d.].

xx, 121 p.; 18 cm.

Dramaturgy.

BIO - CRITICAL NOTICES

Adya Rangacharya. Drama in Sanskrit literature. - Bombay : Popular Prakashan, 1967.

Pp. 13, 16, 51, 58, 63, 73, 78, 84, 87, 89, 133, 141, 152.

Anjum Saifi. Critical and comparative study of Dasarupaka and Natya Darpana / by Saifi Anjum.

Ph.D. thesis approved by the Rohilkhand University.

Aufrecht, Theodor. Catalogus catalogorum .- Weisbaden : Franz Steiner Verlag Gmb. H, 1962.

2 Vols.; 26 cm.

Banerji, Sures Chandra. A Companion to Sanskrit literature. - Delhi : Motilal Banarsidass, 1971.

--------. Sanskrit sahityer itihas. - Calcutta : The Dacca Students Library, [1970?].

In Bengali.

Contents : Dhananjaya. Pp. 129, 146, 152.

Bhattacharya, Biswanath. Sanskrit drama and dramaturgy. Delhi : Sharada Publishing House, 1994.

Bhattacharya, Syamapada. Evaluation of the toics of Sanskrit dramaturgy from the times of Bharata to Dasarupaka / by Syamapada Bhattacharya.

Ph.D. thesis approved by the Burdwan University in 1978.

Bibliotheca Indica, N.S. Fasc 12, 24, 62 collection of oriental works (Vols. 36). Osnabrūck : Biblio Verlag, 1980.

Reprint of the edition, Calcutta 1861-1865.

Introductory chapter furnishes a detailed discussion on the life & work of Dhananjaya.

Dalal, Minakshi L. Conflict in Sanskrit drama. - Bombay : Somaiya Publications Pvt. Ltd., 1973.

Contents : Dhananjaya. P. 42

['The Dasarupaka of Dhananjaya'] -. *Aryan Path* April 1970; Vol. 41 (4); Pp. 194-195.

Book review.

-----. *Journal of Oriental Institue* March 1970; Vol. 19, No. 3; Pp. 298-300.

-----. *Vishveshvaranand Indological Journal,* 1969; Vol. 7, Nos. 1-2; Pp. 184-86.

Encyclopaedia of Indian Literature .- New Delhi : Sahitya Akademi, 1987-1994.

Pp. 201, 490, 890, 993, 2433, 2921, 3569, 3718.

Garg, Ganga Ram. An Encyclopaedia of Indians Literature. - Delhi : Motilal Publishers, 1982. Pp. 91, 99.

Glimpses of Sanskrit literature / ed. A.N.D Haksar. - New Delhi : Indian Council for Cultural Relations, 1995.

Contents : Dhananjaya. Pp. 37, 175.

Gupta, Sangita. Commentaries on Dasarupaka : a comparative study of avaloka, laghutika and dipika / by Sangita Gupta.

Ph.D. thesis in Hindi, approved by the Banasthali University in 1987.

Keith, A. Berriedale. The Sanskrit drama in its origin, development, theory and practice. - Oxford : OUP, 1924.
405 p.; 22 cm.

--------.The Sanskrit drama in its origin, development : theory and practice. - London : Oxford University Press, 1954.

Reprint. Pp. 292, 321, 325, 328, 329, 340, 347.

--------.Sanskrit - natak : udbhav aur vikas : Siddhanta aur prayog / tr. into Hindi by Udaybhanu Singh. - Delhi : Motilal Banarsidass, 1965.

Krishnamachariar, M. and Srinivasachariar. History of classical Sanskrit literature. - Delhi : Motilal Banarsidass, 1989.
P. 746.

Lēvi, Sylvain. The theatre of India / tr. from the French by Narayan Mukherji. - Calcutta : Writers Workshop, 1978.

Contents :

Dhanañjaya : Pp. (Vol. 1) 8, 15, 16, 26,

Daśarupa (ka) Pp. (Vol. I) 5, 11, 13, 14, 16-18, 26, 27, 55, 141, 183, 192, 201, 238; (Vol. II) 29, 81, 102.

Macdonell, A.A. India's past : a survey of her literatures, religious, languages and antiquities. - Varanasi, 1956.

Marasinghe, E.W. The Sanskrit theatre and stagecraft. - Delhi : Sri Satguru Publications, 1989. - (Sri Garib Dass Oriental Series; No. 78).

Moghe, S.G. Citations from the Dasarupaka of Dhananjaya in the commentaries on Sanskrit dramas / by S.G. Moghe. *Journal of Oriental Institute* Dec., 1978; Vol. 28, No. 2; Pp. 7-12.

Muhammad Israel Khan. Samskṛta - natya - siddhanta ke anālocita paksha. - Ghaziabad : Crescent Publishing House, 1985.

Contents : Dhananjaya. Pp. 14-24.

The National bibliography of Indian literature. - New Delhi : Sahitya Akademi, 1962-1990.

5 Vols.; 24.5 cm.

Pandey, Kanti Chandra. Dhanañjaya and Abhinavagupta on śānta rasa : summary. *All India Oriental Conference* XII; Vol. II; 326-330.

Pandey, Satyanarayan. Critical study of Dhananjaya's Dasarupaka and its contribution to Indian Natyasastra / by Satyanarayan Pandey.

Ph.D. thesis in Hindi, approved by the Agra University in 1959.

Poddar, Kanhaiyalal. Sanskrit sahitya kā itihās. - Kashi : Nagari Pracharani Sabha, [sam. 2030] (Ramvilas Poddar Samarak granthamala.)

Raghavan, V. Sanskrit drama : its aesthetics and production .- Madras : Sarada Raghavan, 1993.

Ray, Ashim Kumar and Gidwani, N.N. A Dictionary of Indology (Vol. 2). - New Delhi : Oxford & IBH. Publishing Co., 1984.

Sethi, Atmaram. Anudit Hindi sahitya: vishishta grantha-suchi / by Atmaram Sethi .- Gurgaon : Indian Documentation Service, 1981.

Contents : Sanskrit (Pp. 1-624).

Shekhar, I. Sanskrit drama : its origin and decline. - Leiden : E.J. Brill, 1960.

Pp. 43, 159.

6

Diṅnāga

Diṅnāga, a well known ancient dramatist, flourished before 400. He is the author of Kundamala, an evocating play in six acts on the same theme as Bhavabhūti's Uttararāmacarita. Thus, based on Ramayana, it depicts the exile of Sītā, her discovery and reunion of Rāma and Sīta, alongwith their sons, Kusha and Lava during the Ashvamedha Yajña.

The plot of the play suggests that it might have been written later than the Uttaramacarita and therefore, work is assigned to the 7th century. To some, it seems to have been written earlier than Uttaramacarita.

Neither exact date of the composition of 'Kundamala' could be ascertained nor the scholars could correctly identify the author. Many experts in the domain, however, ascribe the work to Diṅnagā with his other variants. Play is ascribed to Diṅnāga by the Mysore Mss, while the name Dhīranāga is given by the Tanjore Mss.

In the manuscripts, Diṅnāga is thus referred to as Dhiranaga, Viranaga, Ravinga and Nagayya etc.

He seems to be different from famous Buddhist logician and philosopher with the same name belonging from Kanchi.

Some translators have demonstrated that the author of Kundamala was no Buddhist. So majority of the scholars accept the name Diṅnāga, on the authority of the Mysore Mss. and of a quotation in Vallabhadeva's Subhāsitāvali, they conclude that the author of this play was the rival of Kālidāsa mentioned by the commentators.

This great dramatist was a Hindu who had enduring faith in the vedic religion.

Tanjore manuscripts refers to the poet as a resident of Anuparadha, while Mysore manuscript refers to the place as Araralapura. Some holds the view that he might be a native of Sri Lanka. Thus his native place is yet to be identified.

Modelled on the Bhababhuti's Uttararāmacarita', an aesthetically consummate work of lasting literary and dramatic merit, 'Kundamala', was first brought to light by M.R. Kavi and S.K. Ramanatha Sastri who discovered the manuscript and published it in 1923 from Madras. A commentary was later added to it in 1924 by Jayachandra Śastri and appeared in print from Lahore in 1929.

Prof. Saran Dass Bhanot worked on the play for many years. He published his first critical edition of the play with translations, introduction and notes in the year 1932 in collaboration with Prof. Ved Vyas. This edition was very useful to the late Dr. A.C. Woolner when he prepared his English translation.

Kali kumar Datta selected this work as his research topic and broughtout a critical edition in 1964.

Dinnaga made many deviations from the original epic to suit the dramatic plot, especially in the Naimisha forest.

Even many significant episodes are skipped off by the dramatist very easily.

While wandering in the forest, Rama and Lakshmana finds a garland of jasmine flowers 'Kundamala' floating in the waters of the Gomati and Rama at once recognises it as the work of Sita, subsequently they tries to trace the place of its origin and come to the hermitage of Valmiki where Sita is plucking flowers. The garland plays a very significant role in this recognition scene, hence the title of the play Rama's lamentation for Sita is overheard by the latter, but Sīta is invisible because of a boon granted by the sage Valmiki.

However Rama sees her reflected image in the waters of the lake. Rama falls into a swoon and is fanned by the invisible Sita with her scarf which is visible. The Vidushaka inform that it was a trick of the divine nymph 'Tilottama' assuming the guise of Sita.

Adya Rangacharya in his article *'Epics and Sanskrit drama'* observes 'As we read the play we are not struck so much by any greatness of the drsamatist as we are reminded of Kālidāsa and Bhavabhūti. The more we read the play the more we feel that some youngish admirer of Bhavabhūti has tried to make a play by putting together different pieces from the works of those two dramatists.'

Agya Rangacharya further points out that the main scene in the very first act opens like that in Abhijṅana Śakuntala with an identical description of the moving chariot. Further Sīta's speech in this can reminds one of Kālidāsa's verse in Raghuvaṁsa in the same context.

Above all, the presence of a Vidūsaka, friend of Rāma resembles the Vidūsaka (jester of king Duṣyanta) of Abhijñāna Śakuntala Diṅnāga's Rama asks the same question in Act V that if Sita was worthy enough to be still remembered why Viduṣaka did not prevent him from banishing Sita.

The 'Kundamala' motif may remind one of the necklace in Shriharsha's 'Ratnavali' or 'Bakulamalas' in Bhavabhūti's Malatimadhava.

An outstanding play that unveil many incidents and situations in six acts of uneven length that employs all sorts of literary devices.

Written in lucid style, the verses are forceful and rich in thought content.

The sentiment love in separation, ie, the intensity of the 'Vipralambhashringara' is delineated in excellent manner.

Keeping aside the erotic sentiments and the heroic deeds, which were the basis of classical Sanskrit dramas or the recurring rasas. Diṅnāga standsout for his skillful application of some of the finest human feelings.

The play is full of sorrows, and he does not strictly adheres to the classical norms. But he successfully makes his audience happy by uniting Rama with Sīta as a natural culmination of the prolonged sorrows of separated life which he has woven as unithread in earlier acts.

Lakshman Sarup writes that 'The Kundamālā is a notable addition to Sanskrit drama... Diṅnāga, its author is a master of dialogue. He is successful in not only delineating remarkable portraits but has the special gift of painting the characteristic traits in a character by a few simple but effective strokes of pen.

This can be illustrated from Sītā's character which is enhanced and made impressive in a manner which no other Indian dramatist has succeeded in portraying.

A work of high merit, the influence of 'Kundamala' can be noticed in other great works such as Bhoja's 'Shringaraprakasha', 'Saradatanaya's 'Natakalakshanaratnakosha', Ramchandra and Gunachandra's 'Natyadarpana', Vidyakara's 'Subhashitaratnakosha', Shridharadasa's 'Saduktikarnamrita and Vishvanatha's 'Sahitya darpana'.

Reference of this work have been made in Bahurupamishra's 'Rupadipika', a commentary on Dhananjaya's Daśarupaka and in 'Kavyakamadhenu', an anonymous work.

KUNDAMALA

Synopsis

This is the later part of the story of Rāma after his coronation. It depicts the desertion of Sīta, her discovery and reunion with Rāma.

Dramatis Personae

Rāma	-	The hero
Lakṣmaṇa	-	Rama's brother
Sumantra	-	The charioteer
Vālmīki	-	
Bādarāyaṇa	-	Sages
Kaṇva		
Kauśika	-	The jester
Chamberlain.		
Sītā	-	The heroine
Kuśa		
Lava	-	twin sons of Rāma and Sītā
Yajñavedi	-	first maid
Vedavatī	-	another maid belonging to the hermitage.
Kausalyā	-	Royal ladies
Kaikeyi		
Sumitrā		

Earth - The goddess

Stage - Manager (In the prologue)

Female ascetics, heavenly nymphs etc do nto appear on the stage, but are spoken of as present.

Plot:-

After the benedictory verses to Gaṇeśa and Śiva, Sūtradhāra narrate the events relating to the banishment of Sītā.

Though Sita is delighted at the company of Ganges, cool breeze and the songs of swans and shade of the trees, but she is to be abandoned in the deep forest. Sīta is communicated about her exile by the Lakṣmana. Overpowered with deep grief, helpless Sīta submits to her ill fate. But she gets some relief when she comes to knows that Rāma has abandoned her only for fear of public scandal and would never marry again.

In Act one, the abandoned queen of Rāma is reported to Vālmiki by his pupils. Vālmikī employs his yogacakṣus and finds Sītā innocent and therefore decides to take her to his āshram.

The great sage Vālmikī finds her in a pitiable condition and takes her to his hermitage.

On her way, Sīta offer the Ganges, a garland of Kunda flowers everyday for her safe delivery.

This garland becomes an indicator of the auspicious birth of Lava and Kusha who are to be the illuminators of the 'Ikshvaku' family after Rama, it also unfolds to Rama the presence of Sīta in the vicinity of the river Ganges.

In the Second act, the interlude provides information about the birth of Kuśa and Lava and the performance of Aśvamedha Yajña by Rāma in Naimiṣāraṇya.

Then the act opens with a conversation between Vedavanti and Sītā in which the latter express her deep grief over her long separation from Rāma and also remember the happiest moments of her past life.

Third act brings the hero and heroine close. Wreath of Kunda flowers woven by Sīta is carried by the breeze.

Rama while wandering on the bank of Gomati alongwith Lakṣmaṇa in melancholy mood discovers this garland of Kunda flower which comes to the feet of Rama. Rāma at once recognises it as woven by Sītā. However he had to throw it because the 'Kundamala must be an offering to the gods.

In his venture to trace Sita, her foot prints are found on the sandy banks of the river and on which they conclude that Sītā must be around.

Sita was invisible through the grace of Vālmīki, is engaged in plucking flowers hears Rāma's lamentaton for Sita.

Fourth act centres on the forest where Sīta comes to a step well. She has worn the shawl which was given to her by the sylvan deity Māyāvati at Citrakūta. Sīta's presence is, however, not felt by the Rāma. Because the former is not seen due to the boon granted by the great sage Vālmiki, but Rama sees her reflection in water and faints due to his mental agony. Sīta embraces him to bring back to his consciousness. Rāma swoons by not finding her again. With the fringe of her shawl, she tries to fan him. Rama snatches way that shawl. He also throws off his own upper garment which Sīta picks up and finds the garment unscented, she gets relief that Rāmā has not married again. Their longing for each other is beautifully depicted in this act.

The scene becomes more pathetic when Rāma is compelled to believe by the jester that the celestial nymph 'Tilottama' has deluded him in the forest by imitating Sītā's activites.

The Fifth act brings the father and children at one place, as they meet not knowing each other. Kuśa and Lava narrates the story of Rāmāyana from the beginning up to the desertion of Sita.

The Rāma's mental condition is shown here poignantly. Amaged by seeing the children who have strange resemblance to Sita reminds him of his own lost children.

In the Final act, Rāma and Sītā are united. Atlast Vālmiki has to admonish Rāma and she goes through the ordeal to prove her chastity that form the climax of the drama. There after, Rāma accepts his wife, Kuśa is crowned as king and Lava as the heir - apparent.

Dramatic Works : A Biblography

Text

Kundamālā / by Diṅnāga; ed. & tr. by A.C. Woolner. - London : [s.n.], 1935.

Kundamala / by Diṅnāga; ed. by K.K. Datta. - Calcutta : Govt. Sanskrit College, 1956.

Kundamālā / by Diṅnāga; ed. by Kali Kumar Datta. - Calcutta : [s.n.], 1964.

(Sanskrit College Research Series; No. 28).

Kundamālā / by Diṅnāga; ed. by M. Ramakrishna Kavi and S.K. Ramanatha Sastri . Bombay : Tattva - viveka Press, 1923.

84 p. - (Dakṣiṇabhāratī Granthamālā; No. 2).

Kundamala / ed. with a commentary by Jayacandra Śāstrī. - Lahore : Motīlāl Banārsidās, 1929.

xiv, 202, 30p.; 22 cm.

Includes append. & index.

Second edition of this volume contain English and Hindi translation appeared in print in 1937.

Kundamala / by Diṅnaga; ed. with a Sanskrit commentary and English tr. by J. Sastri and S.D. Bhanot .- Lahore : [s.n.], 1932.

Kundamāla / by Diṅnāga; ed. with Sanskrit comm. by J.L. Śāstri and tr. into English by Saran Dass Bhanot and Vedavyas. - Delhi : Motilal Banarsidas, 1983.

xlvii, 360 p.; 22 cm.

Kundamālā / by Diṅnāga; commentary by Narasimhadeva Sastri. - Lahore : Meharchand Laksmanadas, 1930.

242 p.

Kundamala / by Diṅnāga; comm. in Hindi and Sanskrit by Lokamani Dahala. - Varanasi : Chowkhamba Surabharati Prakashan, 1992.

17, 223 p.

[Kundamala=] The Jesmine garland / by Diṅnāga; ed. by K.K. Raja and B. Bhattacharya; tr. by A.C. Woolner. - Lahore : Punjab University, 1935.

(Adaptations)

Kailasanatha. Nātya - kathā - mañjarī. - Lahore : Motilal Banarsidas, [1934/35] 1991 vs.

Includes story of 'Kundamālā' in Sanskrit Pp. 179-216.

Translations

English

The Jasmine garland / tr. from Sanskrit into English by A.C. Woolner. - London: Oxford University Press, 1935.

xiv, 50 p.; 24.5 cm.

(Punjab University Oriental Publications; 27).

Tr. of Kundamālā.

Kundamala / by Dinnaga; tr. into English by Saran Dass Bhanot and Veda Vyas. - Delhi : Motilal Banarsidas, 1983.

Kundamālā / by Diṅnaga; tr. by Satyendra Śarat. - Allahabad : Nilām Prakashan Griha, 1950.

Kundamālā / by Diṅnaga; tr. into Hindi by Vagīśvar Vidyalaṃkār. - Lahore : [s.n.], 1932.

Hindi

Kundamālā / by Dinnaga. - Delhi : Vishva Sahitya Granthamala, 1931.

Kundamālā / by Dinnaga. - New Delhi : Sasta Sahitya Mandal.

Kundamala / by Diṅnāga; comm. in Hindi and Sanskrit by Lokamani Dahala. - Varanasi : Chowkhamba Surabharati Prakashan, 1992.

17, 223 p.

Kundamala / by Dinnaga; ed. with a Sanskrit commentary and English tr. by J. Sastri and S.D. Bhanot. - Lahore : [s.n.], 1932.

Kundamālā / by Dinnaga; tr. by Kailashnāth Bhatnagar. - New Delhi : Saraswati Bhawan, 1955.

Kundamālā / by Dinnaga; tr. by Kṛṣṇakumar Dhawan. - Jullandhar : Bharatiya Sanskrit Bhawan, 1955.

Kannada

Kundamālā / by Diṅnaga; tr. by B. Rama Rao. - Mysore : [s.n.], 1923.

(Karnataka Granthamale; 113)

75 p.; 21 cm.

In prose.

Kundamālā / by Diṅnāga; tr. by Moleyaru Shankaranarayana Bhatta. - Bela, Kasaragudu : Molayaru Subraya Bhatta, 1954.

Prose and verse.

Kundamāla / tr. by Mōḷeyāra Śaṅkaranārāyaṇa Bhaṭṭa .- 2nd ed. - Mangalore : Jñānaprapañca, 1954.

ii, 99 p.; 18 cm.

Kundamālā / by Diṅnāga; tr. into Kannada by B.H. Sridhara. - Mysore : Gita Book House, 1962.

Prose & verse.

Malayalam

Mullamāla / tr. by Kiḷimānūr K. Kṛṣṇa Vāriyar; introd. & notes by E.R. Śrīkṛṣṇa Śarma. - Kozhikode : P.K. Bros., 1951.

xxxviii, 119 p.; 18 cm.

Includes append. & index.

Contains alphabetical index of verses occuring in the work of 'Kundamālā'.

Mullappūmālā / tr. by S.K. Nāyar. - Chittoor : P. Kṛṣṇan Nāyar, 1953.

98 p.; 23 cm.

Virahavirāmam / by Diṅnaga; tr. into Malayam by M.R. Veluppila Sastri.

Tr. of 'Kundamālā'.

Marathi

Kundamālā / tr. by Raṅgācārya Bāḷkṛṣṇācārya Reḍḍī & Rāmcandra Cintamaṇ Śrīkhaṇḍe. - Wai : The translators, 1935.

xx, 78 p. : plate; 18.5 cm.

Telugu

Kandamālā / by Diṅnaga; tr. into Telugu by Akili Sreerama Sarma.

Kundamāla / by Diṅnāga tr. into Telugu by Bulusu Vēṅkaṭēśvarulu. - 3rd ed. - Kakinada : The translator, 1950.

xxxvi, 104 p.; 18 cm.

Kandamālā / by Diṅnaga; tr. into Telugu by Gatti Lakshminarasimha Sastry.

Kundamala / by Diṅnaga, tr. into Telugu by Vaḍḍādi Subbārāyuḍu. - Rajahmundry : [s.n.], 1932.

xvi, 83, 1 p.; 21 cm.

Tr. from Original Sanskrit.

Kundamāla / by Diṅnāga, tr. into Telugu by Vēdamu Vēṅkaṭakṛṣṇaśarma. - Madras : The translator, 1948.

xxvi, 108 p.; 18 cm.

Kandamālā / by Diṅnaga; tr. into Telugu by Veturi Prabhakara Sastry.

BIO - CRITICAL NOTICES

Adya Rangacharya. Drama in Sanskrit Literature. - 2nd ed. Bombay : Popular Prakashan, 1967.

Aggarwal, H.R. A short history of Sanskrit Literature. - 2nd rev. ed. - Delhi : Munshiram Manoharlal, 1963.

Contents : (Dinnaga. P. 182).

Banerji, Sures Chandra. A Companion to Sanskrit Literature. - Delhi : Motilal Banarsidass, 1971.

P. 228.

Bhartiya, Kanti Kishore. Sanskrit Natakkara. - Uttar Pradesh : Prakashan Shakha, Suchana Vibhag, 1959.

(Hindi - Samiti granthamala; 25)

Contents : Dinnaga. Pp. 197 - 199.

Comparative Indian literature (Vol. 1) / ed. by K.M. George .- Trichur : Kerala Sahitya Akademi, 1984.

P. 568.

A Critical inventory of Rāmāyana studies in the world [Vol. 1] / ed. by K. Krishnamoorthy and Satkari Mukhopadhyay. - New Delhi : Sahitya Akademi, 1991.

Pp. 200 - 201.

'The Date of Kundamālā' / by A.C. Woolner. *Annals of the Bhandarkar Oriental Research Institute; 1933-34,* Vol. XV, No. I - II. Pp. 236-239.

Datta, Kali Kumar. Critical survey of Dinnaga's Kundamala in relation to later Ramayana dramas in Sanskrit / by Kali Kumar Datta.

Ph.D. thesis approved by the University of Calcutta in 1960.

De, S.K. [On date and authorship]. *JRAS,* 1924 & 1935.

De, Sushil Kumar. Aspects of Sanskrit Literature. - Calcutta : Firma KLM, 1959.

Contents : 'On Kundamālā' P. 290.

Dinnāga. Kundamāla / by Dinnāga; ed. with a Sanskrit comm. by J.L. Shastri; English tr. with a critical introd. by Saran Dass Bhanot and Veda Vyas. - 3rd rev. ed. - Delhi : Motilal Banarsidass, 1983.

Pp. I - XLVII.

Introd. gives a detailed account of the date authorship and critical study of his work.

Encyclopaedia of Indian Literature . - New Delhi : Sahitya Akademi, 1987.

Pp. 1050-51, 2184-85.

Garg, Ganga Ram. An encyclopaedia of Indian literature. - Delhi : Mittal Publishers, 1982. Pp. 103, 200.

Gera, Vimla. Mind and art of Bhavabhuti. - Delhi : Meharchand Lachhmandas, 1973.

Pp. 254-270.

Kane, P.V. 'The Kundamālā and Bhāsa' / by P.V. Kane.

Annals of the Bhandarkar Oriental Research Institute 1929; Vol. X, Nos. I'- II, Pp. 153-154.

Keith, A. Berriedale. The Sanskrit drama in its origin, development, theory and practice. - Oxford : OUP, 1924.

405 p.; 22 cm.

Keith, A. Berriedale. Sanskrit - Natak : udbhav aur vikas : siddhanta aur prayog / tr. into Hindi by Udaybhanu Singh. - Delhi : Motilal Banarsidass, 1965.

'Kundamala of Dinnaga'. *Journal of Asiatic Society* (Bengal); 1964; Vol. 6, No. 2; Pp. 117 - 118.

Book review.

Levi, Sylvain. The theatre of India / tr. from the French by Narayan Mukherji. - Calcutta : Writers Workshop, 1978.

Contents : Dinnāga. (Vol. 1) P. 143.

Kundamala (Vol. 1) P. 119.

Masterpieces of Indian Literature (Vol. 3) / ed. by K.M. George . - New Delhi : National Book Trust, 1997.

P. 1967.

'On Kundamala' / by S.K. De. *Annals of the Bhandarkar Oriental Research Institute;* 16. 1934 - 35, P. 158.

Pandey, Radhakant. Comparative study of Kundamala of Dinnaga and Uttararamacharita of Bhavabhuti / by Radhakant Pandey.

Ph.D. thesis approved by the Kanpur University in 1974.

Pathak, M.C. Sanskrit nāṭaka men atiprākṛta tattva. - Jaipur : Devanagar Prakashan, [n.d.].

18, 468 p.

'Pratima and Kundamālā / by D.R. Mankad. *Annals of the Bhandarkar Oriental Research Institute; 1930; Vol. XII, No. I,* Pp. 97 - 98.

Sahitya Akademi - New Delhi . The National bibliography of Indian literature. - New Delhi : The author, 1962 - 1990.

5 Vols.

Pp. 16 - 20.

Satyavrat. On some readings in Kundamālā / by Satyavrat. *Vishweshwaranand Indological Journal;* 1978; Vol. 16, No. 1. Pp. 47-54.

Sethi, Atmaram. Anudit Hindi sahitya : vishishta grantha - suchi / by Atmaram Sethi. - Gurgaon : Indian Documentation Service, 1981.

Contents : Sanskrit (Pp. 1 - 624).

Srivastava, Neerja. Critical study of Dinnaga's Kundamala / by Neerja Srivastava.

Ph.D. thesis approved by the Avadh University in 1984.

Subramanya Iyer, K.A. Kundamālā and Uttararāmacarita / by K.A. Subramanya Iyer. *7th All India Oriental Conference;* Pp. 91 - 97.

'Treatment of pathos in Kundamala of Dinnaga' / by Lalita Kuppuswamy. *In* Treatment of pathos in Sanskrit dramas / ed. by Pushpendra Kumar and Kapila Vatsyayan. - Delhi : Nag Publishers, 1981.

Pp. (II : 10) 79-82.

Verma, Jaynarayan and Gupta, Pushpa. Sanskrit sahitya ka itihas. - Ghaziabad : Tarun Prakashan, 1991.

Woolner, A.C. [on date and authorship]. *ABORI*, Vol. XV.

7

Harṣadēva

A multifaceted personality, Śriharsa was a king, emperior, military genius, organiser, patron of letters, poet, dramatist who was born about 590 A.C. Harsa or Harsha - Vardhana was the second son of Prabhākaravarḍhana and Yaśomaṭī. His father was the king of Sthānvīśvara (modern Thāneswar). The king of Sthānvīśvara was in constant conflict with Huns, Gurjaras and Malawas and attained considerable success. His capital was Dhaneswar and Kanauj. But his career was cut short by his unexpected death in A.D. 64.

Harsha's only sister Princess Rājyaśri was married to Grahavarmā, the Kanyakubja ruler of the Maukhari dynasty, who was killed by the King of Mālawa. In an expedition against the King of Mālawa to weak his vengeance for wrongfully confining Harṣa's sister Rājyaśrī, his elder brother Rājyavardhana, though won the battle, but was treacherously stained by the vanquished king's ally, Saśānka, king of Bengal.

After Rājyavardhana the ministers offered the crown to young prince Harsha and he accepted it not without some reluctance at first and not without consult of a Buddhist oracle. He was crowned in 604 A.D. and infact, assumed the royal title only in 612 A.D. The task of his empire building began in October, 606 A.D. at the minor age of sixteen.

After ascending the throne, started for Kanauj to avenge the death of his brother and eventually rescued his sister and within five years he seized the northern parts of India and reigned happily till 647 A.D.

In his Harsacarita, Bāna deals comprehensively with the life and greatness of his patron king Harshavardhana. But his story ends abruptly. He does not tell us whether Harshavardhana could avenge the murder of his brother or not.

He undertook a series of military compaign and came to hold sway over the whole of Ganges basis covering Nepal and whole of the Hindustan including Uttar Pradesh, Bihar, Bengal and Orissa.

He , however, failed in his venture to capture the Southern India and badly defeated at the hands of Chalukya Pulakesin II.

His last compaign was that of bringing under control the Ganjam district on the coast of the Bay of Bengal in 643 A.D., few years before his death. Thereafter, he did not undertake any further compaign, but led a peaceful life. Hiuen Tsang says that he became a Buddhist in his old age and that once in five years he gave away all his money in charity to the needy. In his times, the two rival creeds of Buddhism and Brahmanism were reconciled to some extent and his drama 'Nagananda' bears ample testimony to this fact.

Like his great predecessor Aśoka, he found peace and comfort in religion.

According to historians, Harṣa was a Buddhist, but at the sometime he was liberal in his attitude to other faiths reflections of which we not only find in his writings, but it is said that in the quinquennial assemblies held by him at Prayāga, he used to worship - Śiva, Viṣṇu and Buddha, all in turn.

Dramatist Śri-Harsha should not, however, be confused with the author of the Mahākāvya Naishadha - Charita and the philosophical treatise named Khaṇḍanakhaṇḍakhādya, 'Sri Harsha' who flourished in the second half of the twelfth century A.D. Wilson has suggested the name of another king Harsha of Kashmir who reigned from 1113 to 1125 A.D.

His court was the resort of erudite scholars such as Bāṇa, Ḍivākara, Mātanga and Mayūrabhatta (the author of Suryashataka), on whom he bestowed various prizes and gifts. It is said that Mātanga Diwākara was a Chāṇḍāla by caste but being a poetic genius, he earned a reputation equal to other court poets of Harṣa. Himself a great poet, it is a subject of controvery whether king Harṣ avarḍhana was the author of or patronized the author of three magnificient dramas Nāgānanḍa, Priyadarśikā and Raṭnāvalī.

Several doubts have been raised regarding Harshadeva's authorship of all three plays, especially on the strength of a stray remark of Mammṭa in his Kāvya - prakāśa and the explanation of the same by some of the commentations.

During his visit to India, the Chinese traveller Hieun Tsang visited the capital and offers us an excellent account of his court and administration.

Soddhala listed Śrī Harṣa, Munja, Bhojadeva, Vikramāḍītya etc as Kavīnḍras and eulogises Hārṣa. Jayadeva cites Harṣa alongwith Bāṇa, Rāmila, Saumila etc. Ḍamoḍaragupta uses excerpts from Raṭnāvali and calls it the work of a royal author.

Plays of Shri Harsha occupies an eminent position in the domain of Sanskrit dramatic literature. In all, three dramas namely Ratnavali, Priyadarshika and Nagananda are ascribed to him because of the similarity of ideas and expression in all three. Scholars such as Eltinghausen, Levi, Henry, Windisch accept Hharsha's authorship of all these three dramas.

His plays Ratnavali and Priyadarshika revolve round the same theme ie the Udayana and Vasavadatta legend and main plot is similar, but there are variations in the names of characters and in the events. Bela Bose feels that perhaps dissatisfied with the composition of the 'Priyadarshika' he sought to bringout an improved edition of the play and so came to write the 'Ratnavali'.

Otherwise why should an author would write two plays of a similar character, However, there seems to be consensus of opinion that Ratnavali marks in every way an improvement on the latter.

Scholars feel that the verses of Ratnavali are, as a rule, sweet and melodious and attain the rank of true poetry. Its elegant, straight forward, though somewhat artificial, style shows that the dramatist had great practice in writing. He constructed the plot of Ratnavali in strict comformity with rules of dramaturgy.

An extremely enjoyable play is 'Priyadarshika' which is a light comedy, merry and bright. Here Harsha can not claim any originality for the drama as the same subject matter was handled by Bhasa several centuries before him and in a masterly manner too. Harsha's dramtic genius is not certainly of the same order as Kalidasa's. But he will be reckoned not basically for his dramatic art but for his poetic style.

He is a master of chaste and undorned diction, his delicate use of words and equilibrium in structure gives him greater praise as a poet than as a dramatist.

It is generally agreed that 'Priyadarshika' was written first, then appeared an improved edition of the same under the title 'Ratnavali' followed by 'Nagananda' which was composed when dramatist's Buddhistic learnings became pronounced. This drama is acknowledged as a perfect creation of a mature dramatist.

In Nagananda the playwright changed from a gay to a grave subject which is based on a story narrated in the Kathasaritasagara. This moralised drama was highly revered when it was written. But with the decline of Buddhism in India, the play lost its popularity, The setting of this dramatic piece supernatural. This symbolic drama brings supernatural, human and sub - human characters in the same play. Godess Gauri figures in the play; the hero 'Jimutavahana' himself is super human; human characters like the heroine, Garuda, the tormentor a celestial bird and Sankhachuda the reptile serpent are symbolic of Buddha's love for all living beings. This universal love not only for human beings but also birds and animals has added importance to modern man who realises the importance of the well - being of the flora and fauna or the equilibrium of the co - system. The drama seeks to inculcate the lesson of self - sacrifice, to preach the doctrine of resignation, in the spirit of Buddhist jatakas. The play is, therefore, didactic in its tone.

The play, thus upholds noble traits of human character like self - sacrifice, charity and love for fellow being. This is perhaps the only Sanskrit drama which expounds Buddhists ideals of Universal love, ahiṃsa and brotherhood. The hero sacrifices his life for the sake of snake. The virtue of filiel piety is another dimension of this play. As stated, the Buddhist ideal of happiness for all creatures is the predominant spirit in this play. The hero 'Jjimutavahana' is believed to be a Bodisattiva or Buddha's incarnation. An outstanding drama, 'Nagananda' enjoys a special place in the studies of Buddhism. All important works on Buddhism refer to this drama.

Sri Harsa is also credited with the authorship of two stotras, the 'Suprabhatastotra' and the 'Ashtamahasrichaityastotra, and of a lexicon. Harṣavardhana died in C. A.D. 646.

Nāgānanda

Synopsis

Nāgānanda of Harṣadeva is a drama in five acts on the Buddhist legend of the self - sacrifice of Jīmūtavāhana which is told in the two Sanskrit versions of the Bṛhatkathā.

The hero of this play is Prince Jīmutavāhana, son of the king of the Vidyādharas who falls in love with Malayavati, daughter of the king of the Siddhas; then living in the forest.

In the hermit - grove, while Malayavati was playing upon the lute while attended by a handmaiden, Jimutavahana comes there and enchanted by the music, the prince in concealment praises her art.

The meetings results in love at first sight, but two have had to part for the time being. Tormented by her passion, the heroine seeks comfort in the sandal bower with her maiden, who places sandal - leaves as a balm upon her bosom. In the meanwhile, the hero and his companion approaches.

Through a misunderstanding and lack of communication on their part (which the hero says), the heroine, in despair of having her love requited, tries to commit suicide but is rescued by the Prince who unfolds his passion by a portrait which he has drawn of her and the consummation of their love is assured. Then their marriage takes place, but when the wedding feast was to served, the Jīmutavāhana is led in the fourt act to offer his own life to save that of a snake - deity who is doomed to be devoured by Garuḍa, the bird who is a foe to the serpent race.

In the end the sacrifice is made, but the savage bird is caused to relent, and the hero who is cruelly torn regains his life by the goddess Gaurī. Prince Jīmutavāhana is reunited with his wife and parents.

Dramatis Personae

Male

Atreya	...	The Jester.
Garuda	...	King of birds.
Jimutaketu	...	King of the Vidyadharas.
Jimutavahana	...	Son of Jjimutaketu, the Hero.
Mitravasu	...	Brother of the heroine.
Shandilya	...	A hermit.
Shankachuda	...	A serpent, offered to Garuda as victim.
Shekharaka	...	A voluptuary, Navamalika's lover.

Sunanda	...	Janitor.
Vasubhadra	...	Chamberlain.
Stage Manager, servants, etc.		

Female

Chaturika	...	Maidservant.
Gauri	...	Goddess
Kanakabati		Jimutaketu's queen, 'old lady'.
Malayavati	...	Mitravasu's sister, the Heroine.
Manoharika	...	Maidservant.
Navamalika	...	Do., Shekharaka's sweet - heart.
Old Female	...	Shankhachuda's mother.
		An Actress.

Characters Mentioned

Males

Kaushika	...	Religious preceptor.
King Vishvavasu	...	Mitravasu's father.
Matanga	...	A lord of the Vidyadharas, enemy of the hero.
Vasuki	...	King of serpents.

Females

Mother of Mitravasu.		
Pallavika	...	Garden-keeper.

Plot :

Act One :-

Prologue : Indra Festival

After the benedictory verses, the stage director informs the audience that on the occasion of Indra festival, 'the feudatory king of Sri Harsha has requested him to stage a play entitled 'Nagananda' composed by the Emperor himself. The play deals with the tale of the Vīdyādhara Jātaka. He adds that the dramatist is a clever poet, the audience would appreciate merit and thus he is sure of its success in stage - representation. 'Nāgananda' is dorned with all the required qualities such as attractive theme, skilled performers etc.. He, thus, calls his wife and we learns from him that his aged parents have retired for the penance grove. He also desires to follow them, in imitation of Jimutavahana, the hero of the play and subsequently the hero is introduced on the age.

Main Scene :- The scene is centred in the penance grove near the temple of Gauri. Jimutavahana, the youthful prince of Vīdyādharas accompanied by Artreya, the clown wanders about the forests of the Malaya mountain in search of a suitable place of residence as his father has expressed a desire to stay there. As a faithful son he has given up his own kingdom and would spend his youth in serving the old parents and such services would transcend the enjoyment of the pleasures of kingship. While in power, he had done everything to make his subjects happy and prosperous.

Moving around the mountain, they are struck by the grandeur of the Malaya and decides to stay there. They comes to a hermitage and happen to hear the delicate cadence of music from the Gauri temple of the hermitage and then conceals behind the thicket of Tamāla tree with his companion to find out who was singing. They find the heroine Malayavati is playing on the lute before the Godess Gauri. They overhear the secret conservation between the heroine and her lady - in - waiting. They learn that Malayavatī had a dream in which Goddess Gauri, being pleased with her devotion conferred a boon that her future husband will be the Emperor of Vidyadharas.

At this moment, the hero who is struck by her feminine beauty : is dragged by the jester into the presence of the heroine and love at first sight captures their hearts. The maid welcomes and offers them seals. But as a hermit emerges and takes her away with him (as Malayavati is to return home according to the orders of her father, 'King Visvavasu). From the sage, it is also learnt that Mitravasu has gone in search of Jīmūtavāhana now staying somewhere on the mountain in order to offer him the hand of his sister, Princess Malayavatī in marriage. The latter departs, leaving an indelible impression on his mind.

Act - Two

Interlude :- Two maids of Princess Malayavati hold a conservation which informs us that Malayavati desire to take a rest in the bower of sandal creepers as he was exhausted by the exertion of collecting the flowers and also by the autumnal heat. From the monologue of one of the maids we get a hint that it is not the external heat that troubles her. Malayavati is waiting for her brother Mitravasu, who had gone to Jimutavahana with the marriage proposal.

Main Scene marks a further stage in the development of the love between the Prince and the Princess. The focus is on the heroine which is love - sick, desires to go to the Sandal - bower and eventually reclines on the stone - slab, She confessed before her maid 'Chaturika', the secret of heart. The maid tries to allay her burning torment by applying sandal - juice to her bosom and tries to console her with cheering words. To dispel this torment when Malayavatī seeks her adrice, she suggests that the only remedy is the presence of the Prince.

Now the hero and hte jester approaches and hearing the sound of their foot - steps, both the girls hide behind a red Ashoka tree and observe the passers by. The hero confides to his companion, the jester a dream in which he has seen his beloved as seated on a stone - slab in the Sandal - bower and being angry with him through love and weeping for some unknown reasons. Ultimately they find the stone - slab and portrays the image of his love on the stone slab through his imagination with mineral dyes collected by his friend near the mountain. The heroine and the maid who were listening secretly to the conversation of the hero and the jester are led to believe that the hero has fallen in love with some other girl and consequently Malayavatī becomes very disappointed with the narration of his dream.

At this juncture, Mitrāvasu, the brother of the Princess who was sent by his father to the hero with proposals of marriage comes suddently. The hero at once conceals the painting on the slab with a plantain leaf. He expresses his father's wishes before the Prince, who declines to accept, thinking Malayavatī to be different from his sweet heart. This embarassing situation is saved by the wit of the jester who requests Mitravasu to obtain the consent of Jīmūtavāhana's father in this matter and Mitravasu retires.

Now the dissappointed heroine dismises her maid under some pretext, takes a drastic step to end her life by hanging herself with the noose of a creeper. Suspecting her intention, the maid hides nearby and raises an alarm as soon as she makes an attempt to do so. The hero rushes to the spot and rescues her. She is brought back to the very stone - slab and realizes that his beloved is the same as Malayavati whose hand he had just rejected. Seeing her own portrayal drawn by the hero, the Princess becomes convinced of his love for her. Finally a maid enters to announce that hero's parents have given consent to their marriage that was to be taken plce that very day.

Act - Three

The focus is on the Kusumakara garden, where all the Siddha and Vidyādhara people are enjoying a hearty banquet after the wedding ceremony. The introxicated Viṭa and Cheta enter with wineglass in his hand. Vīta is waiting for his sweatheart Navamālikā. The jester comes with his body wrapt up in red garments like woman to protect himself from the molestation of the bees Unable to control his passion, Vīta mistakes him for her and embraces him. Navamālika comes on the scene at this very moment. At first, she becomes very jealous thinking that he is coaxing some other girl. But the truth is unfolded and both Vīta and Navamālikā make fun of Jester. The helpless Jester prepares to fall at their feet.

After such humorous scene, a quite yet warm love - scene spread before the audience. The hero and the heroine enter. The former is charmed by the Venus - like beauty of his newly - wed bride and compares it to a lotus. However like a fleeting arrow, the happiest moment passes and the excited Mitravasu enters and breaks the sad news that his kingdom is plundered by Matanga and seeks hero's permission to destroy the foe. The hero, however, pained at the thought of punishing the enemy. He feels that even if his kingdom and his life were endangered, he would not grant permission.

They departs, the hero justifies his view point to Mitravasu by glorifying the sun who exerts himself for obliging the world.

Act - Four

Interlude :- Through a brief conversation between the Chamberlain of Mitrāvasu' father and the doorkeeper, the audience comes to know that the Chamberlain has been ordered by the mother of Mitravasu, the Queen to present the red garments to the bride (her daughter) and the bridegroom (the son-in-law) to be worn by them for a period of ten days on the auspicious Dīpāvali festival. Chamberlain adds that Jimutavahana has gone to the beach alongwith Mitravasu and the bride Malayavati was staying with her relations. The doorkeeper who enters at this moment tells us that he has been commanded by king Vishvāvasu to summon his son Mitravasu; as some gift is to be offered to his son - in - law on the occasion.

Main Scene :- The main scene shifts to the sea - shore where Jīmūtavahana and his brother - in - law Mitrāvasu has gone to take a stroll. High over the peaks of the Malaya mountain, they see piles of bones as while as the now - clad Himalayan peaks. From Mitrāvasu, the hero, learns that these are the bones of serpents devoured by Garuda, the king of birds who eats one serpent everyday according to an agreement made by the king of serpents Vasuki in order to save the 'Nāga' (serpent) race from its imminent extermination. Jimūtavāhana is shocked by this horrid news. At this stage, comes the door keeper and summons away Mitrāvasu at his father's request.

The hero is left alone and soon hears the heart - breaking lamentation's of a women. The cause of her wailing is her son, 'Shankhachuda', who was to be offered to Garuda on that day according to the pact. Hearing this, Jimutavahana volunteers to sacrifice his life in place of the young Nāga.

However, by his uncommon nobility 'Shankhachuda' wins the hearts of the audience when he says that he would not bring a stigma on his family and thus disapprove the hero's proposal to carryout the king's command. He decides to bow down to the Lord Shiva at the Southern Gokarna before Garuda arrives and departs with his mother.

There is no concession on Jimutavahana's side who is equally determined to sacrifice his life. He is fortunate enough to have Chamberlain at this crucial moments who enters with a pair of red garments presented by his Inlaws feels that his marriage with Malayavati has proved fruitful. He covers himself with the red garments which is the mark of a victim and he ascends the slaughter stone. Garuda comes and finally takes him away upto the summit of the mountain. The sound of celestial drums is heard and the Gods showere flowers in admiration of this unparallel heroic deed.

Act - Five

In this final act, A door keeper who was sent by the anxious king Visvavasu to ascertain the whereabouts of Jimutavahana, now enters and meets his aged parents accompanied by Malayavati. As he has not returned from the beach so far, all of them starts thinking that some evil might have befallen him. A crest jewel clinging to a peace of flesh smeared with blood falls at the feet of his father. The aged parents of the hero are struck with grief on seeing their son of the verge of death.

Jimutavahana admonishes Garuda from self destruction but advises him to expiate for his sin by abstaining from killing creatures, by diligently collecting merits by indulging in virtuous acts and serving the suffering humanity. Before dying Jimutavahana request Nāga Shankhachūḍa to help fold his hands in an effort to offer his last salutation to his parents. A funeral pyre is prepared and

Shankhachuḍa, Malayavati the aged parents of Jimutavahana are ready to burn themselves to death.

Garuḍa, now a completely a changed soul flies up into the sky to ask Indra to pour down ambrosial nectar to resuscitate the hero and all the lordly serpents previously killed by him. Malayavati invokes Goddess Gauri and the latter emerges on the scene. Pleased by her devotion and the self - sacrifice by Jimutavahana, revives Malayavati's husband and by an additional favour, the title of the Emperor of Vidyādharas is bestowed on him. At this juncture, the shower of nectar falls from the heaven that symbolizes the sincere expression of Garuḍa's atonement and everything ends happily.

Amidst uneasy presentiments, they becomes certain that it must be of Jimutavahana. After workshipping the Gokarṇa, Shankhachuda was hurriedly coming to his previous spot and to his utter disappointment, he finds that the noble one has really sacrificed his body in his stead during his brief absence. He follows the line of blood with tears in his eyes and comes before the anxious parents and informs them that their son has sacrificed his life to Garuda to save him. Unable to bear the pangs of his premature death, they resolve to give up their life. Thus clad in red garments, Shakhachūḍa followed by the three start towards the summit. As both the Nāga and the hero bear the same mark of a victim, Garuḍa is puzzled and is at a loss to know which one of them is his original prey. Garuḍa realizing the blunder committed by himself decides to atone for his sin by entering the fire. Garuḍa could never imagine that he could ever slain a noble and celebrated soul such as Vidyādhara about whom he has on many occasion heard through the hymns sung in glory of him everywhere.

Priyadarśika

Synopsis

'Priyadarśika' is a four-act drama that derives its title from the name of its heroine Priyadarsika or Priyadarśanā, who up to the time of the denoucement is called Aranyaka, ie, from having been found in the forest and is then discovered to have been a princess in disguise. Thus, Priyadarśikā is brought up in early childhood as a captive to the court of King Vatsa Udayana and is looked after by the Queen Vāsavadattā, until she shall be of marriageable age. The king falls in love with her and lateron finds that she is the daughter of a friendly monarch, Dṛḍhavarman, who had been imprisoned by an enemy more than a year ago or at the very moment when Priyadarśikā was accidently captured and brought to King Vatsa's court.

The king restores Dṛḍhavarman to his throne by overcoming his captor, the king of Kaliṅga. Eventually the play ends with the princess Priyadarśika's union with Vatsa Udayana.

Dramatis Personae

Male

Vatsaraja (or Udayana)	...	King of Kausambi, the Hero.
Rumanvat	...	Minister of king Vatsaraja.
Vijayasena	...	General of king Vatsaraja.
Vasantaka	...	Jester, companion of the king.
Vinayavasu	...	Chamberlain of Dridhavarma, king of Anga.
		Chamberlain of Mahasena Pradyot, king of Ujjaini, Hero's father - in - law. Stage Manager.

Female

Vasavadatta	...	Daughter of king Mahasena Pradyot of Ujjaini, Queen of king Vatsaraja.
Aranyaka	...	(or Priyadarshika or Priyadarshini) Daughter of Dridhavarma, king of Anga and first cousin of the Queen, the Heroine.
Samkrityayani	...	A cultured lady of rank.
Indivarika		
Manorama	...	Attendants of the Queen,
Kanchanamala		Attendants of the friends of the Heroine.
Yashodhara	...	Female door-keeper.

Persons Mentioned

Mahasena Pradyota	...	King of Ujjaini, the Queen's father.
Dridhavarma	...	King of Anga, the Heroine's father.
Vindhyaketu	...	Forest-king in whose charge the heroine was placed.

Yugandhara	...	Minister of king Vatsaraja.
Padmavati	...	Another Queen of king Vatsaraja.
Angaravati	...	Queen of Mahasena Pradyota, Vasavadatta's mother.
		A bard, retinue, etc.

Plot :-

Act One:-

In this act Dṛḍhavarman, king of Aṅga (The heroine's father) pledged his daughter in marriage to king Vatsa of Kauśāmbi (the hero). But the heroine Priyadarśikā's had had been repeatedly sought by the king of Kalinga. Disheartened and furious king, therefore, waged war against Dṛḍhavarman, ravaged his kingdom and made him prisoner.

Admist the battle, Dṛḍhavarman's daughter, ie, Priyadarśikā was saved by her father's faithful Chamberlain and was handed over to his ally, the forest - king Vindhyaketu for her safety. Now the Chamberlain left on a pilgrimage, but after a short sojourn he come back to find that Vidhyaketu was killed alongwith his followers by some unknown foes, the camp had been burned and there was no trace of the princess.

In the explanatory scene, all there incidents are narrated by the chamberlain himself who expresses his willingness to join Dṛḍhavarman. He further discloses that the King Vatsa, the hero who had earlier been held a captive by a powerful monarch of Avantī (Ujjain) called. Mahānsena - Pradyota; had by now escaped from bondage and had carried off his captor's daughter Vāsavadatta to whom he got married.

The scene now focuses on the king Vatsa's palace at Kauśāmbī. The King appears alongwith his favourite companion, the Brahman Jester Vasantaka. Their conversations gets interrupted by the entrance of Rumaṇvant, the prime minister and Vijayasena, the general of the army of Vatsarājā, who are the unknown assailant of Vindhyaketu, against whom he had been sent by Vatsa in pursuaance of some unmentioned grudge. He vividly describes his heroic deeds and tells the king that he has brought along a captive maiden, mistaken as the daughter of Vindhyaketu. The king gives an instant order that the young girl shall be looked after by the queen, Vāsavadattā and taught the accomplishments befitting her presumed rank and instructs that he shall be notified when it is time for her to wed, so that an appropriate marriage may be arranged. The first act closes with the King's intention of sending his successful and boon general to wage war against rancorous Kalinga.

Act Two: [A year or so has passed]

Queen Vasavadatta is observing a religious fast. The King is walking in the palace garden with the Jester, Vasantaka to dispel his loneliness. Here he catches sight of 'a beautiful damsel, ie, 'Priyadarsika' (who is known as 'Aryaṇyaka' till the time of the denouncement). Āryaṇyaka is now a fully grownup girl who at the intances of Queen has come to the garden alongwith another attendant 'Indīvarika' to pluck lotuses for an offering in connection with the religious ceremony.

Enchanted by her beauty King with the Jester hide behind a clump of bushes to overhear the conversation between the two maidens. He comes to know that 'Āraṇyaka' is none other than the supposed daughter of his late enemy 'Vidhyaketu'.

In the meanwhile, Āranyaka's companion withdraws to a distance for a while. While picking up the flowers, she is suddenly being attacked by bees lurking in the cluster of lotuses. Frightened Aranyaka calls to Indivarikā for help and covers her face with her mantle. At the initiation of the Jester the King rushes to her rescue and drives off the tormenting insects and gets a chance to embrace the maiden. By disregarding the Jester's advice to remain silent, and in his endeavour to comfort the maiden recites a stanza of impromptu poetry.

Startled Āraṇyakā had thought her rescuer to be Indīvarikā, but now learns that it is the king Vatsa with whom her father Dṛḍhavarman had planned her marriage. Though she is infatuated with the King, but at once calls in alarm to Indīvarikā. This compels Vatsa to go back to hinding again.

Āranyaka retires with her companion in pensive mood. Similarly the King allured by her beauty departs alongwith the Jester with the hope of meeting the damsel again in near future.

Act - Three (Perhaps a few days has elapsed)

Queen Vāsavadattā's friend and a learned lady named Sāṅkṛtyāyanī has penned a dramatic piece for the diversion of her royal mistress. This dramatic performance would based on an incident in the courtship of Vāsavadattā and her husband, the King. The Queen's part is to be enacted by Āraṇyaka, where the role of King Vatsa is entrusted to the Queen's attendant Manoramā. The audience comes to know about all this from Manoramā's monologue in the Introductory scene. Manorama's overhears Āraṇyaka in the garden expressing her eternal desire for the King and who is looking for some means to see the King again. At this moment, the jester appears in search of Āraṇyaka by the instruction of the King and the mutual love of hero and heroine is, therefore, made manifest. Clever and artful Manorama whispers to the Jester the best device for bringing them together.

The scene now shifts to a room in the palace, arranged as a playhouse, where the Queen with her attendants and Sāṅkṛtyāyani comes to witness a scene from the play. Thus the play within the play begins with Āraṇyakā appearing in the role of the Queen, but instead of Manoramā, the King himself enters secretly to assume his own part. This becomes a golden opportunity for him to make love to Āraṇyakā in person. Seeing the King's intense desire, Queen becomes suspicious. Very soon the truth is revealed from the lips of the Jester, who while sleeping in the adjoining room, confesses everything in his drowsiness.

The play is interrupted by Vāsavadatta in anguish and orders that both Āraṇyaka and the Jester should be thrown into prison. King fails in his venture to pacify the Queen who leaves the stage in high dudgeon.

The King also retires for the night planning some means to propitiate his jealous Queen, who has hurried Āraṇyakā and the Jester off to prison.

Act - Four (A short interval of time has elapsed)

In this final act, Aranyaka emerges and reveals that Āraṇyakā is still imprisoned by the Queen and in her despair is meditating suicide. Meanwhile comes another attendant named Kañcanamāla who informs Manorama that the Queen is worried by a letter from her mother telling that King Dṛḍhavarman, husband of her mother's sister is still a captive of the King Kaliṅga and 'more than a year' has elapsed. This shows that the Queen was ignorant about the fact that the King had already sent an expedition against Kalinga months ago to uproot him and thereby, to release Dṛḍhavarman.

The scene shifts to the 'Ivory tower' of the palace where the disconsolate Vāsavadattā is seated. While Queen friend Sāṅkṛtyāyanī desperately tries to assure her of the King's continued affection. The latter appears with the Jester, now released, and discussing the means to appease the Queen to cause Araṇyaka's freedom.

King unfolds before the Queen that he is waiting for the news of his victory over Kaliṇga. At this very moment the general Vijayasena himself enters to announce his triumphal success and brings the tindings of Kaliṅga's death in the battle. Vijayasena is accompanied by Vinayavasu, the old Chamberlain of Dṛḍhavarman who appeared in the Explanatory scene at the beginning of the play. With the victory of Vatsa's forces, Dṛḍhavarman regains his kingdom. In this happy occasion, the Chamberlain. narrates the sad tale of the disappearance of the Dṛḍhavarman's daughter Priyadarśika, who was left in charge of Vindhyaketu in the forest. At this juncture, Queen Vāsavadattā gives orders for Āranyakā's release and deeply touched by the sad news of the loss of her cousin 'Priyadarsika' whose whereabout is not known to anyone. Suddenly Manorama rushes in and breaks the shocking news that in despair, Āraṇyakā' has committed suicide by taking poison. At the instances of the Queen, Āranyakā is brought and led on the stage in a dying condition. As the King is skilled in his use of magic spells, he might be the right person to save her life. The old Chamberlain of the restored monarch recognizes 'Araṇyaka' as 'Priyadarśikā', the lost daughter of Dṛḍhavarman and explains her relatinship to the Queen, who is her cousin. King Vatsa comes to the rescue and by employing his magic formulas, restores the heroine to life. Vāsavadattā is happy to have her couin 'Priyadarśika' and to fulfil Dṛḍhavarman's pledge unites Priyadarśika to the King as another wife and all ends happily.

Ratnavali

Synopsis

The daughter of the king of Ceylon called 'Ratnāvalī' (with which also runs the title of the play) has been destined by a prophecy to become an additional wife to king Vatsa Udayana who is already married to Vāsavadattā. While on her way to consummate this royal alliance, Ratnāvalī (or Sāgarikā) is shipwrecked at sea, but is rescued and brought to King Vatsa's capital. Here his chief minister places her under the care of Queen Vāsavadatta without disclosing her identity as a princess. That is why she is known in the play as 'Sāgarika', because of having been rescued from the ocean (ie, sāgara). In the palace garden, Sāgarīka meets the king by chance that results in mutual love.

This amorous intrigue in which the use of disguise plays a part, is helped on by the damsel's friend and by the King's Jester, but is revealed before the Queen, who causes both Sāgarikā and the Jester to be thrown into prison.

However, a solution to the crisis is soon found. Through a magician's artifice, a fire breaks out in the palace that places the imprisoned maiden in imminent danger, but she is gallantly rescued by the King. At this juncture, enters her royal father's minister, who had escaped from the shipwreck in which the princess was thought to have been lost, results in an instant recognition of Sāgarika as Ratnāvalī, the destined bride of King Vatsa Udayana. Now the Ratnavali is related to the Queen as a cousin and the latter accepts Ratnavali as a co-wife. In this rejoicing moment, another happy news comes that King Vatsa's general Rumaṇvant has triumphed over the rival King of Kosala.

Dramatis Personae

Males

Babhravya	...	The Chamberlain of the King of Vatsa.
Shambarasiddhi	...	A magician.
Udayana	...	King of Vatsa, the Hero.
Vasantaka	...	King's companion, the Jester,
Vasubhuti	...	Prime Minister of the King of Ceylon.
Vijayavarma	...	An Army Officer.
Yaugandharayana	...	The Prime Minister.
The Stage - Manager		

Females

Chutalatika		
Kanchanamala	...	Attendants of the Queen.
Madanika		
Nipunika		
Ratnavali or Sagarika	...	Daughter of King of Ceylon, the Heroine.
Susamgata	...	Attendant of the Queen.
Vasundhara	...	"

An Actress

Persons Mentioned

Kaushambika	...	A female attendant.
Rumanvat	...	General of the King of Vatsa.

Sanjayavarma	...	Elder brother of Vijayavarma.
Shrikhandadasa	...	.. A sage.
Vikramavahu	...	King of Ceylon.

Plot :-

Act - One :-

Prologue (Scene 1 Ratnavali)

At the end of the invocation, the stage - director informs the audience that he has been requested by the feudatory king of Sri Harsha to enact the drama called 'Ratnavali' designed by him. He congratulates himself upon his fortune of having to stage a drama by such a clever poet as Sri Harsha before a distinguished audience as the one in front of him, with the help of expert players. He delighted to present the beautiful story of Vatsaraja on the occasion of the spring festival. He now seeks his wife for the preparations.

But the worried wife is anxious as to how the marriage of their daughter can take place when the bridegroom, to whom she has been betrothed by her father, war in a far - away land. The stage director says that if fortune be favourable, it will of its own accord, somehow effect the desired union, however far removed the object of their desire might be.

At this moment 'Yaugundharāyana'; the minister of Vatsaraja appears on the stage and approvingly repeats his remarks. The stage director introduces the minister to the audience and retires with his wife.

Scene II (The Prelude)

In this scene, Yaugandharayana introduces the audience with the incidents that have occured before the play commences. He declares that a merchant of Kausambi brought the daughter of the King of Simhala (Ceylon) to the capital after saving her from a shipwreck and that he offered her to the care of Queen Vāsavadatta who names her Sagarika (as found in the sea). We also learn from him that Ratnāvali alias Sāgarika is destined to become the consort if a man who would become the ruler of the world according to prophecy, on account of which he solicited the Ceylonese King to give his royal assent to Ratnavali's marriage with Vatsarāja Udayana.

Scene III : The Cupid's festival

Main scene is laid in the Makaranda garden of the king's palace at Kaushambi. The King ascends to the top of his palace alongwith his companion to enjoy the sight of joyous spring festival, the day when his citizens are gay making merrimant and fun. At this rejoicing moment two maids enter, dancing and sing ing and the Jester joins them and makes himself merry for a time. Now these people extend to the King the Queen's invitation to the function of Cupid worship to be performed by her under the red Ashoka tree, the King accepts the invitation with pleasure, desends and starts for the Makaranda garden.

Scene IV : The worship of Kama

The King and the jester appear in the Makaranda garden expressing its beauty. Sāgarikā brings materials for worship of the God. As she approaches the Asoka tree in the garden, the Queen jealously guards Sāgarika and is prevented from falling into the undesirable ken of King Udayana. She sends her away from the place on some pretext, before the King arrives there. Now the worship takes place in the presence of the King. The Queen first worships Kamadeva, next the King and then offers some gifts to the Jester. Desiring to witness the worship, Sāgarika remains in vicinity unseen by Queen Vāsavadattā, she observes the rituals from behind a tree. She mistakes the hero for the God of Love. But soon realizes that the very 'Cupid is King Udayana to whom she was betrothed by her father. Sāgarikā cherishes a secret longing for him. She leaves before the King and the Queen retire from the garden after sunset.

Act - Two :

Interlude (Scene I)

Susangatā, the maid is found to be loitering with a parrot cage in her hand and in search of her fond friend Sāgarikā who has gone leaving the parrot to her, and on the way she meets Nīpuṇika, also a maid, who informs that today the King Udayana is going to make his favourite jasmine putforth untimely blossoms by dint of the secret method he learnt from a medicant and that Sāgarika has been seen by her repairing to the plantain arbour sorrowfully. She is love - sick and is carrying with her some painting materials perhaps to draw a picture of the King to distract her mind from the unbearable sorrow.

Scene II

In the arbour, Sāgarika finds herself deeply in love with the King, but sees no hope of union with him. She feels that she has only to pine away and to divert herself from her hapless condition, she decides to paint the likeness of the King on the painting board.

As she was drawing the picture, Susangatā comes silently from behind and watches the progress of her painting and then suddenly she appears unnoticed and seizes the picture board. Sāgarika now confides the whole story about her love to her, who in turn not only consoles her, but after admiring her aspirations, draws Sāgarikā's picture on the board by the side of the King Udayana. In the meanwhile, a monkey gets loose from the stables and opens the parrot - cage. Eventually the bird flies away, but picks up all the two girls dialogues and repeatedly recites what it has memorized during the two girls conversations. The girls runs after it and in confusion, leaves the picture board in the plantain bower.

Scene III : The first Meeting

The King accompanied by the jester comes to the garden to enjoy the sight of the Jasmine creeper which has put forth blossoms by the efficacy of the treatment and desires that the Queen Vasavadatta should also witness the same with him. On the way they happen to hear the 'parrot perched upon the Bakula tree all the conversations, (containing the confessions of Sāgarika) that it memorized. Hearing this, the jester laughs loudly that frightens the bird away. On entering the bower they find the picture - board and atonce the King's sensuality is roused and his passion is inflamed and is presently fervently enamoured of her. Sāgarika overhears what the King is speaking and now Susangatā emerges and comes to the same bower under the pretext of fetching the picture - board and she presents the King to Sāgarika. The King is struck by her beauty. The two girls are parted by the arrival of the Queen (alongwith Kānchanmāla) who is now out to appreciate the jasmine plant. But the picture board drops down from the armpit of the jester and is offended at the sight. The King tries to pacify her in vain. She walks away to the palace in excuse of a headache.

Act III

Scene I : The Interlude

Before the main scene commences, the audience is aquainted in the form of a short dialogue between Madanika nad Kānchanmālā regarding a secret arrangement that has been contrived by the jester Vasantaka and Susangatā in order to effect a second meeting between the King and Sāgarika in the disguise of the

Queen to the picture - gallery in the evening and the jester will be waiting to take Sāgarika to the King in the Madhavi bower. They further informs us that Vāsavadattā has grown more cautious and suspicious due to the 'picture - board' incident and that Udayana is seized with love - sickness. Kanchanmala has overheard the conversation between the jester and Susangata and new goes to report it to the Queen.

Act III

[Scene II : The Rendezvous]

The love - distracted King waits for the jester Vasantaka. There comes the jester dancing with apparent joy and King becomes glad to hear from him that in consultation with Susangata he has arranged a secret meeting with Sagarika in the Madhavi bower and as a reward, the King offers him his own gold bracelet. The King now reaches the confidential spot and awaits the arrival of Sāgarika in the dark. Vasantaka goes to bring Sāgarika who would be in disguise as Queen and leaves behind the restless King with a longing for her.

To frustrate their plan, the Queen who is now well informed about the cunning plot and goes to the place herself accompanied by Kānchanamāla who makes a secret signal by snapping her fingers at which the jester leads them to the King and informs him that he has brought his love, Sāgarikā. The King with impatient longing unfolds his feelings for her which inturn becomes unbearable for the Queen Vasavadatta. She removes her veil and thereby discloses her identity. For his insolance, he is badly rebuked by the Queen. He lays prostrate at her feet begging for her forgiveness. The Queen, however, departs with her maid without perdoning the King. The King reproves the jester for his inadvertence, but the latter is confused as to how his plan has been failed. He goes for the palace to pacify the angry Queen.

On the way he meets the Sāgarika in the disguise of the Queen. Sāgarika is determined to end her life by hanging herself with a creeper - noose. She feels this act to be much more preferable than to be disgraced at the hand of Queen who is bent upon preventing her union with the King. Her lamentations fall on the King's ears, who at once dissuades her from the attempt and embraces her to his exclusive satisfaction. Repentant of her previous conduct, the Queen returns back only to conciliate the King, but finds them in passionate love - making. Vāsavadattā orders the arrest of Sāgarika and the Jester, who are led away, but leaves the King to bemoan his condition.

Act Four :

Scene I : The Interlude

The forlorn and helpless girls Sāgarika is according to a rumour sent away by the Queen to where God only knows. But infact, she is confind in a secret cell in the palace by the Queen. Susangata has been asked by Sāgarika in prison to give her necklace of gems to any Brahmin as her last present. This is the same jewel necklace which her father gave her when she sent her to Vatsaraja. In the final act, this neclace helps the minister of Simhala in the identification of the heroine 'Ratnavali'.

Pacified by the King, the Queen releases the jester who enters in a gay mood and Susangata offers the precious necklace to him.

Scene II : The Victory

The jester reports to the King that Sāgarikā is been exiled to Ujjayini and disheartened by the news, the King grows inexplicably lonely. The jester also narrates the story of the necklace to the King who examines it and asks the Jester to wear it round his neck so that he may be diverted by it. Before us spreads an altogether different scene. The dramatist skillfully transform the mental condition of the King from disappointment and sadness to joy and expectation. The nephew of Rumanvant is shown in who congratulate the King on the victory of Rumanvant, his commander, over the King of Kosalas. Being asked, he presents meticulously the entire war fare in which the Rumanvant has shown immense courage and finally succeeded in slaying the King of Kosala. Pleased by his heroic deed, the King orders Yaugandharayana to honour his commander in a fitting manner.

Scene III : The Magic

At the Queen's request, a magician of Ujjayini is brought in by Kānchanamālā. Both the King and the Queen enjoy the magical entertainment in pleasant amazement. The show is abandoned abruptly when Vasundhara, a female doorkeeper announces the arrival of Vasubhūti and Bābhravya. The magician leaves with a word that another show will be shown sometime.

Vasubhuti, the minister of the King of Simhala (Ceylon) and Babhravya, the Chamberlain of Vatsaraj had earlier escaped from the shipwreck and joined Rumanvant and comes to Kausambi.

Yaugandharayana feels that it would most appropriate occasion to identify Sāgarika and unite her to the King. He, thus, sends the minister and the Chamberlain to the King. By seeing the neclace on the jester's neck, Vasubhuti recalls which was presented to Princes Ratnavali by the King on parting with his daughter. They relate to the King Udayana and the Queen Vasavadatta the whole story about the ill - fated princess Ratnāvalī, about her betrothal to the King, about the unfortunate journey and her consequent vanishment due to shipwreck.

At this juncture, Yaugandharayana employs the services of the magician to make the palace appear as if on fire. The Queen who was shocked to know of the fate of her cousin and the ill treatment meted out to her, now shows her concern for the Sagarika alias Ratnavali and request the King to save her from the devilish flames. Unmindful of his own safety, the gallant King rushes into the fire and saves her from the terrible fire that brokeout in the harem.

Ratnavali is rescued, the fire miraculously subsides, Ratnavali is brought to the presence of the minister who recognises and identifies her, Yaugandharayana admits that without seeking his master's permission, he tried to effect King's union with the Princess. And finally Vasavadatta accepts her as her co-wife and thus, everything ends happily.

Plays in Performance

From Harṣacharita we learn that the stage formed one of the main entertainments during the age of Harṣa. All the three plays of Harṣa were presented before the imperial audience and on the occasion, many distinguished visitors, guests and feudatories were invited.

Citizens and theatre lovers used to flock to the capital and are all addressed by Sutradhara in the very begining. The Janapada of Sthāṇviśvara was looked upon as a concert - hall by the actors (lāsakaiḥ). These reference to actors are definite evidences of dramatic performances. One of the companions of Bāṇa was a young actor (Śailāliyuva) named Śikhanḍaka. It is mentioned in the biography that women were also interested in theatre. At the courts a stage-manager was employed. This job was also entrusted to a lady. We meet Muktikā, the manager of the drama, who was crying aloud near Rājyaśrī in the Vindhya forest. It appears that the lady was intimately associated with the princess.

Nagananda

I-tsing, the Chinese traveller (671-695) had referred to the play Nāgananda written by King Harsha. He visited India after the demise of Harṣadeva, recalls his contributions in the field of fine arts and literature in his travel accounts. He tells that the King Shilāditya (Harṣadeva) had got staged the story of Bodhisattva Jimūtavāhana with actors and musicians. In his own words :

'King Siladitya versified the story of the Bodhisattava Jimutavahana (Chinese : 'Cloud Brone') who surrounded himself in the place of a Naga. This version was set to music (Lit : string and pipe). He had it performed by a band accompanied by dancing and acting thus popularised it at his times'. (A record of Buddhist religion as practised in India, Pp. 163-164). According to the account of this Chinese traveller I-tsing, the royal author had his drama on the Bodhisattva's self - sacrifice, the Nāgananda (Delight of Snakes), staged during a mela, or religious gathering, that he held Harṣa.

Kūdiyāttam is one of the most ancient and popular of Kerala's entertainments which is generally acted during night. It has pan - Indian importance for in this we have the Sanskrit dramas staged. Here the particular act of the particular drama is enacted. Chākyar's act the chosen act of the chosen drama, because to produce a whole play require the better part of several months. In Kerala, a Kudiyattam performance may take atleast five days or it may extend up to eleven days. Thus, in the partial fashion, the Chākyār's stage few dramas. Though their repertory's forte is Rama plays, but Harsha's Nāgananda is also performed. K. Rama Pisharoti wrote in the *Quarterly Jjournal of the Mythic Society,* April 1922 that their preference for Nāgananda shows, but the impress left upon us by a Buddhist wave which must once have swept over Kerala.

The real importance of Kūṭiyāṭṭam in the history of the production of Sanskrit plays lies in the stage manuals which have been handed down from generation to generation. The language of these stage manuals is the local language of Kerala, Malayāḷam However in case of Nāgānanda (Delight of Snakes), the stage manual is written in Sanskrit giving full details for the direction and production of performances in Kūṭiyāṭṭam form.

Dramatic Association called 'Āndhra Bhāsābhimānī Samājam' was incepted on 31st April 1899 to enact the plays of Vedam Venkataraya Sastry. The eminent Telugu scholars like Sri Poondla Ramakrishnayya, Ganapati Yenadi Reddi and a host of others associated themselves with this organisation. The Samajam felt that Venkataraya Sastry was the dramatist and the other Telugu playwrights were nowhere. The group attracted enlightened graduates, poets, writers and many of the old students of Sri Sastry who happened to settle down at Nellore. Sri Sastry was made the President of the Samajam and under his direction it started enacting his Telugu rendering of Sanskrit classics. It included Harsha's Nagananda (published in 1891). The Samajam functioned upto 1925.

In post-independence phase, under the auspices of the Bharatiya Vidya Bhavan's Kala Kendra, Bombay, the eight Inter - Collegiate Dramatic Competition was held in the first week of September 1958 at the Bharatiya Vidya Bhavan in which three Colleges, Elphinstone College; Wilson College and K.C. College participated. Sriharsha's Sanskrit classic 'Nagananda' was chosen for this competition. Though a students production; there was a record crowd.

A scene from "Nagananda" staged in the Bharatiya Vidya Bhavan Kala Kendra Inter-Collegiate Drama Competition held in Bombay in September 1958.

Performance of Nagananda of Harsha by Kerala Kalamandalam in Kutiyattam idiom is preserved today in the Sangeet Natak Akademi's Audio-visual archive. It was done during the Kutiyattam Mahotsavam of the Akademi from 24-29 March, 1995.

Priyadarshika

The Chinese pilgrim Hiuen Tsang visited Indian during the reign of King Harsha and the latter honoured him by holding two religious assemblies one at

Kanauj and the other at Prayag. It has been surmised that the King's famous dramas 'Priyadashika' and 'Nagananda' were enacted at the first assembly.

Shri Vedam Venkataraya Sastry (21/12/1853 - 18/6/1929) was a dominant figure in the Telugu literary field for over a half a century beginning from the last quarter of the nineteenth century and ending with the first of the twentieth. This literary giant, became a by word for Sanskrit and in 1886, he was appointed as Sanskrit Pandit at the Madras Christian College where he served till 1910. An important factor in the life of Sri Venkataraya Sastry was his dramatic activity as a literary past time. He was not only a playwright but a stage director as well. In the eighties of the 19th century its was his practice to see that every year his students at college enacted the Sanskrit Drama prescribed for that year. Thus he saw Nagananda, Priyadarsika of Harsha; Śākuntala of Kalidasa; Bhavabhuti's Uttararamacarita and the like enacted year after year.

Even outside the educational limits, associations of Sanskrit lovers enacted these dramas in its original form.

Ratnavali

V. Raghavan in his article entitled *'Performance in ancient India'* tells us that at the end of eighth century A.D., Dāmodaragupta, minister of King Jayāpīḍa, a great enthusiast of dance and drama, wrote a poem called *'Kuṭṭanīmata'* in which he described the enactment of the opening act of the classical drama Ratnāvali of King Harṣavardhana. The venue is Banaras. A prince, Samarabhaṭa, who had come there on a pilgrimage, inquires of a dance master what the stage of dance and drama in that city may be. He replies that he migrated to Banaras on the death of the royal dramatist. He has a drama troupe of pupils which is trained in presenting *'Ratnāvali'*. This troupe consists wholly of actresses who play both the female and male roles. His chief pupil is Mañjarī, who plays the title role. In the course of praising her art, the teacher refers to the essential qualities and components of acting : effort and training; natural beauty; skill in different poses and grace of movement; proper intonation of the words of the text; nourishment of rasa that must be conveyed with concentration; identification with the feelings portrayed and the manifestation of the voluntary physical reactions of those feelings (sattva), which earlier the teacher emphasized as the most essential thing in acting; gestures of the hands with the appropriate turns of the arms and many other points. Expert actress that Mañjarī is, she can remove completely from the hearts of the spectators the sense of duality, the character verses the actor, and elicit their exclamations of admiration. While some actions may be common to the pangs of separation in love and actual pathos, she can, with her skill, show the subtle distinction between the two states.

Then the actual presentation of the opening act of Ratnāvali with Mañjari and other actresses begins. The poem describes the setting of the whole orchestra, the entry of the stage manager to the music of the flute and songs relating to his entry (prāveśikī dhruvā), the other typs of songs (dhruvā), and the introduction of the play. It then brings on the characters of the main act - Minister Yaugandharāyaṇa and King Udayana - to witness the spring festival going on in the grounds below. It follows the action of the act step by step. The main and attendant feelings (bhāva) to be portrayed by the different actors are mentioned. Then the explanation of how the festival is to be portrayed by the actors through improvisations of several amorous acts is given. As we read further, we find instructions for the actor on how the text written by the dramatist was to be integrated with music and dance and how a passage or verse was to be interpreted. Two maids of the palace enter dancing and recite a verse about the god of love hitting with his flower - arrows the hearts of lovers already made soft by the spring season. How this is to be rendered in hand gestures and poses of the limbs is set forth. Then the King, looking on and enjoying the dance of the maids in a spring of abadon, praises them in a verse of his own. That the actor playing the King's role is to intepret this verse and bring out its meaning through improvisation, reveals a most important aspect of how the art of acting (abhinaya) functions in Indian drama. The maids are then said to exit behind the curtain and when Queen Vāsavadattā enters with her retinue, the curtain is said to be removed. At the end of the act, the King, along with others, is said to leave the stage to the exit-song, naiṣkrāmikī dhruvā. The producer of the play (nṛtyācārya) receives from the prince a whole village as a present for the performance.

In modern period, in Calcutta Raja Pratap Chandra Sinha became very popular for patronizing the Bengali theatre of his time. On 31 July 1858, 'Belgatchhia Theatre' was opened in Calcutta at the Belgatchhia Villa belonging to brothers Pratap Chandra Sinha and Iswar Chandra Sinha, the Rajas of Paikpara. This private theatre started with Harshadeva's Sanskrit play 'Ratnavali' in Bengali which was rendered by Ramnarayan Tarkaratna. Nearly ten thousand rupees was spent on this massive production. That was witnessed by distinguished audiences such as Sir Fredrick Halliday, Lt. Governor of Bengal, Pandit Iswar Chandra Vidyasagar, Michael Madhusudan Dutt, Peary Charan Mitra, Kishori Chand Mitra, Ramgopal Ghosh, Rajednra Lal Mitra, Harish Chandra Mukhopadhyay, Ramaprasad Ray etc. Michael Madhusudan Dutt wrote an English synopsis of the play for English men. It was a very satisfactory outcome for all involved in this venture. Special mention could be made of Keshab Chandra Ganguli for his portroyal of 'Vidushak'. The music was conducted by Kshetra Mohan Goswami alongwith Jadunath Pal, the first Indian Orchestra played in the theatre. Music director was Maharaja Jatindra Mohan Tagore. The play was a roaring sucess from all angle, be it acting music or direction. The reviews appeared on 4 August 1958 in *Sumbad Prabhakar* and 5 August 1958 in the *Hindu Patriot*. Deeply inspired by the production, Michael went, on to write a play 'Sarmistha' for this theatre in which he discarded classical norms of Sanskrit dramas and adopted his own fresh technique and for the first time in Bengali theatre, the blank verse.

The dramatis personae was chosen by Babu Keshab Chandra Ganguly. He was a man with good taste for theatre, supervised and trained the whole troupe.

Many actors from Oriental theatre took part in it and were trained by Shri Keshavchandra Gangopadhyay. The dramatis personae were :-

King Udayana	:	Priyanath Datta
Vasantaka	:	Keshavchandra Gangopadhyay
Rumnvant	:	Raja Iswarchandra Sinha
Yaugandharayana	:	Gaurdas Basak / Dinanath Ghosh / Tarachand Guha
Babhrabya	:	Nabinchandra Mukhopadhyay
Bāhubhuti	:	Girishchandra Chattopadhyay
Vasavadatta	:	Mahendranath Goswami / Chunilal Basu
Ratnavali	:	Hemchandra Mukhopadhyay
Kanchanmala	:	(A Brahmin of Shri Rampur)
Susangata	:	Aghorchandra Digharia
Bajikar	:	Srinath Sen
Darban	:	Jadunath Ghosh
Sutradhar	:	Kshetramohan Goswami
Chopdar - 1	:	Dwarkanath Mallik
Chopdar - 2	:	Krishnagopal Ghosh

Nati	:	Ramanath Laha
Nartaki - 1	:	Kalidas Sanyal
Nartaki - 2	:	Kaliprasanna Bandyopadhyay

There were six shown of the play and last performance was on 19 October [24 Kartik] 1858. As stated, the music was rendered by Maharaja Jatindramohan Tagore. Eminent musician Kshetramohan Goswami employed many indigenous instruments for the play. The songs were written by Gurudayal Ray.

Keshav Chandra Ganguli who did the role of Vidusaka for 'Ratnavali' staged at Paikpura was regarded by Raja Pratap Narayan Sinha as the best jester that he had seen.

At one place, Jogindranath Basu in his *'Reminiscences of Michael Madhusan Dutta'* has quoted Gaurdas Basak who commented about the performance of Ratnavali by Belgatchhia Theatre in the following words :-

"To say that the Belgatchhia theatre scored brilliant success, is to repeat a truism that has passed into a proverb. It actuated a success unparalleled in the annals of Amateur Theatricals in this country. The graceful stage, the superb sceneries, the stiring orchestra, the gorgeous dresses, the costly appurtenances, the splendid get up of the whole concern were worthy of the brother Rajas and the genius of their intimate friend Maharaja Sir Jyotindramohan Tagore, an accomplished connoisseur. The performance of a single play, Ratnavali, which alone cost the Rajas ten thousand rupees, realized the idea, and established the character of the real Hindu Drama with the improvements suited to the taste of an advanced age".

Ratnavali was again staged in Bengali on 22 March 1873 by the Oriental theatre, Calcutta and the Bengali translation was by Ramnarayan Tarkaratna.

Bengali Theatre, Calcutta which came into being on 7th December 1873 at Calcutta, also staged Ratnavali of Sriharsa on 22 November 1873. The show was repeated on 28 February 1874.

In South, 'Dharwada Nataka Samajam, (from Dharwada, now in Karnataka) a threatrical troup toured the coastal districts of Andhra in the years 1880-81 and created a near sensation and encouraged theatre workers of Andhra to take to serious dramatic activities.

Kandukuri Veeresalingam himself started an association and got one of his Telugu rendering of Sri Harsha's play Ratnāvaḷi in the same thatched shed used as an auditorium by the Dharwada Company at Rajahmundry and left it intact. This was the first theatrical association to perform only Telugu plays.

Sambhuprasad Dhungel's Nepali rendering of 'Ratnavali' (completed at Benaras in 1913) was staged in Darjeeling in the year 1922.

It is interesting to note that the last performance of the Āndhra Bhāsabhimānī Samājam' that was formed in 31st April 1899 to enact the plays of Vedam Venkataraya Sastry was the Telugu rendering of Harsha's Ratnavali (published in 1921). It was staged on the night of the Silver Jubilee Day in 1925. This dramatic Association functioned up to 1925.

Costume Design of Śri Harṣa's Ratnāvalī

Figure 1 - Udayana	:	Figure of king adapted from Badami, Cave III, image of Viṣṇu (C. 578 A.D.) Zimmer, pl. 5, 126-27. His crown from Dr. Motichandra, p 79, No. 26.
Figure 2 - Vidūṣaka	:	Costume visualised from painting in Ajanta Cave No. 2 (7th century A.D.). Vidūṣaka's cap (as per Agrawal V.S. - Trishikhandaka) from Dr. Motichandra, p. 209, Fig. 364.

Figure 3 - Kañcukī

(The Chamberlain) : Costume visualised from Ajanta Cave No. 17 (5th century A.D.). His turban, Dr. Motichandra, p 67.

Figure 4 - Vasubhūti : Costume appraximated from Ajanta Cave No. 17, in the battle of Ceylon, Harringham, pl. VIII, 10.

Figure 5 - Vāsavadattā : The Uttarīya draped in gatrika style. Hairstyle as per Cave 1 Ajanta, from line drawing, Prince of Wales Museum, Mumbai.

Sāgarikā : Costume approximated with hairstyle of one plaite as per NS description (Chapter XXIII, 70). One

(Courtesy : Dr. Tarla Mehta)

Dramatic Work: A Bibiliography

Nāgānanda

Text

Nāgānanda / ed. & tr. into English by Asha V. Toraskar, N.A. Deshpande; Sanskrit commentary by M.R. Kale. - Bombay : Booksellers Publishing Co., 1953.

[265] p.; 21 cm.

Nāgānanda / by Harṣadeva; ed. by G.B. Brahme and S.M. Paranjape. - Poona : [s.n.], 1893.

Nāgānanda / by Harṣadeva; ed. by T. Gaṇapati Śāstrī. - Trivandrum : Government of Travancore, 1917.

iv, 306, [2] p.; 24 cm. - (Trivandrum Sanskrit Series; No. 59).

Includes index.

Text includes the commentary 'Nāgānandavimarśinī' of Śivarāma.

Nāgānanda / by Harṣadeva; ed. with a commentary & notes by M.C. Śaṭhakopācārya. - Kumbakonam : Śrīvidyā Press, 1903.

[230] p.; 21 cm.

Includes an English rendering and introduction by P.G. Sundaram Ayyar.

Nāgānanda / by Harṣadeva; ed. with a commentary 'Sārasvatadadhimathī' by Sundaradās Śastrī. - Bombay : Nirṇaya Sagār Press, 1915.

iii, 138, [2] p.; 22 cm.

Nāgānanda / by Harṣadeva; ed. with an English translation, notes and appendices by R.D. Karmārkar. - 3rd ed. - Poona : Āryabhūṣaṇ Press, 1953.

xxxvi, 269 p.; 21 cm.

First published in 1919.

Nāgānanda / by Harṣadeva; ed. with an introd., Sanskrit commentary, various readings, English translation, notes and appendices by Moreśvar Rāmacandra Kāḷe. - Bombay : Bombay Vaibhava Press, 1919.

lx, [208] p.; 22 cm.

Nāgānanda / by Harṣadeva; ed. with notes, various reading, English translation and introd., by V.R. Nerūrkar and G.M. Jośī. - Bombay : Śrī Lakṣmīnārāyaṇ Press, 1919.

[284] p.; 22 cm.

Nagananda - natakam / by Harshadeva, ed. with the 'Bharavarthadipika' Sanskrit - Hindi commentaries by Baladeva Upadhyaya. - Varanasi : Chaukhamba Sanskrit Sansthan, 1986.

48, 240 p.; 18 cm.

Nagananda - natakam / by Harshadeva; ed. with the 'Kalyani' Sanskrit - Hindi commentaries by Ramanatha Tripathi Sastri. - Varanasi : Chaukhamba Amarabharati Prakashan, 1976.

37, 240 p.; 19 cm.

Naganandam / by Harshadeva; 'Vimarsini' commentary of Sivarama; ed. by T. Ganapati Sastri. - Delhi : Nag Publishers, 1989.

62, 305, 2 p.

Śri Harsha play / by Harshadeva; tr. by Bak Kun - Bae. - Bombay : Asia Publishing House, 1964.

514 p.; 24 cm.

Contains 'Naganandam'.

Translations

Bengali

Sanskrit sahitya sambhar / ed. by Gaurinath Sastri & ed. al. - (Vol. 16) - Calcutta: Navpatra Prakashan, (197-).

Includes Bengali rendering of 'Nagananda' of Śriharsha.

English

Classical triptych : Sakuntala; the little clay cart, Nagananda / tr. into English verse by H.W. Wells. - Mysore : University of Mysore, 1970.

The dramas of Shri Harsha / by Harṣadeva; tr. into English by Bela Bose. - Allahabad: Kitabistan, 1948.

viii, 215 p.; 19 cm.

Contains Nagananda, Priyadarshika and Ratnavali.

Nāgānanda / tr. by Asha V. Toraskar and N.A. Deshpande. - Bombay : Booksellers Publishing Co., 1953.

265 p.; 21 cm.

Gives an account of King Harsha, his plays, sources of the play etc.

Nāgānanda / by Háṛṣa; tr. by Palmer Boyd. - London : [s.n.], 1872.

Nāgānanda / by Harshavardhana; tr. into English by Leela Devi. - Delhi : Sri Satguru Publications, 1988.

xvi, 75 p.; (Sri Garib Dass Oriental Series; No.59).

Introduction gives a glimpse into his life, identity, source of the play and deviations from the original and impact of Buddhism on the play etc.

The recensions of the Nāgananda by Harṣadeva. - New Delhi : Aditya Prakashan, 1991.

Vols.; 25 cm.

Reprint

First published in 1921.

Contents : Vol. 1 The North Indian recension / ed. by Madhabchandra Ghosh and Kṛṣṇakamal Bhaṭṭacharya; tr. by Roland Steiner.

Six Sanskrit plays / ed. by Henry W. Wells. - London : Asia Publishing House, 1964.

xxxi, 487 p.; plates; 21 cm.

Includes 'Nagananda' of Harsha.

Śri Harsha play / by Harshadeva; tr. by Bak Kun - Bae. - Bombay : Asia Publishing House, 1964.

514 p.; 24 cm.

Contains 'Naganandam'.

French

[The plays of Harsha] / by Harshadeva, tr. into French by Alain Danielon.

Gujarati

Nāgānand / by Harṣadēva; tr. into Gujarati by Ramṇik J. Dalāl .- Ahmedabad : Āditya Mudraṇalay, 1927.

ii, 102 p.; 17 cm.

Hindi

Nāgānanda / by Harṣavardhana. - Agra : Laksminarayan Aggarwal, 1927.

Tr. of 'Nāgānandanātakam' into Hindi.

Nāgānanda / by Harṣavardhana. ; tr. by Hardayalusiṃha. - New Delhi : Sasta Sahitya Mandal, [n.d.].

Nāgānanda / by Harṣavardhana; tr. by Sādhurāma. - Delhi : Atmarama & Sons, [n.d.].

Nāgānanda / by Harṣavardhana; tr. by Satyavrata Śāstrī. - Jullandhar : Kohinoor Book Depot, 1958.

Nāgānanda / by Harṣavardhana; tr. by Sītārāma Lālā. - Kanpur : [s.n.], 1900.

Nāgānanda / by Harṣavardhana; tr. into Hindi by Gangādhara Indūkara. - Allahabad : Hindi Sahitya Sammelan, 1946.

Nāgānandanātakam / by Harṣavardhana; comm. & ed. by Baladeva Upādhyāya. - Varanasi : Caukhamba Vidyabhavan, 1956.

Nāgānandanātakam / by Harṣavardhana; tr. & ed. by Omprakāśa. - Jullandhar : Bharatiya Sanskrit Bhawan, 1958.

Nāgānandanātakam / by Harṣavardhana; tr. by Ciranjīva Miśra; rev. by Nārāyaṇadatta Rainā. - Hoshiarpur : Handa Publishing Co., [n.d.].

Tamil

Naganandam / by Śri Harshadevā, tr. into Tamil by Mu. Ku Jagamatharaja. - Madras : Peacock, 1992.

116 p.; 18 cm.

Telugu

Nāgānanda / by Harṣadeva; tr. by Divākarala Veṅkaṭāvadhāni. - Rajahmundry : Tirupativēṅkaṭēśvara Book Depot, 1943.

iv, 80 p.; 21 cm.

Priyadarśika

Text

Priyadarśanā / by Harshadeva; commentary by Nivāsa Jagannātha Svāmin. - Vizagapatnam : [s.n.], 1880.

102 p.

In Telugu characters.

Priyadarśikā / by Harshadeva - [s.l.] : [s.n.], 1870.

56 p.

Priyadarsika / by Harshadeva, a commentary and introd. by Pandit R.V. Krishnamachariar. - Srirangam : [s.n.], 1906.

iv, xlviii, 97 p. - (Sri Vani Vilas Sanskrit Series; No. 3).

Priyadarśika / by Harṣadeva; ed. by G.K. Nariman, A.V.W. Jackson and C.J. Ogden. - Columbia University, 1923 (Columbia University Indo - Iranian Series).

Text in Roman script with English translation and notes.

Priyadarśika / by Harṣadeva; ed. by Jīvānanda Vidyāsāgar. - Calcutta : [s.n.], 1874.

Priyadarsika of Sri Harshadeva / by Harsha; ed. by M.A. Kale. - Delhi : Motilal Banarsidass.

Text with English translation, notes, introduction etc.

Priyadarśikā / by Harṣadeva; ed. by V.D. Gadre. - Bombay : [s.n.], 1884.

Priyadarśikā / by Harṣadeva; ed. with a commentary and introd. by R.V. Kṛṣṇamācārya. - Srirangam : Vāṇīvilās Press, 1906.

[118] p. : plate; 21 cm. - (Vāṇīvilās Sanskrit Series; 3).

Priyadarśika / by Harshadeva; ed. with an English tr. by P.V. Ramanujasvami. - 2nd ed. - Madras : V. Ramasvami Śastrulu & Sons, 1948.

75, 96, 208 p.; 18 cm.

Priyadarśika / by Harṣadeva; ed. with an English translation, notes and critical introd. by R.P. Kāṅgle. - Ahmedabad : Vasanta Press, 1928.

xxiv, 216 p.; 21 cm.

Priyadarśikā / by Harṣadeva; ed. with an introd., English translation, notes and appendices by N.G. Suru. - Poona : The editor, 1928.

xlviii, [188] p.; 18 cm.

Priyadarśikā / by Harṣadeva; ed. with an introd., Sanskrit commentary, various readings, English translation, notes and appendices by Moreśvar Rāmacandra Kāḷe. - Bombay : Bombay Vaibhava Press, 1928.

[204] p.; 22 cm.

Priyadarśika / by Harṣadeva; ed. with introd., English translation and notes by P.V. Rāmānujasvāmī. - Madras : V. Rāmasvāmi Śāstrulu & Sons, 1935.

lxxvi, [304] p.; 19 cm.

Includes appendices.

Priyadarshika : a drama in four acts / by Śri Harsha; ed. with notes by Pandit Jibananda Vidyasagara. - Calcutta : [s.n.], 1874.

61 p.

This edition was based on one very old manuscript, which Vidyāsāgara later claimed to have lost.

Priyadarśikā : a Sanskrit drama by Harsha / tr. into English by G.K. Nariman, A.V. Williams Jackson and Charles J. Ogden. - New Delhi : Orient Books Reprint Corporations, 1984.

cxi, 131 p.

Includes Sanskrit text.

The Priyadarśikā of Śriharshadeva / by Śrī Harsha; ed. with notes and Prākṛta Chhāyā by Vishṇu Dājī Gadrē. - Bombay : [s.n.], 1884.

[95] p.

Gadre based his edition on three manuscripts from the Palace Library at Tanjore.

Sri Harṣa's plays / tr. into English by Bak Kun Bae. - Bombay : Asia Publishing House, 1964.

Includes Sanskrit text.

Published in collaboration with Indian Council For Cultural Relations.

Contains 'Priyadarsika'.

Translations

English

Priyadarśika / by Harshadeva; ed. with an English tr. by P.V. Ramanujasvami. - 2nd ed. - Madras : V. Ramasvami Śastrulu & Sons, 1948.

75, 96, 208 p.; 18 cm.

Priyadarsika / by Harṣadeva, ed. with introd., English tr. & notes by P.V. Ramanujaswami. - Madras : V. Ramaswamy Sastrulu & Sons, 1935.

lxxvi, 96, 208 p.; 19 cm.

Includes appendices.

Priyadarsika / by Harsha; tr. into English by G.K. Nariman, A.V. Williams Jackson and Charles J. Ogden. - New Delhi : Oriental Reprint Corporations, 1923.

Priyadarśikā : a Sanskrit drama by Harsha / tr. by G.K. Nariman, A.V. Williams Jackson & Charles J. Ogden New Delhi : Munshiram Manoharlal Publishers, 1984.

cxi, 132 p.; 22.5 cm.

Gives an account of the life & times of Harsa, Harsa as author & patron.

Priyadarśikā / by Harṣadeva, tr. into English by G.K. Nariman, A.V. Williams

Jackson and Charles J. Ogden. - New York : Columbia University Press, 1923.

cxi, 131 p. : facsim. ; 22.5 cm.

Includes bibliography.

Priyadarsika of Sri Harshadeva / by Harsha; ed. by M.R. Kale. - Delhi : Motilal Banarsidass.

Text with English translation, notes, introduction etc.

Sri Harsa's plays / tr. into English by Bak Kun Bae. - Bombay : Asia Publishing House, 1964.

Published in collaboration with ICCR, New Delhi.

Contains 'Priyadarsika'.

The dramas of Shri Harsha / tr. into English by Bela Bose. - Allahabad : Kitabistan, 1948.

viii, 215 p.; 19 cm.

Contains Priyadarshika, Ratnavali and Nagananda.

French

[The plays of Harsha] / by Harshadeva; tr. into French by Alain Danielon.

Priyadarsika piece attribuce an roi Sriharchadeva, en quatre actes, proccedes dun prologue et d'une introduction / traduite par G. Strehly. - Paris : [s.n.], 1888.

88 p. - (Bibliotheque Orientale Elzevirienne; No. 58).

Gujarati

Natyakathao / ed. by Jivanlal Amarshi Mehta. - Ahmedabad : the editor, 1927.

viii, 104 p.; 16 cm.

Includes Gujarati translation of plays of Harshadeva.

[Priyadarsika] / tr. by Keshavlal Harshadrai Dhruva.

Hindi

Priyadarśikā / by Harṣavardhana; tr. into Hindi by Gangādhara Indūrkara. - Allahabad : Hindi Sahitya Sammelan, 1946.

Priyadarśikā nātikā / by Harṣavardhana; comm. by Rāmacandra Miśra. - Varanasi: Caukhamba Vidyabhavan, 1955.

Kannada

Priyadarśikā nāṭike / by Harṣadeva; tr. by Nañjanagūḍu Śrīkanṭha Śāstri. - Mysore: Karnataka Granthamala, 1905.

viii, 56 p.; 21 cm.

Marathi

Islāmpūrkar, Vāman Śāstrī. Lalitavatsarāj / by Vāman Śāstrī Islāmpūrkar. - Bombay : Vāsudev Moreśvar Potdār, 1889.

2 Vols.; 18 cm.

Novel in Marathi, based on Harṣadeva's 'Priyadarśikā'.

Nepali

Priyardarsika / by Sriharsa; tr. into Nepali by Motirām Bhaṭṭa.

Published in 1959, this Nepali rendering was done in the year 1889-90 with minor alterations and additions of songs and verses composed by the translator.

Priyadarśika / by Sriharsa; tr. into Nepali by Śambhuprasad Dhungel.

Tamil

Piriyatarcikai / by Śrīharsa; tr. from Sanskrit into Tamil by M. Muttuveṅkaṭācalam. - Karaikudi : Selvi, 1989.

xii, 119 p.; 18 cm.

Telugu

Priyadarśika / by Harṣadeva; tr. by Bulusu Pāpayyaśāstri. - Visakhapatnam : [s.n.], 1902.

45 p.; 18 cm.

Priyadarśika / by Harṣadeva; tr. by Cennāpragaḍa Bhānumūrti. - Masulpatam : C.M.S. Dove Press, 1909.

48 p.; 18 cm.

Priyadarśika / by Harṣadeva; tr. by Kommanamañci Jōgayyaśarma. - Waltair : The translator, 1950.

x, 74 p.; 18 cm.

Priyadarśika / by Harṣadeva; tr. by Vēdamu Vēṅkatarāyaśāstri. - Madras : Jyotiṣ mati Press, 1909.

128p., 18cm.

Includes text and notes.

Ratnavali

Text

Ratnāvalī / by Harṣadeva. - Calcutta : [s.n.], 1832.

Ratnavālī / by Harṣadeva; ed. by C. Cappeller. - St. Petersburg, 1877 & 1909.

In Bōhtlingk's Sanskrit Chrestomathie.

Carl Capeller (1840 - 1925)

Carl Johann Wilhelm Capeller was born on 23.3.1840 in Alexkehnen in Eastern Prussia. He began his studies in 1860 in Berlin, where he read Classical languages. Indo-European linguistics, Sanskrit and Lithuanian. He obtained a doctorate in 1868 for his Latin thesis Observationes ad Kalidasae Malavikagnimitram. For 1870 to 1872 Capeller taught Latin, French and English in a school. In 1872, he submitted a thesis Die Ganachandas, Ein Beitrag zur indischen Metrik ("The Ganachandas. A contribution to Indian metrics"). He studied about a thousand verses in Sanskrit and Prakrit and compared the different metres. He also discussed the theory that Sanskrit drama had evolved from Greek drama. This view was held by several scholars of his time. Carl Capeller specialised in Sanskrit drama. He has several critical editions to his credit. He also wrote on poetics. His Sanskrit - German Dictionary for beginners and its revised English edition greatly benefited students of Sanskrit. In his critical editions, Cappeler did not give preference to any one manuscript. He tried to cull the best from each tradition, a subjective method not approved by all scholars. His edition of Harsha's Ratnavali was based on six manuscripts and six Indian editions. It appeared in Boehtlingk's Chrestomatie in 1877 and 1909. Capeller was appointed reader of Sanskrit in the University of Jena in 1872. He became associate professor in 1875. In 1921, when he was 81 years of age, he discontinued giving lectures. He died on 17.7.1925 in Jena.

Ratnāvalī / by Harṣadeva; ed. by K. Joglekar. - Bombay : [s.n.], 1913.

Ratnāvalī / by Harṣadeva; ed. by K.P. Parab and V.S. Joṣi. - Bombay : [s.n.], 1889.

Ratnāvalī / by Harṣadeva; ed. by N.B. Goḍbole and K.P. Parab. - Bombay : Nirnaya Sagar Press, 1882.

Ratnāvalī / by Harṣadeva; ed. by N.B. Godabole and K.P. Parab. - 2nd ed. - Bombay : [s.n.], 1890.

Ratnāvalī / by Harṣadeva, ed. by K.P. Parab with Govinda's commentary. - Bombay : Nirnaya Sagar Press, 1895.

Ratnavali / by Harshadeva; ed by Ramnarayan Sastri. - Pudukkottai : Sugandharam Publications, 1978.

67, 69 p.; 18.5 cm.

Includes Sanskrit text and its English rendering.

Ratnāvalī / by Harṣadeva; ed. by S.C. Chakravarti. - 2nd ed. - Calcutta : [s.n.], 1919.

Ratnāvalī / by Harṣadeva; ed. with an introd., English translation, notes and appendices by C.R. Devadhar and N.G. Suru. - Poona : Śrī Gaṇeś Printing Works, 1925.

xliii, 191 p.; 18 cm.

Ratnāvalī / by Harṣadeva; ed. by Kṛṣṇanāth Nyāyapañcānana with the commentary of Śivarāma. - Calcutta : [s.n.], 1864.

Ratnavali / by Harshadeva; ed. with an English tr. by P.V. Ramanujasvami. - Madras : V. Ramasvami Sastrulu & Sons, 1936.

73, 192, 196 p.; 18 cm.

Ratnāvalī / by Harṣadeva; ed. with an introd., Sanskrit commentary, English translation, notes and appendices by Moreśvar Rāmacandra Kāḷe. - Bombay : Bombay Vaibhav Press, 1921.

[243] p.; 22 cm.

Ratnāvalī / by Harṣadeva; ed. with English and Bengali translations, Sanskrit commentary and annotations by Śrīścandra Cakravaratī. - Dacca : The editor, 1902.

xxxvi, 350 p.; 18 cm.

Includes append.

Ratnāvalī / by Harṣadeva; ed. with notes in English, occasional English translation, various readings and introd. by Vināyak Sakhārām Ghāṭe. - Bombay: Induprakāś Press, 1907.

[187] p.; 22 cm.

Ratnavali nātikā / by Harshadeva. - Bombay : Nirnaya Sagar Press, 1938.

20, 202 p.; 22 cm.

Select Specimens of the theatre of the HIndus / by H.H. Wilson. - 3rd ed. - London : [s.n.], 1871.

2 Vols.

Vol. 2 contains a tr. of 'Ratnavali' (Pp. 255 - 319).

Sri Harṣa's plays / tr. into English by Bak Kum Bae. - Bombay : Asia Publishing House, 1964.

Published in collaboration with ICCR, New Delhi.

Contains 'Ratnavali'.

Translations

Assamese

Ratnavali / tr. into Assamese by Tulasinarayan Sharma. - Jorhat : Annada Sahitya Mandir, 1932.

1, 32 p.; 15 cm.

Bengali

Ratnāvalī / by Sri Harṣa; ed. with Bengali and English translations, Sanskrit commentary and annotations by Śrīścandra Cakravartī. - Dacca : The editor, 1902.

xxxvi, 350 p.; 18 cm.

Includes append.

Four acts drama on the romance of the King Udayana and princess Ratnāvalī.

Ratnabali / by Sriharsa; tr. into Bengali by Haridon Ray.

A free rendering for staging in Bengali Jatra form (a blending of songs and dialogues).

Ratnavali / by Shriharsha; tr. into Bengali by Jadunath Tarkaratna. - 1860.

Ratnavali / by Shriharsha; tr. into Bengali by Jyotirindranath Thakur. - 1900.

Available in Jyotirindranath rachanavali

Ratnavali / by Śriharsa; tr. into Bengali by Michael Madhusudan Datta. [19th cent.].

Ratnavali / by Shriharsha; tr. into Bengali by Nilmani Pal. - Calcutta : [s.n.], 1849-50.

First Bengali rendering of the original Sanskrit play.

Ratnavali / by Shriharsha; tr. into Bengali by Nṛsimhachandra Mukhopadhyay. - 1874.

Ratnavali / by Shriharsa; tr. into Bengali by Ramnarayan Tarkaratna. - 1858?

[Ratnavali] in De, Sabitri. Sanskrit sahityer anubad - dhara. - Calcutta : Chinmay Majumdar, [1983].

Contents : Ratnabali. (Pp. 181 - 194).

Sanskrita sahitya sambhar / ed. by Gaurinath Sastri & et al. [Vol. 3]. - Calcutta : Navpatra Prakashan, [197-].

Includes Bengali rendering of Śriharsha's 'Ratnavali'.

English

The dramas of Shri Harsha / by Harṣadeva; tr. into English by Bela Bose. - Allahabad : Kitabistan, 1948.

viii, 215 p.; 19 cm.

Includes glossary.

Contents : Ratnavali; Priyadarshika; and Nagananda.

Pearl necklace / by Sri Harsa; tr. of 'Ratnavali' into English by G. Tucci.

Journal of the Royal Asiatic Society. 1934.

Ratnavali / by Harshadeva; ed. with an English tr. by P.V. Ramanujasvami. - Madras : V. Ramasvami. Sastrulu & Sons, 1936.

73, 192, 196 p.; 18 cm.

Ratnāvalī / by Harṣadeva; ed. with Bengali and English translations, Sanskrit comentary and annotations by Srish Chandra Chakravarti. - Dacca : The editor, 1902.

xxxvi, 350 p.; 18 cm.

Includes append.

Ratnavali / by Harsha; English tr. by C. Sankara Sastri. - Madras : [s.n.], 1935.

Ratnavali or the Necklace / by Harṣadeva; tr. from the original Sanskrit by H.H. Wilson. - Calcutta : Society for the Resuscitation of Indian Literature, 1901.

x, 66 p.; 15 cm.

Four acts play on the romance of King Udayana and Ratnāvalī, a princess.

Select specimens of the theatre of the Hindus / tr. into English by Horace Hayman Wilson. - 3rd ed. - New Delhi : Asian Educational Services, 1984.

Includes English rendering of Harṣadeva's drama in four acts entitled 'Ratnāvalī'.

Sri Harsa's plays / tr. into English by Bak Kum Bae. - Bombay : Asia Publishing House, 1964.

Published in collaboration with ICCR, New Delhi.

Contains 'Ratnavali'.

French

[The plays of Harsha] / by Harshadeva; tr. into French by Alain Danielon.

Ratnāvalī / by Harṣa; tr. into French by M. Lehot. - Paris : Institut de Civilisation Indienne, Collection Emile Senart, 1933.

German

[Ratnāvalī] / by Harṣadeva; tr. into German by Ludwig Fritze. - Chemnitz : [s.n.], 1878.

Gujarati

Ratnāvalī - nāṭak / by Harṣadeva. - Bombay : Nirṇaya Sāgar Press, 1886.

xxi, 85 p.; 23 cm.

Ratnāvalī nāṭikā / by Harṣadēva; tr. by Ratipatirām Udaymrām Paṇḍyā ; ed. by Jīvaṇlāl Amarṣī Mahētā. - Ahmedabad : Jñānvardhak Pustakmāḷā, 1921.

xxvii, 79 p. : plate, map, 17 cm.

Vindhya van - nī kanyakī athavā Priyadarśanā / by Harṣadēva; tr. by Kēśavlāl Harṣ adrāy Dhruv. - 4th ed. - Ahmedabad : Vilōcan Kēśavlāl Dhruv, 1939.

viii, 196 p.; 19 cm.
Includes append.

Tr. of Sanskrit play 'Ratnāvalī nāṭak'.

Hindi

Ratnāvalī / by Harṣavardhana. - Allahabad : Government Press, 1895.

Ratnāvalī / by Harṣavardhana. - Bombay : Nirṇayasagara Press, 1895.

Ratnāvalī / by Harṣavardhana. - Calcutta : Bangabashi Office, 1898.

Ratnāvalī / by Harṣavardhana; ed. & tr. by Nāharasiṃha Solanki. - Eta?: [s.n.], [n.d.].

Ratnavali / by Harṣavardhana; tr. into Hindi by Balmukund Gupta. - 1898.

Ratnavali / by Harṣavardhana; tr. into Hindi by Bharatendu Harishchandra. - 1868.

Ratnavali / by Harṣavardhana; tr. into Hindi by Devdatta Tiwari. - 1872.

Ratnavalī / by Harṣavardhana; tr. into Hindi by Gangadhara Indūrkar. - Allahabad: Hindi Sahitya Sammelan, 1946.

Ratnāvalī / by Harṣavardhana; tr. by Rāmacandra Miśra. - 2nd ed. - Varanasi : Caukhamba Vidyabhavan, 1952.

Ratnāvalī / by Harṣavardhana; tr. by Rāmeśvara Bhatta. - Bombay : Venkateshwar Press, 1895.

Ratnāvalī / by Harṣavardhana; tr. into Hindi by Bālamukunda Gupta. - Calcutta : Bharat Mitra Press, 1959.
Reprint.

Ratnavalī / by Harṣavardhana; tr. into Hindi by Śivarāja Śāstrī. - Meerut : Sahitya Bhandar, [n.d.].

Italian

[Ratnāvalī] / by Harṣadeva; tr. into Italian language by Francesco Cimmino. - Naples : [s.n.], 1894.

Kannada

Karnataka Ratnavali natike / by Harṣadeva; tr. into Kannada by Basavappasastri. - Mysore : Sri Panchacharya Electric Press, 1954.
96 p.; 16 cm.

Maithili

Ratnavali natika / by Harshadeva tr. into Maithili by Parmanand Jha. - Darbhanga: Pathak & Sons, 1956.

xiv, 96 p.; 18.5 cm.

Malyalam

Ratnāvali / by Harṣdeva; tr. by A.P. Paramēśvaran Piḷḷa. - Trivandrum : Press Rāmses, [n.d.].
93 p.; 19 cm.

Ratnāvali / by Harṣadeva; tr. by K.P. Gōvinda Piṣāraṭi .- Madras : Bālamanōhara Press, 1935.

Ratnāvali / by Harṣadeva; tr. by M. Rāmavarma Rāja. - Trivandrum : Kṛṣṇavilāsam Press, 1923.

97 p.; 19 cm.

Nepali

Ratnavali / by Śriharsa; tr. into Nepali by Pahalman Singh Swar.

Ratnāvalī / by Harṣadeva; tr. by Sambhuprasād Ḍhungel. - Varanasi : Viśvarāj Harihar Śarma, 1915.

62 p.; 17 cm.

Translated from Sanskrit original into Nepali.

Oriya

Ratnavali / by Sriharsa; tr. into Oriya by Birmitrodaya Simhadev, 1894.

This was the first work of the Prince Birmitrodaya Simhadev of Subarnapur.

Sindhi

Ratnāvalī / by Harṣadeva; tr. by Kauromal Khilnāṇī .- 2nd ed. - Karachi : Ratan Sāhitya Manḍal, 1938.

102 p.; 17 cm.

First published in 1888.

Swedish

[Ratnāvalī] / by Harṣadeva; tr. into Swedish by H. Andersson. - [s.l.] : [s.n.], 1892.

Tamil

Sri Harsha's Ratnavali / tr. by P.V. Ramanujaswami. - Madras : V. Ramaswamy Sastrulu & Sons, 1936.

73, 192, 196 p.; 18cm

Gives his early life, conquest, later life, religion, his contribution as a poet himself as a patron of Letters.

Telugu

Ratnāvalī / by Harṣadeva; tr. by Kandukūri Vīrēśaliṅgamu. - 5th ed. - Rajahmundry: Hitakāriṇī Samājamu, 1950.

vi, 95 p.; 21 cm.

Ratnāvalī / by Harṣadeva, tr. by Madhunāpantula Satyanārāyaṇa - Śāstri. - Rajahmundry : Satyavōlu Gunnēśvararāvu Bros., 1947.

iv, 74 p.; 21 cm.

Ratnāvaḷī / by Harṣadeva; tr. by Yarasūri Mallikārjunarāvu. - Rajahmundry : The translator, 1952.

95 p. : plate; 18 cm.

Thai

[Ratnavali] / by Śri Harsha; tr. into Thai by Dusdie Malakun.

Other Works

Liṅgānuśāsana / by Harṣadeva; critically ed. with an introd. by V. Veṅkaṭarāma Śārmā. - Madras : The University of Madras, 1931.

xliv, 138 p. : fascim; 24 cm.

Madras University Sanskrit Series; 4

Grammatical treatise on gender. With the commentary 'Sarvalakṣaṇā by Pṛthvīśvara. The appendices contains the Liṅgānuśāsanas of Pāṇini and Śākatāyana and the Liṅgaviśeṣavidhi of Vararuci.

Text of the work also appeared in 'Die Indischen Genuslehren mit dem Text der Liṅgānuśāsana's des Śākaṭayāna, Harṣavardhana, Vararuci' by Otto Franke, Kiel, 1980.

BIO - CRITICAL NOTICES

Adya Rangacharya. Drama in Sanskrit literature. - 2nd rev. ed. - Bombay : Popular Prakashan, 1967.

Pp. 41, 61, 69, 70, 78, 121, 155 - 164.

Aggarwal, H.R. A short history of Sanskrit literature. - 2nd rev. ed. - Delhi : Munshiram Manoharlal, 1963.

Contents : (Harsa. P. 182-).

Aggarwal, Vasudevasharan. Harshacharit : ek samskritik adhyayan. - Patna: Bihar Rashtra Bhasa Parishad, 1953.

xxiv, 224, 24 p. : 22.5 cm.

Includees twenty eight plates.

Agrawala, V.S. Description of Harsa as darpasala by Bana / by V.S. Agrawala. *Vishveshvaranand Indological Journal;* Sept. 1964; Vol. 2, No. 2; Pp. 247 - 253.

Aufrecht, Thedor. Catalogus catalogorum. - Weisbaden : Franz Steiner Verlag Gmb. H, 1962.

2 Vols.; 26 cm.

Bānabhatta. Andhra Harṣacaritramu / by Bāṇa Bhaṭṭa.; tr. into Telugu by Mēḍēpalli Vēṅkaṭaramaṇācāryulu. - Vizianagaram : The translator, 1929.

vii, 158 p.; 24 cm.

Bāṇabhatta. Harṣacarita / by Bāna; ed. by Śuranāḍ Kuñjan Pilla. - Trivandrum : Trivandrum Sanskrit series, 1958.

--------. tr. into English by Cowell and Thomas. - London : Royal Asiatic Society, 1897.

One of the best translations of any Sanskrit text.

--------. Harṣacarita / by Bāṇa Bhaṭṭa; ed. with a commentary 'Bālabodhinī' by S.D. Gajendragaḍkar. - Poona : A.P. Bāpat & Bros., 1917 - 18.

2 Vols.; 24 cm.

Includes notes, appendices etc.

--------.Harṣacarita / by Baṇa Bhaṭṭa; ed. with a Hindi tr. by Sūryaṅarāyaṇ Caudhurī. - Purnea : [s.n.], 1948 - 50.

2 Vols. ; 18 cm.

--------.Harṣacarita / by Bāṇa Bhaṭṭa; ed. with an introd. & notes by P.V. Kāṇe. - Bombay: The editor 1917 - 18

2 Vols. ; 21 cm.

Includes appendices and index.

--------.Harṣacarita / by Bāṇa Bhaṭṭa; ed. with critical notes by A.. Fuhrer. - Bombay : Government Central Press, 1909.

iv, 342 p.; 23 cm. - (Bombay Sanskrit & Prakrit Series; No. 66).

Includes commentary 'Saṅketa' by Śaṅkara Kavi.

--------. Harshacharita; tr. into Bengali by Prabodhendunath Thakur. - Calcutta : Rupa & Co., 1986.

12, 361 p.; 22 cm.

First published in 1978.

--------. Calcutta : Ranjan Publishing House, 1951.

viii, 324 p. : col. plates; 24 cm.

--------. Harṣacarita / by Baṇa Bhaṭṭa; tr. into English by E.B. Cowell & F.W. Thomas. - London : [s.n.], 1897.

--------. Harsa carita / by Bānabhatta; tr. into Nepali. - Varanasi : Hitaiṣī Co., 1950.

156 p.; 22 cm.

Reprint.

Tr. from the original Sanskrit.

--------. The Harshacarita of Banabhatta : text of uchchhrasas I - VIII / ed. by P.V. Kane. - Delhi : Motilal Banarsidass, 1986.

li, 645 p.; 23 cm.

--------.Harṣa caritam / by Bāṇa; tr. by Kuṇḍalagiriyācārya. - Mysore : Karṇāṭaka Granthamala, 1900.

iv, 142 p.; 21 cm.

Tr. into Kannada.

--------. Harshacharitam / by Banabhatta; ed. by Kaśināth Pānduranga Parab with Śankarakavi's 'Sanketa'; rev. by Narayan Ram Ācarya. - 7th ed. - Bombay : Nirnayasagar Press, 1946.

258 p.; 22 cm.

--------. Harṣacaritasārasaṅgraha / by Baṇa Bhaṭṭa; ed. by T. Śrīnīvāsācārya. - Trichinopoly: St. Joseph's College Press, 1907.

iii, 110 p.; 18 cm.

Abridged edition.

--------. Harṣacaritramu / by Bāṇa Bhaṭṭa; tr. by Tirupativēṅkaṭēśvarakavulu. (Part I). - 3 rd. ed. - Rajahmundry : Tirupativēṅkaṭēśvara Book Depot, 1939.

vi, 108 p.; 18.5 cm.

In Telugu.

Bandyopadhyay, Sureschandra. Sanskrit sahityer itihas. - Calcutta : The Dacca Students Library, [1970?].

Banerji, Sures Chandra. A companion to Sanskrit literature. - Delhi : Motilal Banarsidass, 1971.

Pp. 96 - 97.

Banerji, Nani Gopal. Sri - Harsa the king pret *Indian Historical Quarterly.*

Sept. 1936; I. 12 (3); Pp. 504 - 510.

-; Dec. 1936; II. 12 (4); Pp. 701 - 713.

Bhartiya, Kanti Kishore. Sanskrit natakkar. - Uttar Pradesh : Prakashan, Śakha, Suchana Vibhag, 1959.

(Hindi - Samiti granthamala; 25).

Contents : Harshavardhana. Pp. 123 - 134.

Bhatt, S.C. Drama in ancient India. - New Delhi : Amrit Book Co., 1961. Pp. 81 - 85.

Bhattacharya, Bimanchandra. Sanskrit sahityer ruprekha. - 5th ed. - Calcutta :

Vidyodaya Library Pvt. Ltd., 1922.

In Bengali.

Bhattacharya, Biswanath. Sanskrit drama and dramaturgy. - Delhi : Sharada Publishing House, 1994. Pp. 229, 339, 351.

Bhattacharya, D.C. Udayanācārya and Śrīharṣa. Siddha Bharati II.

Bhattacharya, Hillol. Tragedy : ek bicchinnatar itihas *Syas Natya Patra - 16;* 1999.

In Bengali.

Bose, Bela. The dramas of Shriharsha. - Allahabad : Kitabistan, 1948.

Introductory chapter deals with the life and works of the dramatist.

Chakravarti, Chintaharan. King Harsa and Aihole inscription. *Indian Historical Quarterly;* June 1926; Vol. 2 (2); P. 384.

Chandra, Veena. Study of the dramas by Harsha / by Veena Chandra.

Ph.D. thesis approved by the Patna University in 1980.

Chatterjee, Asoke. On the interpretation of a passage of Harsacarita. *Indian Historical Quarterly;* June - Sept. 1961; 37 (2 & 3); Pp. 210 - 214.

Chattopadhyay, Sudhakar. Kanauj after Harsa's death *Indian Historical Quarterly* June 1954; 30 (2); Pp. 160 - 166.

Cimmino, Francesco. Il terzo atto del dramma indiano Priyadarcika. *Atti dell Accademia Pontaniana;* 31, 1 - 18, Naples, 1902.

-----. Sui Drammi attribuitī ad Harshadeva. Naples : [s.n.], 1906.

15 p.

Comparative Indian literature. (Vol. 1) / ed. by K.M. George. - Trichur : Kerala Sahitya Akademi, 1984. P. 567.

The Cultural heritages of India [Vol. V] / ed. by Suniti Kumar Chatterji. - rev. ed. - Calcutta : The Ramakrishna Mission Institute of Culture, 1978. Pp. 239 - 242, 250.

Dalal, Minakshi L. Conflict in Sanskrit drama. - Bombay : Samaiya Publications, 1973. Pp. 206 - 211, 254 - 260.

Das, Sarbeshwar. The comic and romantic in Sanskrit dramas with special reference to Bhāsa, Kālidāsa, Harsa and Bhavabhūti *Summary of Papers : All*

India Oriental Conference (Bhubaneshwar); 1959; Vol. XX.

Dictionary of oriental literatures (Vol. II) : South and South - East Asia. - Delhi : Vikas Publishing, 1975.

Encyclopaedia of Indian literature (Vol. II). - New Delhi : Sahitya Akademi, 1988.

Pp. 1558 - 1560.

Ettinghausen, Maurice, L. Harṣa - Vardhana : emperior et poete de l' Inde septentrionale. - Louvain : [s.n.], 1906.

A comprehensive work of Śri Harṣa.

Frazer, R.W. A literary history of India. - London : T. Fisher Unwin, 1898. P.293

Garg, Ganga Ram. An encyclopaedia of Indian literature. - Delhi : Mittal Publishes, 1982. Pp. 408 - 409.

Glimpses of Sanskrit literature/ ed. by A.N.D. Haksar. - New Delhi : Indian Council for Cultural Relations, 1995. Pp. 116 - 118.

Roy, Ashim Kumar and Gidwani, N.N. A dictionary of Indology (Vol. 2). - New Delhi : Oxford and IBH Publishing Co., 1984.

Goyal, S.R. The date of the Harshacharita of Bana' / by S.R. Goyal *Quarterly Review of Historical Studies;* 1978 - 79; Vol. 18, No. 4.; Pp. 246 - 249.

Harsha. The dramas of Shri Harsha / tr. by Bela Bose. - Allahabad : Kitabistan, 1948. Pp. 1-20.

Short sketch on the life and works of Harshadeva.

Harsa. Nāgānand of Harshadev / ed. by Asha V. Toraskar and N.A. Deshpande; Sanskrit commentary by M.R. Kale. - Bombay : Bookseller's Publishing Co., 1953.

Pp. 1 - 38.

Contains an account of King Harsha, the authorship of the three plays, the synopsis and critical appreciation of his play.

Harsha. Naganandam by Harshavardhana / tr. into English by Leela Devi. - Delhi : Sri Satguru Publications, 1988. Pp. vii - xvi.

Introductory chapter deals with Harshavardhana, the identityof Harsha, critical examination of his play 'Naganandam'.

Harsha. Priyadarśika : a Sanskrit drama / by Harsa; tr. into English by G.K. Nariman, A.V. Williams Jackson & Charles J. Ogden. - New Delhi : Oriental Books Reprint Corporation, 1984.

Translation with text in transliteration contains chapters on life and times of Harsha; critical insights into his play Priyadarshika, plots of other dramas and a detailed bibliography.

Harsha. Ratnavali / ed. with introd., tr., notes and appendix by P.V. Ramanujaswami. - Madras : V. Ramaswamy Sastrulu & Sons, 1936. Pp. 1 - 72.

Introduction contains sections on origin of Sanskrit drama & its secular origin; Śri Harsha : his early life, his conquests, his later life etc; his three dramas, their similarities, identity of their authorship etc.

I - Ch'ing [I - Tsing]. A Record of the Buddhist religion in India and the Malay Archipelago / tr. by J. Takakusu. - Oxford : [s.n.], 1896.

Contains references to Harsha on pages 163-164.

Jackson, A.V. Williams. 'Time analysis of Sanskrit plays : the drama of Harsha' / by A.V. Williams Jackson. *JAOS;* 1900; 21. Pp. 88 - 108.

Jhala, G..C. A note on Bana's Kadambari and Harsa's Priyadarsika' / by G.C. Jhala. *Indian Antiquary;* January 1967; Vol. 2, No. 1; Pp. 40 - 41.

Jharkhandi, S.N. Coronation of Harsa : miscellany. *Indian Historical Quarterly;* March 1936; Vol. 12, No. 1; Pp. 142 - 144.

Katar, Usha Kiran. Comparative study of the depiction of 'Love' in the works of Bhavabhuti and Harsha / by Usha Kiran Katar.

Ph.D. thesis approved by the Rohilkhand University in 1983.

Keith, A. Berriedale Sanskrit - natak : udbhav aur vikas : siddhanta aur prayog / tr. into HIndi by Udaybhanu Singh. - Delhi : Motilal Banarsidass, 1965.

Konow, Sten. Dass indische drama. - Berlin : [s.n.], 1920 - (Grundriss dev Indo - Arischen Philologie und Altertumskunde; Vol. 2, part 2 D).

Pp. 73 - 77.

Covers invaluable discussions on Harsha and his plays.

Krishnamachariar, M and Srinivasachariar. History of classical Sanskrit literature. - Delhi : Motilal Banarsidass, 1989. Pp. 583 - 589.

Lal, P. Ratnavali / by P. Lal *Illustrated Weekly of India* ; August 1967; Vol. 88, No. 30; P. 39.

Levi, Sylvain Une Poesie inconnue du Roi Harṣa Ciladitya' / by Sylvain Levi *In Actes du dixieme congres international des orientalistes;* 1894; Part -2 , Sec - 1. Pp. 189 - 203. - Leiden : 1897.

Lēvi, Sylvain. The theatre of India / tr. from the French by Narayan Mukherji. - Calcutta : Writers Workshop, 1978.

Contents :

Harsavardhana Pp. (Vol. I) 5, 8, 137, 143, 161 - 171, 184, 188, 239; (Vol. II) 30, 32, 55, 68, 75, 89, 93, 118.

Nāgānanda. Pp. (Vol. I) 166 - 171, 184; (Vol. II) 30, 32, 33, 62, 67, 68.

Priyadarśikā. Pp. (Vol. I) 146, 164 - 166; (Vol. II) 89.

Ratnāvalī. Pp. (Vol. I) 2, 134, 137, 146, 152, 162 - 164, 253; (Vol. II) 84, 89, 93, 95, 101.

Macdonell, A.A. India's past. - Varanasi : Motilal Banarsidass, 1956.

Pp. 94, 112, 135 - 136, 254, 275.

Majumdar, R.C. Harsa era. *Indian Historical Quarterly* Sept. 1951; Vol. 27, No. 3; Pp. 183 - 190.

-----. Sept. 1952; Vol. 28, No. 3; Pp. 280 - 285.

Marasinghe, E.W. The Sanskrit theatre and stagecraft. - Delhi : Sri Satguru Publications, 1989. - (Sri Garib Dass Oriental Series; No. 78).

Masterpieces of Indian literature [Vol. 2]. - New Delhi : National Book Trust, 1997.

Contents : Nagananda (Sriharsha). Pp. 1201 - 1203.

Masterpieces of Indian literature (Vol. 3) / ed. by K.M. Geroge. - New Delhi : National Book Trust, 1997.

P. 1968.

Mirashi, V.V. Harsa and Bhatika eras : miscellany. *Indian Historical Quarterly* June 1953; Vol. 24, No. 2; Pp. 191 - 195.

Mishra, Anand Svarup. Mahakavi Shri Harsha tatha unka Naishadkavya. - Lucknow : Sulabh Prakashan, 1988.

xxxvi; 423 p. : ill.; 24.5 cm.

Mishra, Bechan. Critical study of the dramas of Harsha / by Bechan Mishra.

D. Litt. thesis in Hindi approved by the K.S. Darbhanga University in 1982.

Nārāyaṇa Śāstrī, T.S. Sriharsha : the dramatist. Madras : [s.n.],

1902

Dissertation.

Pandey, Mahatma Prasad. Critical study of the dramas of Harshavardhana / by Mahatma Prasad Pandey.

Ph.D. thesis approved by the Agra University in 1976.

Pannikar, K.M. Sri Harsha of Kanauj : a monograph of the history of India in the first half of the 7th century A.D. - Bombay : [s.n.], 1922.

Pant, Deepa. Critical study of the dramas of Harsha in the light of Sanskrit aesthetics / by Deepa Pant.

Ph.D. thesis in Hindi approved by the Rajasthan University in 1987.

Parikh, J.T. Sanskrit comic characters. - Surat : Popular Book Depot. 1952.

Contents : Humour of Harsa : Vasantaka : Ātreya.

Pathak, M.C. Sanskrit nāṭaka meṅ atiprākṛta tattva. - Jaipur : Devanagar Prakashan, [n.d.].

18, 468 p.

Pisharoti, K.R. Extracts from the Ratnavali : miscellany. *Indian Historical Quarterly;* March 1949; Vol. 25, No. 1; Pp. 66 - 73.

Prabha Kiran. Critical study of the dramas of Harsha / by Prabha Kiran.

Ph.D. thesis in Hindi approved by the Bihar University in 1977.

Pusalkar, A.D. Śri Harṣa's plays / by A.D. Pusalker. *Annals of the Bhandarkar Oriental Research Institute;* 1964; Vol. XLV.

Review of English tr. by Bak Kun Bae.

Pp. 167 - 169.

Raghavan, V. Performance in ancient India' / by V. Raghavan. *In* Sanskrit drama in performance / ed. by Rachel Van M. Baumer and James R. Brandon. - Hanolulu : The University of Hawaii, 1981. Pp. 16 - 18.

Sahasrabudhe, Sheela. Harsha, the dramatist : a study of the Sanskrit dramas / by Sheela Sahasrabudhe.

Ph.D. thesis approved by the Banaras Hindu University in 1949.

Sahitya Akademi - New Delhi : The National bibliography of Indian literature. - New Delhi : The author, 1962 - 1990.

5 Vols.

Sanskrita sahitya sambhar / ed. by Gaurinath Sastri & et al. [Vol. 18]. - Calcutta : Navpatra Prakashan, [197-].

Contains 'Harṣacarita' of Baṇabhatta.

Schuyler, Montgomery, Jr. A Bibliography of the plays attributed to Harṣadeva / by Montgomery Schuyler, Jr. *Verhandlungen des xiii. Internationalen Orientalisten - Kongresses* (1902). - Leiden, 1904. Pp. 33 - 37.

Schuyler, Montgomery, J.A. Bibliography of the Sanskrit drama. - New York : [s.n.]; 1906. - (Columbia University Indo - Iranian Series; Vol. 3).

-----. The Origin of the Vidūṣaka and the employment of this character in the plays of Harṣadeva / by Montogomery Schuyler, Jr. *JAOS,* 1899; No. 20. Pp. 338 - 340.

Sethi, Atmaram. Anudit Hindi sahitya : vishishta granthasuchi / by Atmaram Sethi - Gurgaon : Indian Documentation Service, 1981.

Contents : Sanskrit (Pp. 1 - 624).

Sharma, Baijnath. Harṣa and his times. - Varanasi : Sushma Prakashan, 1970.

xxxii, 527 p.; 25 cm.

Shastri, Aiyaswami N. Nāgānanda and its social background *All India Oriental Conference* XV (Summary); Pp. 62 - 63 *Annals of the Bhandarkar Oriental Research Institute* 1951; Vol. 31; Pp. 233 - 238.

Shastri, Gaurinath. Sanskrit sahityer itihas. - Calcutta : Sarasvata Library, 1969? [Aśvin 1376].

Shastri, H.G. The Ancient kings mentioned in the sixth ucchavāsa of the Harṣ acarita [of Bāṇa]. *All India Oriental Conference* XVII; Pp. 325 - 329.

Shastri, Raghavara Mithulal. Was Śrīharsa a Bengali? *All India Oriental Conference IV;* Vol. I (Summaries; 48).

Shekhar, I. Sanskrit drama : its origin and decline. - Leiden : E.J. Brill, 1960.

Pp. xxv, 72, 116, 135, 148, 161, 171 - 175, 177 - 179, 193, 194.

Sircar, Dines Chandra. Harsa's accession and era : miscellany. *Indian Historical Quarterly;* Dec. 1951; Vol. 27, no. 4; Pp. 321 - 327 & March 1953; Vol. 29; No. 1; Pp. 72 - 79.

Smith, Vincent A. Early history of India. - 3rd ed. - Oxford : [s.n.], 1914. Pp. 335 - 359.

Deals with the reign of Harsha.

Smith, Vincnet A. Oxford history of India. - Oxford : [s.n.], 1919. Pp. 165 - 171.

Covers the reign of Harsha.

Tirtha : the treasury of Indian expressions / ed. by Vijaya Ghose. - New Delhi : CMC Ltd., 1992. P. 206.

Varadpande, M.L. Religion and theatre / by M.L. Varadpande. *Sangeet Natak Akademi Journal;* July - Sept. & Oct. - Dec. 1979; Vols. 53 - 54. Pp. 5 - 13.

Verma, Jayanarayan and Gupta, Pushpa. Sanskrit sahitya ka itihas. - Ghaziabad : Tarun Prakashan, 1991.

Warren, S.J. Koning Harsha van Kanyākubja. - The Hague : [s.n.], 1883.

8 p.

Extract from *Bijdragen tot de Taal -, Land-, en Volkenkunde van Neerlandsch - Indiē.*

Winternitz, M. History of Indian literature (Vol. 3) / tr. from German into English by Subhadra Jha. - Delhi : Motilal Banarsidass, 1985.

8

Jayadeva

Historians have placed Sanskrit dramatist Jayadeva in the thirteenth century. He is the author of famous Rama play 'Prasannaraghava' and is distinct from Gitagovinda fame poet Jayadeva and also several other Jayadeva's known to literary world such as Jayadeva of 'Śṛngāramādhavīya - champu or the sixteen century A.D. Sanskrit author of Ratimañjari, a work on erotics etc.

From his drama, we learn that Jayadeva was the son of Mahadeva and Sumitra and of Kuṇḍinya Gotra.

In the *'History of Sanskrit literature'*, Sri De writes that the dramatist was proficient in logic and in the domain of poetry. But his identity with the logician Jayadeva Prakashadhara of Mithila lacks evidence, but it is certain that he penned 'Prasannaraghava' and also credited with a book on poetics entitled *'Candraloka'* from which he probably took the surname of Pīyūshavarsha.

He was a pupil of Harimiśra and probably a native of Vidarbha in Northern India. A Śaiviṭe in religion, he was an ardent devotee of Rāma.

Ramaranjan Mukherjee opined that being born in an age of decadence, Jayadeva was not able to demonstrate his dramatic talents to the full, but his 'Prasanna - Raghava' is certainly one of the best of the Rama plays that cropped up in imitation of the Rama story. Therefore, as far as dramatic quality is concerned, the play, undcubtedly shows sign of decline when the Sanskrit drama writing itself was passing through a decadent phase. However, because of the lyrical etement, this play is reckoned as one of the noteworthy plays that deal with the story of Rāma.

He takes up dramatic from to show his metrical skill and his expertise in the use of figure of speech and so many other things.

In the play, author prefers longmetres, though the 'Vasantatilaka' is his favourite and then comes the Sārdulavikrīḍita, Sloka, Sikhariṇī and Sragdharā.

Biswanath Bhattacharya in his *'Sanskrit dama and dramaturgy'* wrote : 'The entire drama suffers from an exuberant display of rhetorical skill. The prose of Jayadeva is typical of the decadent period and both verse and prose indicate that the playwright was a skilled master of rhetorics. Dramatic art, however, did not receive any impetus from him. Jayadeva's Nāṭaka is a typical product of the period of stagnation of the dramatic art'. He further commented that 'The Nāṭaka had maintained a very living tradition upto the times of Bhavabhuti after which it began to show signs of degeneration which reached its lowest level by the time of Jayadeva. Therefore, he is the last dramatist during the period in question.

Based on the Rāmāyana epic, the theme is modelled slavishly upon Murāri's Nāṭaka and thereby, the dramatist shows little originality in it. He, however, made several modifications in the original story to give dramatic effect such as in the first act, the demons Bāṇa and Rāvaṇa are brought together as Śītā's suitors and ridiculed. The concluding act introduces a pair of Vidyādharas who narrate the battle and the purification and restoration of Sītā.

At several places, the Hindi poet Tulasīdāsa was greatly influenced by Jayadeva. In his Rāmacharitamānasa he had directly borrowed the garden - scene from the play 'Prasanna Rāghava'. The proud dialogues between Parashurāma and Lakshmaṇa had motivated Tulasīdāsa to incorporate this thrilling context in his work.

A. Berriedale Keith feels that one merit of the drama is its Act V where the spectacle of the river goddesses grouped round the ocean affords admirable scope for an effective tableau, but it is wholly out of harmony with dramatic action.

In the prologue to his play, Jayaḍeva eulogises Bāṇa, Bhāsa, Cora, Kāliḍāsa and Mayūra.

Verses from this drama are quoted in Jalhaṇa's *Sūkṭimukṭāvali*, a composition of 1247 A.D. There are commentaries on 'Prasanna - Raghava' by Lakṣ mīdhara, Venkatārya, Raghunanḍana, Lakṣmaṇa, Narasimha or Rājarāya.

Rajendra Mishra commented that Prasannarāghava is an epoch - making literary creation, which may attract the common public towards the Rāma episode.

Prasannaraghava

Synopsis

A play in seven acts, Prasanna - Raghava depicts the life of Rāma that begins from his wedding after breaking of Śiva's bow and end with his return from Laṅkā in the aerial car and his coronation.

Dramatis Personae

(In order of appearance)

Sutradhar

Nata

Dalbhyayan

Manjiraka

Nūpuraka

Puruṣa

Ravaṇa

Baṇasur

Tapasa

Bhikshu

Rāma

Lakṣmaṇa

Sīta

Sakhi

Cetī

Vamanaka

Kubjaka

Vishvamitra

Shatananda.

Janaka

Pratīharī

Muni

Kanchukī

Jamadagnya

Taṇdyayana

Bhargava

Gaṇga

Yamuna

Saryu

Ubhe

Kalhamsa

Tistra

Hansa

Sagara

Godavari

Tundangbhadra

Trijata

Hanuman

Pulsatyaśiṣya

Karalaka.

Prahasṭa

Mandodarī

Vidyadharī

Vidyadhara

Bibhiṣaṇa

Sugrīva.

Plot:-

In the First Act, Yājñavalkya's disciple enters and repeats from the speech of two bees heard behind the scene the news they are discussing. For the hands of Sīta, the Asura Bāṇa is to rival Rāvaṇa. Two heralds emerge to narrate the suitors for the maiden's hand; They are interrupted and insulted by a gross and rough arrival who casts a contemptuous eye on the bow which the suitor is supposed to bend; and forcibly seize the prize. The heralds soothe him, but he takes ten headed monstrous form of Ravaṇa. Then emerges Bāṇa who tries to bend the bow in vain, insults Rāvaṇa and exists. In Act II, focus is on Rāma who watches Sītā and her friend; both Rama and Sīta decribes the beauties of the union of the Vāsantī creeper and the mango - tree that reflects their own state of mind and confronted shyly whisper love. Act III depicts a number of compliments exchanged by all the parties, 'Vishvamitra, Shatānanda, Janaka, Dasaratha, Rama and Lakṣmana. Vishvamītra asks Rama to bend Sīva's bow; through a message from Parashurama deprecates such an insult.

Rama succeds in breaking the bow. This is a rejoicing moment and eventually the marriage is celebrated.

In Act IV, Parashurama appears in person; his great feats are set out in a dialogue of Rāma and Lakṣmana; Parashurama encounters them, heated arguments are exchanged. Janaka, Satananda and Visvamitra tries to dissuade them from battle, but when Vīsvāmitra is being humiliated, the Rama can not resist himself and ultimately they fight in which Rāma becomes victorious, but falls at his rival's feet and asks his blessing.

In Act V, the Rama story is told through the various river goddesses and the god Sāgara (ocean). It begins with Yamuna who tells Ganga of her grief at Vālin's act in exiling his brother, Sugriva. Sarayu enters and narrates Rama's fate until his departure for exile; now emerges her flamingo who breaks the further news until Rama's fatal departure to hunt a golden deer. The rivers anxiously proceeds toward the ocean, Sāgara, to learn the news; here they find Godavari narrating the tells right from Sitā's rape, the death of Jatayu, the fall of Sīta's jewels to their transport to Ṛṣyamukha. The Tungabhadra brings the news that Rāma has slain Valin and made alliance with Sugriva and Hanumant. All of a sudden, a great mass flies over the ocean. Sāgara goes out to find whether it is Himālaya or Vidhya? The rivers approaches the ocean.

In Act VI grief striken Rama goes out madly in search of his beloved and asks the birds, the moon for Sita. At this juncture, two vidyadharas by magic art presents the incidents that occur in Lanka; Sīta emerges, saddened lest Rāma suspect or be faithless to her; Ravana proposes her but Sita despises him and this insult breaks down Ravana's patience and he reaches out his hand for his sword to slay her, but surprisingly receives in it his son Aksa's head who got slained by 'Hanumant and also has leaped the ocean and attacked Lanka. Sita is now desperate to end her life by burning herself on a funeral pyre, but even the coal changes to pearl, and finally she is being consoled by Hanumant and tells about Rama's fidelity.

In Act VII, Prahasta presents a picture sent by Malayavant to Ravana that portrays the details account of enemy's attack and the bridge; he refuses to regard it as mere painter's fancy. At this moment, his wife, Mandodari appears and tells that she has received an oracular response that terrifies both her and Prahasta, but Ravana ignores it. But at last to realizes that the city is attacked and thus, sends atonce both Kumbhakarna and Meghanada to defend but they meet their death. Finally he himself issues forth to die. His fate as well as the purification and restoration of Sita is told by Vidyadhara and his mate. After this appears Rama, Sita, Laksmana, Vibhisana and Sugriva. They all describe in turn the setting of sun and the rise of moon. The nataka ends with Rama's journey to Ayodhya in the aerial car and on their way, they describe a few points of interest in the country over which they passes and then in turn describes the rising of the sun in solemn manner.

Dramatic Works : A Bibliography

Text

Prasanna - rāghava / by Jayadeva; commentary 'Bhāvabodhini' by Ganganatha Upadhyaya. - Kashi : Medical Hall Press, 1986.

130 p.

Prasanna - rāghava / by Jayadeva; commentary by Venkatacharya Upadhye; ed. by Shivarama Raoji Khopakar. - Bombay : Nirnaya Sagar Press, 1894.

277, 18 p.

Prasanna - rāghava / by Jayadeva; ed. by Govindadeva Sastri. - Banaras : Medical Hall Press, 1868.

157 p.

Prasanna - rāghava / by Jayadeva; ed. by Jivananda. - Calcutta : [s.n.], 1872.

168 p.

Prasanna - rāghava / by Jayadeva; ed. by K.P. Parab. - Bombay : Nirnaya Sagar Press, 1893.

-----. Bombay : Nirnaya Sagar Press, 1914.

140, 6 p.

Prasanna - rāghava / by Jayadeva; ed. by S.M. Paranjape and N.S. Pause . - Pune: Shiralkar & Co., 1894.

209, 106 p.

Includes introd. & notes.

Prasanna - rāghava / by Jayadeva; ed. by S.S. Palande. - Bombay : Ganapat Krishnaji, 1859.

Includes Marathi translation.

Prasannaraghava / by Jayadeva; ed. by Vasudeva Lakshana Panasikara. - New Delhi : Meharchand Lachhmandas, 1982.

122, 6 p.; 21 cm.

Prasannarāghava / by Jayadeva; ed. with a commentary 'Bhāvabodhini' by Gaṅgānāth Jhā. - Allahabad : Medical Hall Press, 1906.

150 p.; 18 cm.

Play in seven acts.

Prasannaraghava / by Jayadeva; the 'Vibha' Sanskrit and Hindi commentaries by Ramanatha Tripathi Sastri and Ramakanta Tripathi. - Varanasi : Chaukhamba Amarabharati Prakashan, 1977.

40, 547 p.; 18.5 cm.

Translations

Hindi

Prasannarāghava / by Jayadeva; tr. by Śeṣrāj Sharma Regmī. - Varanasi : Caukhamba Vidyabhavan, 1956.

Prasannaraghava / by Jayadeva; the 'Vibha' Sanskrit and Hindi commentaries by Ramanatha Tripathi Sastri and Ramakanta Tripathi. - Varanasi : Chaukhamba Amarabharati Prakashan, 1977.

40, 547 .; 18.5 cm.

Malayalam

Prasanna - rāghava / by Jayadeva; tr. into Malayalam by Velutheri Kesavan Asan.

Marathi

Prasanna - rāghava / by Jayadeva; ed. & tr. into Marathi by Shriram Shastri Palande. - Bombay : Ganapat Krishnaji, 1859.

Telugu

Prasanna - rāghava / by Jayadeva; tr. into Telugu by C. Ramanuja Das.

Prasannarāghava / by Jayadeva; tr. by Kākarla Koṇḍalarāvu .- Eluru : Rāmā Press, 1929.

xiv, 181 p.; 22 cm.

Tr. of Sanskrit drama.

Prasanna Raghava / by Jayadeva; tr. into Telugu by Kokkonda Venkataratnam .- Madras : V. Ramasvami Sastri, 1945.

108 p.; 20.4 cm.

Prasannarāghava nāṭakamu / by Jayadeva; tr. into Telugu by Mantripragaḍa Bhujaṅgarāvu. - Eluru : The translator, 1928.

viii, 142 p.; 18 cm.

Prasannarāghava nāṭakamu / by Jayadeva; tr. into Telugu by B. Subrahmaṇya Śarma. - Mopidevi : The translator, 1953.

Prasanna - rāghava - nāṭya - prabandham / by Jayadeva; tr. into Telugu by Bodducharla Timmaya.

Telugu rendering by a 16th century author whose style takes a mixed form of poetic composition and a dramatic presentation.

Other Works

Text

Candraloka / by Jayadeva; ed. with Hindi tr. Sanskrit commentary etc. by Subodhacandra Panta. - Delhi : Motilal Banarsidass, 1981.

[15], 238 p.

Candraloka / by Jayadeva; ed. with 'Paurnamasi' & 'Kathabhatti' Sanskrit & Hindi commentaries by Nandakiśora Śarma. - Varanasi : Chowkhamba Sanskrit Series Office, 1950.

30, 304 p.; 18 cm.

Candralokah / by Jayadeva; the commentary 'Saradagama' by Pradyotana Bhattacharya; ed. with Sanskrit and Hindi commentary... by Gangasagara Raya. - Varanasi : Chaukhamba Sanskrit Sansthan, 1985.

16, 260 p.

Verse with commentary, on Sanskrit rhetoric and poetics.

Candralokah : with the Sanskrit commentary 'Sakha' / by Jayadeva; ed. with commentary by Candramauli Dvivedi. - Varanasi : Bharatiya Vidya Sansthan, 1991.

47, 332 p.

Translations

Hindi

Candraloka / by Jayadeva; ed. with Hindi tr., Sanskrit commentary etc. by Subodhacandra Patna. - Delhi : Motilal Banarsidass, 1981.

[15], 238 p.

Candrāloka / by Jayadeva; tr. into Hindi by Brajaratnadāsa. - Allahabad : Rāmanarayanlal, 1933.

Chandrāloka / by Jayadeva; tr. into Hindi by Gaurīśankara Śarmā. - Varanasi : Master Kiladilal, 1954.

Candrāloka / by Jayadeva; tr. into Hindi by Nandakiśora Śarmā. - Varanasi : Caukhamba Vidyabhavan, 1954.

BIO - CRITICAL NOTICES

Aufrecht, Theodor. Catalogus catalogorum. - Weisbaden : Franz Steiner Verlag Gmb. H., 1962.

2 Vols.; 26 cm.

Adya Rangacharya. Drama in Sanskrit literature. - Bombay : Popular Prakashan, 1967.

Pp. 44, 194.

Bhyartiya, Kanti Kishore. Sanskrit natakkar. - Uttar Pradesh : Prakashan Śakha, Suchana Vibhag, 1959.

(Hindi - Samiti granthamala; 25).

Contents : Jayadeva. Pp. 201 - 202.

Bhattacharya, Biswanath. Sanskrit drama and dramaturgy. - Delhi : Sharada Publishing House, 1994.

Chandrana, Urmil. Critical study of Prasannaraghava of Jayadeva / by Urmil Chandrana.

Ph.D. thesis approved by the Punjab University in 1986.

Deolia, Asha. Comparative study of the heros of the Sanskrit dramas : from Bhasa upto Jayadeva / by Asha Deolia.

Ph.D. thesis approved by the Rajasthan University in 1972.

Encyclopaedia of Indian literature. - New Delhi : Sahitya Akademi, 1987 - 1994.

Pp. 964, 1102, 1104, 1205, 1421, 1814 - 16, 1948, 2073, 2347, 2491, 2499, 3026, 3036, 3236, 3323, 3570.

Garg, Ganga Ram. An Encyciopaedia of Indian literature. - Delhi : Mittal Publishers, 1982-

Pp. 75, 157, 303 - 304.

Gera, Vimla. Mind and art of Bhavabhuti. - Delhi : Meharchand Lachhmandas, 1973.

Contents : Dinnaga [Pp. 254 -270].

Glimpes of Sanskrit literature / ed. by A.N.D. Haksar. - New Delhi : Indian Council for Cultural Relations, 1995.

Contents : Jayadeva Pp. 6, 108 - 9, 122.

Kadian, Khazani Devi. Comparative study of Ullagha Raghava and Prasanna Raghava / by Khazani Devi Kadian.

Ph.D. thesis in Hindi approved by the Kurukshetra University in 1983.

Keith, A. Berriedale. The Sanskrit drama in its origin, development, theory and practice. - Oxford : OUP, 1924.

405 p.; 22 cm.

Keith, A Berriedale Sanskrit - natak : udbhav aur vikas : siddhanta aur prayog / tr. into Hindi by Udabhanu Singh. - Delhi : Motilal Banarsidass, 1965.

Krishnamachariar, M. and Srinivasachariar. History of classical Sanskrit literature. - Delhi : Motilal Banarsidass, 1989.

Pp. 645 - 646.

Lēvi, Sylvain. The theatre of India / tr. from the French by Narayan. Mukherji. - Calcutta : Writers Workshop, 1978.

Contents: Prasannarāghava. Pp. (Vol. I) 136, 157, 243 - 245, 249, 261 - 266, 274; (Vol. II) 90.

Mishra, Mahendra. Prasannaraghava : a literary study / by Mahendra Mishra.

Ph.D. thesis in Hindi approved by the Magadh University in 1971.

Mishra, Mrigankabhushan. Literal study of Prasannaraghava / by Mrigankabhushan Mishra.

Ph.D. thesis in Sanskrit approved by the K.S. Darbhanga University in 1975.

Mishra, Radheyshyam. Critical study of Jayadeva as a rhetorician / by Radheyshyam Mishra.

Ph.D. thesis approved by the Allahabad University in 1969.

Prabha Devi. Study of commentaries on Chandraloka / by Prabha Devi.

Ph.D. thesis in Hindi, approved by the University of Delhi in 1983.

Purang, Shashi Prabha. Comparative and critical study of the dramas of Murari and Jayadeva / by Shashi Prabha Purang.

Ph.D. thesis in Hindi, approved by the Agra University in 1972.

Sahitya Akademi - New Delhi. The National bibliography of Indian literature. - New Delhi : The author, 1962 - 1990.

5 Vols

Sharma, Devichandra. Comparative study of Anargharaghava and Prasannaraghava / by Devichandra Sharma.

Ph.D. thesis in Hindi, approved by the Meerut University in 1975.

Shekhar, I. Sanskrit drama : its origin and decline. - Leiden : E.J. Brill, 1960.

Vedam Venkataraya Sastry. Andhra Prasanna Raghava Nātaka Vimarśanam. 1898, Vedam Venkataraya Sastry wrote 'Āndhra' Prasanna Rāghava Nātaka Vimarśanam in his *Śāradā Kānchika*, a voluminous criticism of over three hundred pages, where in the unworthiness of the Telugu translation of Jayadeva's Prasanna Rāghava Nāṭaka by Sri Kokkonda Venkata Ratnam Pantulu, a Telugu Pandit of the Madras Presidency College, and a leading writer of the day and the excellence of the original well broughtout.

Vinod Chandra. Jayadeva : a critical study as Acharya and natakkar / by Vinod Chandra.

Ph.D. thesis approved by the Agra University in 1973

9

Krishna Mishra

Kṛṣṇa Miśra is the author of the one of the earliest known allegorical dramas. There are some evidences that makes us believe that Krishna Miśra belonged to the latter half of the eleventh century. Such as the prologue of his work. 'Prabodha - chandrodaya (Rise of the moon of knowledge) that gives an account of the victories of king Kīrtivarman of the Chandella dynasty and his general Gopāla over the armies of Chedi king Karṇadeva. The King Kīrtivarman ruled between 1049 and 1100 and his victory over Karṇadeva was about 1065. The play was written at the instance of Gopāla.

An inscription of A.D. 1042 mentions Karna, and another of 1098 mentions Kirtivarman, the Chandela King.

The genealogies of the Kamakoti Pitha record that Krishna Miśra was contemporary of Chandrashekhara Saraswati, the 47th pontiff of the Pitha.

The dramatist was a stern disciplined devotee of god, an ascetic of the Haṁsa order, a staunch follower of Śaṅkara and missionary for the propagation of Avaita doctrines.

Jagirdar writes that Kṛṣṇa Miśra composed the play at a period when the religious atmosphere in India was in a chaotic condition. Buddhism and Jainism had demoralised to a great extent, and various forms of Hinduism were unsuccessful in inspiring confidence among the people. Rising above class distinction several religious leaders from the lower ranks gave a new interpretation to the old beliefs and contributed to the revival of the Bhakti movement. Therefore Kṛṣṇa miśra's play gives useful information about the fading face of the Buddhist and Jain faiths, demoralisation of Paṇḍitas in Banaras, the orgies in which monks participated, the existence of certain sects allowing the slaughtering of animals, the scenes of gambling and chess - playing.

The credit of composing the first allegorical drama goes to Kṛṣṇamiśra. that inspired many works modelled on it, but are not of high order. Such as Vedantadeśika (12th cent.) who makes the subject matter of his *'Saṁkalpasūryodaya'* (Imaginary sunrise) in favour of Viśīṣṭādvaita philosophy, *'Mohaparajaya'* of Yashahpala (the Defeat of Love) (13th cent.). *'Chaitanyachandrodaya* (1572) of Kavikarnapura. *'Vidyāpariṇaya'* by Ānandarāyamakhin (18th cent.). *Śivaliṅgasūryodaya* of Mallāri Ārādhya (18th cent.).

Besides Prabodha candrodaya, no other work of this author is known. Though author never intended it to be such, this is hailed as one of the best satires in Sanskrit literature; what he has written in the play makes every Hindu not to be born in Benares. Similarly the demoralisation of Buddhist and Jaina orders is meticulously drawn by the merciless caricature of the monks at the hand of the playwright.

Entire play is a glorification of the Vishnu cult as a form of orthodox Brahmanism, much as the allegorical plays of the Spanish poet Calderon exalt the Catholic faith.

Prabodhacandrodaya is in six acts and has in all 191 verses that show the mounting interest the playwright of ancient period displayed in composing stanzas. His verses are much simplier than his prose. The author shows his poetical skill and sometimes employs rimed verses in Prakrit.

Macdonell opined that the main strength of the play lies in the effectiveness of its moral and philosophical stanzas, but the action of its allegorical figures can not said to show any dramatic power. Dialogue of the play is sometimes not without humour. Though the diction of the play suffers from artificiality but are not so tedious. The play shows his commendable grasp of dramatic art and the language is lucid.

Kṛṣṇa Miśra moved away from romantic theme and preferred to employ Śānta Rasa by choosing the allegorical theme of the triumph of discrimination (Viveka) over his rival confusion (Mahāmoha) to illustrate it.

Abstract notions such as religion, reason and knowledge are personified as characters in this play. Therefore in the play, some are mythical or abstract conception and symbolical figures.

With abstract ideas of an essentially religious and philosophical nature, he successfully wrote an allegorical play that evokes interesting reading. The psychological analysis of the states of mind shows playwrights profound perception and critical judgement.

Beneath apparent exterior of erotic ideas, the play upholds the supreme truth of Advaita Vedānta and rejects the tenets of other school of philosophy.

According to Biswanath Bhattacharya, Kṛṣṇa Miśra may be successful in presenting his theme, but the want of human interest in the play is fatal. Such abstract ideas as constitute one's moral being can not attain a life like reality and consequently, inspite of admirable presentation, the Nāṭaka fails to appeal.

On the other hand, I. Shaekhar in his essay entitled '*A rapid survey of decadent features in post Kālidāsan dramas writes*'... After Murari and Rājaśekhara the flame of drama does not show any glow except in the case of Prabodha candrodaya of Kṛṣṇamiśra, when it suddenly lights up to illumine the allegorical play momentarily.

Prabodhacandrodaya

Synopsis

Play dwells on a conflict between two attitudes. One attitude propel man to acquire real knowledge and the other retards it. King Mind has two consorts, Pravritti (Activity) and Nivritti (Repose). The former gives birth to Moha (Delusion), the latter to Viveka (Discrimination). Moha has as his attendants Kama (Love) and his wife Rati (Pleasure), Krodha (Anger), Himsa (Injury), Ahamkara (Egoism) and his grandson Dambha (Deceit) born of Lobha (Greed) and Trishna (Desire).

The retinue covers Mithyadrishti (Heresy, depicted as a courtesan, and the materialist Charvaka. Viveka has, as his followers, Mati (Reason), Dharma (Duty), Karuna (Compassion), Maitri (Friendliness), Shanti (Peace) and her mother Shraddha (Faith), Kshama (Forgiveness), Santosha (Contentment), Vastuvichara (Judgement), Bhakti (Devotion etc.).

A very fierce battle starts between these two related familites. A rumour is spread that a terrible female demon will be born with the Moon - Rise of knowledge (Prabodha candrodaya) from the union of King Discrimination (Viveka) with his wife Revelation (Upanishad), who will destroy the whole family of confusion (Moha).Religion and Reason, accompanied by all virtues are banished from the Kingdom. But with the help of Faith and wisdom the Good wins over Evil. Thus this battle, the old Wisdom becomes victorious. Through Divine Love (Vishṇu - bhakti), the Revelation (Upnishad) becomes pregnant. From her womb a daughter, Science (Vidya) and son, Rise of knowledge (Prabodhodaya) are born.

A voice is heard that announces the emergence of terrible Science (Vidya) from the breast of the mind (Manas) and that she has swallowed king confussion (Moha) with his retinue. At this juncture, there appears 'Rise of knowledge' (Prabodhodaya) and greets with reverance the original Spirit (Purusha) who with great pleasure takes him within his arms.

The drama brings about the eventful unification of Viveka and the Upanishad the latter gives birth to Prabodha (True Knowledge) and Vidya (Spiritual Wisdom) and the over coming of Moha.

Dramatis Personae

Sutradhara	(Stage - manager)
Viveka	(Discrimination) as the King.
Mati	(Reason) (Viveka's wife).
Dharma	(Duty)
Karuṇā	(Pity) (Śanti's wife)
Maitrī	(Good - will)
Śānti	(Peace)
Śraddha	Śānti's mother (Faith)
Ksmā	(Forgiveness) (Vivekadāsī)
Santoṣa	(Contentment)
Vastuvicāra	(Judgement)
Bhakti	(Religious Devotion) and others as his followers.
Moha	(Confusion) : as the rival of Discrimination
Kāma	(Love) (King of Benares)

Puruṣa	(Upaniṣatpatiḥ)
Prabodhodayaḥ	(Upaniṣadutpannapuruṣah putraḥ)
Rati = Kama's wife	(Pleasure)
Krodha	(Anger)
Hiṃsā = Krodha's wife	(Injury)
Lobha	(Greed)
Tṛṣṇā = Lobha's wife	(Desire)
Dambha = son of Lobha and Tṛṣṇā	(Deceit)
Ahaṃkāra	(Egoism)
Father of Greed.	
Mithyādṛsti	(Heresy) Mohajaya etc.
	described as courtesan Carvaka
	to represent materialism (Mohamitram).
Manaḥ	(Saṃkalparupam)
Digambarabhikśukapalikaḥ	(Bauddhajainadi matapravaratāḥ)
Batuh, Śiṣyaḥ, puruṣah, Dauvarikaḥ,	Pariparśaka, purusaḥ, Sarathi, Pratihariṇaḥ.
Vairagya - nididhyasanasaṃkalpaḥ	(Manasa utpannaḥ).
Nati	(Sutradhar's wife)
Upaniṣat	(Vedantavidya)
Sarasvatī	(Viṣṇubhaktisakhi)
Vibhramavati	(Underline is female characters).

Plot:-

Prologue :-

The play begin with the usual Pastāvana. The Sūtradhāra tells audience that the King Gopāla has asked him to stage a Nāṭaka of Śānta Rasa to please his friend, Kīrtivarman who is fed up with the Vīra after a Surfiet of warfare. He then goes on to name the play and playwright and calls upon the Nati to arrange for the performance. In his attempt at removing the wonder of Naṭī as to the desire of the King to enjoy Śānta Rasa, he recites a verse which proclaims that the king has van quished Confusion with the assistance of Discrimination and true knowledge (Prabodha) has revealed itself to him. Śūtradhāra's statement is vehemently opposed by one from of stage, whom the Sūtradhāra recognises to be Love (Kāma) and tells the audience that Love with his wife Pleasure (Rati) is coming in an angry mood. Sūtradhāra departs and the play commences.

Act I opens with king Discrimination (Viveka) and his Queen Reason (Mati) who are deeply concerned at the increasing sway of confusion.

The king desires, and the Queen consents that he should take as his consort Upaniṣad - Devi that a son - Prabodha - Awakening may be born. The king decides to take definite steps so that True knowledge can be born and in order to persuade Upanisad Devi to marry him, he appoints Sama, Dama. The Act, thus, presents the begining of the action.

Act II takes us to the enemy's camp. Deceit reports that king confusion will capture Banares by over coming king Discrimination and his forces.

Playwright aptly chose Banares, the hub of spiritual culture as the centre for the contention between two parties. Deceit announces that he has successfully carried out the orders of his king and Benares is fully under his control. In the meanwhile appears Egoism who after a brief conversation with Deceit recognises Deceit as his grandson and the reveals before him that he has come to Benares to investingate the prevailing situation at the instances of king Confusion. Now they retires to meet the king.

In this Act, Benares Pundits get a scathing criticism where wicked men like Dambha (Arrogance) and Ahamkāra (Vanity) conspire to present the birth of Prabodha.

Here king Confusion is presented who laughs at the folly of the religious men. He propagates his doctrine of 'eat, drink and be merry'. Materialim (Cārvāka) comes with a disciple. The king recognises him to be his friend and greets him.

Cārvaka unfolds that Kurukṣetra has been won over by him to the side of confusion. He, however, adds that Devotion being very strong and invincible, Cārvaka could not overcome him. The latter news purturbs the king who atonce orders the messanger to send Love, Anger, Greed etc to kill Devotion.

From Kaliṅga, a messenger comes who reports that Peace along with her mother, Faith (Śraddha) has gone to lady Upaniṣad as heralds of King Dscrimination to persuade her to marry Discrimination.

Not only this, Duty (Dharma alongwith ground Asceticism (Vairagya) is also gaining. The news adds fuel to the fire. The infuriated king orders the messenger to ask Love to capture Duty and put him behind the bar. He then sends Anger and Greed to overcome Peace, the daughter of Peace. He plans to alienate Faith from Upanisad.

Mithyādṛṣti (Heresy / False understanding), the courtesan is commission to achieve the goal. Śānti (Peace), Śraddhās daughter is to be killed by felons like Krodha (Anger) and Lobha (Avarice) etc or die of sorrow.

Act III begins with Peace and his friend 'Pity'. Peace is sad without her mother and decides to commit suicide. But she is prevented from such act by her friend. Now they go out in search of 'Faith'. Here they come in contact with Jaina and Buddhist monks. If the Pundits of Benares are condemned as immoral hypocrites. Then these Buddhism, Jainism or Kāpalikas get no better treatment here.

All of them claim to own Faith. But Peace and Pity atonce recognises these Faiths as tāmasa and rājasa in nature and lacking sāttvika Faith.

Kāpālika who represents Soma cult wins over Jainism and Buddhism not by means of superiority of his cult but by allurement which he achieves from the charming embrace of his Faith in the form of Kāpālini. In the interest of king Confusion, the three Bohemians drink wine and decide to abduct Sāttvikī Śraddhā (Pure Faith) who is supposed to be living in the company of one Viṣnubhakti (Devotion of God Viṣṇu). Thus, by means of their astrological knowledge they come to know that Faith is to be found only in the hearts of good men, along with Devotion and Duty. Followers of Confusion retires to capture Faith. The Third Act ends with the departure of Peace and Pity only to convey all these happenings to Devotion.

In Act Four Good will (Maitrī) and Faith are discussing among themselves. Faith states about her recovery from the clutches of Mahābhairavi, an assistant of the Kāpālika, referred to in the third Act, in which she was helped by Devotion. Faith reports that she is going to pass on Devotion's message to king Discrimination, the message being an exhortation to the king to defeat the forces of Confusion and a promise of help in the action. It is also revealed that she has already sent some goddesses to persuade lady Upanishad to give birth to True Knowledge.

Good will expresses her willingness alongwith her sisters to support King Discrimination and wants to see King's success, as ordered by Devotion. Faith states that King Discrimination is at the moment is on meditation on the banks of

Ganges at Cakratīrtha in the country of Rāḍha (Bengal) for the fulfilment of his union with Upanisad.

Thereafter, the focus is on king Discrmination who as advised by Devotion considers ways and means of defeating the attendants of Confusion. He orders Judgement to fight with and win over Love. Judgement obeys the command and leaves atonce.

In order to defeat Anger, he chooses Forgiveness (Kṣamā) to take over the task He asks contentment (Santoṣa) to oust Greed and set out immediately for Benares and sends all his forces to chariot and proceeds towards Benares.

Act V describes the battle and its consequences. Here Devotion, Peace and Faith are presented. They unfold the total defeat of confusion and his followers. The reaction of it on Mind, the father, is disheartening who decides to die asks Will make funeral pyne. This Act proper thus presented Mind and Will (Saṅkalpa). The former is unable to bear pangs of separation as his wife Activity (Pravṛtti) has also abandoned him. He is in deep sorrow at the death of his favourite sons. Now Saraswati slowly appears and make him seek refuge in Vairāgya. Wisdom draws upon him which changes his outlook and to him appears Vairāgya. Vairāgya consoles his father, Mind, makes him friendly towards. Discrimination. Saraswati advises him to accept Repose (Nivṛtti) as his consort and to be favourable towards his son, Discrimination and his followers. Mind, thus, takes the side of king Discrimination. In this Act, however, without the birth of true Knowledge success is not fully attained.

Act VI: Attainment of Result (Phalāgama) is shown in this final Act. Peace and Faith relate that Mind is leading a peaceful and happy life and king Discrimination is waiting for Upaniṣad to whom Peace has been sent as a messenger. Confusion is defeated by Logic and has thus failed to win over Puruṣa who is willing to meet Discrimination on her advice and all this is known to the audience through Faith.

Puruṣa is presented after this. To him appears Upaniṣads and Peace, King Discrimintion and Faith, one after another. Upanisad narrates how she suffered at the hands of the Heretics and her ultimate rescue by Viṣṇu. Puruṣa, now realises that he is the Soul, the Supreme being and a happy union of Puruṣa, Upaniṣad and Discrimination occurs. Devotions now sends messenger who conveys to Upanisad that she should go to Devotion alongwith Discrmination and that Wisdom and True Knowledge will, therefore, come into being. Wisdom will be given to mind and True Knowledge to Puruṣa. Accordingly both King Discrimination and Upaniṣ ads obeys the command. The birth of Prabodha is announced from behind the stage. Soon true knowledge emerges and he pays homage to Puruṣa, who embraces him. Devotion now enters to greet and blesses Wisdom and True Knowledge. The last benedictory verse, the Bharatavakya is uttered by Puruṣa after all the learned and philosophical quest for awakening and the play ends.

Dramatic Works : A Bibliography

Text

Prabodhacandrodaya / by Kṛṣṇa Miśra; the commentaries 'Candrikā' by Nāṇḍilagopa Mantriśekhara and 'Prakāśa' of Rāmadāsa Dīkṣita; ed. by Vāsudev Lakṣman Śāstri Paṇaśīkar. - Bombay : Nirnaya Sāgar Press, 1935.

viii, 244 p.; 22 cm.

Prabodhacandrodaya of Kṛṣṇa Miśra is philosophical allegory, in six acts, based on advaita.

Prabodhacandrodaya / by Kṛṣṇamiśra; ed. by Hermann Brockhaus .- Leipzig : [s.n.], 1835 - 1845.

2 Vols. in 1.

Includes Latin Translation.

Hermann Brockhaus (1806 - 1877)

German scholar Hermann Brockhaus was born on 28-1-1806 in Amsterdam. He was a full professor at Leipzig University and had specialised in Indian drama and narrative literature. Brockhaus became popular with his edition of Prabodha Chandrodaya from Leipzig in 1835, thus making the first allegorical Sanskrit drama available to the West. This edition was accompanied by a Latin translation. He stayed in Leipzig till his death on 5-1-1877.

Prabodhacandrodaya / by Kṛṣṇamiśra; ed. by Hrishikesh Śāstrī. -. Calcutta : [s.n.], [n.d.].

Prabodhacandrodaya / by Kṛṣṇa Miśra; ed. by K. Sāmbaśiva Śāstrī. - Trivandrum: Govt. of Tranvancore, 1936.

vi, 210, [4] p.; 24 cm.

(Trivandrum Sanskrit Series; 122).

Includes index.

Contains Govindāmṛta Bhagavān's commentary entitled 'Nāṭakābharaṇa'.

Prabodhacandrodaya / by Krishna Miśra; ed. with a commentary 'Pakaśa' by Ramachandra Miśra. - Vaanasi : Chowkhamba Vidya Bhavan, 1955.

15, 253 p.; 18 cm.

Translations

Bengali

Atmatwatta Kaumudi — [Calcutta] : [s.n.], 1822.

Tr. of 'Prabodhachandrodaya' into Bengali.

Bodhenduvikas / by Krishna Miśra; tr. into Bengali by Ishvar Gupta. - 1863.

Tr. of 'Prabodhacandrodaya'.

De, Sabitri. Sanskrit sahiter anubad - dhara. - Calcutta : Chinmay Majumdar, [1983].

Contents : Prabodhachandrodaya (Pp. 175 - 178).

Prabodhacandrodaya / by Krishna Miśra; tr. into Bengali by Adyanath Sharma. - Vidyabhusan 1893.

Prabodhacandrodaya / by Krishna Miśra; tr. into Bengali by Bishvanath Nyayratna. - 1871.

Originally translated in 1839, this is the first rendering in Bengali.

Prabodhacandrodaya / by Krishna Miśra; tr. into Bengali by Kaśināth Tarkapanchanan, Gadadhar Nyayratna and Ramkinkar Shiromani. - 1862.

Sanskrita sahitya sambhar / ed. by Gaurinath Sastri & et. al. [Vol. 6]. - Calcutta : Navpatra Prakashan, [197-].

Includes Bengali rendering of 'Prabodhacandrodaya'.

German

Prabodha Chandrodaya oder die Geburt des Begriffes / tr. into German by Theodor Goldstuecker.

Theodor Goldstuecker was born on 18-1-1821 in Koenigsberg. He was a Sanskrit professot at the University College in London. He held this post until his death on 6-3-1872. Goldstuecker's first work, published anonymously was the drama translation of Prabodha Chandrodaya oder die Geburt des Begriffes ("Prabodha Chandrodaya or the birth of concept").

Hindi

Prabodhacandrodaya / bý Kṛṣṇamiśra; tr. into Hindi by Ayodhyaprasad Chaudhuri 1885.

Prabodhacandrodaya / by Kṛṣṇamiśra; tr. into Hindi by Bhavadevji Dubey. 1886.

Prabodhacandrodaya / by Kṛṣṇamisrra; tr. into Hindi by Devidin. 1885.

[Prabodhacandrodaya] Grantha Prabodhanca nātaka satika / by Kṛṣna Miśra; tr. by Gulabsiṃha Kavi. - Lahore : [s.n.], 1908.

Tr. of 'Prabodha Candrodaya' into Hindi.

["] Pākhanda vidamban / by Kṛṣṇa Miśra; tr. by Bhāratendu Hariścandra. - Varanasi: Banaras Printing Press, 1873.

Prabodh candrodaya / by Kṛṣṇamiśra; tr. from Sanskrit by Brajvāsīdās. - Barabanki : The translator, 1903.

134 p.; 18.5 cm.

Prabodh Candrodaya / by Kṛṣṇamiśra; tr. from Sanskrit by Gulābsiṃha. - Bombay : Veṅkaṭeśvar Press, 1905.

180 p.; 24 cm.

Drama in verse form.

Also published in 1923.

Prabodh Candrodaya / by Kṛṣṇa Miśra; tr. from Sanskrit by Jasvantasiṃha; ed. by Somnātha Gupta. - Jaypore : Rajasthan Sahitya Akademī, 1963.

Prabodhcandrodaya / by Kṛṣṇa Miśra; tr. from Sanskrit by Maheshcandra Prasād. - Patna : The author, 1935.

Vijñānvibhākar / by Kṛṣṇa Miśra; tr. by Biharilāl Janī. - Varanasi : Sarsudhanidhi, 1879.

Kannada

Prabōdhacandrōdaya nāṭakam / by Kṛṣṇamiśra; tr. by M. Kṛṣṇappa .- Mysore : Karṇāṭaka Granthamālā, 1910.

viii, 100 p.; 21 cm.

Allegorical play translated from Sanskrit original that gives the essence of Vedānta.

Latin

Prabodh Candrodaya / by Kṛṣṇamiśra; ed. by Hermann Brockhaus. - Leipzig : [s.n.], 1835.

Includes Latin translation.

Malayalam

Prabōdhacandrōdayam / by Kṛṣṇa Miśra; tr. by C.A. Nāṇuvayyā Śāstri. - Trivandrum : T.P. Co. Press, 1900.

51 p.; 19 cm.

Allegorical drama, tr. from Sanskrit original.

Prabōdhacandrōdayam / by Kṛṣṇa Miśra; tr. by N. Kumāran Āśan. - Quilon : V.V. Press, 1930.

170 p.; 19 cm.

Marathi

Prabodh Candrodaya / by Kṛṣṇamiśra; tr. into Marathi. - 1851.

This is the first translated Marathi drama from original Sanskrit.

Nepali

Prabodh Chandrodaya / by Krishna Miśra; tr. into Nepali by Bhuvanprasad Dhungel.

[Work yet to be traced].

Prabodh Chandrodaya / by Krishna Miśra; tr. into Nepali by Harinarayan Upadhyay.

Punjabi

Prabodh Candar nāṭak / by Kṛṣṇa Miśra; tr. by Paṇḍit Gulāb Singh; commentary by Sant Javālā Dās. - Amritsar : Gurmat Press, [n.d.].

552 p.; 25 cm.

Telugu

Prabōdhacandrōdayamu / by Kṛṣṇa Miśra; tr. by Ākoṇḍi Vyāsamūrtiśāstri. - Kakinadha : Sujanarañjani Press, 1911.

114 p.; 18 cm.

Prabōdhacandrōdayamu / by Kṛṣṇa Miśra; tr. by Kandukūri Vīrēśaliṅgamu. - Rajahmundry : Hitakāriṇī Samājam, 1950.

vii, 114 p.; 21 cm.

Prabodh Candrodaya / by Krishna Misra; Tr. by Nandimallaya and Ghatasingaya; ed. by N. Venkata Rao. - Hyderabad : Andhra Pradesh Sahitya Akademi, 1977.

103 p.; 20 cm.

Prabōdhacandrōdayamu / by Kṛṣṇa Miśra; tr. by Tatvānanda Svāmi. - Tenali : Ōṅkārāśramamu, 1933.

94 p.; 18 cm.

BIO - CRITICAL NOTICES

Adya Rangacharya. Drama in Sanskrit literature. 2nd ed. - Bombay : Popular Prakashan., 1967.

Pp. 198 - 199.

Aggarwal, H.R. A short history of Sanskrit literature. - 2nd rev. ed. - Delhi : Munshiram Manoharlal, 1963.

Contents : (Kṛṣṇamiśra. P. 182-).

Aufrecht, Theodor. Catalogus catalogorum. - Weisbaden : Franz Steiner Verlag Gmb. H., 1962.

2 Vols.; 26 cm.

Basu, Manomohan. [Bodhendubikas]. *Madhyastha;* [Paus 1280]. P. 618.

On Ishvar Gupta's Bengali adaptation of Krishna Miśra's Sanskrit play 'Prabodacandrodaya'.

Bhartiya, Kanti Kishore. Sanskrit natakkara. - Uttar Pradesh : Prakashan Shakha, Suchana Vibhag, 1959.

(Hindi - Samiti granthamala; 25).

Contents : Kṛṣṇa Miśra. Pp. 199 - 200.

Bhattacharya, Biswanath. Sanskrit drama and dramaturgy. - Delhi : Sharada Publishing House, 1994. Pp. 294, 303 - 305, 311.

Comparative Indian literature (Vol. 1) / ed. by K.M. George. - Trichur : Kerala Sahitya Akademi, 1984. P. 570.

The Cultural heritages of India [Vol. V] / ed. by Suniti Kumar Chatterji. - rev. ed. - Calcutta : The Ramakrishna Mission Institute of Culture, 1978. P. 252.

De, S.K. History of Sanskrit Literature.

Deva, Nakul Chandra. Critical study of the Prabodha Chandrodaya of Krishna Misra / by Nakul Chandra Deva.

Ph.D. thesis approved by the Gauhati University in 1985.

Encyclopaedia of Indian literature. - New Delhi : Sahitya Akademi, 1987. Pp. 2148, 3312.

Garg, Ganga Ram. An encyclopaedia of Indian literature. - Delhi : Mittal Publishers, 1982.

Pp. 193, 300, 301.

Keith, A. Berriedale. The Sanskrit drama in its origin, development, theory and practice. - Oxford : OUP, 1924.

405 p.; 22 cm.

Keith, A. Berriedale Sanskrit - Natak : udbhav aur vikas : siddhanta aur prayog / tr. into Hindi by Udaybhanu Singh. - Delhi : Motilal Banarsidass, 1965.

Krishnamishra. Prabodhacandrodayam / by Srikrishnamishra; commentary by Ramachandra Mishra. - Varanasi : Chowkhamba Vidya Bhavan, 1955.

Pp. 3 - 13.

Gives glimpses on his, life, his date & work in Hindi.

Lēvi, Sylvain. The theatre of India / tr. from the French by Narayan Mukherji. - Calcutta : Writers Workshop, 1978.

Contents : Kṛṣṇa Miśra. Pp. (Vol. I), 133, 207 - 213; Prabodha - candrodaya. Pp. (Vol. I) 1, 114, 207 - 213.

Macdonell, A.A. India's past : a survey of her literatures, religions, languages and antiquities. - Varanasi : Motilal Banarsidass, 1956.

P. 116.

Panda, P.K. Contribution of Orissa to Sanskrit. - Delhi: Pratibha Prakashan, 1987.

Contents : Prabodhachandrodaya nātaka. P. 91.

Pathak, Kailash Nath. Critical study of Prabodhachandrodaya / by Kailash Nath Pathak.

Ph.D. thesis in Hindi, approved by the Banaras Hindu University in 1983.

Sahitya Akademi - New Delhi : The National bibliography of Indian literature. - New Delhi : The author, 1962 - 1990.

5 Vols.

Sastri, Gaurinath. Sanskrit sahityer itihas. - Calcutta : Sarasvata Library, 1969? [Ashvin 1376].

In Bengali.

Sethi, Atmaram : Anudit Hindi sahitya : vishishta granthasuchi / by Atmaram Sethi. - Gurgaon : Indian Documentation Service, 1981.

Contents : Sanskrit (Pp. 1 - 624).

Shekhar, I. Sanskrit drama : its origin and decline . - Leiden : E.J. Brill, 1960.

Pp. 142, 172, 194, 195

Vidyalankar, Jaidev. Krishnamisra's indebtedness to Mahendravikramavarman's Mattavilasam / by Jai Dev Vidyalankar. *Visheshvaranand Indological Journal;* March - Sept. 1975; Vol. 13, Nos. 1 - 2; Pp. 119 - 126, ft - n.

Warder, A.K. Indian kāvya literature (Vol. 6). - Delhi : Motilal Banarsidass Publishers, 1992.

Contents : Krishnamiśra.

Pp. 355 - 612. (Chapter XLVIII).

10

Murārī

Son of Vardhamānaka and Tantumati, Murārī lived under the Kālācuris ie Kalacur dynastry and of the Cediterritory, and by the middle of the 8th century A.D. Kalacuri kings had left Māhīṣmati and became settled in two lines at the capitals Tṛpurī and Raṭnapura. So hẹ could be placed to the end of the eight century A.D. and to the begining of the 9th century A.D. Ratnākara (middle of the 9th cent.) makes a clear reference to him in his 'Haravijaya'.

On the basis of references made by Ratnākara and Maṅkha, it is be assumed that he probably figured towards the end of the 9th century. Murarī belonged to Mouḍgalya goṭra. This ancient playwright is hailed as 'Bala Vālmīki' for his masterly treatment of the story of Rāmāyaṇa in his seven acts play 'Anargharaghava' and from the beauty of a particular verse he is known as Indru Murārī. The play has been considered a standard for poetic criticism and grammatical learning. Nagojibhatt in his *Siḍḍhānta - Kaumudi* cites Murari's expressions as authority.

Unfortunately the European critics have failed to appreciate his greatness and even Wilson is wrong while commenting that Hindu Pundits have shown Murāri an unjust preferences.

In the mangalacharana of Anargharaghava, the dramatist prays Lord Purushottama who bears 'Jyotismatilochane' or eye rounded like sun and moon.

His play contain no less than 540 stanzas of great length without any scope for actions and the portrayal of human sentiments. His mentrical skill and unlimited capacity to produce verses is evident in this work. Only for the sake of information, he used meagre prose.

The play is written in ornamental language and the poetical descriptions is evident throughout the work having most modern dramatic sequences. Composed in different metres, it comprises of about 567 verses.

His diction is chaste and learned and verses show lyrical harmony and style is characterized as magnificient and employs unusual gramnatical forms.

Critics observes his similes as often original, strike one as peculiar but they are quite natural all the same. Hence Sarangadhara declares :

Bhavabhutimanadritya Nirvanamatina maya,

Murari padachintayamida madhiyate mana.

One can find supernatural element in his play. Murarī has introduced dhruvā in his drama. Regardly performance value, though his play was not capable of being staged, but in all likelihood, it may have been recited in parts. In the words of T.G. Mainkar 'Murārī's poetic gift deserves some appreciation, but as dramatist his performance is poor. The play was performed at the Yātrā of Purushottama.

Therefore, though the work has little to commend it as a drama but has undoubtedly enriched our literary heritage.

It is said that after Murāri and Rājasekhara the flame of drama does not show any glow, except the allegorical play of Kṛṣṇa Miśra.

He was greatly inspired by Bhavabhuti's Uttaramacarita. He too treats the conflict, between Rama and Ravana, brought about through the schemes of Mālyavat, as political strife. It dramatises the traditional narrative of the Ramāyana with some alternations.

I. Shekhar has aptly commented that Murārī could have easily composed a 'Kāvya' on the traditional account of Rāma but, probably, he wanted to surpass Bhavabhūti with the aid of the same theme. It may be assumed that Bhavabhūti's plays must have attracted the attention of the learned and his fame may have left Murāri envious if not jealous. Therefore, Murārī used the drama as an instrument to demonstrate his poetic skill and verbosity to the fullest advantage.

According to Keith 'As a dramatic piece the defects of Anargharāghava are too obvious. The author had no regard for presenting a sound plot full of incidents of the epic pattern. In short he aimed at presenting a miniature Rāmāyana squeezed into a play - length composition with description loaded mercilessly. Hyperbole is his fork and high - sounding expressions are his passion."

One critic said that he has no eye for plot, no taste for dialogues and no regard for consistency and balanced treatment of situations. He himself is guilty of introducing stereotyped characters using pompous expressions marked with hyperbole.

Anargharaghava is the first sanskrit work on Ramayana available so far in Orissa. A number of palmleaf manscripts of Anargha Raghava copied in different centuries have been found from different parts of Orissa and some of them are with detailed commentary.

It may be added here that there are quite a sizeable number of commentaries on the play 'Anargharaghava'. To name a few, commentaries of Pūrṇasarasvaṭ i, Harihara, Mānavikrama; Rucipaṭiḍaṭṭa, Ḍharmānaṇda, Kṛṣṇa (son of Varaḍa), Lakṣmidhara alias Rāmānandāśrama, Viṣṇupandiṭa, Visṇubhatta (son of Mukṭ inātha), Lakṣmaṇasūri, Jinaharṣagani, (Śrīniḍhi, Puruṣoṭṭama, Ṭripurāri, Naracanḍra (Abhirāma by Bhāvanāṭhamiśra), by Dhaneśvara, son Uḍaya and one atnonymous. A very famous drama, the Anargharaghava has, thus, numerous commentaries of which the commentary of Kaviratna Purusottama Mishra (1690 - 1750 A.D.) is highly popular in Orissa.

Anargharaghava

Synopsis

Anargharāghava (Raghava, the Invaluable) is an excellent attempt to dramatize Ramayaṇa. This seven acts play presents the life of Rāma from his breaking the bow of Śiva at Mithilā to his return from the forest after fourteen years and coronation at Ayodhya. Cantowise the names of the topics are : Munidra - sambada, Kumarvikrama, Dhanubhanga, Dasarathavipralambha, Sugrivabhiseka, Dasagrivanigraha and Nayakananda.

Plot:-

Perturbed sage Viśvāmitra comes to take Rama and Lakshmaṇa to crush demons who have been troubling his hermitage. Though intially Daśaratha disagrees; but later allows him to take sons to the forest. In the forest, Rāma kills the demoness Tāḍaka by overcoming his hesitation to slain a female.

In Act Two, Vīśvamitra expresses his willingness to visit to Raja Janaka and after a brief description of both the king and the charms of the famous city of Mithilā, two disciples of Vīśvamitra enlighten the audience with the history of all the characters of Ramayana even before Rāma is married to Sita.

Sīta has now attained the age for marriage and Rāvaṇa seek her hand. Rāma is received by Janaka and Satānanda. But Janaka is hesitant in putting Rāma to the rigorous test involved in bending Śiva's bow.

Rāvaṇa's messenger arrives to demand Sītā's hand, but he is being informed that his master would have to bend the bow and Rama is allowed to do the same.

Report comes that Rāma has succeeded in bending the bow. Subsequently he is promised Sitā's hand and other son's of Daśaratha are also married off to Sitā's sisters. Mālyavant, the Ravana's minister laments the failure of his scheme to win Sītā and plans another move. Here playwright employs Śūpaṇakhā as Manṭ harā having no epic sanction. Rāvaṇa's sister is asked to assume the disguise of Mantharā.

After a wordy duel between Rāma and Paraśurāma, a settlement is reached and Daśaratha expresses his intention of resigning the throne in favour of Rāma, Laksmaṇa brings the disguised Manthara voicing Kaikeyi's demands spoils the whole scheme. (Bidding Daśaratha grant the two boons of the banishment of eldest son Rāma and to crown Bharata as King).

The advent and activities of Rama in the forest is reported through the conversation between Jāmbavanta and an ascetic Śravaṇā. The latter approaches Sugrīva to bespeak a kindly welcome for wayfarers. A conversation between a juggler (Rāvaṇa in disguise) and Lakshmana is overheard by Jāmbavanta. The vulture Jaṭāyu reports the appearance of Rāvana and Mārīcha in the forest. Sugriva is being warned of the ensuing danger by Jāmbavanta, while Jaṭāyu sees Sītā being carried away by Rāvaṇa and pursues him.

In grief, Rāma and Lakshmana searches her in vain. Soon they hear a cry and much to their surprise find the friendly chief 'Guha' being assailed by the headless Kabandha.

Lakshmana while rescuing him, knocks off the tree on which is suspended the skeleton of Duṇdubhi. In the meanwhile Vālin appears who is annoyed by Lakshmana's act. After a lengthy dialogues, he challanges Rāma to battle. The fight is narrated by Lakshmana and Guha and the death of Vālin is reported. Then follows the coronation of Sugriva; his promise to help Rāma in the recovery of Sīta, the killing of all Kumbhakarna, Indrajit and the Rākṣasa forces Rāvana's departure for the battle field which is announced through a frequent employment of voices behind the curtain or through two spies of Rāvana. Ravana goes for the battle. Here the playwright introduces two Vidyādhara characters to report the death of Rāvana Devoid of action, the entire act takes the form of a narrative.

In Act - Seven, Rāma and his associates while returning to Ayodhyā from Lanka and seated in the celestial car vividly describes the scenic beauty of the entire Indian sub - continent and also of the aerial regions, The description in verses (numbering 133) is put in their mouth that makes, the act more like canto than an Act.

The play comes to an end when Rama alongwith Sītā, Lakshman Vībhīshaṇa and Sugrīva depart from Lanka. He comes down from the vimāna (Kubera's car) and meet Vaśiṣtha, Bharata and Śatrughna, etc at Ayodhyā. Finally the sage performs the coronation ceremony to crown Rama and as usual the drama closes with the Bharat - vākya spoken by Rāma.

Anargharaghava in Performances

A landmark on the history of Orissa was the inception of a Pītha by Śaṅkara at Jagannatha. History unfolds that it led to the revival of Sanskrit learning and literature in this region. A few years of Śaṅkara's visit to this place, Murāri's popular drama 'Anargharāghava' was enacted at Puri before erudite pundits, at the time of a festival (Yātrā) of Lord Jagannātha, the consort of Kamalā, who was being worshipped in the Tamāla forest on the seashore as evident from the speech of the Sūtradhāra in the first act.

Dramatic Works : A Bibliography

Text

Anargha - Rāghava / by Murāri .- Madras : Sarasvati Venkata Varadacharya, Sarasvatinidhi Press, 1880.

102 p.

Telugu script.

Anargharāghava / ed. by Durgāprasād & Vāsudev Lakṣmaṇ Śāstrī Paṇaśīkar. - 5th ed. - Bombay : Nirṇayasāgar Press, 1937.

iv, 395 p.; 18 cm. - (Kāvyamālā; 5).

Includes 'Rucipati' commentary.

Anargha - Rāghava / by Murāri; commentary by Rucipati; ed. by Durgaprasada and Kashinath Pandurang Parab. - 2nd ed. - Bombay : Nirnaya Sagar Press, 1894.

Anargharāghava / by Murāri; ed. with Rucipati's commentary by Durgāprasād and Paṇśīkar. - 5th ed. - Bombay : Kavyamala, 1937.

Anargha - Rāghava / by Murāri; ed. by Hassan Narasimha Sastri. - Mysore : Cakravarti Iyangar, 1905.

920 p.

In Telugu script.

Contains commentary 'Iṣṭārthakalpavallī of Rāmānandāśrama, Pañcikā' of Viṣṇubhaṭṭa and Anāmikā of Harihara Dīkṣita.

Anargha - Rāghava / by Murāri; ed. by Jivananda Vidyasagar . - Calcutta : Saraswati Press, 1875.

178 p.

-----. 2nd ed. - Calcutta : Saraswati Press, 1889.

474, 4 p.

Anargha - Rāghava / by Murāri; ed. by Premachandra Tarkavagisa. - Calcutta : Sudharṇava Press, 1866.

241 p.

Anargha - Rāghava / by Murāri; ed. by R. Misra. - Banaras : Chowkhamba, 1960.

Also includes commentaries in Sanskrit and Hindi.

Anargharāghava / by Murari; ed. with a metrical Telugu translation by Satyavolu Kāmeśvara Rāya Kavi; foreword & introd. by Callapella Veṅkaṭa Śāstrī & E.V.V. Rāghavācārya. - Kakinada : Ranga & Co., 1937.

liv, 305 p.; 21 cm.

In Telugu script.

Translations

Hindi

Anargharāghavam / by Murāri; Sanskrit - Hindi comm. by Rāmacandra Miśra. -

Varanasi : Caukhamba Vidyabhavan, 1960.

Malayalam

Anargha - Rāghava / by Murāri; tr. into Malayalam byKummanam Govinda Pillai.

Anargha - Rāghava / by Murāri; tr. into Malayalam by P.K. Krishnan Nambiar.

Telugu

Anargha - Rāghava / by Murāri; tr. into Telugu by Akondi Vyasa Murthy Sastry.

Anargha - Rāghava / by Murāri; tr. into Telugu by Gadiyaram Venkata Sesha Sastry.

Anargha - Rāghava / by Murāri; tr. into Telugu Malladi Viswanatha Kavi.

Anargha - Rāghava / by Murāri; tr. into Telugu Mantripragada Bhujanga Rao.

Anargharāghava / by Murāri, ed. with a metrical Telugu translation by Satyavolu Kāmeśvara Rāya Kavi; foreword & introd - by Callapella Venkata Śāstrī & E.V.V. Rāghavācārya. - Kakinada : Ranga & Co., 1937.

liv, 305 p. ; 21cm

In Telugu script

Anargha - Rāghava / by Murāri; tr. into Telugu by Uppugunduru Venkatapati.

In poetic diction Rāghavakṛti.

Śrīmadāndhra Anargharāghavamu / tr. by Bhuvanagiri Vijayarāmayya. - Guntur : The translator, 1949.

xxiv, 165 p.; 21 cm.

Tr. in Telugu of 'Anargharāghava of Murārī Bhaṭṭa.

BIO - CRITICAL NOTICES

Banerji, Sures Chandra. A Companion to Sanskrit literature. - Delhi : Motilal Banarsidass, 1971.

Pp. 73, 132

Bandyopadhyay, Sureshchandra. Sanskrit sahityer itihas. - Calcutta : The Dacca Students Library, [1970?].

In Bengali.

Bhartiya, Kanti Kishore. Sanskrit natakkar. - Uttar Pradesh : Prakashan Shakha, Suchana VIbhag, 1959.

(Hindi - Samiti granthamala; 25).

Contents : Murari. Pp. 184 - 189.

Bhattacharya, Biswanath. Sanskrit drama and dramaturgy. - Delhi : Sharada Publishing House, 1994. Pp. 293 - 297.

Comparative Indian literature (Vol. 1) / ed. by K.M. George. - Trichur : Kerala Sahitya Akademi, 1984. P. 569.

The Cultural heritages of India [Vol. V] / ed. by Suniti Kumar Chatterji. - rev. ed. Calcutta : The Ramakrishna Mission Institute of Culture, 1978.

P. 252.

Dictionary of oriental literatures (Vol. II) : South and South - East Asia. - Delhi : Vikas Publishing, 1975.

Garg, Ganga Ram. An encyclopaedia of Indian literature. - Delhi : Mittal Publishers, 1982.

Pp. 16 - 17, 254.

Gera, Vimla. Mind and art of Bhavabhuti. - Delhi : Meharchand Lachhamandas, 1973. Pp. 254 - 270.

Keith, A. Berriedale. The Sanskrit drama in its origin, development, theory and practice. - Oxford : OUP, 1924.

405 p.; 22 cm.

Keith, A. Berriedale Sanskrit - natak : udbhav aur vikas : siddhanta aur prayog /

tr. into Hindi by Udaybhanu Singh. - Delhi : Motilal Banarsidass, 1965.

Krishnamachariar, M. and Srinivasachariar. History of classical Sanskrit literature. - Delhi : Motilal Banarsidass, 1989. Pp. 637 - 640.

Lēvi, Sylvain. The theatre of India / tr. from the French by Narayan Mukherji. - Calcutta : Writers Workshop, 1978.

Contents : *Anargharāghava*.

Pp. (Vol. I), 243, 249, 259 - 261; (Vol. II) 90.

Murari : Pp. (Vol. I) - 243, 249, 253, 258, 261, 273, 279; (Vol. II) 28.

Marasinghe, E.W. The Sanskrit theatre and stage craft. - Delhi : Sri Satguru Publications, 1989. - (Sri Garib Dass Oriental Series; No. 78).

Mishra, Padmakar. Critical and comparative study of Murari's Anargharaghava by Padmakar Mishra.

Ph.D. thesis approved by the Allahabad University in 1971.

Musafir Singh. Critical study of Anargharaghava by Murari / by Musafir Singh.

Ph.D. thesis approved by the Banaras Hindu University in 1972.

Panda, P.K. Contribution of Orissa to Sanskrit. - Delhi : Pratibha Prakashan, 1987.

Contents : Anargharāghava nātakam. Pp. 89 - 90.

Pathak, M.C. Sanskrit nāṭaka meṅ atiprākṛta tattva. - Jaipur : Devanagar Prakashan, [n.d.].

18 , 468 p.

Purang, Shashi Prabha. Comparative and critical study of the dramas of Murari and Jayadeva / by Shashi Prabha Purang.

Ph.D. thesis in Hindi, approved by the Agra University in 1972.

Panda, Bhagaban Sanskrit works on Ramayana in Orissa / by Bhagaban Panda. *In* 'The Ramayana in eastern India / ed. by K.C. Mishra. - Bhubaneswar : Institute of Orissan Culture, 1987. Pp. 48 - 49.

Ray, Ashim Kumar and Gidwani, N.N. A Dictionary of Indology (Vol. 1). - New Delhi : Oxford & IBH Publishing Co., 1983.

P. 77.

Sahitya Akademi - New Delhi : The National bibliography of Indian literature. - New Delhi : The author, 1962 - 1990.

5 Vols.

Sastri, Gaurinath. Sanskrit sahityer itihas. - Calcutta : Sarasvata Library, 1969? [Aśvin 1376].

In Bengali.

Sethi, Atmaram. Anudit Hindi sahitya : vishishta granthasuchi / by Atmaram Sethi. - Gaurgaon : Indian Documentation Service, 1981.

Contents : Sanskrit (Pp. 1 - 624).

Sharma, Asha. Comparative study of Mahaviracharita of Bhavabhuti and Anargharaghava of Murari / by Asha Sharma.

Ph.D. thesis approved by the Kanpur University in 1979.

Sharma, Devichandra. Comparative study of Anargha-raghava and Prasanna-raghava / by Devichandra Sharma.

Ph.D. thesis in Hindi, approved by the Meerut University in 1975.

Sharma, Visnu Kumar. Special study of Anargharaghava by Murari in relation to important dramas on Rama / by Vishnu Kumar Sharma.

Ph.D. thesis approved by the Vikram University in 1979.

Shekhar, I. Sanskrit drama : its origin and decline. - Leiden : E.J. Brill, 1960. Pp. 121, 133, 139, 143, 145, 162, 163, 165, 171, 172, 186 - 189, 194.

Singh, Hemalata. Study of Anargharaghava from the angle of Natyasastra / by Hemalata Singh.

Ph.D. thesis in Hindi, approved by the Avadh University in 1983.

Sternbach, Ludwik. Verses attributed to Murāri / by Ludwik Sternbach.

Vishveshvaranand Indological Journal; March - Sept. 1979; Vol. XVII, Nos I - II. P. 313 - 315.

Book review by K.V. Sharma.

11

Rājaśekhara

A dramatist of considerable merit, Rājaśekhara was also a poet, rhetorician and political mentor of the Gurjara - Pratihara dynasty. He probably lived between 880 to 920 A.D.

His writings give us sufficient informations about his ancestors, his wife 'Avantisundari', his education, his travels, his faith and those who patronized his works.

In Kavya Mimamsa, which was planned in eighteen books and of which only the first one is extant deals with a wide ranging topic related to poetics. In this magnum opus, he offers us an excellent account of the various literary activities of his time and derives or quote copiously from several established and even unknown rhetoricians and poets, including, his own wife 'Avantisundari'. Though only a small part of the work is handed down to us, but is a remarkable contribution in the domain of poetics as well as in furnishing authentic data about a bygone era. Son of Duhika or Durduka (who held the rank of chief minister) and Shilavati, this great writers of Prakrit and Sanskrit spent much of his life as preceptor of king Mahendrapala and his son Mahipala of Mahodaya (Kanauj) and for sometime as a protege of the Kalachuri ruler of Tirupati called 'Yuvaryadeva'.

His family originally hailed from Maharashtra, perhaps Vidarbha.

Rajaśekhara belonged to a family of the Yayavaras with a literary tradition in which were born poets and erudite pundits like Kādarbani Rāma, Surananda,

Tarala, Kavirāya and Akālajadada (his great - grandfather, famed in the anothologies).

The dramatist's wife 'Avanti sundari' was a reputed Kshatriya lady of the Chahamana family who had much poetic tallent and who helped him in establishing his rhetorical theories whom he quotes with respect in his great work 'Kavya-mimamsa' and at whose beliest the celebrated Prakrit play 'Karpuramanjari' was written? and eracted.

Though he was a Shaiva, but his praise of Vishnu in his major work of literary criticism, i.e., 'Kavya-mimamsa' proves his religious tolerance and reverance to other faiths.

Rajaśekhara had profound knowledge of the various branches of learning, including the shastras, like Vedanta, Dharmashastra, etc. and classical literature of his predecessors such as Kalidasa, Shriharsa, Bana and Bhavabhuti etc.

He had specialized in poetics and made a mark for himself for his command of Sanskrit, Prakrit and Apabhramsha that entitled him to the claim of 'proficiency in all languages' andn earned the title 'Balakavi' for his six 'prabandhas'.

He had travelled extensively in countnries of the south, west and north. In the royal court of Mahendrapala, he wrote

(i) *Balaramayaṇam* (In 10 acts)

(ii) *Haravilasa* (epic)

(iii) *Karpuramanjari* (Nātika)

In Balarāmāyanam he refers to his six earlier works. After Mahendrapala's death in AD 910 and the exile of Mahipala, he left Kanauj and sought the patronage of the Kalachuri king Yuvarajadeva at Tripuri when he wrote

(iv) *Viddhashalabhanjika* (Nātikā)

In c. AD 914, after the restoration of Mahipala to the throne, he returned to Kanauj and penned

(v) *Bhuvana - kosha* dealing with the topics of general geography and

(vi) *Kavya mimamsa*. In *Kavya mimamsa* he refers to his work Bhuvana - Kosha.

(vii) *Balabharatam* or *Prachaṇḍapāṇḍavam* (of which only two acts are extant).

Among his creative outputs, his *Shatprabandhah* (six compositions), *Bhuvanakosha*, and *Haravilasa* are lost.

The '*Bālabhāratam*' or 'Mahābhārata for boys' is also introuduced by another title called '*Pracaṇḍapāṇḍava*'. This is a mercifully unfinished play with just two acts that are now available to us. Bālabhārata, though incomplete, but even in its present state contains not less than 143 slokas. Critics feels that it could have been another 'Mahanātaka' and would have surpassed even the Bālarāmāyaṇa in proportion to the Mahābhārata story. The play 'Bālabharata evokes little interest, though one can find some verses of literary tastes.

'*Bālarāmāyanam*' is living testimony to his poetic talent and linguistic beauty. This mahānāṭaka has 741 stanzas, and of these approximately 203 are in the 19 syllable Shārdulavikrīdita andn 89 in the Sragdharā, which has two more syllables in each pada or 84 in a stanza.

The dialogues in the play are witty and enjoyable and the dramatist made several modifications in the basic Rāma episode and his imaginative splendours is evident at many places. However, T.G. Mainkar opined that there is no selection of incidents, no dramatic or skilful arrange and no poetry worth the name.

After he established himself as a Sanskrit poet of eminence and his great skill in the employment of artificial metres, the dramatist might have wanted to prove that he was equally at case to deal with the most difficult metres in Prākrit. This prompted him to write one of the best comedics that Indian literature has so far produced. This is '*Karpūra-mañjarī*, the only extant popular drama entirely composed in Prākrit.

According to Keith, his ability to handle elaborate Prākrit metres is undeniable; in 144 stanzas in the *Karpūramañjarī* he has 17 varieties. If poetry consisted merely of harmonious sound, he must be ranked high as a poet. He is fond of proverbs... he introduces freely words from verraculars, including Marāthī. He rightly observed that vernaculars had advanced beyond the Prākrits of the drama.

As regards his dramatic abilities, Keith feels that the playwright is devoid of power to create character, the haroine is without merit, the intrigue is poorly managed and the confusion of exits and entrances is difficult to follow and is unsuitable for acting.

In *Karapūramañjarī*, instead of allowing the love to grow through a natural course of events, the playwright has chosen to rely on tantrism, magic, underground passages, and absurd games of hide and seek, writes a critic.

Instead of the Vidushaka, there is a magician 'Bhairavānanda', the spiritual guide of the queen, who coducts the entire plot.

Karpuramanjari is a Sattaka in Prakrit having 4 acts. This is the earliest available Śattaka, the credit of introducing a new genre of dramatic composition goes to him. His play was a model for many writers of later period such as *Rambhamanjari* of Nyaychandra (14th century); Ruḍraḍāsās *Canḍralekta* (17th century) work, a Sattaka in four acts that depicted the story of the marriage between Canḍralekhā and Manaveḍarāja; the *Vilasavati* of Markandeya (17th century); the *Śhṛingāramañjari* of Viśveśvara (18th century), the *Anandasundnari* of Ghanashyam (18th cenntury) who is known to have composed two more similar Śattakās.

In composing this Sattaka, Rājaśekhara came under the strong spell of Kalidasa's Malavikagnimitra and some scenes, incidents and even character such as master magician from Śriharsha's 'Ratnavali'. However he did not succeed in his attempt in the borrowing.

By the time of Rajasekhara's *Karpuramanjari* (c. 1000 AD), it is evident that the pure drama had given place to the musical play, which was perhaps known earlier but had not become very popular with the dramatists. The growth of the musical play later on generally determined the dance - drama forms of the regional languages in the later medieval period. *Karpuramanjari* therefore presents before us a kind of drama which was very much akin to what is today known as the operatic dance - drama, observes Sunil Kothari.

There are commentaries on *Karpūramañjari* by Kāmarāja, Dharmadāsa, Pīṭāmbara, Dharmacanḍra, Vāsuḍeva, J. Vidyāsāgara, Kṛṣṇasūri, Nṛsimharāja, and Ananṭadāsa.

Viddhaśālabhañjikā of Rājaśekhara is a drama on the amorous court life centering round Vidyādharamalla, King of Karpūravarṣa and Mṛgāṅkāvalī, daughter of King Candravarman, of Lāṭa. In concept and execution, the play '*Viddhaśālabhañjika*' is similar to *Karpūramañjarī*.

An outstanding writer of comedy, Rājaśekhara's play '*Viddhasalabhañjika or the statue*' contains ample comic situations for which the fact that the heroine is a girl disguised as *boy affords* abundant opportunities.

He comes under the strong spell of Sriharsha in this Prakrit play, but he could not be as successful as him in handling this form, his plot construction and characterization.

According to I. Shekhar 'In plot construction and general treatment *Viddhasalabhañjikā* fares better though it is influenced by Harsa's Ratnāvalī. The dramatist has made use of a better use in deceiving the queen by ushering in a girl dressed in the garb of a boy as it heightens the effect of the sentiment of wonder. The plot is poorly developed and the characters introduced are stereotyped and feeble..."

These are commentary on it by Nārāyaṇa, by Ghanaśyama and by his wives Sundarī and Kamalā, by Saṭyavraṭa, by J. Viḍyāsāgara, and by a pupil of Karuṇakara, and by Vāsudeva.

A.A. Macdonell who was an Emeritus Professor of Sanskrit in the University of Oxford writes that "Rājasekhara's plays deserve to be studied for the correctness of their diction and the smoothness of their verses both in Sanskrit and Prākrit, as well as for the proverbial sayings with which they abound and the allusions which they contain to the customs prevailing in his days."

Balabharatam or Pracandapaṇḍavam

Synopsis

This is an incomplete play and the only two extant acts deals with the marriage of Draupadi and the gambling scene of the epic in which she was dragged by her hair before the assembly by one of the Kauravas and disgraced. The drama closes with the departure of the Pandavas to the forest.

DramatisPersonae

Male Cast

Stage Manager

Vyasa

Valmiki

Yudhisthira

Vimasena

Arjuna

Nakul

Sahadeva

Dhṛṣṭadrumna

Bandī (Prisoner)

Droṇa

Vidura

Puruṣa

Śakuni

Duryodhana

Duhśasana

Vikarṇa

Female Cast

Draupadi

Sakhī (Draupadi's friend)

Sunanda

Surekha

Bālabhāratam in Performances

After the restoration of Mahipala to the throne in c. AD 914, the successor of Mahendrapāla who was previously exiled, Rajaśekhara returned to Kanauj where he gave a stage performance of his play 'Balabharata or' Prachandapandava' before the subjects of this city with king Mahipala himself presiding. It is believed that the full play might have been presented, but today we have just two acts extant.

Balarāmāyana

Synopsis

Bālarāmāyana is a mahanataka that treats at excessive length the entire Rama story in ten acts with prologue that itself goes to the length of an act. In the play the love of Rāvana and his longing for Sita dominates.

Plot:-

Act One :- Rāvana appeares in person in the First Act but refuses to test himself by drawing Shiva's bow, and departs, menacing evil to any husband of Sītā.

Act Two :-Rāvaṇa who is Rāmā's rival for the hand of Sīta seeks the aid of Parashurama, but is humiliated and a battle barely prevented by intervention of friends.

Act Three :- The marriage of Sīta is enacted before lovesick Rāvaṇa to distract his amorous sorrow, but the attempt fails, because Rāvaṇa interrupts and eventually the scene is broken off.

Act Four :- In this act the duel of Rāma and Parashurāma is disposed of.

Act Five :- In Act Five, effort is made again to amuse Rāvaṇa. Here dolls with parrots in their mouths are presented to him as Sītā and his foster sister; he is deceived until he finds that his grasp is on wood; distracted, he demands his beloved from nature, the seasons, the streams and the birds.

The emergence of Sūrpaṇakha, his sister who has badly wounded from her attack on Rāma, makes him furious.

Act Six :- Act carries matter down to the death of the disheartened Daśaratha.

Act Seven :- The problem of inducing the ocean to accept burden of the bridge is solved in Act Seven. Dadhittha and Kapittha, two monkeys enlighten Rama on the contruction of this bridge. By stratagem of Mālyavant, the severed head of Sīta seems to be flung on the shore that results in momentary terror. But soon the fraud is revealed and it is found that it was none other than the head of the speaking doll.

Act Eight :- In Act Eight, we see Rāvaṇa's impressions as disaster after disaster is announced. He even sends out Kumbhakarṇa but also sees him helpless despite his magic weapons, before Rāma.

Act Nine :- This act deals with the last desperate duel of Rāma and Rāvana which is described by Indra himself.

Act Ten :- In Act Ten, a survey of the universe is arranged on the celestial car that ends with the inevitable consecration.

Karpūramañjari

Synopsis

Karpūramañjari is a Prakrit drama on the conventional theme of King Caṇḍapāla's amour with a lovely maiden who lends her name as the title of the play. The drama while describing the love-lorn condition of the King, shows the jealousy of the queen with the consequent impediments and ends with the lover's marriage.

Dramatis Personae

Male Caste

Sutradhar (Stage Manager)

Pariparśvika

Chandrapal (Rājā / The King)

Kapinjal (Viduṣaka / Jester)

Ratnachaṇda (Vaitālik)

Kanchanchandra (Vaitalik)

Bhairavananda (Tantrik sage)

Female Caste

Karpūramanjari (Princess of Vidarbhanagar)

Devi / Vibhramlekha (Queen / Wife of the King Chandrapal)

Vicakśhana (Cetī)

Pratiharī (Maid)

Kurangika (Karpūramanjari's friend)

Sarangika (Maid)

Charchari (Dancers)

Plot:-

Act One :- In Act I, the king's jester, Kapinjala enters to announce the arrival of Bhairavananda, a magician (miracle-maker) at the door. After the permission is granted, he enters bragging of his Yogic attainments. As directed, he displays a damsel named Karpūramañjari, to the King Chaṇdapala of Kanauj. The apparition tells her tale and queen takes her as an attendant. The king and the maiden fall at once in love.

Act Two :- In Act II we find that in a letter the damsel avows her passion, but the queen finds out the love. The damsel is imprisoned and thus, kept under strict vigilance of the queen and her other attendants. The love-sick king seeks the help of his jester to make an arrangement to secretely meet his beloved. Vichakshana, the maid comes with a letter from the Kuntala princess avowing her love for the King. The unfortunate damsel has been assigned by the queen two important tasks : a play on the swing and the task of satisfying the 'longings' of three trees, Tilaka, Kurabaka and Ashoka in the ladies park.

This becomes an opportunity for the King to see his beloved. Vichakshana directs the king and the jester to wait near the Emerald - bunch. There the king watches the swing play of the princess with great delight. He also observes the embracing of the Kurabaka the eyeing of the Tilaka and the kicking of the Ashoka plant, all this tasks is carried out by the princess to fulfil their 'longings'. The trees put forth flowers at once. As evening approaches, the time of appointment for the first meeting of the king and the princess.

Act Three :- Act III depicts the love - sick king who had a dream in which he was flirting with his beloved who was standing at a arm's distance from his bed and as he tried to seize her by the skirt of her garment, the maiden disappeared.

When the night falls, the king and the jester goes near the detention house where the king's beloved is confined by the queen.

The jester puts out the lamp and as per his direction, the king goes out in the open in the ladies park as there is total darkness. The king leads the princess holding her by hand and enjoys the flirtation in the garden. The act closes with the hue and cry of the guards at the detention house.

Act Four :- Act IV shows that the image opening on the garden is blocked and the detention house is guarded heavily. Sarangika is placed in charge of the damsel and Vichakshana ad her sister Sulakshana is discharged.

In the absence of Vichakshana the jester takes the help of Bhairavananda for the king, for he (Bhairavananda) wields great impact, as that of a Guru, over the credulous queen. He consented to receive the gift and proposed by the way a marriage of the princess Ghanasaramanjari, the daughter of the Lata king. The queen is induced to demand that the king shall marry her, by whom her husband will be a paramount monarch, least suspecting that Ghanasaramanjari is no other than Karpūramañjari a cousin of the queen. The wedding is fixed for celebration that very evening. The king is directed to remain present at the sanctuary of Chamunda under the banyan tree.

Now another passage is made to the sanctuary of Chāmunda, the entrance being concealed behind the statue. This passage enables the princess to play a game of hide - and - seek with the queen as directed by the magician. Finally, Bhairavananda discloses the identity of Ghanasaramanjari. The queen a victim of this mean tricks unwittingly accomplished the lover's desire.

The jester acts as the priest of the ceremony and the marriage goes on merrily.

'Karpuramanjari' in Performances

History tells us that at the behest of Rajaśekhara's learned wife 'Avantisundari', the Kshatriya lady of the Chahamana family, the premier performance of the Prakrit play 'Karpuramanjari' was produced for the delight of his contemporary elite.

Viddhaśālabhañjika

Synopsis

The play '*Viddhaśālabhañjika*' is the saga of love of king Vidyādharamall, his longing for a princess Mṛgāṅkavallī who comes to his palace dressed as a boy under the name 'Mṛgāṅ-kavarman.

It is the minister Bhāgurāyana who conducts this plot, arranges usual secret meetings, which has the dreams and the statue etc. To seek revenge, the queen marries him to the boy, but the king ultimately gets the girl of his choice by this marriage.

Plot:-

Act One :- One night the king dreamt of a beautiful maiden who casted a collar of pearl necklace round his neck. The necklace is not 'such stuff as dreams are made on'. He keeps it with deep longing for the maiden of his dream. He is haunted by her that makes the queen very jealous. Ignoring queen's feelings, he goes on describing his love to the jester. He even finds her in sculptured form 'Śāla-bhañjikā' in the picture gallery and lucky enough to have a further glimpse of her in the disguised Lāṭa prince. This Lāṭa prince is none other than the

'Mrigāṅkavallī' in the guise of Lāṭa king Chandravarman's son and hier Chandravarman sends to the court of his overlord Vidyādharamalla, the king of Karpūravarsha.

Act Two :- In Act II we learn that the queen proposes to marry Kuvalayamāla of Kuntala to the pretended boy i.e., the Lāṭa Prince (actually the princess). Vīdūṣ aka is also promised by her foster - sister, Mekhalā, marriage with a lady named 'Ambaramāla (Air Garland). But the girl turns out to be a servant of the royal household. The disgusted Vidūṣaka plans for a retaliation; the king has to calm him and together they watch in hiding Mṛgānkavallī playing in the garden and hear reading a letter of love. The heralds proclaim the evening hour.

Act Three :- In Act III we are told that the dream of the king was reality devised by Bhāgurāyaṇa, his minister, who predicted that the daughter of king Chandravarman will be maried to the king of kings and thus brings the only daughter of the king to the palace of his own king.

The Vidūṣaka is successful in making Mekhalā kneel down before him. He bids a woman hide herself and callout a warning to Mekhalā of evil to befall her unless she crawl between a Brahmin's, limbs. The queen requets the Vidūsaka to permit this ceremony, and it over, he avows the plot to the great indignation of the queen. The Vīdūṣaka and the king then have an interview with the heroine.

Act Four :- In Act IV, the queen plots to punish the king, she induces him to marry the sister of the pretended boy, meaning that he would find that he has ultimately married a boy. The king agrees and the marriage is completed.

Message comes from Chandravarman that a son is born; he begs the queen to dispose in marriage of his daughter, who may resume her sex. Though the queen is tricked and deceived, but with dignity she bestows on her husband both Mṛgāṅkavallī and Kuvalayamāla. It is also unfolds that the last rebels are subdued and the king's suzerainty is recognized everywhere.

DRAMATIC WORKS : A BIBLIOGRAPHY

Balabharatam or Pracandapandavam

Text

(Bālabharatam) / by Rajasekhara. - Delhi : Motilal Banarsidass, 1983. The play is included in author's Prakrit play 'Karpuramanjari'

Pracandapandavam natakam : with the 'Prakasa' Hindi commentary / by

Rajasekhara; e.d. by Haridatta Sastri. - Varanasi : Chowkhamba Sanskrit Series Office, 1969.

19, 79 p.; 18 cm.

Play is also known as 'Balabharatam.

Pracandapandapa / by Rajasekhara, e.d. by Carl Capeller.

Strassburg, 1885

Carl Capeller (1840-1925)

Carl Johann Wilhelm Capeller was born on 22.3.1840 in Alexkehnen in Eastern Prussia. He began his studies in 1860 in Berlin, where he read Classical languages, Indo-European linguistics, Sanskrit and Lithuanian. He obtained a doctorate in 1868 for his Latin thesis Observations ad Kalidasae Malavikagnimitram.

From 1870 to 1872 Capeller taught Latin, French and English in a school. In 1872, he submitted a thesis Die Ganachandas, Ein Beitrag zur indischen Metrik ("The Gannachnadas. A contribution to Indian metrics"). He studied about a thousand verses in Sanskrit and Prakrit and compared the different metres. He also discussed the theory that Sanskrit drama had evolved from Greek drama. This view was held by several scholars of his time.

Capeller was appointed reader of Sanskrit in the University of Jena in 1872. He became associate professor in 1875. In 1921, when he was 81 years of age, he discontinued giving lectures. He died on 17.7.1925 in Jena.

Carl Capeller specialised in Sanskrit drama. He has several critical editions to his credit. He also wrote on poetics. His Sanskrit-German Dictionary for beginners and its revised English edition greatly benefited students of Sanskrit.

In his critical editions, Capeller did not give preference to any one manuscript. He tried to cull the best from each tradition, a subjective method not approved by all scholars. Capeller edited the Pracandapandava by Rajasekhara, Strassburg 1885. This edition was based on two manuscripts. According to the prologue, the title should be Balabharata, corresponding to Balaramayana. Since the play has only two acts, this led some scholars to conclude that the play was a fragment. In the preface Capeller argued that the poet wanted to dramatise some episodes from the epic. He thought that the play was not in an unfinished state.

Bālarāmāyana

Bālarāmāyana / by Rājaśekhara; commentary Tattvāloka by Lakṣmaṇa sūri.- Tanjore: Purnacandrodaya Press, 1899,

198p.

Bālarāmāyaṇa / by Rājaśekhara; ed. by Govindadeva Sastri. - Banaras : Medical Hall Press, 1869,

312 p.

Reproduced from *Pandit Old Series;* 3 (1868-69).

Bālarāmāyaṇa / by Rājaśekhara; ed. with a comm. Jivananda. - Calcutta : Nutana Valmiki Yantra, 1894,

703 p.

Bāla Rāmāyanam / by Rājaśekhara; ed. with Hindi tr. by Ganga Sagar Rai. - Varanasi : Chaukhamba Surbharati Prakashan, 1984.

xxxii, 382 p.; 22-5 cm.

Translations

Hindi

Bāla Rāmāyanam / by Rājaśekhara; ed. with Hindi tr. by Gannga Sagar Rai. - Varanasi : Chaukhamba Surbharati Prakashan, 1984,

xxxii, 382 p; 22-5 cm.

Telugu

Bālarāmāyanamu / by Rājaśekhara; tr. by Tirupati Vēṅkaṭēśvara Kavulu.- Kakinada : Bālasarasvatī Press, 1902-03,

2 Vols.

Karpūramañjarī

Text

Karpūramañjarī / by Rājaśekhara; critically ed. in the original Prakrit with a glossary, Index and an essay on the life and writings of the author by Sten Konow.- Cambridge (Mass.) : Harvard University Press, 1901,

xviii, 288, 8p.; 27 cm.

Also contains an English translation and notes by Charles Rockwell Lanman.

Karpūramañjarī / by Rājaśekhara; critically ed. with an introd. and notes by Manomohan Ghosh.- Calcutta : The University of Calcutta, 1939.

lxxvi, 94p.; 21 cm.

Includes bibliography and append.

Karpūramañjari / by Rājaśekhara. - Delhi : Motilal Banarsidas, 1983.

181 p.

Reprint of Nirnaya Sagar ed.

Includes the commentary of Vasudeva and Balabhāratam.

Also contains playwright's drama Bālabharatam.

Karpūramañjari / by Rājaśekhara; ed. by Nārāyaṇ Rām Ācarya.- 4th ed.- Bombay : Nirṇaya - Sagar Press, 1949.

xvi, (165) p.; 18 cm.

Contains Vāsudeva's Commentary that follows author's 'Bālabhārata'.

Karpuramanjari / by Rājaśekhara; ed. by Rama Kumara Acharya. - Banaras: Chaukhamba Vidya Bhavan, 1955, 216 p.; 18 cm.

Karpūramañjari / by Rajaśekhara; ed. by Sten Konow; tr. into English by Charles Rockwell Lannman.- Delhi : Motilal Banarsidass, 1963,

xxvi, 288 p.; 24 cm. - (Harvard Oriental Series).

Karpūramañjarī / by Rājaśekhara; with commentary (incomplete) of Vāsudeva. - Bombay : Nirnaya Sagar Press, 1887,

(Kāvyamālā; 4).

Karpūramañjarī / by Rājaśekhara. Text approved in *'Pandit', old Series;* Vol. 7; 1872-73.

Karpūramañjarī : with the Sanskrit commentary of Vasudeva and Bala Bharata.- Delhi : Motilal Banarsidass, 1983, (181) p.

Translations

Bengali

Bharatiya Sahitya ratna samkalan / Comp. by Dhirendranath Banerjee.-

Calcutta : Sanskrit Book Depot, 1980.

Contents : 'Karpura-manjari' Bengali rendering of Rajaśekhara's classic (Excerpt) Pp. 249-254.

English

Karpūra-mañjarī / by Rājasekhara, Critically ed. in the original Prakrit, with a glossarial index, and an essay on the life and writings of the poet by Stenn Konow, and tr. into English with notes by Charles Rockwell Lanman.- Cambridge (Mass): Harvard University Press, 1901.

xxviii, 289 p.; 25.5 cm.- (Harvard Oriental Series; 4).

Rajsekhara's Karpura-mañjari / by Rājasekhara; ed. by sten Konow; tr. into English by Charles Rockwell Lanman.- Delhi : Motilal Banarsidass, 1963.

xxvi, 288 p.; 2 cm.- (Harvard Oriental Series).

Hindi

Karpuramanjari / by Rajasekhara; tr. into Hindi by Bharatendu Harish Chandra, 1876.

Nepali

Karpuramanjari / by Rajasekhara; tr. into Nepali by Sambhuprasad Dhungel.

Viddhaśālabhañjikā

Text

Viddhasalabhanjika-natika / by Rajaśekhara.- Varanansi : Chaukhambha Orientalia, 1976.

169 p.; 21 cm.

Viddhaśālabhañjikā / by Rājaśekhara; critically ed. with an introd. by Yatīndra Vimal Caudhurī.- Commentaries 'Camatkārataraṅgiṇī of Sundarī & Kamalā & Prāṇprātiṣṭhā of Ghanaśyāma.- Calcutta : Calcutta Oriental Series ; 30, & Contribution of Women to Sanskrit Literature; No. 1.

Viddnhaśālabhañjika / by Rājaśekhara; ed. by Bh. R. Atre.- Poona : (s.n.), 1886.

Viddhaśālabhañjikā / by Rājaśekhara; ed. by Vāmanācārya. Paṇḍit, Old Series; Vols 6 & 7; 1871 - 73.

Translations

Bengali

Sanskrita Sahitya Sambhar / ed. by Gaurinath Sastri and et at (Vol. 17) - Calcutta: Navpatra Prakashan, (197-?).

Includes Bengali rendering of Rajasekhara's 'Viddhaśalabhanjika'.

English

Viddhaśālabhañjikā / by Rājasekhara; tr. by Louis H. Gray. *JAOS*. 1906, Vol. 27; Pp. 1-71.

Telugu

Viddhaśālabhañjika / by Rājaśekhara; tr. by Janamañci Vēṅkaṭarāmayya.- Rajahmundry : The trannslator, 1942.

viii, 112 p.; 18 cm.

Viddhaśālabhañjika / by Rajasekhara; tr. into Telugu verse by Manchana.- 1300 A.D.

Original title : Keyurabāhu Charitam.

Other Works

Kāvyamīmāṁsā

Kavyamimamsa / by Rajasekhara; ed. by C.D. Dalal and R.A. Sastry; rev. & enl. by K.S. Ramaswamy Sastri.- Baroda : Oriental Institute, 1934.

lii, 314 p.

Kāvya - mīmāṁsā of Rājaśekhara / by ed. by Ganga Sagar Rai 3rd ed. Varanasi : Chowkhamba Vidya Bhawan, 1982.

Introductory essay on the life and works of Rājaśekhara.

Kāvyamīmāṁsā / by Rājaśekhara; ed. with a commentary 'Candrikā' by Nārāyaṇ Sāstrī Khiste. - Banaras : Vidya Vilas Press, 1931

68 p.; 22 cm.- (Kaāśī Sanskrit Series; 86)

Contains Pt. 1, adhyāyas 1-5 only.

Kāvyamīmāṁsa / by Rājaśekhara; ed. with a commentary 'Madhusūdanī' by Madhusūdana Miśra.- Banaras : Chaukhamba Sanskrit Series Office, 1931-32.

2 Vols.; 22 cm.- (Kāsī Sanskrit Series; 86 & Haridās Sanskrit Series; 14).

Kāvyamīmāṁsā / by Rājaśekhara; ed. with an introd. & notes by C.D. Dalal & R. Ananta-kṛṣṇa Śastrī.- Baroda : Government of Baroda, 1916.

xxxvi, (152 p.) : facsim.; 24 cm.- (Gaekwad's Oriental Series; 1).

Only the first 'adhikarana' of this work on rhetoric is available which shows that the author planned a very large work.

Kavyamimamsa / by Rajasekhara ; ed. with 'Prakasa' Hindi commentary by Ganga sagar. Raya.- Varanasi : Chowkhamba Vidya Bhawan, 1982

(344) p.

Kavyamimamsa / by Rajasekhara ; Hindi tr. by Kedaranatha Sarma Sarasvata.- Patna : Bihar Rashtrabhasa Parishad, 1965.

49, 350 p.

Translations

Hindi

Kavyamimamsa / by Rajasekhara; Hindi tr. by Kedaranatha Sarma Sarasvata.- Patna : Bihar Rashtrabhasa Parishad, 1965.

49, 350.

BIO - CRITICAL NOTICES

Adya Rangacharya. Drama in Sanskrit literature. 2nd ed.- Bombay : Popular Prakashan, 1967. Pp. 90, 196, 197, 202, 203.

Aufrecht, Theodor. Catalogus Catalogorum.- Weisbaden : Franz Steiner Verlag Gmb. H, 1962, 2 Vols. ; 26 cm.

Banerji, Sures Chandra. A Companion to Sanskrit literature.- Delhi : Motilal Banarsidass, 1971. Pp. 82, 150, 151, 373.

Bandyopadhyay, Sureshchandra. Sanskrit Sahityer itihas.- Calcutta : The Dacca Students Library, (1970?)

Includes a critical insights into Karpuramanjari.

Bhartiya, Kanti Kishore. Sanskrit natakkar.- Uttar Pradesh : Prakashan Shakha, Suchana Vibhag, 1959.

(Hindi - Samiti granthamala; 25)

Contents : Rājaśekhara. Pp. 190-194.

Bhattacharya, Biswanath 'Rajasekhara's Karpuramanjari' / by Biswanath Bhattacharya *Visvabharati Quarterly*; 1973-74. Vol. 39, No. 3-4; Pp. 288-298.

Bhattacharya, Biswanath Sanskrit drama and dramaturgy.- Delhi : Sharada Publishing House, 1994. Pp. 148, 152, 153, 352, 354-358, 388.

Chakrabarti, Nagendranath. Rajsekhara Kavyamimamsa / by Nagendranath Chakrabarti. - Calcutta : Visvabharati, 1960.

136, 288 p.; 24.5 cm.

Comparative Indian Literature (Vol. 1) / ed. by K.M. George.- Trichur : Kerala Sahitya Akademi, 1984, P. 569.

De, Sushil Kumar Aspects of Sanskrit literature.- Calcutta : Firma KLM, 1959.

Pp. 107, 221, 270.

Dictionary of oriental literatures (Vol. II) : South and South - East Asia. Delhi : Vikas Publishing, 1975.

Encyclopaedia of Indian literature.- New Delhi : Sahitya Akademi, 1987 - 1994.

Pp. 294, 815, 828, 1095, 1102, 1104-1106, 1486, 1998-1999, 2028-30, 2248, 2471, 2496, 3112, 3516-17, 3570, 4171, 4573.

Garg, Ganga Ram. An encylopaedia of Indian literature.- Delhi : Mittal Publishers, 1982.

Pp. 34-36, 332, 488.

Gera, Vimla. Mind and art of Bhavabhuti.- Delhi : Meharchand Lachhmandas, 1973.

Contents : Rajasekhara Pp. 254-270.

Ghosh, Manmohan Ghosh.

Ph.D. thesis approved by the Calcutta University in 1938.

Ghosh, Manmohan, The Language of Rājāśekhara's Karpūramañjarī. *All India Oriental Conference* X, Summaries, 50.

Glimpses of Sanskrit literature / ed. by A.N.D. Haksar.- New Delhi : Indian Council for Cultural Relations, 1995.

Pp. 8, 51, 108, 115, 122.

Joshi, Shambhu Dutt. Critical edition of Viddhasalabhanjika of Rājaśekhara with an unpublished commentary of Vasudeva with an elaborate introduction / by Shambhu Dutt Joshi.

Ph.D. thesis aprroved by the Punjab University in 1969.

Keith, A. Berriedale. The Sanskrit drama in its origin, development, theory and practice.- Oxford : OUP, 1924.

405 p. ; 22 cm.

Keith, A. Berriedale Sanskrit - natak : udbhav aur vikas : Siddhanta aur prayog / tr. into Hindi by Udaybhanu Singh.- Delhi : Motilal Banarsidass, 1965.

Krishnamachariar, M & Srinivasachariar. History of Classical Sanskrit literature.- Delhi : Motilal Banarsidass, 1989.

Pp. 625-630, 742-744.

Lēvi, Sylvain. The theatre of India / tr. from the French by Narayan Mukherji.- Calcutta : Writers Workshop. 1978.

Contents :

Rājaśekhara Pp. (Vol. I) - 51, 136, 137, 139, 160, 206-207, 223-230, 242, 243, 248, 253, 272, 273; (Vol. II) 28, 80, 90.

Bālarāmāyaṇa Pp. (Vol. I) 51, 116, 120, 157, 160. 207, 223, 242, 248, 253-257; (Vol. II) 36, 80, 90.

Karpūramañjarī Pp. (Vol. I) 126, 146, 228-230.

Macdonell, A.A. India's past : a survey of her literatures, religions, languages and antiquities.- Varanasi : Motilal Banarsidass, 1906.

Pp. 105, 114, 115.

Majumdar, Manjula. Studies in the dramas of Rajasekhara / by Manjula Majumdar.

Ph.D. thesis approved by the Calcutta University in 1973.

Ojha, Sarla. Critical study of dramas of Rajasekhara / by Sarla Ojha.

Ph.D. thesis approved by the Banaras Hindu University in 1978.

Pathak, M.C. Sanskrit nāṭaka meṅ atiprākṛta tattva.- Jaipur : Devanagar Prakashan, (n.d.) 18, 468 p.

Poddar, Kanhaiyalal. Sanskrit Sahitya ka itihās. - Kashi : Nagari Pracharani Sabha, (Samvat 2030) (Ramvilas Poddar Smarak granthamala).

Rajasekhara. Karpuramanjari / ed. by Ram Kumar Acarya.- Varanasi : Chowkhamba Vidya Bhavan 1955.

Preface contains brief account of his life and works.

Rajasekhara Karpūramañjari and Bāla Bharata. - Delhi : Motilal Banarsidass, 1983.

Preface gives brief biographical sketch.

Rajasekhara Kārvyamīmāṁsā of Rājaśekhara / ed. by C.D. Dalal and R.A. Sastri; rev. & enl. by K.S. Ramaswami Sastri.- 3rd ed.- Baroda : Oriental Institute, 1934.

Introduction Contains information about author's life & works.

_____. Kavyamīmamsā / by Rajaśekhara; tr. into Hindi by Kedarnath Sharma Sarasvati. 2nd ed.- Patna : Bihar - Rastrabhasa - Pariṣad, 1965.

Introduction contains short account of the life and works of Rajaśekhara.

_____. Pracaṇḍapāṇḍava nāṭaka of Śrī Rājaśekhara / ed. by Śrī Haridatta Śāstri.-

Varanasi : Chowkhamba. Sanskrit Series Office, 1969.

Introduction gives informations on the life and literary outputs of this classical writer.

Ramesh Chand. Humour and satire in Sanskrit dramas : Bhasa to Rajasekhara / by Ramesh Chand.

Ph.D. thesis approved by the Punjab University in 1985.

Sahitya Akademi - New Delhi. The National bibliography of Indian literature.- New Delhi : The author, 1962 - 1990, 5 Vols.

Sastri, Gaurinath. Sanskrit Sahityer Itihas.- Calcutta : Sarasvata Library, 1969? (Ashvin 1376).

Sen, Amulyachandra. Karpuramanjari : miscellany. *Indian Historical Quarterly* Sept. 1928; Vol. 4, No. 3; Pp. 567-570.

Sethi, Atmaram. Anudit Hindi Sahitya : vishishta grantha - suchi / by Atmaram Sethi.- Gurgaon : Indian. Documentation Service, 1981.

Contents : Sanskrit (Pp. 1-624).

Sharma, Hanuman V. Study of the works of Rajasekhara / by Hanuman V. Sharma.

Ph.D. thesis approved by the Osmania University in 1987.

Sharma, Ram Nihal. Kavi-siksha in Sanskrit literature and Rajasekhara's contribution to it / by Ram Nihal Sharma.

Ph.D. thesis approved by the Sagar University in 1963.

Shekhar, I. Sanskrit drama : its origin and decline.- Leiden : E.J. Brill, 1960.

Pp. 7n, 42, 60, 72, 90n, 116, 129, 133, 139, 142, 143, 145, 149, 162, 163, 163n, 165, 171-173, 175, 189-194.

Sternbach, Ludwik. 'An Attempt to reconstruct a "lost" work of Rajasekhara' / by Ludwik Sternbach *Annals of Bhandarkar Oriental Research Institute* 1980, Vol. 61, Nos. 1-4, Pp. 21-38 ft-n.

Sushama Kumari. Rajasekhara as a poet and critic / by Sushama Kumari.

Ph.D. thesis approved by the University of Delhi in 1977.

Tripathi, Bhaskaracharya. Critical and comparative evaluation of the Bala Ramayana of Rajasekhara.

Ph.D. thesis approved by the Allahabad University in 1965.

Tripathi, Bhuvanachander. Critical study of the works of Rajasekhara / by Bhuvana - Chander Tripathi.

Ph.D. thesis in Sanskrit, approved by the Sampoornanand Sanskrit Vishva Vidyalaya in 1974.

Tripathi, Radhavallabh. 'Marriage rituals as described by Rajasekhara' / by Radhavallabh Tripathi. *Madhya Bharati* Part (i) sec. (A), 1976-1977, Nos. 24-25, Pp. 39-41.

______. 'Rajasekhara's contribution to Indian theatre' / by Radha Vallabh Tripathi. *Sangeet Natak Akademi Journal*; Jan-March 1979; Vol. 51. Pp. 45-52.

Varma, Jaynarayan and Gupta, Pushpa Sanskrit Sahitya ka itihas.- Ghaziabad : Tarun Prakashan, 1991.

Varma, Shyama. Acharya Rajasekhara.- Bhopal : Madhya Pradesh Hindi Granth Akademi, 1971.

291 p.; 22 cm.

______. Rajasekhara's Sanskrit literary contribution / by Shyama Varma.

Ph.D. thesis in Hindi, approved by the Vikram University in 1968.

Warder, A.K. Indian kāvya literature. (Vol. 5).- Delhi : Motilal Banarsidass, 1988.

Contents : Rājaśekhara. Pp. 413-532.

Zambare, Vasant Triyambak Rajasekhara : critical study / by Vasant Triyambak Zambare.

Ph.D. thesis approved by the University of Poona in 1957.

12

Rūpa Gosvāmin

Rūpa Gosvāmin was a dramatist, poet and rhetorician of high order. Of the age of Rūpa Gosvāmin little can be affirmed positively as no authentic information is available to us. But we come to know that by nature of a religious disposition, he came closer to Chaitanya Mahāprabhu and became his follower. From his association with this great religious leader and from the dates of composition recorded at the end of his few writings, it can be said that his literacy activities might have started as early as 1495 A.D., but most flourishing period occured between 1533 to 1550 A.D.

Śrī Jīva Gosvāmin has given us the early history of the family of Rūpa Gosvāmin. He tells us that Sarvajña Jagadguru of the Bhāradvāja Gotra was a prince Karṇāṭaka. His son Aniruddha was a wellknown Prince too. He fathered two sons Rūpeśvara and Harihara, by his two wives. The first one became an erudite scholar while the second son took to evil ways and turned out his elder brother from his principality. In the east, Rūpeśvara had a son named Padmanābha, who settled down on the banks of the Ganges at Navahaṭṭa Grāma and performed a sacrifice (Yajña). Out of his five sons, the youngest called 'Mukunda' had a quarrel with his relatives and subsequently family dispute compelled him to leave Navahaṭṭa Grāma and finally moved to Fateyābad. Mukunda had a son named Śrīkumāra who was immensely rich and appears to have three sons.- Amara, Santosa and Vallabha, to whom Chaitanya Mahāprabhu gave new names Sanātana, Rūpa and Anupama respectively.

Amara alias Sanātana learnt Sanskrit from a scholar of Navadvīpa called Raṭnākara Vīdyāvāchaspati. He became a high official of Hussain Shah, the Muslim ruler of Bengal (Gauḍa) and settled at the village Ramakeli with his two brothers. Rūpa also had the distinction of holding some position at the same court.

They were bestowed with the title of Davir Khās. They came in contract with Chaitanya Mahaprabhu at Gauḍa on his way to Vṛndāvana and were so much influenced by his teaching that they left home and became a devout Vaiṣṇava. As an ascetic, Rūpa spent life at Vṛndāvana. He was respected as one of the six Gosvāmins of the region.

The term *gosvāmī,* literally, "owner of cows" is a title of respect applied initially to the six learned teachers of Vṛndāvana whose writings constitute the most authoritative literature of the Gaudīya Vaiṣṇava school. It is learnt that task of recovering the deserted sacred sites of Vṛndavana was accomplished through their influence.

Rupa Gosvāmin's love for Kṛṣṇa is evident from his poetic compositions as well as drama.

In the field of drama, his *Vidagdha-mādhava* (7 Acts), *Lalita-mādhava* (10 Acts), and *Dānakeli-kaumudi* (Bhāṇika, ie, without acts division) are the devotional plays having refined erotico religious elements and reflects Kṛṣṇa-bhakti produced by the influence of the Chaitanya movement.

According to Sukumar Sen, Rūpa's dramas have indeed been read through the years by Vaiṣṇavas, not simply as works of literature, but as vehicles of religions truth. He wrote more for literary and theological point of view than really to give them dramatic effects.

Rūpa perceived and articulated through his writings, the intimate relation of aesthetics and religious realization (devotion), both in the worship of Kṛṣṇa generally and in the Gauḍīya Vaiṣṇava movement in particular.

Among Rūpa's works, The *Vidagdhamādhava* in particular rewards sustained attention. Of his two full length dramas which are considerably longer and more elaborate than their classical exemplars., *Vidagdhamādhava* has been the one more highly treasured by members of the Gauḍīya Vaiṣñava community.

The *Vidagdhamādhava*, according to Donna M. Wulff, provides a concrete picture of Rūpa's vision of the religious life that is far more vivid and accessible than the rather abstract reflections found in his theoretical works.

The three printed editions of the Vidagdhamādhava contains the date Saṁvat 1589 (= 1532 - 1533 A.D.) Vidagdhamādhava is written both in Sanskrit and literary Prakrit. Sanskrit is spoken by Kṛṣṇa, Nanda, (his foster father) and Balarāma, (his elder brother) as well as by Paurṇamāsī and Vṛndā (both of whom partake to some degree of divinity).

With the exceptions of the Stage - Manager (Sūtradhāra) and his assistant, rest of the characters speak Prakrit, except in verses, for which they almost always use Sanskrit.

The Lalitamādha text gives the date Śaka 1459 (= 1537 A.D.). Babulal Shukla Shastri observes: Lalita Mādhava Nāṭaka is mostly based on traditional Nāṭaka and Nāṭikā style and does not reveal so much of originality. Rūpa Gosvāmin certainly possesses considerable literary skill, and it is always elegant, often picturesque and sometimes touching. The poverty of action and weakness of characterisation are characteristics common enough in the latter decandent Sanskrit dramas, but Rūpa Gosvāmin, out of respect for texts and traditions, writes more for literary and theological than really to dramatic efects. The central idea of the superiority of the Vṛndāvana Līlā, no doubt, supplies a dramatic motive, but inspite of the unity of action which imparts, the works are really a series of narrative episodes loosely strung together by a semblance of dramatic form. Here, as elsewhere, most of the important incidents are reported instead of being represented.

Regarding his dramatic compositions Babulal Shukla Shastri further finds that the old Kṛṣṇa - legend is modified in the light of the conception of Chaitanya sect and the works are deliberately composed in conformity with its own Rasa Śāstra in order that they may illustrate the hundreds of niceties of its elaborate scheme of devotional sentiments... These works are rightly held in high esteem by the devotees of the faith... They are remarkably brilliant on the poetic side. Nomally these dramas are peculiars types of composition in which the Vidagdha and vidvat combine with the Rasika and Bhakta."

His '*Nāṭaka - chandrikā*' deals with dramaturgy that follows Bharata's *Nāṭ ya - Śastra* and the *Rasārṇava - Sūdhākara* but rejects the *Sāhitya - darpaṇa*, being opposed to Bharata's views. The work is distributed into 8 sections. It begins with the general characteristics of a drama and takes into account the Hero in second section; the divisions of the Rūpaka in third section; fourth part deals with elements in the action annd their classification; Arthopakshepakas and their divisions, (viz. Vishkambhaka, etc) are included in fifth chapter; Divisions of acts and scenes are highlighted in chapter six. This is followed by distribution of dialects in seventh chapter and the last section offers styles of dramatic composition annd their adaptation to the several Rasas. The illustrations are copiously takes from the Vaishṇava writings.

The lack of order and the errors in the work *'Sahityadarpaṇa'* of Visvanātha Kavirāja, are made the basis of criticism by Rūpa Gosvāmin in the early part of the sixteenth century, in his own treatise on drama, *'Naṭaka candrika'* could show little improvement on the work of his predecessor, whence it draws much of its material; as Keith puts it, its real purpose is to eulogize the saint Caitanya, whose disciple Rūpa was and in whose honour he composed dramas of no merit.

His magnum opus is the *Ujjvala - nilamaṇi*, a treatise on poetics. This Vaiṣ nava Rasa - Śāstra depicts classes and conditions of lovers and the several stages and modes of their affection. The work is profusely illustrated with verses in praise of Kṛśṇa; there are several commentaries on it.

His *Bhaktirasāmṛta - sindhu is* another work on poetics, a delightful book on Vaiṣṇava Rasa - Śastra. It contains a date Śaka 1463 = 1541 - 1542 A.D.

Haṁsadūta and *Uddhava* are two poems of message, composed on the lines of Meghadūta.

He had compiled an anthology entitled *'Padyāvali'* comprising of 386 verses from over 125 authors. All the verses are in glory of Kṛśṇa and his love-sports.

Ujjvala - chandrikā is a dialogue between Chaitanya - chandra's sister Rādha and her friend about Kṛṣṇa.

In *Harināmāmṛta*, he introduces religious elements in grammer and this grammer is still in vogue among the Bengal's Vaishnavites.

His *'Saṃkṣepta - bhāgavatāmṛta'* deals with Vaiṣṇava thology and philosophy.

His other notable works are *Yamunā - stotra; Gandharava - prārthanā - stotra; Gaurāṅgastava - kalpataru, Kusumastabaka; Mukundamuktāvalī, Chātupushpānjalistava; Utkalikāvallari; Laghu - Bhagavatāmrta; Ānanda - mahodadhi* and *Mathurā - mahimā* etc.

Dāna - Keli - Kaumudi

Synopsis

This is an one - act play of the Bhāṇikā type. Vasudeva is performing a sacrifice. Rādhā accompanied by other Gopis, is carrying ghee. Kṛṣṇa alongwith his attendants obstructs their way and demands toll on the ground that he is the lord of the forest through the girls are passing. This results in a quarrel and finally Rādhā is proposed by one of her friends to be given as a toll.

Lalita - Mādhava

Synopsis

Kṛṣṇa līlā at Vṛndāvana, and Dvārikā is depicted in the Sanskrit drama 'Lalita - Mādhava' in which the dramatist has made several modifications in the old legend. This is more extensive being in ten acts with a complicated theme and plot. It has aptly been said that the play is more narative than dramatic in conception and execution because there a great deal of dialogue but little incident.

Dramatis Personae

Male

Sūtradhara

Śrī Kṛṣṇa

Madhumangal

Rāma

Uddbhav

Bhīṣma

Abhimanyu

Sunanda

Krathakaiśikau

Suparṇa

Govardhana

Nārada

Śankhacūḍa

Viśvakarmā

Kañcukī.

Female

Naṭī

Rādhikā

Candrāvalī

Padmā

Lalitā

Viśakhā

Mādhavī

Navavrindā

Bakula

Vṛndā

Paurṇamāsī

Gārgī

Kundalatā

Yaśodā

Rohiṇī

Jatilā

Mukharā

Bhāruṇḍā

Vṛddhā

Śarad

Sukaṇṭhī

Mālatī

Tulasī

Pingalā

Plot :-

Prologue :- In the prastāvana of the Lalitamādhava, Śiva is represented as commanding Rūpa in a dream, to perform the Lalitamādhava for the group of

Vaiṣṇavas who have assembled on the bank of the Rādhā kuṇḍa for the worship of Mount Govardhana at the beginning of the Divālī festival. The origin of Chandrāvali and Rādhikā is unfolded by Paurṇamāsī, mother of Sāndīpani Muni and disciple of Devarṣi Nārada Muni. Chandrāvali and Rādhikā are infact two daughters of Vindhya Giri about which they themselves were unaware. Demoness Pūtāna had stolen the infant Chandrāvali, an emissary of Kaṃsa - Rāja fell from her hands in a stream and was found by the king of Vidarbha named Bhiṣmaka. She grew up as his own daughter. Rukminī, (Chandravali) and Rādhā's story is ascribed later on to the Sixteen thousand and one hundred Gopīs, who worshipped Kātyāyanī Devī and Kāmākhyā Devī of Kāmrūpa Deśa and received the boon of obtaining Śrikṛṣ na as their husband. The other chief Gopīs such as Bhadrā, Lakṣmaṇā, Lalitā, Nāgnijiti, Śaivyā, Śyāmalā or Mādra were all originally Princesses, while Viśākha was the incarnated river Yamuna, daughter of the Sun God. We are further told that a regular marriage of Chandrāvali and Rādhikā with Śrī Kṛṣṇa was solemnized, who were already the wives of Gopās named Govardhana and Abhimanyu respectively : by the effect of Māyā. The same is true of other Gopīs, when their so - called husband, ie, the Gopās could never treat as their wives.

Act One :- The sole aim of this act is to describe purvarāg with reference to Chandrāvali and Rādhikā. Act shows the returning home of Śrīkṛṣna in the evening after tending cows all the day and his meetings, separately with both Chandravali and Rādhikā. But the meetings are interrupted by the vigilance of Bhāruṇḍā and Jaṭilā, their respective mother - in - laws.

Act Two :- Begins with the next morning that depicts Śrīkṛṣṇa's nocturnal sports with the Gopis. Here dramatist present Pādmā and Śyāmalā, two companions of Chandravali as Vipralabddha and Svādhīnbhartikā heroines respectively.

In this act the demon Śaṃkhachūda is stayed by Śrīkṛṣna behind the scene and on account of this event, the act is called 'Shaṃkhachuḍavadha'. The demon is sent by Kaṃsa to kidnap Rādhikā, who is reported to have been married to Śrīkṛṣ ṇa and who is enthroned as the chief of the Gopīs. When she goes to worship the Sun God, Śrīkṛṣṇa emerges as a Brāhmaṇa kumāra, in disguise as the priest to perform the ceremony, but this brief humorous situation is spoiled by the reported arrival of Śaṃkhachūḍa and whom Śrikṛṣna eventually kills.

Act Three :- Focusses on the departure of Śrīkṛṣṇa and Balaram to Mathura. Akūra come to fetch them and the grief the Gopīs at their departure is portrayed. However the act is called 'Unmatta Rādhika' as the main scene revolve around the frantic Rādhika who is in search of her beloved Kṛṣṇa. Unable to withstand the pangs of separation, wailing Rādhikā jumps into the river Yamunā and is lost with Viśākhā, but a devine voice tells us that she has gone to the other world by passing through the orb of the Sun. Her companion Lalitā also jumps from the top of the hill to end her life in despair.

Act Four :- Fourth Act shift from Vṛndavana to Mathurā where Śrīkṛṣṇa is also heart broken due to his separation from Chandrāvali, Radhikā and other Gopikās. Meanwhile Chandravalī who is actually Rukminī has been abducted by her brother Rukmin. Being ashamed of her, he brings him to Vṛndāvana in order to perform her marriage with Śiśupāla, king of Chedi. By this time Vṛndāvana might have been a desolated region, as the sixteen thousand and one hundred Gopikās are forcibly carried away by the Narakāsura.

Now a play within play commenses at the instance of Pauraṇamāsi to entertain sorrowful Śrikṛṣṇa. The play describes the incidence of Śrīkṛṣṇa's sports at Vṛndāvana, in which Śrīkṛṣṇa deceives Jaṭilā, mother-in-law of Rādhikā by assuming the disguise of Abhimanyu, her son and Rādhikā's husband and thus, the permission is granted to sport with Rādhikā.

Act Five :- Focusses on the tactful abduction of Chandrāvalī at Kuṇḍina - Nagara, instigated by Paurṇamāsī. Śrīkṛṣṇa alongwith Suparṇa (Garuḍa) enters and takes away Chandrāvalī against the wishes of her brother Rukmin, However with the silent consent of Bhīṣmaka, her father.

Act Six :- The Sixth Act deals with the winning of Satyabhāma, daughter of king Satrājita and recovery of the Syamantaka Jewel.

Satyabhāmā is none other than the transformed Rādhikā, who alongwith the Syamantaka Jewel, was gifted to king Satrājit by the Sun God. Viśvakarman, father-in-law of Sun God (ie father of Saṁjñā) builds a Nava-Vṛndāvana at Dwārikā, where Chandrāvalī is installed as the queen and Satyabhāma is left in her protection.

Satyabhāma will be recognised as Rādhikā only when Śrikṛṣṇa presents her with the Syamantaka gem recovered from Jāmbavata, alongwith Jāmbavatī (Lalita), his daughter.

Act Seven :- This act centres on the secret meeting of Satyabhāma with Śrīkṛṣṇa is where the latter shows her a speaking image of Rādhikā made by Viśvakarman. But the meeting is interrupted due to sudden appearance of Chandrāvalī.

Act Eight :- It also carries love - episodes at Dwārikā in a new milieu with little humour. A comedy of errors is shown which is based upon Chandrāvalī's jealousy of Satyabhāmā by exchange of two caskets of jewelleries made by Viśvakarman for these two ladies. Incidently this is related to the rescue of Viśākhā, reborn as a woman ascetic by Śrīkṛṣṇa. The latter brings her to Dwārikā.

Act Nine :- This act primarily deals with the presentation of reminiscent love by Śrīkṛṣṇa for Rādhika (now Satyabhama) to whom he shows a series of cave-frescoes made by Viśvakarman, bearing on the Vṛndāvana - Līla. The act also reports about the rescue of Rādmā, Bhadra, Śyamalā and all sixteen thousand one hundred Gopīs.

Act Ten :- In the Final Act, the Syamantaka gem atlast is sent by Satrājita King. The role of one of the maids sent by the king with Symantaka gem, but the truth is revealed. This leads to the Chandrāvalī's recognition of Rādhikā. The play terminates happily with reunion affected by the efforts of Nanda, Yaśodā and others who arrives at Dwārikā, which is now transformed into a really Nava Vṛndāvana.

Vidagdha - Mādhava

Synopsis

The entire episodes of the Vṛndāvana - līlā of Rādhā - Kṛṣṇa is dramatised by Rūpa Gosvāmin in his 'Vidagdha - Mādhava. The composition of this seven acts was completed in Saṃvat 1589.

Dramatis Personae

Abhimanyu	...	Radha's husband (through the illusion cre ated by Yogamāya).
Aghamathana	...	"Destroyer of sins / the demon Agha", an epithet of Kṛṣṇa.
Candrāvalī	...	Rādhā's rival; wife of Govardhana who is the superintendent of Kaṁsa's herds.
Govinda	...	A name of Kṛṣṇa 'Cowherd', ie, one who finds the cows.
Hari	...	"Tawny", a name of Kṛṣṇa.
Jaṭilā	...	Rādhā's mother-in-law, Elderly mother of Abhimanyu.

Kakkhaṭikā (Kakkhaṭi)	...	Old female monkey.
Kaṁsāri	...	"Kaṁsa's enemy", an epithet of Kṛṣṇa.
Karālā	...	Candrāvalī's maternal grandmother.
Kṛṣṇa	...	Supreme Lord of the universe; youthful cowherd who is the lover of the gopīs.
Lalitā	...	Rādha's girlfriend.
Mādhava	...	"The Springtime", a name of Kṛṣṇa.
Madhumaṅgala	...	Brahmin friend and confidant of Kṛṣṇa.
Madhusūdan	...	"Slayer of the demon Madhu (Bee)", an epithet of Kṛṣṇa.
Mukharā	...	Rādhā's maternal grandmother; nurse to Yaśodā.
Mukunda	...	"Giver of release", a name of Kṛṣṇa.
Murabhid	...	"Destroyer of the demon Mura", an epithet of Kṛṣṇa.
Nanda	...	Faster father of Kṛṣṇa; Head of the cow-herd village.
Nāndīmukhī	...	Grand - daughter and assistant to Paurṇamāsī.
Padmā	...	Candravalī's girl friend.
Pāripārśvika	...	Sūtradhāra's assistant.
Paurṇamāsī	...	Grandmother of Madhumaṅgala; Saintly go-between.
Rādhā	...	Abhimanyu's young bride; gopī (most beloved of Kṛṣṇa).
Rāma (Balarāma)	...	Elder brother of Kṛṣṇa.
Raṅginī	...	Rādha's deer.
Śaivyā	...	Candrāvalī's girl friend.
Sāraṅgī	...	Jaṭilā's young niece.

Śrīdāman	...	Kṛṣṇa's friend.
Subala	...	Kṛṣṇa's close friend.
Suraṅga	...	Kṛṣṇa's deer.
Sūtradhāra	...	Stage manager.
Śyāmala	...	"Dark one", an epithet of Kṛṣṇa.
Tāṇḍavika	...	"Dancer", Kṛṣṇa's peacock.
Viśākha	...	Radha's girl friend.
Vṛndā	...	Goddess of the forest Vṛndāvana (which she beautifies for Kṛṣṇa).
Yaśodā	...	Kṛṣṇa's foster mother

(Only prominent epithets of Kṛṣṇa is included in the list).

Plot :-

Prologue :- Unlike other classical plays, in *Vidagdhamādhava,* the playwright in his role as sūtradhāra tells his assistant that he was directed to enact the amorous sports of Kṛṣṇa by Lord Śrīśaṅkaradeva (Śiva), a bhaktavatāra in order to resuscitate few of his devotees who were expiring because they were separated from their Lord.

The Sūtradhar or Stage Manager who speaks as author then goes to state the theme of the drama, ie, the unique love of Rādhā and Kṛṣṇa at the backdrop of Vṛndāvana ad their union brought about through the efforts of Paurṇamāsī. Once she is introduced, both the stage Manager and his assistant departs. Then enters Paurṇamāsī with her grand-daughter named Nāndīmukhī. In this Introductory Scene (Viṣkambhaka), through their conversation it is learnt that Rādha has been taken from Gokula to Bhānutirtha out of fear of king Kaṁsa, who must have heard of her unparalled beauty. They are deeply concerned that Rādhā's husband Abhimannyu poses for the realization of Paurṇamāsī's purpose, but reach no decision. If Abhimanyu takes Rādha away from the pastoral Vṛndnāvan (the cowherd village) then that would prevent her union with Kṛṣṇa. This is followed by Nāndimukhī's vivid description of Rādhā's pūrvarāga, first blossoming of her love for Kṛṣṇa. Both Paurṇamāsī narrates the spontaneous quality of Rādhā's supreme love through a devotional verse. She unfolds her stratagem before Nāndimukhī. The latter is to instruct Viśākhā to draw a portrait of Kṛṣṇa that will soothe Rādhā's eyes and Paurṇamasī herself would contrive to entrance Kṛṣṇa with the sweet sounds of Rādhā's name.

We further come to know that Kṛṣṇa is approaching Vṛndāvana accompanied by his brother Balarama and friends caressed by his loving parents. Thus before Paurṇamāsī leaves the stage with Nāndīmukhī, we learn of Kṛṣṇa's radiance from the verses of Paurṇamāsī, his eyes; his forest ornaments; his crest of peacock feathers, his garland of wild flowers, his necklace, the campaka blossoms that adorn his ears, his bejeweled flute etc.

Act One :- Now the main act begins with Kṛṣṇa's emergence with his foster parents Nanda and Yaśodā, whose great affection for him is evident from their words and gestures. Here comes Kṛṣṇa's humorous companion and confidant named Madhumaṅgala who begins with an apparently innocuous verse about Kṛṣṇa, which the latter approves smilingly but soon he realizes that the stanzas hints at Kṛṣṇa asks his friend to stop, but Madhumaṅgala bluntly refuses and tells that he would reveal everything before Kṛṣṇa's mother. Nevertheless Kṛṣṇa's embarrassment soon changes to relief when he finds the concluding verse merely describe Kṛṣṇa's rowdy pastimes with his fell cowherds and nothing else.

Kṛṣṇa asks his parents to return to the village as the hungry cows are waiting for him to take them out to pasture.

Giving this excuse, he and his companions proceed toward the verdant field and groves of Vṛndāvana and on the way he plays his flute. His elder brother Rāma (Balarāma) and Madhumaṅgala describe the seductive sound of the flute and their effects on the cows and also upon the rocks and streams. A divine voice from the sky tell us about the cosmic repercussions of Kṛṣṇa's flute - playing and at this juncture a humorous event occurs when the gods who approach at the sound of the flute are mistaken for demons by the terrified Madhumaṅgala. As they proceed further, appears Paurṇamāsī with a plate of sweets when enquired about the reason behind this unexpected gift, Paurṇamāsī tells that the sweets come from Mukharā, whose grand daughter Rādhā has just been married to Abhimanyu. Hearing Rādhā's name from Paurṇamāsī, Kṛṣṇa begins to temble and being unable to conceal his emotion, he tries to change the subject, but Paurṇamāsī deliberately brings the same topic, ie, about gopīs and mentions Rādhā's name. Madhumaṅgala teases Kṛṣṇa about Rādha and having succeeded in his venture, satisfied Paurṇamāsī leaves them. After their departure, she moves ahead and meets Rādhā who is taking to her close friend Lalitā. While proceeding Vṛndāvana, Lalitā informs Rādha that this is the place of Kṛṣṇa's līlā.

At the name "Kṛṣṇa", Rādha gets excited annd requests Lalitā to repeat it. At this moment, the sound of Kṛṣṇa's flute is heard and Radha is utterly captivated. Now enters Vīśākhā who brings with her the picture of Kṛṣṇa that she had painted and to have a glimpse at it, all of them goes into a grove.

Act Two :- A rumour is spread that Rādha is seriously ill and to findout the truth, at the request of Paurṇamāsī; Nāndimukhī goes in search of Mukharā. Yo one's utter disbelief, she find Mukhāra weeping because of Rādha's terrible state who has fallen prey to Kṛṣṇa's beauty. As they leave the stage, enters Rādhā accompanied by her two closest friends who are pestering her to unfold the cause of her consternation. Rādhā put blames on Viśākhā for her suffering because it was she who showed her the painting. She is so fascinated by Kṛṣṇa that like half - crazy she describes a meeting with Kṛṣṇa as if it had already taken place. She expresses her intention to take her own life because, for she is under the impression that she is in love with three men : The bearer of the name 'Kṛṣṇa', the flute player, and the extra ordinary beautiful and handsome youth in the picture. But finally there is a sigh of relief with her friends statement that these are not three men, but one. For how could the gopīs love anyone except Kṛṣṇa? At this juncture enters Nandīmukhī in the bamboo grove and meets Rādhā. She atonce recognizes Rādhā by her appearance who has been affected by "the Kāma of Vṛndāvana, ie, Kṛṣṇa. She is informed by Viśākhā of all that has transpired and leaves to bring Paurṇamāsī. Rādhā is goining through on emotional turmoil. There is the conflict between the dharma of respectable women and the infatuation towards "the Prince of Nāgaras." Soon Nāndīmukhī return with Paurṇamāsī and Mukharā. The latter is astonished at the strange behaviour of Rādhā and feels that it may be caused by an evil spirit. Paurṇamāsī is of the opinion that it must be Kāmsa and his fellow demons, who, she adds, have been looking for Rādhā. This interpretation enables Paurṇamāsī to offer a radical solution, ie, she should be treated by exposure to the glance of Kṛṣṇa, the enemy of demons. Mukharā says that with such a remedy, Jaṭ ilā would not be happy. Thus, Paurṇmāsī agrees to create a Kṛṣṇa by her magical skills.

Mukhara leaves and both Paurṇamāsī and Nāndīmukhī discuss Rādhā's longing for Kṛṣṇa and realizes that "the tree of her love is firmly rooted". Paurṇamāsī asks her to write a love-letter to Kṛṣṇa. The scene shifts to Kṛṣṇa who is shown in his single - minded preoccupation with Rādhā. However, with the appearance of Madhumaṅgala, Kṛṣṇa tries in vain to conceal his emotions. Finally he admits before his suspecting frined about his deep love for Rādhā and expresses her beauty and grace (though he had seen her from afar).

Their conversation is interrupted with the emergence of Lalitā and Viśakhā, who brings the love - letter and present it to Kṛṣṇa. The latter is highly delighted when Madhumaṅgala loudly recites its contents.

Kṛṣṇa, however, hides his true feelings and outrightly denies that he would have anything to do with a woman. Lalitā argues that how he, who gives delight to all the inhabitants of Gokula, can cause Rādhā alone unhappy. Viśākha puts Rādhā's necklace of Guñjā berries around Kṛṣṇa's neck and conveys the Rādhā's longing for him. Kṛṣṇa denies his feelings either for the young maidens or for the neck-lace. By mistake, he takes off his own Raṅgana garland instead of Rādha's neck-lace and gives it to Viśakhā. The latter atonce hides it and gladly leaves with Lalita. Soon after their departure, Kṛṣṇa starts repenting for the indifference shown to the maidens. He fears that this may cause Rādhā to withdraw from the world or even to take her own life. The two friends discuss the matter and it is finally decided that Kṛṣṇa would write a love - letter to Rādhā in return and goes out immediately to pluck flowers to make the ink.

Distressed Rādhā is given the Raṅgana garland of Kṛṣṇa by Viśakhā and informs her about their encounter with Kṛṣna. Rādha still thinks of committing suicide without the latter. Viśākhā says that Radha has been robbed of all her good qualities by "Tena dhūrtena" (that villain) ofcourse, refers to Kṛṣṇa.

While looking for flowers, Kṛṣṇa and Madhumaṅgala sees Rādhā and Viśākha and in order to overhear their conversation hides at once.

Rādhā's sincere devotion and love brings Kṛṣṇa to tears and when Rādha closes her eyes to meditate upon his form, appears Kṛṣṇa in front of her. Soon she realizes that she is not dreaming. But her delight is short lived due to untimely emergence of Jaṭilā, who has come to enquire Viśākhā about the Pūjā preparation. She is surprised to find Kṛṣṇa there. She challanges him and is hardly affected by Madhumaṅgala's insults and Kṛṣṇnā's insolence. Through double meanings, both Kṛṣṇa and Viśākhā manager to communicate. The former's love for Rādhā. Jaṭilā concludes that this Kṛṣṇa is an apparition brought about the Paurṇamāsī's magical power, but admits that his glance is indeed powerful and she can see that Rādhā is greatly recovered. She takes Rādhā and Viśākhā to the pavilion of Sūrya to perform Pūjā. Then to find Paurṇamāsī, Kṛṣṇa and Madhumaṅgala goes out.

Act Three :- Both Paurṇamāsī and Lalitā are wondering about Kṛṣṇa's reluctannce to meet Rādha. The former spies Kṛṣna in conversation with Madhumaṅgala and easily makes out that Rādhā is the object of his preoccupation.

Kṛṣṇā greets Paurṇamāsī, who teases him about his relations with the gopīs and as their conversation advances, the mutual love of Kṛṣṇa and Rādhā is unfolded. Paurṇamāsī enquires why he is not accepting Rādhā's love, when the latter has over come for his sake three obstacles, ie, dharma, Abhimanyu (her husband), and the elders. Madhumaṅgala says that Kṛṣṇa's objection to a meeting with Rādhā is only feigned.

They arranges a secret meeting, and Paurṇamāsī and Lalitā set out to find Rādhā. Now emerges Rādhā in conversation with Viśākhā. The former reveals her longing for union with Kṛṣṇa. Paurṇamāsī, after indicating to Lalitā that she wants to induce Rādhā to express her love, tells Rādhā that Kṛṣna has refused to see her. But after realizing the intensity of Rādhā's emotion and her complete devotion, as expressed by her wish to die and be reborn as a bee on Kṛṣna's forest garland, solely intent upon the fragrance of his face. This impels Paurṇamāsī to admits that she has misled Rādha so that her true feelings may becomes manifest.

She then tells Rādhā her good fortune, because Kṛṣṇa has himself become desperate to ṣee Rādhā, the same Kṛṣṇa for whom, just to have a glimpse, even Lord Śiva and the other gods perform penance. Bewildered Rādhā and Lalitā go to the grove to meet Kṛṣṇa.

Viśākhā comes back to the mango tree, where she finds Kṛṣṇa eagerly waiting for Rādhā. Kṛṣṇa expresses his apprehension because night has come, but no one has yet arrived to take him to his lady love. Viśākha play a mischief and with feigned sorrow tells that Abhimanyu has taken Rādhā to Mathura. This makes Kṛṣṇa half crazy and confesses that he cannot bear even an instant without Rādhā. Viśākhā admits that it was a mere joke and starts narrating the manifestations of Rādhā's love at Kṛṣṇa's request.

Analogous to Kṛṣṇa's emotional emotional state, Rādhā is also tormented by doubts, because Viśākhā has delayed in bringing Kṛṣṇa. Finally when she steals a glance at Kṛṣṇa, she literally faints with joy. But Lalitā request her to be bold enough to meet him. Both Lalitā and Viśākhā talks to the Kṛṣṇa and alleges that he has stealed their friend's heart and demands that his should prove his innocence by touching the central jewel of Rādhā's necklace without being affected. Rādhā protests to this and tries to escape but Lalitā stops her and as Kṛṣṇa follows Rādhā, Lalitā restrains him with a description of the obvious signs of his excitement. When Kṛṣṇa succeeds in holding Rādhā's hand. The latter protest against his behaviour and disappear among the trees.

Lalitā and Viśākha request Rādhā to cooperate in playing a trick on her lover and Lalitā tells him that Rādhā is afraid to transgress dharma by meeting him. By hearing this, Kṛṣṇa becomes utterly disappointed, but doesnot give up without an argument and eventually he realizes that Rādhā's protest is largely pretense. But Rādhā is still shy and her friends on the one hand forcing her to satisfy Kṛṣṇa's desire and on the otherhand, at the same time resisting all his actions.

Kṛṣṇa explains the ways in which he will serve her in their love making. But Rādhā, as usual pretends to be shocked, once again tries to flee.

At this moment, appears Mukharā in search of Rādhā. Disappointed by seeing Kṛṣṇa, Mukhara tell that how she can have any peace so long as his flute continues to lure the gopīs from their homes. Mukharā urges him to leave, but Kṛṣṇa pretends departure, but soon comes out once again from his hiding place and pulls Rādhā's sari. Mukhara protests against this indicency, but Lalita convinces her by stating that Rādhā is seeing the Tamāla tree on the banks of the Yamunā, and suddenly Mukharā feels dizzy and retires to sleep. But a playful exchange with Rādhā goes on. Here friends teases her and at Viśākhā's mention of the Raṅgana garland, Kṛṣṇa becomes envious of this fortunate garland, which is close to Rādhā's bosom.

The latter now asks for her Guñjā necklace, with great affection, Kṛṣṇa puts it around her neck. At Kṛṣṇa's touch, they again cut jokes with her.

Rādhā gives a sidelong glances at Kṛṣṇa that incite Lalitā and Viśākha to leave the place. Atlast Kṛṣṇa helps Rādhā to overcome her shyness with verses professing his prompt response to her supreme love and the two proceed towards the garden.

Act Four :- As directed by Lalitā, Nāndīmukhī enters to ask Subala to remind Kṛṣṇa of Rādhā at every opportunity. Even Lalita had seen Kṛṣṇa going toward the direction in which Candrāvalī lives. At this moment Padmā appears and ask Nāndīmukhī how she can appease Candrāvali who is despressed because Kṛṣṇa no more visit her. Nāndīmukhī assures Padmā that Kṛṣṇa is approaching Mount Govardhaṇa, so she can console Candravalī with this good news. Even she herself hurries off to find Subala. Padmā recognises the voice of Vṛnda from the wings and alleges that this forest goddess is keeping Candrāvalī from meeting Kṛṣṇa at the behest of Candravalī's grandmother. Again Vṛndā's voice is heard, in which she warns Candrāvalī not to go out, lest she will fall prey to Kṛṣṇa's bewitching sidelong glances and would become mind as Rādhā has done. Candrāvalī enters and seeing her gloomy face, Padma console her with the news that the lord of the Yadus, ie, Kṛṣṇa is verymuch in the vicinity. At this moment Kṛṣṇa arrives and tells Subala that he is longing for Candrāvalī's love. Kṛṣṇa plays the flute and Candravalī is deeply moved by his ever refreshing tones. After requesting Subala's help in securing Candrāvalī's favour, affecionately he approaches her and makes lame excuses for nights he had spent elsewhere. But Candrāvalī accuses that he is as fickle as a bee, always seeks new companionship. Kṛṣṇa flatters with the statement that Candrāvalī is herself always new and in his effort to appease her, he clarifies that to cool the heat of his separation from Candrāvalī, he took recourse to a stream ie, dhāra. But accidently he uttered the word "Rādha" instead of "dhārā". This makes Candrāvali envious and annoyed. Atonce Kṛṣṇa denies having mispoken. Pādmā urges Candrāvalī to accept her fate and breaks the news that Kṛṣṇa is in love with Rādhā.

Disheartened Candrāvalī however pretends as if she has forgiven Kṛṣṇa and then departs with Padmā.

Kṛṣṇa takes refuge to Subala to find ways to appease Candrāvalī. He sends Subala to Lalitā to arrange a meeting with Rādhā. However, Padmā and Madhumaṅgala who appears on the scene making plots to arrange a tryst for a union between Kṛṣṇa and Candrāvalī. They overhear Kṛṣṇa's words of joyfal anticipation and wrongly assume his disperation to be for Candrāvalī. Padmā expresses his confidence to Madhumaṅgala by stating that Candrāvalī will soon calm down and get over her anger.

Madhumaṅgala tells Kṛṣṇa that he would soon bring his beloved. Both Padmā and Madhumaṅgala return shortly with Candravalī. Eagerly waiting Kṛṣṇa is delighted to hear the jingling of the anklets and mistakes her as Rādhā, he rushes and in verse, he expresses Rādhā's glory and even mentions her name, where he intends "Maṅgalabhā, rādhikā (ie, Rādha with beautiful or auspicious radiance).

Hearing Rādhā's name, Candrāvalī's anger is renewed. But clever Madhumaṅgala saves the situation when he splits the same worlds as "maṅgala - bhāra - adhikā (ie, filled with great auspiciousness) and in haste, Kṛṣṇa finishes the verse that appears to be explicitly for Candrāvalī. When Padmā and Madhumaṅgala leaves, Kṛṣṇa takes Candravalī elsewhere, fearing that Rādhā may arrive at any moment.

Shortly Rādha and Lalitā enters the grove to find Kṛṣṇa. Lalita tells Rādhā that she has utterly forgotten the world, otherwise how could she put on all her ornaments on wrong in the confusion of her great eagerness to meet Kṛṣṇa?

Lalita's anxiety grows, when they fail to find Kṛṣṇa there. But Rādhā suggests that Kṛṣṇa must be hiding somewhere and playing a joke on them. After a series of search, finally they give up and concentrate on preparing the love bower. Rādhā is worried that Kṛṣṇa must have been detained by Padmā. When Kṛṣṇa does not arrive, they leave the grove. When Kṛṣṇa comes to the grove, it is already dawn. He realizes that Rādha must have been very upset because of his failure to meet her. An idea springs up and he picks up some nāgakesara flowers so that he may claim that he had been waiting at nagakesara bower all night for Rādha. Rādhā, Viśakha and Lalitā comes. Seeing Kṛṣṇa, Lalita tells that Rādhā has become "hard like a gold statue". He lies before them that he meant "the nagakesara bower" and not "the Kesara bower" and shows Rādhā and Lalitā the nāgakesara flowers.

He further accuses Lalitā who has caused him to spend a sleepless night in the Kesara grove. Lalita does not believe him, for Rādhā spent the whole night waiting for him in the grove. Rādha's friend accuse him of being fie and fickle. Kṛṣ ṇa alleges that Rādhā's love must not be enduring. In the course of deliberation, Kṛṣṇa puts his flute into the añcal (the end of the sari) alongwith the nāgakesara flowers (which he offered her to adorn her hair). All this happens accidently because of Rādhā's bewitching side long glance.

Rādha and her friends whisper to one another of their utter delight at this unexpected achievement. At this point, appears Madhumaṅgala who tries to appease Rādhā with a verse that desacribes the power of her glance upon Kṛṣṇa. In the course of their conversations, Madhumaṅgala misinterprets Rādhā's verse by taking it to mean that she saw Candrāvalī andn Kṛṣṇa in the grove. Thus, he decides to accept the fact that Kṛṣṇa truly spent the night with Candrāvalī, but soon he realizes his mistake when Kṛṣṇa stops him in the middle of his verse. Kṛṣṇa tries to resolve the crisis in vain by completing the verse in such a way that it suggests that the moon served to console him in his separation from Rādhā. The truth is unfolded and Lalitā points to the signs of enjoyment on Kṛṣṇa's limbs. Rādha feels dejected and despite Viśākhā's request and Kṛṣṇa's efforts to appease her such as by offering the jasmine garland brought by Madhumaṅgala, Rādhā is not pacified. Mukharā arrives at this crucial juncture and feels sorry for her grand daughter Rādhā having fallen prey to the villain who is none other than Kṛṣṇa. In response to her remark, Madhumaṅgala brashly compare her vapidness to that of Kṛṣṇā's flute. Hearing this, Kṛṣṇa suddenly realizes that his flute in missing and puts the blame on Rādhā for stealing it. Rādhā vehemently protests and their arguments continues. Mukharā asks Kṛṣṇa to leave the place immediately and threatens that Kaṁsa would punish him for the humiliation meted out to Rādhā. She exists, followed by Rādhā and her two friends. Kṛṣṇa is left alone to ponder over the Rādhā's conflicting emotions towards him.

Act Five :- Paurṇamāsī is plunged in serious thoughts and looks worried. Madhumaṅgala and Vṛndā enter and ask her about the cause of her grief. She reveals that Abhimanyu is very angry because he has seen on her body the marks of love - play with Kṛṣṇa and thus, he is taking his family along. Even his mother Jaṭila torments her.

Now Vṛndā also informs about Kṛṣṇa's dejection caused by Rādhā's anger and Madhumaṅgala puts the blame on Lalitā. During their deliberations, Subala enters and they all makes an arrangement for Rādhā's meeting with her lover. Lalita tells Paurṇamāsī about Rādhā's true feelings for Kṛṣṇa. Paurṇamāsī advice them not to blame Kṛṣṇa and the two hides near the mango tree to overhear Rādhā's expression of her love.

Radha is lamenting as she did not accept Kṛṣṇa's apology. In grief, she regards the bees and other creatures of Vṛndāvana as Kṛṣṇa's messengers and converse to an imaginary Kṛṣṇa, who she thinks is embracing her closely. At this point, enters Lalita and asks her as to whom she is addressing. Rādhā realizes that Kṛṣṇa's is not there. Now Viśākhā comes with a letter given to Subala by Vṛndā. From the contents, it is learnt that due to Rādhā's rejection, Kṛṣṇa is amusing himself elsewhere. This makes Rādhā much more distressed and fears that she is going to loose her lover.

Soon her anxiety changes to relief, when Nāndīmukhī breaks the news that like a yogi, Kṛṣṇā is meditating or more precisely consentrating upon Rādhā's beautiful face. Rādha is happy and as told by Viśākhā she helds Kṛṣṇa's flute toward the wind and it automatically emits a sweet sound that confirms its super natural powers. But Lalita at once refrains her from doing so, otherwise Kṛṣṇa's followers would definately hear it.

The sound of the flute reaches Jaṭilā who comes rushing up, thinking to find Kṛṣṇa there. She snatches the flute from Rādhā that scares them all. Vṛndā however assures Paurṇamāsī that she would soon recover it. Subala informs Jatila that the old female monkey is going toward her house for yogurt. Paurṇamāsī adds that the monkey must have been sent by Vṛndā as a distraction. To stop the monkey, Jaṭilā throws the flute at that direction, who picks it up and climbs a tree. She asks Subala to get it and he tells her to bring her nephew Viśāla, who lives some distance away. When all obstacles are removed and the coast is the perfect venue for Rādhā's tryst, an unexpected crisis emerges. Mukhara brings the message of Abhimanyu, who summons Rādhā to join him atonce for Caṇḍī pujā.

Therefore, Paurṇamāsī directs Subala to go with Vṛndā to console Kṛṣṇa. Subala fears that will not be pacified, and to amuse him they agrees to disguise themselves (instigated by Vṛnda).

Next scene focuses on Kṛṣṇa's desire for union with Rādhā. Madhumaṅgala hears the tinkling of anklets and requests Kṛṣṇa not to worry. Enters Subala and Vṛndā in disguise as Rādhā and Lalitā. Kṛṣṇa is excited, but they maintains distance. Viśāla's sister Sāraṅgi enters with a message from Mukharā, who wants to know why Rādhā is to be blamed, when she did not take his flute, which is in the old monkey's possession.

Kṛṣṇa in reply says he has found it, as he had spied his flute in Subala's hands. From the back stage, the voice of Subala (impersonating Rādha) is heard, and Sārangi believing it to be Rādhā's voice, enquires why she did not obey Abhimanyu's summons. Sāraṅgī is humilated by Vṛndā (impersonating Lalitā) and she leaves in a greate rage to tell Jatilā. Vṛndā as Lalitā then snatches the flute from Subala as Rādha and posses it towards Kṛṣṇa, but Madhumaṅgala quickly collects it.

Meanwhile Jaṭilā emerges and presuming Subala and Vṛndā as Rādhā and Lalītā, takes them away. Kṛṣṇa sends Madhumaṅgala atonce to witness what transpires, shortly returns Madhumaṅgala and informs Kṛṣṇa that when Jaṭila brought Rādhā before elderly village women, Rādhā removed her veil and emerged as Subala. The entire village folk made fun of the whole episode that impelled Jatila to flee in embarrassment. Now Kṛṣṇa realizes that everything was plotted by Vṛnda for Kṛṣṇa's amusement. So he atonce desires to see both Vṛndā and Subala in their disguises and subsequently plays his flute. Interestingly this time,. the real Rādhā and Lalitā appears Kṛṣṇa urges Rādha whom he takes to be Subala, to embrace him so that he may enjoy the same delight that he received while touching Radha. Vṛndā arrives at this point and requests Rādhā to give Kṛṣṇa what he desires. Overwhelmed with joy, Kṛṣṇa still wonders that it is none other than Rādhā herself who stands before him. But both Rādhā and Lalitā are still accuses him of his unfaithfulness. Rādha feels cheated and breaks down. Kṛṣṇa wipes her tears away annd admits his involvement with other gopīs, but at the same time emphasise that Rādhā is the dearest of all.

Kṛṣṇa expresses his desire to frolic with Rādhā in the forest. Vṛnda causes all the flowering creepers to bloom. Both Madhumaṅgala and Lalitā starts a teasing argument and infanct the puns begins with the different blossoms. Even Vṛndā and Kṛṣṇa also joins and the punning rivalry is carried on by two parrots. The Śuka (male) and Sārī (female), the former criticizes the gopis and takes Kṛṣṇa's part, while the latter favour Rādhā.

Vṛndā collects lotuses from the river to adorn Kṛṣṇa and he places them behind Rādha's ears. From a lotus bud, a bee emerges and alights on one of these lotuses that frightens Rādhā. Immediately Madhumaṅgala drives it away with his stick and informs Rādhā about the bee's disappearance. But Rādhā misinterprets his statement, taking Madhusudana (slayer of Madhu, the demon) (also, "bee"), epithet of Kṛṣṇa. Rādhā is confused and wonder why Kṛṣṇa would abandon her. Disheartened Rādhā is about to lose all control when Kṛṣṇa comes to her rescue. The latter was always there in front of her. Rādha regains her composure. In a series of verses, the playwright display Rādhā and Kṛṣṇa's literary skill. When Madhumaṅgala tries to alert them about Jatilā's staff, Jaṭila arrives there to reclaim it. Frightened Rādhā hastily leaves followed by Lalītā and Vṛndā. This time, Jaṭilā takes Rādhā as Subala in disguis, and departs without any hassle. With Kṛṣṇa and Madhumaṅgala's return to Gokula, closes this act.

Act Six :- In the morning from the rāsa dance (a circular dance performed by Kṛṣṇa and the gopīs) of the previous night, Viśākhā looks exhausted. Enters Jaṭ ilā who hears that Rādhā is wearing a yellow garment and becomes suspicious because of the colour worn by Kṛṣṇa. Jaṭilā instructs Viśākhā to call Rādha, who appears rubbing her eyes. Jaṭila is dumb-stuck to see Radha wearing Kṛṣṇa's yellow upper garment. But Viśākhā saves Rādhā from this grave situation. She attributes the yellow colour to turmeric - water thrown by the young gopīs during the festival and trusting her Jalita leaves the compound. Meanwhile enters Lalita accompanied by Padmā, who gives her a letter from Kṛṣṇa. Lalitā reads the coded message in which Kṛṣṇa has requested her to bring Rādhā to him. But she waits until Padmā leaves. The latter engages both Lalitā and Vīsākhā, starts asserting the superiority of their heroine's love Kṛṣna and of his corresponding favour.

With Padma's exit, Lalitā takes Rādhā to Kṛṣṇa under the pretext of collecting flower for Sūrya worship.

The monsoon rains has enhanced the beauty of Vṛndāvana. Both Kṛṣṇa and Madhumaṅgala enters eulogizing it. But Kṛṣṇa feels sad that Rādhā is not there. He plays his flute and shortly there after appear Rādhā followed by Lalitā and Viśākhā. The two friends tease Rādhā about her desperation, but she tries to conceal her feeling for Kṛṣṇa and in turn, accuses them of their dalliance with Kṛṣṇa.

At this moment Rādhā sees a dark tree at a distance and thinking it Kṛṣṇa, he tries to flee hastily Viśākhā says that the 'trailokya', ie, the whole world apears Kṛṣṇa to her. Rādhā reels about dizzily after hearing the sound of the flute again and eventually catch hold of a kadamba tree. Lalitā acknowledges her gratefulness to the flute that it unfold Rādhā's deep love for Kṛṣṇa. But Rādhā curses it for causing her so much agony. Kṛṣṇa is in high praise for Radha's natural beauty which appears to him as the moon without its mark. As if hypnotised, Madhumaṅgala support him as he comes closer to his beloved Rādha also comes under the spell of Kṛṣṇa's radiant beauty but at the same time feeling apprehensive, subsequently takes refuge in Lalitā's protection. The latter refrains Kṛṣṇa from approaching Radha who suggests that they take the flowers they have collected and go to the banks of the Yamunā. But Kṛṣṇa, who is unable to bear the pangs of separation, blocks the path and asks Rādhā how she can be so cruel as to leave with the bandhūka flowers (the life of a friend, ie, Kṛṣṇa). Rādhā also expresses her feelings in verses asking him no to behave like a snake in their path and to take her into his arms. Kṛṣṇa misinterprete her remark and to keep her request, he tries to embrace her, but Lalitā resists his act. Cleverly Madhumaṅgala and Kṛṣṇa demands payment for the flowers that they are taking from Kṛṣṇa's Vṛndāvana. The mode of payment would be an equal number of gems from the girls neckiaces.

Viśākhā warns Kṛṣṇa to keep away and expresses Rādhā's readiness for battle that have another meaning, ie, her eagerness for meeting Kṛṣṇa. The later, thus, tries to approach Rādha again. In despair, Kṛṣṇa offers a bribe that he will cheat Rādhā and spend the night with her. Lalita, however, rejects the offer and when been asked what bribe would satisfy her. Lalitā asks him to adorn Rādhā with flowers. When Kṛṣṇa proceeds to comply with her request, Lalitā again shields her and says that Rādha had a purificatory bath in preparation to worship Sūrya.

In reply, Kṛṣṇa tells that he too had a ceremonial bath. Though Lalita is convinced, but Rādhā reminds her of the Sūrya worship. Madhumaṅgala also expresses their willingness to perform worship. They stay awake at the altar formed by the grove of trees, collects flowers for puja offerings, and concentrate on the jingling of anklets. There after, the two goes to gather peacock feathers to make a crest for Rādhā. As soon as they departs, Rādhā hides in a nearby grove of trees. When they return, Lalitā informs that Rādhā has left for her home. Love sticken Kṛṣṇa in his great distraction, mistakes a land-lotus golden with pollen and later a yellow flower, for the golden - hued Rādhā. Lalita also misleads him and as instructed by her, he goes to the grove of Kadamba trees, but finds it empty.

Madhumaṅgala say that he has seen Rādhā and makes a promise that he would deliver her into Kṛṣṇa's hand. Infact he simply handsover a leaf in which two syllables, are inscribed, ie, 'Rā-dhā'. But Kṛṣṇa is not depressed, because even very name of his beloved gives him much delight that manifest the depth of the passion of Kṛṣna for Rādhā.

Finally Kṛṣṇa locates her in a grove of aśoka trees. Their sportive rivalry continues and when Lalitā boasts of Rādha's superiority, Kṛṣṇa suggests that he would see whether they can continue to brag when he is out of sight. Thereby, he hides and Rādhā and Lalitā begin the search. But from the behaviour of the animals and trees, Rādha easily makes out the direction that Kṛṣṇa has taken and subsequently she finds the tamāla grove where Kṛṣṇa is hiding.

In order to escape, Kṛṣṇa freezes, but is detected by Rādha who atfirst pretends not to recognize him. Kṛṣṇa urges that their teasing eachother serve no purpose, but would do bring more harm by separating them. They agrees to retire to the grove of saptaparṇa trees.

By seeing their foot prints, Lalita and Viśākhā speculate the union of Rādha with Kṛṣṇa. Later when the two find her in the grove, in dishevelled condition, the inference is confirmed. Kṛṣṇa emerges and gives explanation himself by stating that he had hidden in the forest to get rid of the ravages of Rādhā's passion. Radha in turn accuses her beloved of being a master in blaming others for his deeds. At this moment, the voice of Madhumaṅgala is heard from the back ground.

While describing the saptaparṇa trees, Madhumaṅgala spells out the word Jaṭilā in a misleading manner that frightened Radhā. She hastily leaves with her companions to avoid detection by her mother - in - law. When Kṛṣṇa hears the rest of the verse (only after Rādhā and her friends have left), he realizes their mistake. In great distress, he disappears that bring the act to a close.

Act Seven :- The final act begins with Vṛndā who describes the beauty of the forest during monsoon session. She notices Abhimanyu talking to Paurṇamāsī and waits till they finish their conversations before meeting the old lady. She overhears that Abhimanyu has come to seek permission from Paurṇamāsī to take Rādhā to Mathura, as he is distressed over the rumors of his wife's dalliance with Kṛṣṇa.

Paurṇamāsī, however, warns Abhimanyu that taking Rādhā to the royal city would be risky. She fears that his wife would fall a prey in the hands of the wicked king Kaṁsa. Eventually the old lady succeeds in manipulating Abhimanyu who decides to wait until he receives firsthand evidences against Rādhā's bearing on her infidelity. He requests Paurṇamāsī for intitiating Rādhā to worship Caṇdi.

Paurṇamāsī cleverly answers that Rādhā would soon worship one who is truly the bringer of auspiciousness to all (especially Rādhā), ie, Kṛṣṇa. After Abhimanyu's departure Vṛndā shares with Paurṇamāsī her happiness over the affairs of Rādhā and Kṛṣṇa. But she is disappointed because of Rādhā's anger over Kṛṣṇa over Kṛṣṇa's has expressed his desire to meet Rādhā on Saudhāgyapūrṇimā. She also brings to the notice of Paurṇamāsī that Padmā has deliberately misconstrued Kṛṣṇa's request, making it seem to refer to Candrāvalī.

At this moment, Lalitā emerges tearfully to tell that she has seen Padmā wearing the very garland that Rādhā had lovingly presented to Kṛṣṇa. But she is relieved when Vṛndā informs (which she has learned from the old monkey) that while Kṛṣṇa was having his bath, Padmā had stolen the garland.

Still they all worry that Padmā may tactfully take Candrāvalī to Gauritīrtha, where Kṛṣṇa is to wait for Rādhā. Meanwhile Viśākhā brings the happy news that Candrāvalī is to join her husband Govardhana for this festival day, as ordered by Karālā, her grandmother. Seeing their path clear they set out to bring Rādhā to Kṛṣṇa. But realizing that Candrāvalī's friends in the vicinity of Gaurītīrtha. They decides to wait till Paurṇamāsī comes.

Śaivyā who is dejected on account of Karālā's order is consoled by Pādmā. They hear it again from the off stage and suddently an idea strikes in her mind. Padmā finds a solution that by taking Candrāvalī to Gaurītīrtha, which is next to Mount Govardhana, they will obey the letter if not the spirit of Karālā's command. Whey they hasten there, Padmā tells that she has given Madhumaṅgala the offering for Gaurī. Her verse anticipates the sight of union of Candrāvalī with Kṛṣṇa that is parroted by the old monkey, who leaves with a threat. Enters Kṛṣṇa and Candrāvalī, as Padmā narrates their moment of meeting.

Kṛṣṇa teasingly obstructs Candrāvalī's way mistaking her to be his beloved Rādhā. But the moment Padmā and Śaivyā arrives and take her part, Kṛṣṇa is puzzled to see that it is Candrāvalī instead of Rādhā, but soon he saves the situation by resolving to please Candrāvalī. From the behaviour of his pet deer, Kṛṣṇa learns that Rādhā has reached Gaurītīrthā, but he deliberately waits that the girls may not approach her. Thus, he rather prefers to exchange puns with Padmā and Candrāvalī, Lalitā and Vṛndā also joins. Padmā and Śaivya argues with Lalita and Vṛnda, each side asserts the superiority of their heroine's love for Kṛṣṇa through riddles and puns. Exhausted Pādmā reminds Candrāvalī of their intention to worship Gaurī. But Karālā emerges in a rage and abuses them for their violation of dharma. Impelled by Lalitā she angrily looks at Padmā, who and the latter tells that she was simply following Karālā's orders. Her confusion of Mount Govardhana with Candrāvalī's husband is explained by Vṛndā who succeeds in pacifying Karālā. The latter departs with Candrāvalī and Śaivyā, followed by Padmā in search of Jaṭila.

Kṛṣṇa delightfully receives the campaka flowers from Vṛndā, sent by Rādhā and promises to meet his beloved soon. Vṛnda and Lalitā moves towards Gaurītīrtha, the former states that she is envious of the Kadamba tree, whose blossoms adorn Kṛṣṇa continually and then, thrilled to see Rādhā, an embodiment of natural beauty and love. From offstage, Paurṇamāsī praises Kṛṣṇa as the embodiment of Yaśodā's motherly affection.

Both Vṛndā and Lalitā observe their sports. Lover's, however, soon disappears into the grove that debarring them from the wondrous vision of their love-making. Vṛnda is astonished to find that how a mere girl has won the heart of the Lord of the entire universe. Finally they sees the pair as Rādhā making request to Kṛṣṇa to adorn her. Vṛndā observes Kṛṣṇa's dishevelled condition, his every features speak of their happy union. Their descriptions compel Kṛṣṇa to appear before them. He praises Rādhā's radiant beauty and places in her hair the blossoms given by Lalitā and Vṛndā. Now Kṛṣṇa plans to play a joke on Rādhā. Lalitā is engaged in collecting more flowers. He, therefore, asks Vṛndā to enlist the old monkey's help and feigns a slip of the tongue, pretending to address Rādhā as Candrāvalī. Rādhā's suspicion is confirmed by monkey act. Kṛṣṇa enjoys her angry mood and tries to appease her half - heartedly without fruition. Rādhā departs in a great rage. He tells Vṛndā that he would now disguise himself as a beautiful damsel of fair complexion and win her back. In the meanwhile Madhumaṅgala arrives to remind Kṛṣṇa that the offering for Gaurī presented by Padmā contains everything that he will need. Kṛṣṇa requests Vṛndā to address him as her sister and leaves for the sanctuary of the Gaurī temple for their arrival.

Vṛndā then come upon Rādhā as she is narrating Lalitā and Viśākhā what has just happened to her. She is consoled by her friends that Kṛṣṇa would never utter the name of another woman in hr presence and fears that their rivals might take advantage of the situation. Seeing Vṛndā, they seek her aid immediately. Vṛnda pretends to scold Rādhā for her envious nature and informs that Kṛṣṇa is in the temple of Gaurī and talking with `Nikuñjavidyā'. Hearing this unknown name, the girls get confused. Vṛnda mischievously identifies Nikuñjavidyā as her sister and asks them to enlist her help to win back Kṛṣṇa. They all enters the temple.

Vṛndā, at first looks in and seeing Kṛṣṇa in disguise, informs the girls that "the deity of Bhāṇdira" is alone. Rādhā proposes to go inside and enquire Kṛṣṇa where abouts from her.

At this juncture, Jaṭilā emerges there, as he hears from Padma that Rādhā is at Gaurītīrtha to perform Guarī puja. She is pleased to her about her daughter - in law act and intends to bless her. In the countryward, she finds Rādhā's pet deer. But suddenly spying Kṛṣṇa's peacock there, she departs in anxiety to look for her son Abhimanyu.

In the temple sanctuary, Rādhā meets the "fair one" and is captivated by her beauty. She ask her where Kṛṣṇa is. In response, a voice from the interior of the temple asks a series of questions with teasing verses. Rādhā in despair, urges Nikuñjavidyā to help her win Kṛṣṇa's love. But Rādhā's efforts bring no result and subsequently blames Vṛnda for her misguidance.

At this moment, enters Jatilā alongwith her son Abhimanyu, who intends to take Rādhā to the Royal city (Mathurā). They reaches the entrance of the temple and stops to observe the happenings. Kṛṣṇa, in the role of Gaurī, teasingly advises Rādha not to ask for something unattainable. Suddenly Abhimanyu appears in rage and announces that Rādhā has been caught red-handed. Jaṭila asks her son about the identity of this women with fair complexion and unearthly beauty.

Abhimanyu (unable to suspect Kṛṣṇa in disguise) tells that it must be the goddess who must have appeared in response to Rādhā's plea. His view is supported by both Lalitā and Viśākhā. Abhimanyu questions what Rādhā was requesting of Gaurī. Vṛndā promptly answers that Abhimanyu is in great danger and is soon to be sacrificed to Bhairava by king Kaṁsa and that is why Rādhā has fallen prostrate before the image. Frightened Jaṭila joins Rādhā and begs the Goddess to have mercy on her son.

Radha in her plea address Kṛṣṇa as ballavīkuladevatā, ie, the deity of the gopīs and requests that she should never be separated from Nātha, Rādhā means the Lord, ie, Kṛṣṇa, again. But Abhimanyu naturally understand it to refer to him, her husband.

Kṛṣṇa also repeats in his ambiguous language that what Rādhā is asking is all but impossible, but at the sometime appreciates Rādhā for her sincere devotion and finally gives his consent to fulfil her desire, if she remain forever in Gokula and worship him. Abhimanyu who was in utter terror, takes oath that he would never take Rādhā to Mathura, accuses Subala (who assumed the role of Radha in disguise) for causing false scandal about Rādhā's liaison with Kṛṣṇa and exists with his mother.

In the final scene, Paurṇamāsī emerges and is delighted to see Kṛṣṇa in disguise as a woman and express her sense of gratitude at being spared the pain of separation from his beloved. Paurṇamāsī makes two final heartfelt petitions that Kṛṣṇa would ever engage in sports with Rādhā in Vṛndāvana and that whoever hears of the unique līlās of Rādhā and Kṛṣṇa may realize the charm of supreme love for the Lord. Kṛṣṇa assures that her request will be granted. He then expresses his desire to return to his village in order to delight his foster parents and with this ends this devotional play.

Dramas in Performances

Scholar Donna M. Wulff of Harvard University says it is possible that Rūpa's dramas have never been performed in their original versions. In particular, it is not known whether they were enacted in Vṛndāvana during him life time - even informally, without elaborate costumes or make-up. My questioning of scholars in Bengal and Brindavan felicited surprisingly, strong opinions on both sides of this issue but no knowledge of any direct evidence either way. There are, so far as I have been able to determine, no references in the Sanskrit or Bengali biographies of Caitanya to such a performance, not even in the voluminous *Caitanya caritāmṛta* of Kṛṣṇadāsa, who was a disciple of the gosvāmīns annd lived for much of his life in Vṛndavana. What Kṛṣṇadāsa does give us is an account of two occasions in Puri on which verses from Rūpa's dramas were allegedly read or recited. The first was by Caitanya himself, who is described as having read aloud a verse of the Vidagdhamādhava (I.15) just after Rūpa had finished writing it. The second was by Rūpa who, at the urginng of Caitanya and Rāmānanda Rāya, is said to have recited a number of verses from both plays for them annd a group of Caitanya's disciples. On each occasion the response of Caitanya and the others to Rūpa's poetry was one of great joy".

Modern scholar Mayadhar Mansimha writes that the play Lalita - Madhava by Rupa Goswami was staged in the Radhakan Math famous as Chaitanya's home at Puri. This appears to be a command - performance as it is on record that all the expenses were met from the State treasury. The ruins of the stage where this play was staged still exist.

DRAMATIC WORKS : A BIBLIOGRAPHY

Text

Dānakeli kaumudī / by Rūpa Gosvāmī.- Berhampore, Bengal : (Rādhāramaṇ Press?), 1881.

Danakelikaumudī / by Rūpa Gosvāmī; ed. by Purīdās.- Aloya, Mymensingh : Śacīnāth Rāycaudhurī, 1947.

x, 44p; 25 cm

Includes index

Drama of the `bhāṇika' type on the love and sports of Kṛṣṇa and Rādhā in Bengali script.

Lalitamādhavañaṭakam / by Rūpa Gosvāmī; ed. by Purīdās.- Aloya, Mymensingh : Śacīnāth Rāycaudhurī, 1947.

viii, 120, [20] p.; 25 cm

First published in 1902.

Includes index.

Drama in ten acts on the love of Kṛṣṇa and Rādhā; in Bengali script.

Lalitamadhava natakam : with the commentary of Narayana / by Rupa Gosvami; ed. by Babulal Sukla Sastri.- Varanasi : Chowkhamba Sanskrit Series Office, 1969/

28, 278 p.

Lalitamādhavanāṭakam with a commentary / by Rūpa Gosvāmī; ed. with a Bengali tr. of Rāmānārāyaṇa Vidyāratna. - 2nd ed.- Murśidābad : the translator, 1901 [1309 Sāl]

First published in 1880 [1288 Sal]

Natakacandrika / by Rūpa Gosvami; ed. by Purīdās.- Mymen Singh : Śacīnātha Rāyachaudhurī, 1948.

Nāṭakacandrīkā of Sri Rūpa Gosvāmin / by Rūpa Gosvāmī; ed. with the `Prakāśa' Hindi comm. and critical notes by Bābūlāl Śukla.- Varanansi : Chowkhamba Sanskrit Series Office, 1964 (Chowkhamba Sanskrit Series, No. 97).

Vidagdhamādhavanāṭakam / by Rūpa Gosvāmī.- Berhampore, Bengal : Rādhāraman Press, 1924.

Vidagdhamādhavanāṭakam / by Rūpa Gosvāmī; comm. by Viśvanātha Cakravarti; the Bengali padāvalī by Yadunandana, the Bengali tr. by Rāmanārayana Vidyāratna.- 2nd ed. - Murśidābād : the translator, 1988 [1307 Sāl]

Vidagdhamādhavanāṭakam / by Rūpa Gosvāmī; ed. by Purīdās.- Aloya, Mymen Singh : Śacīnāth Rāycandhurī, 1947.

xxiv, 108p.; 25 cm.
Includes indexes.

In Bengali script.

Vidagdhamādhava naṭakam / by Rūpa Gosvāmī; ed. with a commentary by Banandatta Śāstrī and Kāśīnāth Pāṇḍuraṅga Parab.- Bombay : Nirṇayasāgar Press, 1903.

iii, 219, [6] p.; 21 cm
Devotional play on `Kṛṣṇa bhakti'.

Vidagdha - mādhava of Śī Rūpadeva Gosvāmī : with a commentary / by Rūpagosvāmī; ed. by Bhavadatta Sāstrī and Kāsīnāth Pāṇḍurang Parab.- 2nd ed.- Bombay : Nirṇaya Sāgar Press, 1937.

(Kavyamāla; No. 81)

First published in 1903.

Translations

Bengali

Danakeli / by Rupagosavamin; tr. into Bengali by Sri Jamunadas. [17th cent.]

First rendering.

Lalitamādhava / by Rūpagosvāmin, tr. into Bengali by Rāmanārāyana Vidyāratna.- Murśidābād : [s.n.], 1880 [1288 Sāl]

Naṭaka - Candrikā / by Rūpa Gosvāmī; ed. with a Bengali tr. by Rāsavihārī Sāṅkhyatirtha.- Cossimbazar : Mahārājā Maṇīndracandra Nandī, 1907.
vi, 226 p.; 19 cm

In Bengali script.

A work on `Alaṅkāras' pertaining to drama with illustrations mainly from the authors own drama `Lalitamādhava'.

Vidagdhamādhava / by Rūpa Gosvāmin; tr. into Bengali by Yadunanandanadāsa.

Published in the first part of the seventeenth century.

Vidagdhamadhava / by Rupagosvamin; tr. into Bengali for the first time by Sri Jamuna Das. [17th cent.]

Vidagdhamādhava / by Rūpa Gosvāmī; comm. by Viśvanātha Cakravartī; ed. & tr. into Bengali by Satyendranāth Basu.- Calcuttta : Basumatī Sāhitya Mandir, [n.d.]

English

Wulff, Donna M. Drama as a mode of religious realization : the Vidagdhamādhava of Rūpa Gosvāmī.- Chico, Calīfornia : Scholars Press, 1984.

x, 270 p.; 22.5 cm

Includes an annotated English rendering of Act No. 7 with summary of the play.

Hindi

Vidagdhamādhavam / by Rūpa-gosvāmī; tr. by Ramākamta Jhā.- Varanasi : Caukhamba, 1970.

Manipuri

Bidagdha Mādhab nāṭakam / by Rūpa Gosvāmī; tr. from Sanskrit original by Hāobam Kulabidhu Simha.- Imphal : Māibam Candrahās Simha, 1976.

142 p.; 22 cm

Oriya

Bidagdhamādhaba nāṭaka Pt. 1 / by Rūpa Gosvāmī; tr. by Baiṣṇaba-caraṇa Dāsa.- Cuttuck : Dāśarathi Dāsa, 1930.

x, 163 p.; 18 cm

Tr. from Sanskrit the acts one of three.

Bidagdhamādhaba nāṭaka Pt. 1 / by Rūpa Gosvāmī; tr. by Gobindacandra Tripāṭ hī.- Cuttuck : Harekṛṣṇa Beherā, 1931.

104 p; 18 cm

Adaptations

Vidagdhacintāmaṇi / by Abhimanyu Sāmanta Simhara Siṅgāra.

Oriya poetry seen in 1921 in Puri by the late Dīnśaran Dās of Brindavan; poet makes no mention of the Vidagdhamādhava as the prototype for this work, but the similarily of title suggests such a relation. Besides Donna M. Wulff feels that this is an Oriya version of the Vidagdhamādhava. This Oriya poet whose notable devotional poem `Bidagdha - cintamani' illustrate the doctrinal nuances of the emotional `bhakti' in terms of the old romantic Krishna - legend. Title of the work is culled out from Rupa Goswami's drama `Vidagdha Madhava'. Some portions of the poem also includes the subject matter of the classics.

Other Works : A Bibliography

Ānanda mahodadhi

Aṣṭādasā chhandas

[stotra]

Aṣṭakālikaślokāvalī.

Bhakti - Ratnākara quotes some traditional verses from which this work is added to the literary output of Rupa gośvamin.

Bhaktirasāmṛtasindhu / by Rūpa Gosvāmī, commentaries by Jīva Gosvāmi, Mukunda dāsa Gosvāmī, and Viśvanātha Cakravartī; ed. by Harīdās Das. 2nd ed.- Navadvip : Haribol Kutī, 1961 [475 Gaurābda]

First published in 1948 [462 Gaurābda]

Bhaktirasāmṛtasindhuḥ / by Rūpa Gosvāmī; ed. by Bhaktisiddhānta Sarasvatī.- Mayapur, Navadvip : Nadiā - Prakāś Press, 1931.

lxvi, 148 p.; 18 cm.

Includes index.

In Bengali script.

Treatise on the bhakti cult of Śrīkṛṣṇa.

Bhaktirasāmṛtasindhu / by Rūpa Gosvāmī; ed. by Purīdās.- Aloya, Mymensingh : Śacīnnāth Rāyacaudhurī, 1946.

xxii, 136, [46] p.; 25 cm.

Includes indexes.

Work on `Vaiṣṇava alaṅkāra' in Bengali script.

Chātupush pañjalistava.

Gandharavaprārthanā

[stotra]

Gaurāṅgastavakalpataru

Govinda - birudāvalī

[stotra]

Haṁsadūtam / by Rūpa Gosvāmī; ed. by Purīdās.- Aloya, Mymensingh : Śacīnāth Rāycaudhurī, 1946.

ii, 10, [6] p.; 25 cm

Includes index

In Bengali script.

'Dūta - Kāvya' in which a swan is sent as messenger by the Gopīs of Vṛndāvana to Kṛṣṇa at Mathurā that incidentally illustrates the `Rasaśāstra' of the Gauḍiya Vaiṣṇavism.

Kṛṣṇa janmatithi vidhi.

Bhakti - Ratnākara quotes some traditional verses from which this work is added to the literary efforts of Rūpagośvāmin.

Kuswmastabava.

Mathurāmāhātmyam / by Rūpa Gosvāmī; ed. by Purīdās.- Aloya, Mymen singh : Śacīnāth Rāycandhurī, 1946.

xii, 30 p.; 24 cm

Includes index

In Bengali script.

Compilation of verses from authoritative works on the religious sanctity of Mathurā, a second place of the Vaiṣṇavas, and the rites to be performed therein.

Mukunda muktāvalī

Pādyāvali / compiled by Rūpa - Gosvāmin.- Dacca : [s.n.], 1934.

Padyāvalī / by Rūpa Gosvāmī ed. by Purīdās.- Aloya, Mymen Singh : Śacīnath Rāycaudhurī, 1946.

xl, 58 p.; 25 cm.

First published from Murshidabad in 1884.

Includes indexes.

In Bengali script; an anthology of Vaiṣṇava verses, with sources.

Padyāvalī / by Rūpa Gosvāmī; critically ed. with an introd. by Suśīl Kumar De. - Dacca : The University of Dacca, 1934.

cxlv, 296 p.; 25 cm.

(Dacca University Oriental Publication Series; 3)

Includes appendices and indexes and notes in English on the authors cited in the text.

The Padyavali : an anthology of Viasnnava verses in Sanskrit / comp. by Rupa Gosvami; ed. by Sushil Kumar De. - New Delhi : Navrang, 1990.

cxliv, 296 p.

Prayuktākhyāta chandrikā.

(Bhakti - Ratnākara quotes some traditional verses from which this work is added to the author's works).

Premendu sāgara

[stotra]

Rūpacintāmaṇi / by Rūpa Gosvāmī; commentary and Bengali tr. by Viracandra Gosvāmī ed. by Atulakṛṣṇa Gosvāmī.- Calcutta :Vaṅgavāsī Press, 1927.

iv, 36 p.; 16 cm

In Bengal script.

Vaiṣṇava treatise on the process of meditation on Śrīkṛṣṇa.

Saṅkṣepa Bhāgavatāmṛtam / by Rūpa Gosvāmī; ed. by Purīās.- Aloya, Mayen singh : Śacīnāth Rāycaudhurī, 1946.

xxviii, 48 p.; 24 cm

Includes indexes.

Vaiṣṇava work in verse being a synopsis of Sanātana Gosvāmī's Bṛhadbhāgavatāmṛta, an exposition of the doctrine of the worship of Śrikṛṣ ṇa as set forth in the Bhāgavatapurāṇa.

Sarasan grahah / by Rupa Gosvami; ed. by Krishna-gopal Gosvami Sastri.- Calcutta : University of Calcutta, 1949.

lxxx, 225 p.; 25 cm

A work on Gaudiya. Vaisnavism.

Shribhaktirasamrita sindhu / comp. by Rupa Goswami.- Vrindavan : Vrajagaurav Prakashani, 1981.

Various paginations; 25 cm

Contains 'Durgasangamani' by Jiva Gosvami, Bhaktisara - pradarshini by Vishvanatha Chakravarti & Harikripa - bodhini Hindi notes.

Smarana maṅgalai kādaśa.

(Ascribed to Śrī Rūpa Gosvāmin)

Śrī Gaṇoddeśa dīpika or Rādhākṛṣṇa Gaṇoddeśa dīpika

[Both bṛhat and Laghu]

Bhakti Rātnākara quotes some traditional verses from which this work is added to the list of Rūpa Gosvāmin's literary output.

Stavamālā / by Rūpa Gosvāmī, ed. by Jīva Gosvāmī.- Bombay : Nirnaya Sāgar Press, 1913

(Kavyamala; No. 84).

Stavamālā / by Rūpa Gosvāmī; ed. by Bhavadatta Śāstrī and Kāśīnāth Pāṇḍuranga Parab.- Bombay : Nirṇaya Sāgar Press, 1903.

vi, 306 p.; 19 cm.-

(Kāvyamālā; 84)

Contains the commentary of Jiva Gosvāmī

Stavamālā / by Rūpa Gosvāmī; ed. by Purīdās.- Aloya, Rāycaudhurī, 1946.

iv, 84, [52] p.; 25 cm.

Includes append & indexes.

Collection of Vaiṣṇava hymns in Bengali script.

Uddhavasandeśaḥ / by Rūpa Gosvāmī; ed. by Purīdās.- Aloya, Mymensingh : Śacīnāth Rāycaudhurī, 1946.

viii, 10 p.; 25 cm.

In Bengali script

Includes index

`Sandeśa - kavya' based on the Bhāgavata episode of Uddhava.

Ujjvalanilamanih / by Rupagosvami.- Delhi : Chaukhamba Sanskrit Pratisthan, 1985.

Includes commentaries of Jivagosvami and Viśvanatha Chakravarti.

Nirnaya Sagar ed. reprinted.

A treatise on Sanskrit poetics emphasizing on the erotic sentiment on divine level of devotion.

Ujjvalanilamanih / by Rupa Gosvami; commentariens by Jiva Gosvami and Visvanatha Chakravarti; ed. by Durgaprasad Sarma and Vasudeva Panasikara.- Delhi : Chaukhamba Sanskrit Pratisthan, 1985.

21, 608 p.

Ujjvalanīlamaṇi / by Rūpa Gosvāmī; commentaries `Locanarocanī' by Jiva Gosvāmī and `Ānandacandrikā' by Viśvanātha Cakravarti; ed. with a Bengali tr. by Rāmanārāyaṇa Vidyāratna.- 2nd ed.- Murśidabad : The Editor, 1887 [1295 Sāl]

Ujjvalanīlamṇi / by Rūpa Gosvāmī; comm. `Svātmapramodinī' by Viṣṇudāsa Gosvāmī; Bengali tr. by Haridās Dās; ed. by Kānāilāl Adhikarī.- Navadvip: Haribol Kuṭī, 1964 [478 Gaurābad].

Ujjvalanīlamaṇi / by Rūpa Gosvamī, ed. by Durgaprasād and Vāsudev Laxman.- 2nd ed. - Bombay : Nirnaya Sāgar Press, 1932.

(Kavyamālā; No 95)

Includes commentaries of Jīvagosvāmī and Vishvanātha Chakravarti.

Ujjvalanīlamaṇi / by Rūpa Gosvāmī; ed. by Kedārnāth and Vāsudev Lakṣmaṇ

Śāstrī Paṇaśīkar.- Bombay : Nirṇaya Sāgar Press, 1913.

xx, 498 p.; 21 cm.- (Kavyamālā; 95)

Includes commentaries of Jiva Gosvāmī & Viśvanāt Cakravartī.

Work on poetics, as applied to the love of Kṛṣṇa.

Ujjvalanīlamaṇi / by Rūpa Gosvāmī; ed. by Purīdās.- Aloya, Mymen singh : Śacīnāth Rāycaudhurī, 1946

xiv, 104, [38] p.; 25 cm

Includes index

In Bengali script.

Ujjvalanīlamaṇi / by Rūpa Gosvāmī, ed. by Rāmnārāyaṇ Vidyāratna with Bengali translation.- Murshidabad : [s.n.], 1873.

Ujjavalanilamani : Hindi vyakhya / by Rupa Gosvami; ed. by Shyamnarayan Pandey.- Kanpur : Grantham, 1986.

vii, 121, 455 p.; 22 cm.

Upadeśāmṛtam / by Rūpa Gosvāmī; ed. by Vimalāprasād Siddhānta.- Sarasvati. - Mayapur, Navadvip : [s.n.], 1914.

44 p.; 18 cm.

In Bengali script.

Contains eleven verses on the cult of Śrī Kṛṣṇa, with Rādharamaṇ Dās's commentary, Kedārnāth Bhaktivinod's Bengali exposition and a Bengali super-commentary by Vārṣabhānāvīdayitadāsa.

Utkalikā vallarī.

[stotra]

Yamunā - stotra.

Translations

Bengali

Śrī - Rūpacintāmaṇi / by Rūpa - Gosvāmī; ed. by Atūlkṛṣṇa Gosvāmī; a commentary and Bengali tr. by Vīracandra Gosvāmī.- Calcutta : Baṅgavāsī Press, 1927.

iv, 36 p.; 16 cm

In Bengali script

A Vaiṣṇava treatise on the process of meditation on Śrī Kṛṣṇa.

Hindi

Bhaktirasamrit sindhu / by Rup Gosvami, tr. into Hindi with notes by Vishveshar.- Delhi : The University of Delhi, 1963.

xlviii, 501 p.; 22.5 cm.

Manipuri

Bhakti - rasāmṛta - sindhu / by Rūpa Gosvāmī; tr. by Vairokpam Bhagīrath Siṃha.- Nambol : Gambhini Devī, 1966-67.

2 Vols.; 22 cm.

Vol. 1 has 127 p.

Vol 2 has 122 p.

Tr. from Sanskrit original.

BIO - CRITICAL NOTICES

Agarwal, Deepa Rani. Contribution of Rupa Goswami to Sanskrit alamkara sastra with special reference to Bhakti / by Deepa Rani Agarwal.

Ph.D. thesis in Hindi, approved by Allahabad University in 1978.

Aufrecht, Theodor. Catalogus catalogorum.- Weisbaden : Franz Steiner Verlag Gmb. H, 1962.

2 Vols.; 26 cm.

Banerji, Sures Chandra. A Companion to Sanskrit literature.- Delhi. Motilal Banarsindass, 1971.

Bhatt, Achyuth Lal. Rupa - Goswami and his works : a comparative and critical study / by Achyuth Lal Bhatt.

Ph.D. thesis approved by the Agra University in 1972.

Chatterji, Jayasri.

`The Philosophical and theological background of the drama Vidagdhamadhava' / by Jayasri Chatterji. *Our Heritage;* July - December 1976; Vol. 24, No. 2; Pp. 1-26 ft-n.

The Cultural heritage of India [Vol. IV]/ ed. by Haridas Bhattacharya.- rev. ed.- Calcutta : The Ramakrishna Mission Institute of Culture, 1956.

Pp. 187, 189, 191n, 192n, 195n - 197n, 205, 265, 473, 518.

De., Sushil Kumar. Aspects of Sanskrit literature.- Calcutta : Firma KLM, 1959.

142 f, 144-149.

De. S.K. Early history of the Vaiṣṇava faith and movement in Bengal.- Calcutta : [s.n.], 1961.

Devotional poets and mystics [Vol. 2] - New Delhi : Publication Division, 1979.

(Cultural Leaders of India/ ed. by V. Raghavan).

Encyclopaedia of Indian literature.- New Delhi : Sahitya Akademi, 1987-1994. Pp. 434, 623, 1105, 1205, 1420, 3717-18.

Garg, Ganga Ram. An Encyclopaedia of Indian literature.- Delhi : Mittal Publishers, 1982. Pp. 88, 204, 358, 488.

Jha, Durga. Critical study of the dramas of Rupagoswami from the angle of Aucitya bheda abheda / by Durga Jha.

Ph.D. thesis in Hindi, approved by the K.S. Darbhanga University in 1984.

Joshi, Pramod Shankar. Rupa - goswami and his dramatic works : a critical study / by Pramod Shankar Joshi.

Ph.D. thesis approved by the Punjab University in 1982.

Keith, A. Berriedale Sanskrit drama in its origin, development, theory and practice.- Oxford : OUP, 1924.

405 p.; 22 cm.

____ Sanskrit natak : udbhav aur vikas : siddhanta aur prayog / tr. into Hindi by Udaybhanu Singh.- Delhi : Motilal Banarsidass, 1965.

Kiran. Rupagoswami's contribution to Sanskrit literature / by Kiran.

Ph.D. thesis approved by Vikram University in 1969.

Kundu, Bisweswar. Survey of the three dramas of Rupa Goswami / by Bisweswar Kundu.

Ph.D. thesis approved by the Jadavpur University in 1982.

Lēvi, Sylvain. The theatre of India / tr. from the French by Narayan Mukherji.- Calcutta : Writers Workshop, 1978.

Contents : Rupa Gosvami Pp.

(Vol. 1) 17, 18, 215-16.

Medieval religious literature in Sanskrit / ed. by Jan Gonda. - Wiesbaden : Otto Harrassowitz, 1977.

(A History of Indian Literature) P. 22.

Mukhopadhyay, Herendranarayan. On a critical and comparative study of the Ujjavalarasa in the Gaudiya Vaishnava kavyas with special reference to Rupa Goswami's Ujjvalanilamani / by Herendranarayan Mukhopadhyay.

Ph.D. thesis approved by the University of Calcutta in 1966.

Poddar, Kaanhaiyalal. Sanskrit Sahitya kā itihas.- Kashi : Nagari. Pracharani Sabha, [Sam. 2030]

(Ramvilas Poddar Smarak granthamala)

[Rūpagośvāmin]. *Journal of Dept. of Letters,* Calcutta, 1931.

Sahitya Akademi - New Delhi. The National bibliography of Indian literature.- New Delhi : The author, 1962-1990.

5 Vols.

Sastrī, Surendranath. `Sri Rupa Goswamin's "Dana Keli Kaumudi" : a critical introduction' by Surendranath Sastri. *Journal of Bharati Research Institute*; July 1979; Vol. 1, No. 1; Pp. I-XX.

Sastri, Vedanta. Rūpagosvāmi and garbhāṅka. *All India Oriental Confernence XIV* (Summary); Pt. i; Pp. 46-47.

Sastri, Vedanta. Rūpa's conception of Rasa. *All India Oriental Conference* IX (Summary), P. 195.

Sethi, Atmaram. Anudit Hindi sahitya : vishishta grantha - suchi / by Atmaram Sethi.- Gurgaon : Indian Documentation Service, 1981.

Contents : Sanskrit (Pp. 1-624)

Sharma, Prem Lata. Studies in Bhakti rasa based on Rupa Goswami / by Prem Lata Sharma.

Ph.D. thesis approved by the Banaras Hindu University in 1954.

Singh, Urmila Literary study of Lalithamadhavam of Rupa Goswami from the point of view of Natya Sastra / by Urmila Singh.

Ph.D. thesis in Hindi, approved by Kanpur University in 1982.

Srivastava, Geeta. Critical study of Lalithamadhava and Vidaghdhamadhava of Rupagoswami / by Geeta Srivastava.

Ph.D. thesis approved by the Banaras Hindu University in 1980.

Upadhyay, Ramji. Adhunik Sanskrit natak.- Varanasi : Chowkhamba Vidyabhavan, 1991.

(Vidyabhavan Pracyavidya granthamala; 36)

Contents : Rupa Goswamin kā natya sahitya (A literary study of his plays Vidagdhamadhava, Lalitamadhava and Dankelikaumudi). Pp. 1-45.

Upadhyaya, Suwalal. Rupa Goswami's contribution to Vaishnava dharma and Sanskrit literature / by Suwalal Upadhyaya.

Ph.D. thesis in Hindi, approved by the Jiwaji University in 1970.

Wulff, Donna M. Drama as a mode of religious realization : the Vidagdhamādhava of Rūpa Gosvāmī.- Calīfornia : Scholars Press, 1984.

x, 270 p.; 22-5 cm.

Includes bibliography

An indepth study of the play.

13

Śaktibhadra

Śaktibhadra was a major playwright of ancient Sanskrit drama who belonged to Deccan. He was a native of the Nambudiri Brahmin settlement of Chengannur n Kerala. Śaktibhadra was greatly revered in Malabar and is believed to have lived in the 8th or 9th century. Tradition says that he was pupil of Śaṅkarāchārya.

There is a legend that being the disciple of Sankaracharya, the great Advaita teacher, he once read out his play *'Aścaryacuḍamani'* (The wonderful crest-jewel) to the guru to elicit his comments, but the master did not respond since he had been observing silence for a year. In despair, Shaktibhadra threw the manuscript into the fire. At the close of the year, when Sankara saw him again, he enquired about the play. Śaktibhadra narrated the whole incident to him. Hearing this, Sankaracharya reproduced the whole play from memory. The story might not be authentic but it is established that he was a conemporary of Sankara.

It is established that besides Ādi Śankara of pre-Christian era, Śankarācāryas of equal fame lived in the 8th and 9th centuries. Therefore, if Śaktibhadra was a pupil of Ācārya of that epoch, then he must have flourished during 800 A.D.

It is to be observed that there is significant similaries in the idea and expression of few verses of Cūdāmaṇi annd Bhattanārayana's Venīsamhāra which may show that Śaktibhadra was well familiar with Veṇīsamhāra. These evidences goes to prove that a likely date for Saktibhadra would be the fall of 8th and the early 9th century, but the date is conjectural.

Prior to Śaktibhadra's drama, king Mahendravikrama Pallava of Kāñcī (7th cent.) has handed down to us two one - act farces. Therefore Śaktibhadra's claims that his is the very first play to be written in South India would be wrong, but again if Śaktibhadra's use of the word 'nāṭaka' is emphasized, then it can be accepted that his work was the first of the heroic class called 'nāṭaka' to be composed in South India.

L.D. Barnett hails *Āścaryacūḍāmaṇi* of Śaktibhadra as one of the best of the Rama plays and one that deserves to be included in the list of classics and studied as such.

Though the play is based entirely on Rama story but playwright introduced several interesting and important dimensions to the basic theme of conflict between good and evil. The most important of these is the use made of the miraculous powers of tāpas, embodiel by the sages on the hero's side, to counter the evil māyā of the demons.

Equally interesting is the political orientation given to the theme of conflict within the milien of statecraft. The play has been aptly described as an improvisation on the Rāmāyaṇa story from the view point of Kautilya's politics in Arthaśāstra.

A crest jewel with miraculous power is employed in the play to add to the dramatic effect. Infact this Cūḍāmani (tiara) of Sita helps to bring about the union of Rāma and Sitā. The device used in the drama is remarkable and is dramatically effective.

One of the norms of Sanskrit play is that 'Adbhuta Rasa' (wonder) can not be the principal sentiment of a play. Śaktibhadra stands out here for his deviation from this norm by making his play endowed with 'Adbhuta Rasa' as the dominant sentiment. The play is also excellent for its easy diction.

With regards to playwright's style and expression, celebrated sanskritist, V. Raghavan writes : Śaktibhadra is said to follow the Vaidarbhī style (characterized by simplicity and clarity, sweet and graceful expression, dignity and freedom from exaggeration) but his work is not as excellent an example of this style as the works of Kālidāsa and Daṇḍin. In the *Āścaryacūḍamaṇi* clarity and adequacy of expression are sometimes lacking, some lines are elliptical; some are very involved and complex in construction. It is refreshing to note that however that Śaktibhadra's style did not develop in the same direction as the style of other post

Bhavabhūti Rāma playwrights such as Murāri and Rājaśekhara. Compared with the language of the Ānargharāghava and the Bālarāmāyaṇa, that of the *Aścaryacūḍamaṇi* is considerably simplier and more straight forward. Also, the play does not become merely a poem in a different form, acting and movement are not neglected.

There are some expressions in the play that seems to echo Viśākhadutta's play '*Mudrārāksas*', Bharabhuti's *Uttararāmacarita* and Bodhayana's *Bhagavadajjukīya*. Apart from the story and its events as furnished by Vālmiki, his ideas and similes are copiously adopted by the playwright and throughout the length and breadth of the drama, one can notice the influence of Kālidāsa's works.

His '*Ascharya cudamani*' resembles Bhasa's plays in many respects such as the entry of Sutradhara after the benedictory verse is over and the introduction of the play with 'sthapana' rather than 'prastavana'.

The 'Ascharyacudamani' is rated as a play of high order by both ancient and modern scholar. Critic Winternitz opined that 'as regards dramatic action and appropriateness for the stage, Shaktibhadra's drama surpasses even the 'Uttararamacarita'.

T.G. Mainkar, however holds different view. According to him, the episodes from the Rāmayana have not been well - knit in it and the play is mediocre.

It is interesting to note that apart from *Āścharya - chūḍāmani*', the '*Pratijṇā - yaugandharāyaṇa* which is ascribed to Bhāsa is held by some as the work of Śaktibhadra under the title '*Unmāda - Vāsavadattā*'. This has been referred to by the playwright himself as his own drama.

The *'Vīṇāvāsavadattā'* an anonymous and incomplete work is regarded by few Sanskrit scholars as the lost *Unmāda - Vāsavadattā*.

Verses from '*Aścharya cudamaṇi*' are also found quoted in '*Subhashitavali*' of Vallabhadeva of Kashmir belonging to 12th century.

In some works on poetics and dramaturgy, there are few known quotation from the *Āścaryacūḍāmaṇi*. In an erudite Kerala anonymous commentary (not earlier than the 14th century) entitled '*Sākuntalacarcā*', two quotations from the play is used. Only one work that deals in depth with *Āścaryacūḍāmaṇi* is another anonymous work called '*Naṭāṅkuśa*' in which a number of passages from the play are quoted. The date of the *Naṭāṅkuśa* is not known, but it is apparently a late work. *Natankusa* (yet unpublished, Manuscript R. No. 3003, Madras Government Oriental Manuscripts Library, Madras, severely criticizes various aspects of the Kuṭiyāṭṭam tradition. (The presentation of the *Āścaryacūḍāmaṇi* by the Cākyār actor).

Āścharya - Chūdāmani

Synopsis :-

Āścharya - chūdamaṇi or *Chūḍamaṇi* is a Sanskrit play in seven - act and is considered by some as the oldest extant South Indian drama which derives its name from the miraculous crest - jewel and ring given to Rāma and Sītā by the hermits. Therefore, this is a Rama play [Sundarakāṇḍa] that depicts the advent of Śurpaṇakhā into Rāma's cottage, physical damage caused to her, the abduction of Sītā by Rāvana, Hanumān's visit to Laṅka, and the finally the triumph of Rāma over Rāvaṇa and asceraining Sītā's purity by the five - ordeal.

The play that begins with the activities of Rama in the forest, finally ends with his reunion with Sītā.

Dramatis Personae

(In order of appearance)

Sutradhar	Mandodarī
Nati	Chetī (Maid servennt)
Laksmana	Varsavar (Chamberlain)
Śūrpaṇakha	Hanūman Amatya (Minister)
Rāma	Vidyādhara
Sītā	Saudāminī
Ṛṣi (Young Hermit)	Jāmbavān
Vṛddha (Old Hermit)	Vibhīṣaṇa
Mārīca	Sugrīva
Ravaṇa	Narada
Sūta (Charioteer)	
Jaṭāyu	

Plot:-

Act One :- *Parṇaśālāṅkam (The Act of the leafy hut)* In the first act, Lakṣmaṇa is seen engaged in building a hut when Śūrpaṇakha (in the guise of a damsel) comes to him. She expresses her love and longing for Lakṣmana. But the latter outrighty rejects her advances. But desperate Śūrpaṇakhā lies that Rāma has ordered her to give company to Lakṣmana. Seeing no option, Lakṣmaṇa asks her to wait and goes to Sītā and Rāma. The act ends with their meeting.

Act Two :- *Surpaṇakhāṅkam (the Śūrpaṇakhā Act)* In this act, after being rejected by Lakṣmaṇa, dejected Śūrpaṇakhā comes to Rāma to satisfy her passion. But the real nature is soon exposed and she lifts Lakṣmana up to kill him. However, Lakṣmana severes her nose and ears and leaves Rākṣasī in this terrifying form. Rāma approves of the action of his worthy brother Lakṣmaṇa and weeping Rākṣasī runs away to report and show her pathetic condition to her brothers, threatening the human beings with dire consequence.

Act Three :- *Māyāsītāṅkam (The Act of the false Sītā)* This is a lengthy act where at the outset, the author employs a Viṣkambhaka to report the killing of the demons. Khara, Duṣana etc and the coming of Rāvana annd his persuasion of the unwilling Mārīca to come to his help. The real drama begins with the presentation of the wonderful crest jewel and magic ring to Sītā and Rāma respectively by Lakṣmaṇa as a gift from the rishis. The strange power of the above mentioned jewels is that by their very touch, the delusion caused by the demons will disappear and they will be exposed in their real nature and form. After accepting the gifts, Rāma places the jewel in the crest of Sitā and the ring in his finger. In the meanwhile, illusory deer (Māyamṛga) emerges. In order to fulfil Sītā desire Rāma follows it with his bow and leaving Sītā in the company of Lakṣmana for her safety.

The focus is now on the Rāvana and Śūrpaṇakhā on a chariot. Rāvana decides to carry off Sītā by force after slaying her husband. The act continues upto the departure of Rāvaṇa with Sītā as his captive. In between, a series of events occurs as found in the original epic, with some innovative alterations. Here the playwright presents Rāvaṇa in the disguise of Rāma, Śūrpaṇakhā in that of Sītā and taking the guise of Lakṣmana and grasping the chariot (reins), the 'charioteer unhesitakingly approaches Rāvaṇa and with great dramatic skill Shaktibhadra excels in depicting the carrying away of Sītā.

Act Four :- *Jaṭāyuvadhāṅkam (The Act of killing of Jaṭāyu)* The fourth Act is a very brief one where Ravana approaches Jātāyu, friend of Daśaratha, who tries to stop the chariot and asks Rāvana to release the devoted wife of the warrior (all occurs off the stage and even the killing of Jaṭayu at the end). The Act closes with the Rāvana's command to the charioteer to drive the horses fast and the chariot runs to Lanka.

Act Five :- *Aśokavanikāṅkam (The Fifth Act of the Aśoka Grove)* takes us to the Laṅka. Maṇdodari enters with her maid servant. The former is disturbed by a very inauspicious dream and narrate it to her handmaid. She decides to go to the Aśoka grove and conceal herself behind the creepers to see, love sick Rāvaṇa's actions, inspired by lust toward the woman who does not love him. Then the Rāvana enters with his retinue to induce Sitā to love him. His minister tries his level best to dissuade Rāvana from such immoral act. Rāvana orders him to appoint spies to bring reports of Rāmā's designs and then enters the Aśoka - bower and he even prostrates himself at Sītā's feet to express his love but Sita draws her feet away. In a rage, Ravana rises precipitately and tries to kill Sitā. Realising that Sītā is a chaste wife, Maṇḍodarī comes forward and stands between the two and refrain Ravana from killing her. Seeing his queen Maṇḍodari, Ravana stands with face downcast and soon retires with his retinue. Sītā, decides to commit suicide by drowning herself to the nearby pond, purify herself and then realise herself from this misery and exists.

Act Six :- *Angulīyāṅkam (The Ring Act)* Hanumān enters with the ring in his hand. He walks round the stage and looks around in search of a simśapā tree under which he might find Sītā. He enters the garden and listen to Sītā's lamentation who enters soon. Soon Hanūman meets Sīta and removes her suspicion about him. Sita gives up her idea of committing suicide. As a memento, she gives her crest - jewel (The blessing of the ascetics) to Hanūman to give it to Rāma and keeps the ring herself. Sita resort to the Śiṃśapa tree as before and wait for her husband's news and bids farewell to Hanūman.

Act Seven :- Before the actual act commences, by a brief Viṣkambhaka, it is reported that the Rāvaṇa and his entire party have been killed. Therefore, the actual fight is skipped. Infact the death of Rāvaṇa at the hand of Rāma is told by a pair of Vidyādhara (A supernatural being possessed of magical powers) and they goes to convey the same to Indra. Then Rāma, without his military equipment, enters with Lakṣmana, Vibhiṣana and Sugrīva. Rāma asks Sugrīva to lead Bibhīṣ ana into the palace. They start but Sugrīva returns immediately and says to Rāma that Bibhīṣana has taken vow that he won't enter the palace until Sītā is being freed from the Aśoka-vana. Hearing this, Rāma asks him to bring Sītā.

On her arrival, Rāma asks Lakṣmaṇa to call Hanūmān and then says to Sugrīva that this lady was never seen by him, but none understands the import of Rāma's words.

The brilliantly clad Sītā appears and Rāmā makes mockery by saying that such a gorgeous and rich dress really befits one who has been long separated from her consort. Sitā realises that the boon of Anasūyā has been turned into a curse on her. Even Hanūman is astonished to see the lady who he saw in the Aśoka-vana.

Sīta expresses her willingess to enter into the fire. Rama commands Lakṣ mana to carryout the wish of this chaste lady. They both Lakṣmana and Sīta departs. Soon Lakṣmana reappears with horripilation of his entire body. He narrates the strange happenings of her entering into and coming out of fire unharmed. The divine sage Nārada appears, who shows to Rāma the assembled dieties, rishis and the dead ancestors to whom Rāma and Lakṣmana pay their respects. The mystery of Sītā's brilliant appearance is revealed by him. As the purity is now vindicated by the gods, sages and fathers, the Sītā is called back and welcomed heartily by Rāma. Then Vibhīṣana, whose coronation has taken place, enters and informs that the people of Laṅkā are condemnig Rāma's act of suspecting Sītā saying that how could darkness stain the light? Rāma is comforted at hearing this. Narada blesses Rāma and at his instance all of them ascend the puṣpakavimāna of Kubera to set journey for Ayodhyā. The Nāṭaka ends with final Benedictory verse : May the oblation offered with prayers to the lord of the Gods be for the descent of auspicious rain; let the God of Love, the archer, desist from rashly aiming his shafts in immoral directions; may kings bear the weight of their crowns with their minds directed toward the duties proper to them; let intellect shake off its inner dormant state of inexpressiveness and attain composure and clarity.

Āścaryacūḍamaṇi in Performancne

V. Raghavan in his introduction to the English translation of the play writes that the Kerala on the southwest coast of India is the heaven where the only surviving form of the traditional Sanskrit theatre has been maintained by a special hereditary class of actors and their patrons : the temples, the princes, and the Nambūtiri Brahmaṇa-s. The traditional Sanskrit theatre of Kerala is called 'Kūṭiyāṭṭam'. It may be mentioned here that the *'Āścaryacūdamaṇi'* is still very popular in the Kūṭ iyāṭṭam tradition and is one of the most significant plays within this living repertoire.

The temple theatre tradition, ie, Kūṭiyāṭṭam has survived essentially intact in the hands of the Cākyār community for at least some thousand years.

There are numerous royal inscription of the Chola period which mention the Cākyār's as actors performing in the temples of Tamil Nadu. However this community of actors disappeared from the Tamil area subsequent to the 13th century and Cākyār community and their dramatic art survive only in Kerala *Āśharya chūḍāmani* is a play that is highly appreciated by the Cākyārs, the professional players of Malabur who frequently performs this play alongwith Bhāsa's plays such as *Abhiśekha naṭaka or 'Pratimā - nāṭakas'* with which it exhibits similar peculiarities of dramaturgy.

Āścaryacūḍāmaṇī is the first of the three plays forming a cycle known as Rāmāyaṇa nāṭaka comprising of *Āścarya cūḍāmaṇi*, *Pratimānāṭaka and Abhiṣ ekanāṭaka* form a series of twenty-one acts which according to traditional belief, were performed in the temple through out the full year preceding the coronation of the kings of Cochin. Today, although the three plays are not performed any longer as a complete cycle, they are still performed separately in excerpt form in the temples.

In modern times, Kerala has offered us great Cākyār actors such as late Paiṇkulam Rāma Cākyar, head of the Training Program fo the State Academy who died in 1980 and today, we have Shri. M.M. Cākyār of the village Lakkadi on whom Padma Shri was bestowed. Another well known performer in the domain of Kūṭiyāṭṭam is Mādhavan Cākyār of the town of Iriñjālagada.

Guru Ammannur Madhava Chakyar, the foremost exponents of Kutiyattam today

Kūṭiyāttam is genenrally acted only during night. As said before, is one of the most ancient and popular of Kerala's entertainments. It has pan-Indian importance for in this we have the Sanskrit dramas staged. Here the particular act of the particular drama is enacted. Chākyār's act the chosen act of the chosen drama, because to produce a whole play require the better part of several months. In Kerala, a Kūtiyaṭṭam performance may take atleast five days or it may extend upto eleven days. Thus, in partial fashion, the Chākyar's stage few dramas and Shaktibhadra's. *Aścaryacūḍamani* or the *Wonderful Crest* is one of the dramas from which acts are chosen for the enactment.

Six acts are chosen from *Ascharyachuḍamani* for Kutiyattam performances.:-

(i) Parnasala

(ii) Soorpanakha

(iii) Mayasita

(iv) Jatayuvadha

(v) Asoka Vanika

(vi) Anguliya

To perform the play '*Āścaryacūḍamaṇi*' we have medieval production manuals from the tradition of Kūṭiyāṭṭam Sanskrit Drama is now available in English translation that appeared in print by the joint collaboration of Oxford University Press and American Instintute of Indian Studies in 1984. The book comprising of the text, translation (by V. Raghavan) and production manual is edited by Clifford Reis Jones.

The forehead marks for the characters (Young Ascetics / Kuris) in *Ascharyachudamani*, as prescribed by the production manual of the Kuṭiyāṭṭam Sanskrit Drama.

Svastikam

Worn by the Sūtradhāra in the Prologue; also sometimes worn by the Young Ascetic in Act 3.* Black on a rose-red base.

Urdhvapuṇḍra

Worn by Vibhīṣaṇa and by Narada in Act 7. A red center field out-lined in black surrounded by white. On a green base for Vibhīṣaṇa; on a natural base of clarified butter for Nārada.

Kulaśaṅkha

(*Three conch shells joined*)

Worn by Sugrīva in Act 7. Black surrounded by white on a rose-red base.

Śulam (Trident)**

Worn by Śurpaṇakhā in Acts 2 and 3 in her form of demoness. White on a black base.

Gōpi

Worn by the Young Ascetic in Act 3.* Black on a rose-red base.

Śaṅkha

(Conch shell)

Worn by Jaṭāyu in Act 4. Black surrounded by white on a rose-red base.

Candrakala

(*Half-moon*)

Worn by the Minister in Act 5. Red surrounded by white on a green base.

* The manual gives connflicting instructions for the *kuri* of the Young Ascetic. The word

gōpi is not used in the manual but is the common name for this *kuri* as used in Kerala today.

** The Sanskrit word *Sūla* means spear and the word *triśūla* means trident, which would be the proper way to describe this *kuri*. However, the word *śūlam* is in common use in Kerala to mean trident.

In modern times, Śūrpaṇakhā, or the Amorous Demoness, Act II of the Kūṭiyāṭṭam version of the Wonderful Crest Jewel was produced at Michigan State University in the spring of 1976. It was directed by Farley Richmond, a Fulbright scholar and the then Associate professor of theatre and director of Asian theatre research at Michigan State University. He presented his paper in the International Conference on Sanskrit Drama in Performance where he discussed among other things the lighting techniques. In his own words 'It seems certain that oil lamps or torches were used in the ancient Indian theatre, just as a large oil lamp is still used in some traditional Kūṭiyāṭṭam performances to illuminate the actors and the stage. However, in accordance with contemporary fire regulations, open flames may be prohibited. Should a modern director wish to produce a Sanskrit play using oil lamps or torch light, an alternative would be to perform outdoors or to seek permission to use open flames indoors. In his production of Śaktibhadra's the Wonderful Crest Jewel, he shared his experience regarding the use of light where in the late afternoon sunlight coupled with oil lamps served as the major sources of illumination. A large grassy field between two knolls on the campus of the university was chosen as the playing area. When the weather became too cool to perform out of doors, it was played in the University's Area Theatre which had a ten-foot high ceiling. Richmond's effort was some what marred when the smoke produced by the lamps became so thick that it was irritating to the spectators. He also risked covering the ceiling and the lighting instruments with a heavy residue of soot. Needless to say, audiences and actors much preferred the production when it was outdoors. Presuming that modern lighting facilities are available, he suspect that contemporary directors will use these facilities with discretion, bearing in mind the style of the production envisioned.

It is important to add here that an hour and a half colored video cassette of the performance was done in a studio and is available for rental or sale by writing Instructional Television Services, Michigan State University, East lansing, Michigan 48824.

Trivandrum Cultural Society's Kutiyattam Kalotsavam's brochure of July 1985 informs us that some decade ago, the Chakyars had combined Bhasa's

'*Pratima*' and '*Abhisekha*' with Saktibhadra's '*Ascaryacudamani*' and presented it as Ramayana. This programme, comprising of twenty one acts, took a whole year to perform.

From 16 to 25 July 1985, Trivandrum Cultural Society organised "Kootiyattam Kalotsavam" to focus public attention on this classic art form. The venue was Sri Chitra Hindu Religious Central Library Auditorium, Trivandrum. On this occasion Kerala Kala Mandalam performed 'Jatayu vadhakam' from *Ascharyachudamani* of Saktibhadra on 21 July 1985.

Under the direction of Guru Ammannur Madhava Chakyar '*Soorpankhamkam*' was performed at the Natana Kairali, Ammannur Chakyar Madhom, Irinjalakuda, Trichur Dist., Kerala on 12 January 1995 on the occassion of Eight Kutiyattam Festival, organised by the Ammannur Chachu Chakyar Smaraka Gurukulam with the help of the Sangeet Natak Akademi, New Delhi.

The Dramatis personae were :-

Sri Rama	...	Sooraj Nambiar
Lakshmana	...	Ammannur Rajaneesh
Sita	...	Usha Nangiar
Lalita	...	Kalamandalam Sailaja
Soorpanakha	...	G. Venu.

The Accompanists were :-

Mizhavu	...	V.K. Hariharan, C.K. Krishnan Nambiar, Kalamandalam Rajeev, Kalamandalam Narayanan, Ramesh.
Idakka	...	Kalanilayam Unnikrishnan
Talam	...	Subhadra Nangiar, Nirmala Paniker etc.
Make-up	...	Kalanilayam Parameswaram

The six-day festival of Kutiyattam and Nangiar Kuttu was organised by Sangeet Natak Akademi, New Delhi from 24-29 March 1995 as an extension of the Akademi's project of "Support to Kutiyattam". The festival featured almost all the leading artists of Kutiyattam and Nangiar Kuttu including Akademi Awardees Guru Ammannur Madhava Chakyar and Guru Kochukuttan Chakyar, and the

Mizhavu expert Guru P.K. Narayana Nambiar. Together with the performances, a series of lecture - demonstrations on 'Aspects of Kutiyattam' was also held from 25-27 March 1995 at the Meghdoot Theatre in the Rabindra Bhavan Complex, New Delhi.

The festival featured eleven performances presenting different acts and scenes from four well-known ancient Sanskrit dramas namely *Ascharyachudamani* of Śaktibhadra, *Abhisekanatakam* of Bhasa, *Bhagavadajjukiyam* of Bodhyana; and *Subhadradhananjaya* of Kulasekhara Varman.

Lakshmana (P.V. Ramachandran) and Surpanakha (Rama Chakyar) in Surpankhankam (from *Ascharyachudamani*) (Act II) of Shaktibhadra (Kerala Kalamandalam)

'*Surpanakhankam*' from *Ascharyachudamani* (Act II) of Shaktibhadra was performed by Kerala Kalamandalam, Cheruthuruthy on 26 March 1995 at Rabindra Bhawan Lawn, Ferozeshah Road, New Delhi.

'*Mayasitankam*' from the same play (Act III) was staged by Margi, Trivandrum on 27 March 1995in the ame lawn.

However, *'Jatayuvadhankam'* from *Act IV* was a combined presentation by artists of Margi, Trivandrum; Kerala Kalamandalam, Cheruthuruthy; Ammannur Chachu Chakyar Smaraka Gurukulam, Irinjalakuda in the Kairali (the Uttara Guruvayoorappan) Temple in Mayur Vihar, and was performed on 29 March 1995.

The *Udayana Pravesam' from Ashokavkaṁkankam, Ascharyachudamani (Act V)* of Śaktibhadra was produced by the Ammannur Chachu Chakyar Smaraka Gurukulam, Irinjalakuda on 24 March, 1995.

All the performances and lecture - demostrations were recorded by the Sangeet Natak Akademi, New Delhi for its archives.

Presented below is an account of the text, text of performance, Cast, Accumpanists, Make-up and Costumes, Troupe :-

SURPANAKHANKAM from *Ascharyachudamani* (Act II) of Shaktibhadra

Plot :-

Surpanakhankam, the Second Act of *Ascharyachudamani,* deals with the life of Rama, Sita and Lakshmana in Panchavati and the episode of the disfigurement of the demoness Surpanakha at the hands of Lakshmana. Surpanakha, torn by pangs of love for Rama, approaches him in the guise of a lovely damsel and requests him to accept her. Rama expresses his unwillingness to do so and sends her to Lakshmana. Spurned by Lakshmana, she returns to Rama, only to be sent back to him again. When rejected once more, Surpanakha reveals her real nature as a demoness and Lakshmana disfigures her by cutting off her ears, nose and breasts. Blood- stained and furious, Surpanakha leaves, to report the matter to Khara and Dushana.

Text of performannce : Sounding the Mizhavu followed by *goshti* drumming the curtain is held up : Enter Srirama and Sita. 'Aha! I am now very happy. How is that? When I went to the harmitage of Sage Agastya, I promised to all the sages who came there that all the demons will be killed. After accepting the weapons given by Sage Agastya who was pleased, I made friends with Jatayu on the way to Panchavati. I reached Panchavati with Sita and Lakshmana. The sages had already told this that his Panchavati is full of cruel demons and wild beasts. None of them are now to be seen here. Let me tell Sita about this : *vaidehi vaidehi vidhure saivam vismayaniyataya stuyate! pasya*

[Sita, all objects in the distances listen with amazement.]

Sloka:

Saitayamibhirambuvaha
nivahaccharyaistriyamacharaih
Sevya panchavatiti me matrirabhududvela
kautuhala

Seyam devi cirocitamupanayatyudyanayogyam
sriyam
Srotur vismayaniya vatuvisayassailatavisagarah

"[Hearing that Panchavati was inhabited by demons as tall as mountains and having the colours of clouds, my mind has been filled with wonder. Devi, that Panchavati is now, due to fimiliarity, like a garden. People who live at a distance are filled with surprise when they hear about mountains, forests or seas.]"

Sita: My Lord, I feel eager to astound the womenfolk in the palace by talking to them again and again about the wonders of the forest.

[Srirama and Sita withdraw into the *nepathya*]

[Surpanakha in disguise as Lalita]

[Lalita enters. She enacts being attracted to Srirama, describes Srirama's *panchanga* (five parts of the body): Matted hair, eyes, face, chest and feet, is overcome by passion, faints, wakes up and leaves the stage.]

[Srirama and Sita enter. Lalita (Surpanakha) goes to them, salutes Srirama]:

May my lord prosper !

Srirama : O beautiful lady, have you met Lakshmana?

Lalita (Surpanakha) : Yes, I saw him.

Srirama : Has he listened to my words.

Surpanakha : Just listened only.

Srirama : What answer did he give?

Surpanakha : You have become a hindrance to me in looking after my lord performing the duties of a hermit.

Srirama : [smiles to himself] He will have said exactly this. [Aloud] I advise you, my lady, to make one more attempt.

Surpanakha : My lord should not speak like that. I shall stay here worshipping your feet.

Sita : This humble one is good, out of love for my lord.

Srirama : [Looking at Surpanakha] Lady, I respect your opinion just expressed. But it was out of regard for my father's desire that in the presence of sage Vasishta and with the holy fire as witness that I married this one. Even she is an obstacle to my situation. This is my situation. Now you may decide as you please.

Surpannakha : If that is to, I shall sacrifice my life here. I don't have the strength to go anywhere else.

Sita : My Lord, it is not proper to reject her apeal.

Srirama : I request you, my lady, to go to Lakshmana once again.

Surpanakha : Alas! By listening to my lord's words, I violated the moral code of women.

Srirama : Lady, that is not correct. Don't think that courtship is not proper for ladies according to Sanatana *dharma*. Ganga dwells on the matted hair of Shiva; and yet doesn't she go to join the sea, the husband of rivers?

Surpanakha : [To herself] All right. If he rejects me unkindly this time also, I'll show them my colours.

[After enacting entry and the characteristics of a demoness, exit]

[Srirama and Sita enter and listen to off-stage voice]

Offstage : [from the *nepathya*] Stop, you demoness!

Srirama : [listening] It seems to be the voice of Lakshmana

Sita : Yes, it is his voice.

[Srirama and Sita exit]

[Enter Surpanakha and Lakshmana. They together enact the entry]

Lakshmana : Stop, demoness, stop!

[When Surpanakha is about to grab Lakshmana the latter rushes back to the *nepathya,* followed by Surpanakha]

[Enter Srirama and Sita]

Srirama : [listening and seeing] What is this, Lakshmana? Ferocious canine teeth, copper-coloured hair, a mountainous figure, cloud colour.It causes fear in me, who has killed Tataka

Sita : My lord, stop the demoness, stop her.

Srirama : Devi, no need to fear. Haven't you seen before the figure of the demoness on the wall?

[Srirama and Sita exit]

[Surpanakha enters]

Surpanakha : I who am fed up with eating the flesh of hermits, have just got soft and sweet food. Having eaten up these ones, I shall make a gift of her to Ravan. [Leaves]

[Enters Lakshmana]

Lakshmana : Here, is she rushing towards me. She waves her hands long enough to touch the clouds and turn around so as to make the earth's surface undulating.

She is rushing towards us with her mouth like the gate of an open fort.

[Enter Srirama and Sita]

Srirama : Here, she leaps into the sky. Again she is on the earth making twist and turns running and jumping about and straightening herself. With the tips of her nails sharp like swords she tears the clouds to pieces.

Sita : My lord, stop the demoness, stop her.

Srirama : Devi, don't be afraid, don't be afraid, O! fair one, this is only a machine whose inside is hollow. Not a demoness. If my weapon touches her, she will at once fall to the ground and start walking.

Lakshmana : Brother, be pleased, I shall stop her myself. [He intervenes]

Surpanakha : Alas, alas! These humans which are my food are attacking me!

Lakshmana : I will slice you up into bits for birds to eat.

Surpanakha : Let me first devour this cruel-hearted one.

Srirama : Stop, stop! We are not hermits to forgive your atrocities. Give up your present attempt. You demoness, our arrows are least merciful to demons.

[Surpanakha grabs Lakshmana]

Lakshmana : Here, because of a small blunder, I have fallen into her grip.

Surpanakha : Mountain peaks are lighter compared to him. [Surpanakha goes up into the sky carrying Lakshmana.]

[Enter Srirama and Sita]

Srirama : Devi, give up your fear; gather courage and leave me. The demoness is carrying Lakshmanna into the sky.

Sita : Who is there to protect me, lord?

Srirama : Who will protect Lakshmana?

Sita : Hasn't he got a weapon in his hands?

Srirama : For one who is in the grip of the demoness, what use is his weapon? [Sits down upset] Even as I look on, the demoness has taken hold of Lakshmana and disappeared into the sky. [He enacts getting ready for a fight, strings his bow, picks up from the quiver an arrow] What holy weapon has to be used against her!

Offstage : [from the *nepathya*] Oh! I have been thrown to the ground. Help me, O! Lord, help me!

Srirama : [after enacting listening to the offstage voice] This is a female voice I hear. What is the reason for this earthquake? Lakshmana has brought the demoness to the ground?

Sita : I too guess the same.

Srirama : Devi, hold on to my hand and come with me. Let me look for Lakshmana.

Sita : I'll try. Both walk about in a stylized manner. [*chellunti natakkuka*]

Srirama : What is this ? Is it water rushing oozing the mineral reserves of the mountains, flowing from the rivers into the forest? Is it the clouds of the deluge making an offering of blood red as the rising sun?

[Then enters Lakshmana. He enters standing on the *pitha*. He is coming down from the sky to the earth]

Lakshmana : Alas! I violate myself by using a weapon for the first time against a woman. Or perhaps, there is nothing to regret in this. Seeing the enmity of the demoness and my brother's determination, I cut off her nose and ears with great difficulty. Let me now go to my brother.

[Lakshmana withdraws into the *nepathya*. When Srirama and Sita enter the stage, Lakshmana goes to them]

Lakshmanna : May you prosper, my Lord.

Srirama : [embracing him with pleasure] O, my mind! be comforted. Lakshmana is all right. Because of him, I remain as happy in the forest as in Ayodhya. Brother, where is that demoness?

Lakshmana : What am I to say? [Stands with head bowed down]

[Then enters Surpanakha wailing aloud - The scene of 'Ninam']

Surpanakha : O my lord Ravana! My lord Kumbhakarna! My lord Vibhishanna! Save me, O, save me from the violence of humans dressed up as hermits!

Srirama : Behold Lakshmana : Like a row of scarlet clouds at eventide, like the part of a mountain full of minerals, like a row of green trees drenched in morning light here is seen the demoness, her red body soaked in blood.

Lakshmana : [to himself] By my good luck my lord has himself found out the heinous act.

Srirama : Lakshmana, you have done what had to be done. This is the right punishment for a woman in place of killing. It is heard she is Surpanakha, the elder sister of Khara and Dushana who live in Dandaka forest and the younger sister of Ravana.

Surpanakha : O, men, remember your violence. You will see the consequence of this from today.

Lakshmana : O, you get away quickly.

Surpanakha : Let me show my condition to Khara and Dushana. [Exit Surpanakha]

Sita : Look my Lord! It seems as if the sun colours the tree tops with the blood of the demoness in the guise of the scarlet rays of the setting sun.

Srirama : [there the day ends] Put the sword in the sheath. Untie the bowstring. Let us bathe in the dust-free water, hold the breath in the wet limbs and perform the evening ritual reciting the *mantras*.

Lakshmana : As my lord orders.

[Srirama, Sita and Lakshmana hold their hands together and walk in a stylized manner - *Kalappurathu* - and retreat to the *nepathya*]

Cast

Srirama : Sivam Namboodiri

Sita : Shylaja

Lalita : Girija

Lakshmana : Raveendran

Surpanakha : Rama Chakyar

Accompanists

Mizhavu : P.V. Iswaranunni, A.N. Hariharan

Edakka : M. Narayanan Namboodiri

Make-up & costumes

P.M. Rammohan, A.S. Rangan, M. Kunjan

Troupe

Kerala Kalamandalam, Cheruthuruthy

MAYASITANKAM from *Ascharyachudamani* (Act III) OF Shaktibhadra

Plot :-

In a deliberate departure from Valmiki's version of Ramayan, the play presents Ravana and his charioteer disguising themselves as Rama and Lakshmana and abducting Sita. Surpanakha also disguises herself as Maya Sita. Ravana (as Maya Rama) concocts a story about Bharata being in danger from his enemies and needing help at Ayodhya. An unsuspecting Sita falls prey to this evil strategy for her abduction, and follows Ravana into the chariot.

Text of performance : After the traditional salutation to the Mizhavu, Sita sits on the *pitha* in a state of extreme anxiety and foreboding. She recites: Api namaryaputrena Lakshmana *samgamsyate* (I pray that Lakshmana may meet my beloved husband.) She fervently prays that Lakshmana may meet Rama and help him out of any possible danger he may be in.

The *nepathya* drumming stops and she hears, *Sita tvamapi mann upekshase* (Oh, Sita! Have you too left me alone and absolutely helpless?)

She exclaims, *Ham adanya khalvaha aryaputram svarena annvichami.* She enacts: "Alas! what do I hear? I am really unfortunate. What can I do? I shall move in the direction from which I heard my husband's cry for help." After repeating the lines, she moves pitha away, moves in the stylised manner and goes to the *nepathya* (symbolic of moving towards Rama).

Scene 2: Enter Ravana, Surpanakha and Suta (charioteer). Ravana stands in front of the lamp. Suta to his right and Surpanakha to his left. Ravana enacts the popular sequence in Kutiyattam known as Panchanga (the description of the five parts of the physique - the head, face, eyes, breast and feet). Following this he enacts being smitten by Kama's arrows and continues his lovelorn contemplation of Sita's beauty.

Surpanakha recites : *"Arya, Pasya, Pasya - panita yantrkam ratnam svayameva gacchat"* and enacts : "Oh brother, the gem that was kept far away and inaccessible to you is now approaching you voluntarily."

Ravana recites : *"Nayam upeksakala; Ramaupenainam ardhapathe pratibadhuami."* He enacts. "I should not lose this chance. This is the most opportune moment. I shall disguise myself as Rama and accost her midway."

Surpanakha recites : *"Sustvaryo bhanati. Ahamapi taved Ramam Sitarupena nivrttipathe vilambayisye."* She enacts: "I too shall disguise myself as Sita and delay the return of Rama to Sita's side."

Ravana says : *"Badham prathamah kalpah"*. He enacts : "Yes, the first step."

Now Surpanakha says : *"Ita param kim maya kartavyam"*, and gesticulates, "Beyond this I have nothing more to do." Exit Surpanakha.

Suta [the charioteer] asks Ravana, *"Ayusman, kim mayedanim kartavyam?"* He enacts, "My lord, what service has to be rendered by me?"

Ravana whispers in Suta's ear, *"evam iva."* He enacts: "Oh, Suta, you must disguise as Lakshmana, get into the chariot and approach Sita in order to make her trust you and speak to her."

Suta recites, *"Yadajnapayatyayusman"*, and enacts, "My lord, I shall do as ordered." Repeats the lines and continues as an aside after some contemplation, *"aho balavan bhartrpinda; idamapi maya kartavyamasil."* He enacts : "Wonderful succour that my master provided me with-so I am bound to do as bidden." Repeats the lines and enacts, "It is not enough that I serve solely as his charioteer; I am also bound to cheat this chaste woman, an action which is despicable and cowardly." He enacts the stylized movements of driving a chariot and exits.

Ravana places the *pitha* in the middle of the stage. The *yavanika* (curtain) is held low. Ravana stands on the *pitha*. Maya Rama (Ravana in disguise as Rama) holding bow and arrow stands behind Ravana. Ravana enacts the chanting of magic hymns (*mayamantra*). The curtain is raised - Ravana exits and Maya Rama stands on the *pitha*. The curtain is removed. Maya Rama moves towards Sita.

Sita is walking in the stylised manner, symbolic of movement from one place to another. On seeing Maya Rama (she naturally mistakes him for the real

Rama), she expresses her boundless joy and recites, "*hum, aryyaputra, jayatuaryyaputra,*" Enacts, "It is really astonishing, my lord has come back. Again moving closer, she says "*jayatuaryyaputra;*" and enacts, "Hail my lord, be victorious!"

Ravana speaks, "*devi, ita, ita*", and enacts, "Respected lady, this way, this way." Then he says,

mayabalena balinam ksanadacaranam

jihvatale karatalodari vartamanam

ivam Laksmana: katham upeksitavan katham tvam
ittham gatasi mrduna carana dvayena.

He enacts the bare outline of this *sloka*. Then acts out the meaning in detail by taking up individual words, phrases etc. for elaboration, thus:

"Oh, charming lady, I instructed Lakshmana to be with you for your protection. Why did he leave alone and go away? It was not proper of him to have done so. You are in the minds of cruel *raksasas* of this forest (the *raksasas* covet you) and these *raksasas* are to be found everywhere here. They could reach you without any resistance and harm you. It was because I was aware of this that I insisted on Lakshmana remaining with you, and thereby ensure your safety."

"What are the traits of these *raksasas?*" He recites "*mayabalinam*", and gesticulates 'by the powers of magic they assume the forms of different creatures and move about - an art in which they are very clever. Due to this power invested in them, no one can really divine their real nature. You are in the midst of such *raksasas*. Therefore I had instructed Lakshmana to remain with you and ensure your safety. Why did he go away from you, disregarding my definite instruction?"

He recites : "Even if Lakshmana had left you alone disregarding your security, you should have remained in the hermitage. Instead, you are walking about in the forest without any fear, stepping on the thorny bushes and sharp stones wiih your tender feet - why is it? I want all the reasons in full detail." He recites the latter half of the *sloka*.

Sita stands for a while in an extremely sorrowful mood and then says, "*hum, adhanyaya mayopalabdha, kumarakimiti mantrayate?*" and enacts, "Alas, the sinner that Iam! I insulted Lakshmana in a variety of ways. How does he feel about it? Alas!"

Ravana, contemplating for a while and acts as if he has taken a decision. He recites, "*nunam vipralabdhasi mayamrgasvarena*" and enacts "that magic deer's cry has deceived you, I am sure." Repeats the lines.

Sita, brightening up, says, "*aryyaputra, kutra sa mayamrga:*" She enacts, "My beloved lord! Where has that magic deer gone?"

Ravana recites, "*pathi vipratipanna, svayam evagamisyati*", and enacts : "Oh, my charming lady, when I tried to catch that deer and came close to it, it hid itself in the dense jungle. Therefore I could not catch it. But I am sure that it will show up again. I have decided to kill it then. Deciding thus I left it and came to meet you."

The word "*Ayamayamagacchami*" is heard from the *nepathya*. Sita hears it and enacts : "Do I hear the words 'I am coming'."

She recites, "*ham aryyaputrasyeva svara*", and enacts : "Alas! What do I hear? It is the voice of my beloved husband."

Then Ravana says, "*manye, purvvam api svara sadrsyena vancitasi*" and gesticulates, "You were deceived by a similar voice earlier too. I fear so."

Sita exclaims, "*nanu tena kumaropi mayopalabdha.*" and enacts : "Oh hearing such a voice earlier, I uttered harsh words insulting Kumara (Lakshmana)."

Then Suta (charioteer) enters disguised as Lakshmana, enacting in the stylized manner the action of driving horses harnessed to the chariot. He approaches Maya Rama (Ravana) and pays obeisance. He then says, "*prasidatvarya*". While saying thus, he uses "*ayusman*" instead of "*aryya*" as he was wont to do as a mere charioteer. He realises the slip and hurriedly corrects it to "*aryya*" and becomes quite upset in the process. He then enacts : "Oh *aryya,* the respected brother be pleased with me". He then requests: "Please get into the chariot, Oh, respected brother" and enacts : "Oh my revered brother, please get into the chariot along with my revered sister-in-law, quickly:.

Ravana says, "Lakshmana, *kim idam*" and enacts, "Lakshmana, who provided you with this chairot? We are dwellers of the forests. Of what use is a chariot to use?"

Maya Lakshmana says, "*aryya, samadhi caksusa Bharatasya paracakra bhayam upanatam drstva turnam yusmabhi: abhigantavyam iti tapasa ratham nirmaya mahyam datva Vanantaresvantarhitas - tapasvi jana*". He enacts the meaning "Oh, my elder brother, the great sages around here have divined by means of their mystic power that our brother Bharata (now ruling Ayodhya) has been attacked by enemies and advised me that we should proceed to Ayodhya to rescue him. To enable us to do so post haste, they, using their divine power, created this chariot, horses and all accoutrements and have them to me. The sages then disappeared into the forest for continuing their penance."

Sita speaks aside, "*yujyate, nanu purvamapyasya haste dattam paramascaryacudamani, adbhutanguliyakam*" and enacts : "What Lakshmana said is true. He has brought *chudamani, anguliyar* and *kavacha* given by the sages earlier."

Ravana says, "*devi, kastavabhipraya*" and enacts the meaning, "Respected lady, what is your opinion?"

Sita replies, "*nanu mayapyesta vyo Bharatasya vyasananaso, vandanan guru janasyo ca.*" She enacts: "I wish to see Bharata helped out of his miserable situation and also pay my respects to our elders in the family."

Ravana says, "*Lakshmana, prathamam devimarohaya ratham*" and enacts : "Lakshmana, to begin with, help Sita to get into the chariot."

Maya Lakshmana recites, "*yadajnanpayati aryya*" and enacts, "As ordered by my respected brother". He requests Sita, "Oh, my sister-in-law, please get into the chariot" by gesticulation.

Sita says, "*distya raksasa vancananmocita bhutva gacchama*", and enacts,"Fortunately we escape being cheated by *raksasas.*"

Sita enters the chariot followed by Maya Rama (Ravana) and Maya Lakshmana (Suta). They move around in a stylised manner suggesting the movement of chariot. Maya Rama, in the stance of holding bow and arrow, stands in front of the lamp, looks at Sita and expresses joy and enacts, "What can I do to make her enjoy this moment?" He considers the means for a while nad expresses as if he has found a way out.

He speaks to Maya Lakshmana, "*Prasanna devi, Lakshmana turnam codayasvan*" and enacts "Terminating the stay in the forest, we return to Ayodhya - this revered lady is very happy at the moment. Drive the horses fast."

Maya Lakshmana says, "*Yadajnapayati aryya*" and enacts, "As ordered by my brother".

They move about in a stylised manner symbolic of a ride in a chariot. Ravana (Maya Rama) stands in front of the lamp. He looks amorously at Sita and wants to enjoy the pleasure of touching her. He moves backward to the left corner to the stage and takes rhythmic steps backwards and forwards. Repeats the movements and turns around. He stands for a while with an expression of indecision.

Ravana : [to himself]

mayi budhyapyasannigdham

imam no sprstamutsahe

Aho tatpurvvadrstanam

kastah strinam samagamah

He enacts, "She firmly believes that I am Rama. Still, I am not bold enough to touch her even though she stands close and in front of me. It is really a very difficult matter to establish physical contact with a woman whom you have not seen (been acquainted with) before". They move around once again in a stylised manner, suggesting the movement of a chariot and exit from stage.

Cast

Surpanakha	:	M. Kochukuttan Chakyar
Maya Lakshmana	:	Margi Madhu
Maya Rama	:	Margi Narayanan
Ravana	:	Margi Raman
Sita	:	Margi Usha

Accompanists

Mizhavu : Kalamandalam Unnikrishnan Nambiar, Kalamandalam Ramana Unni, Kalamandalam Achuthanandan, Kalamandalam Mohanan

Edakka, Thimila : Subramonian Potti, Margi Venugopal

Tala : Margi Sathi

Make-up & costumes

Margi Somadas, Margi Raveendran

Troupe

Margi, Trivandrum

JATAYUVADHANKAM from *Ascharyachudamani* (Act III) of Shaktibhadra

Plot :-

Ravana in disguise as Maya Rama is carrying away Sita in a chariot. The charioteer (Suta) is in disguise as Maya Lakshmana. When in the chariot, Sita's hand, while tying her hair chances to touch Ravana. By the power of the 'Choodamani' (magic gem given to Sita by Rama for protection against harm) which Sita is wearinng on her finger, Ravana's evil spell is removed and his 'maya' cease to work. The 'maya' Rama form is lost and Ravana appears in his true form. But, Ravana does not realise his change of form.

Text of performance : As the curtain is removed, Ravana appears in his true form. Sita is frightened. She says, "This is not my lord (Rama). Ravana - "Respected lady not be afraid, I am Rama only, Am I not your beloved husband?" Ravana turns to Maya Lakshmana (Suta or charioteer) and asks him, "Why is this (confusion)?"

Sita cries - "I am doomed."

Maya Lakshmana replies to Ravana, "What is the fun of your saying you are Rama. You are 'Rama' by words only.

After *sloka,* Maya Lakshmana acts. "Your disguise as Rama has failed. Now you have the protruding canine teeth (of Raksasas or demons). They put to shame the crescent moon in beauty. You appear cruel looking and huge as the Himavan (mountain), quite dark as the rain bearing clouds. Your ten heads look in ten different directions. You are terribly charming and enchanting, being in your natural form. Ravana, quite surprised and embarrassed (at his foolish affirmation that he is Rama only) says, "How did this (change of form) happen?"

Muses for a while, then manages to cover his embarrassment cleverly and says, "I am sorry I disguised myself as that worthless Rama. Really despicable! Now I have cast aside that unpleasant disguise andn recovered my worthy self," laughs and roars loudly. Enacts holding the 'Chandrahasa' swrod proudly. Looks at Sita, who is to his right and standing terror sticken and weeping. Gestures, "Alas, she is grief stricken and weeping. I shall console her," says - "Respected lady, be not afraid. Why? I shall explain."

Recites *sloka* and enacts its meaning thus: "Oh charming lady do not be afraid of me. There is none else in the three worlds as charming and virtuous as you. You don't have to fear anything. You can live with me with all comforts." He watches her, thinks, and asks, "Why are you so sorrowful? When you are with me, even the celestial world is in my control." Watches and continues, "You worry unnecessarily. You need not hope that your husband or any one else will rescue you. So do not worry." Continues, "When I am the enemy to be won over, there is none in the three worlds to release you from my hold. Even a combined effort of the Devas (Gods) and Asuras (Demons) will fail. They would not even contemplate such an atempt. Why?" Recites *sloka* and enacts.

"On my expeditions I have tested my strength against the celestial elephants guarding the cardinal points of heaven, one by one. In this trial of strength, their tusks tried to pierce my chest in vain. They could leave only scars on my chest, which are here (on my chest) for you to see for yourself. Who is there to challenge such a person as me and try to rescue you?

Sita cries, "My revered husband, please rescue me, Lakshmana, save me."

Suta (Charioteer) in disguise as Maya Lakshmana, "Why should I alone be in disguise? I shall also assume my real form." So sayinsg he turns around thrice and exits. The real Suta takes the stage and says aside, "He is not Lakshmana." She is terrified and cries. She exclaims, "Oh my beloved husband, Oh my Lakshmana, please rescue me from the clutches of the raksasa (demon)."

Now Jatayu (the divine bird and friend of Rama) exclaims from the *nepathya,* "I am coming." Suta looks around, fixes his eyes on the back left corner of the stage and enacts the approach of a huge bird (vulture). He reports to (his master) Ravana, "Oh my lord! See, see!" Recites *sloka* and enacts its meaning. "Oh lord, a bird approaches to interrupt our forward movement. How does he look? His beak is like a hook. His neck is like a golden stem. His eyes are as red as cut rubies. The huge air currents caused by the movements of his wings, cause the trees to swing wildly and shed their flowers and even flower buds, which fall to the ground. See such a terrible bird."

Sita, crying, says, "Who is there to save me. Whom should I approach for refuge."

The curtain is held on the raised portion of the stage, Jatayu enters (a lighted lamp and rain of flowers accompany his entry). His makes ritualistic movements inside the curtain.

The curtian is removed.

'Pravesikam' and 'Pakshistobham' (entry and the characteristic bird stances) are enacted to the accompaniment of special rhythm pattern - termed as 'Lakshmi *thala'.*

Jatayu acts as being seated atop the 'Prasravana' mountain and gestures, "What do I hear? Is it? 'Who is to save me? Who is to save me? Who is my refuge?' It is Sita crying?"

Recites and enacts. "Sita. I am here to save you. Don't worry and cry. I am a close friend and comrade of the great King Dasaratha of the solar race. I am Jatayu. It is just to save you that I am here. I am coming."

Turning to Ravana, "Oh Ravana stop your chariots. You let free Sita, beloved of Rama, the great hero. You set her free and go away. If people make mistakes unknowingly, I correct them and forgive them. So if you want to be alive, set her free and be gone!"

Ravana stands pensive for a while and asks, "This bird says, he won't mind my mistakes!" With a contemptuous gesture, orders the charioteer. "You whip him away and clear the way for us to proceed. He does not know how invincible I am."

Jatayu, "I know, I know everything about you. Recites *sloka* and enacts. "Oh wicked Raksasa (demon) your valour is all too well known. When you lifted Kailasa mountain, it fell on your chest and hurt your pride. I know it. King Karthaveeryarjua tied your hands annd threw you into prison. I know that too. Bali had you tied inextricably with his tail. Your hands still retain the marks of that strangulation by Bali's tail. Thus you are known throughout the three worlds as 'Dhoomakethu', a symbol of everything inauspicious. I fully know your greatnenss.

Ravana, indignantly, "This bird raves a lot". Recites *sloka* and enacts, "Oh Suta, drive the horses. Why so? Let Sita witness my powers. I will cut the wings of this haughty bird while moving along in the sky as I did to Mahendra mountain long long ago."

Jatayu [entering] says, "Let us see what happens." Recites *sloka* and enacts. "Oh Ravana, in the presence of this Kshatriya lady Sita, I will peck your ten faces with my sharp beak and make deep cuts. I will throw the pieces of flesh in all the ten directions. How do you look? You are as dark as the clouds at the time of Pralaya (deluge) and as big as the mountain in your stature. Your heads appear as if they are the peaks of Anjana mountain with wild fire burning brightly over them in the dark night; with ruddy hair waving in the wind. Again, when I peck at your neck with furious thrusts, the veins will open up and the blood torrenting out will add its red hue to the entire environment." Enacts pecking at him fiercely and cries out, "See."

After *sloka,* proceeds to stop Ravana. Ravana stops him and they are engaged in fighting pecking with beak, wounding with claws, beating with wings etc. As the fight goes on Ravana thinks, "This bird can not be defeated by straight fighting. He must be cheated and killed. What can I do?" Enacts, "Yes, there is a trick to play." He enquires of Jatayu, "Where is your most vulnerable part (*marma*) The gullible Jatayu replies with candour, "It is in my right wing. Now could you tell me the vulnerable part of your body?"

Ravana dishonestly answers, "It is my big toe in my right leg." The fight continues. Jatayu tries to peck at the big toe of Ravana's right leg. Using this chance, Ravana cuts off the right wing of Jatayu, holding the wing with his left hand. Jatayu falls wounded. He tries to fly with left wing; but in vain and breathes heavily.

As Jatayu falls, Sita cries. She screens her eyes with her hands; not being able to stand the pitiable sight.

Suta enacts - "This bird has been cut with the mighty divine sword. This vulture is cut." Recites *sloka* and enacts its meaning thus : "Here the bird, with its body covered with drops of blood and muddy in appearance, with its neck turned around due to exhaustion, lies. It appears like an evening cloud in the sky." Sita, weeping, recites and enacts, "Alas, God is unkind. Unfortunate that I am, the bird came to save me, taking pity on me. By another misfortune it was also killed. The bird too had to fall a prey to the wickedness of Ravana."

Ravana orders, "Suta (charioteer), drive the horses.

Suta, "As ordered, my Lord."

Suta continues, "How is this master of mine?"

Recites *sloka* and enacts its meaning thus: "To the dictates of Dharma (righteous conduct), wordly wisdom, means of salvation to the other world, tenets of the Dharma *shastras* (ethics), action according to the need of the times etc., which are to be scrupulously adhered to, he does not listen. What is the state of Kamadeva? Those under the influence of amorous passions, do not listen to the relative merits of good and evil conducts. Because of this there is (absolutely) no use in advising him about them."

Acting thus and after recitation of the *sloka,* the three characters enact the stylised movements symbolic of moving about in a chariot.

[The performance ends with a ritual termed 'Mudi Akkitta' which is enacted at the end of a full act in Kutiyattam].

A joint presentation by artistes of Margi, Trivandrum; Kerala Kalamanndalam, Cheruthuruthy; Ammannur Chachu Chakyar Smaraka Gurukulam, Irinjalakuda .

UDYANA PRAVESAM from *Ashokavanikankam, Ascharyachudamani* (Act V) of Shaktibhadra in Kutiyattam form.

Text : *Ascharyachudamani* is one of the most important plays in the repertoire of Kutiyattam today, and has retained its popularity through the many centuries of the existence of this theatric form. Divided into seven acts, the elaborate staging of each act of the play seems to have had considerable influence on the composition and stage techniques of other plays in the same category. Its popularity on the Kerala stage is evident from the fact that *Natankusq,* a critical work belonging to the 15th century, quotes at length from the text and directs its criticism of Kutiyattam by citing several instances of the stage acting of *Anguliyanka,* an act from the text. The plot of *Ascharyachudamani* covers the story of Ramayana from the arrival of Rama, Sita and Lakshmana in Panchavati to Rama's victory over Ravana and his subsequent return to Ayodhya.

Plot :-

The scene depicts Ravana's passion for Sita whom he had abducted and taken captive in the Asoka grove. On a moonlit night, Ravana, decked in regal finery approaches Sita (represented on the stage by a lighted lamp) and implores her to accept him, but Sita angrily spurns his advances. Frustrated and angry, Ravana draws his sword to kill Sita but Mandodari, his wife, appears on the scene, catches hold of his sword and averts the tragedy.

Text of performance : Ravana feels an uncontrollable passion for Sita. Dressed in regal finery and accompanied by his retinue, he proceeds to Asoka - Vanika (The Asoka Grove) to woo Sita.

Ravanan : How does Sita, the daughter of king Janaka, appear at this time?

He elaborately depicts the *kesadipada* (head-to-foot description) of Sita. The description concentrates on Sita's curly hair falling over her forehead, her eyebrows, eyes, nose cheeks, ears, lips, face, neck, chest, breasts, hands, belly, line of hair on the belly, three creases on the belly, navel, waist, garment, thighs, calves, feet, nails and the inner surface of the feet. (Torn by the arrows of Kama, burnt by the rays of the moon, his feeling of love accentuated by a soft breeze, he swoons, and regains consciousness.)

Ravana : Varshavara, lead me to Asoka-Vanika. I am not ordering you, but requesting you. What does Varshavara say? [Listens] "As your Majesty commands - this way, this way." [Mandodari and Chedi appear].

Mandodari : My maid, what did you say? Did you tell me that my husband, dressed in royal finery, went to Asoka-Vanika to see Sita? Maid, come, unseen by my husband, we will hide behind the creepers in the garden. We will observe his erotic excesses towards Sita, who does not reciprocate his feelings. Come, let us have some amusement.

Chedi : As the Queen orders. My friend, let us go to Asoka-Vanika. This way please - this way.

Ravana : This garden is enchanting, indeed. I have not seen another garden like this. Beautiful! Varshavara, Sita is sitting under the Simsapa tree, isn't she? [Listens to his reply : "Yes, my Lord, Sita is sitting under the Simsapa tree".] Sita casts scornful glances at me. When I try to woo her with sweet words, she closes her ears. When I stand before her with folded hands, she addresses Rama and weeps. I don't know how to please her and get a favourable response from her.

I stand near her, dressed attractively, and cast loving looks on her, with all my twenty eyes. I would feel happy only if she glanced in my direction at least once; but instead, she looks at me with scorn. I go near her and tell her : "Look, Sita, you need not sit here brooding; you take a bath, eat food, put on lovely dresses. Oh,, beautiful woman, don't you hear my words?" But all these sweet words are lost on her; she closes her ears with the palms, unable to bear my words.

I stand before Sita, joining the palms of my twenty hands, requesting her to have some mercy on me. Disregarding my words, Sita addresses Rama thus : "Oh, Aryaputra, please come at once and rescue this helpless wife of yours from her sad predicament. I have no other refuge but you. Please come at once and save me."

Every day I thus come and stand before Sita and repeat these supplications; but all this has been futile. I do not know what else I should do. I know how to please ordinary women. But I don't know how to win the favour of this woman.

Mandodari : My maid, there stands His Majesty. We shall now see what he has in mind. [Ravana places rich presents before Sita. Overcome by lust, he cuts arecanut and places it before Sita on betel-leaves smeared with lime.]

Ravana : Lovely one, take your bath in the water of Ganga; put on the celestial robes and ornaments offered by the trees there; enjoy the luxuries of heaven on Mount Kailasa or in the gardens of heaven - luxuries which cannot be won even by the hardest *tapas*. (All this can be yours.) But alas! your chastity bars the path to heaven.

Sita* : Fie upon your path to heaven! I have vowed devotion to my husband and to fulfill that vow I would rather enter hell.

(* Sita's lines are recited by the Nangiar sitting on the side of the stage.)

Ravana : My lady, for your sake I will abandon my entire harem.

Mandodari : Let His Majesty remember these words!

Sita : No, not only your harem; for my sake you will have to give up your very life.

Mandodari : Ah, human beings speak very harshly indeed.

Ravana : True, the God of Love is taking away my life.

Sita : No, my husband who is far more beautiful than the God of Love.

Ravana : Ha, ha, ha! It is not reasonable to say that the weapon of grass wielded by your husband - the degraded Kshatriya wandering in the forest - cannot be borne on the field of battle by Ravana who bore on his chest the mighty weapon of Indra as though it were a tender leaf - the weapon with which Indra chopped off the wings of mountains.

Mandodari : Why does His Majesty make all this effort? Sita cannot be won by any such means.

Ravana : My lady, I make this supplication with folded hands. My entire harem composed of Gandharva, Asura, Sura, Yaksha and Naga women will wait upon you as servants. Will you not show me some favour?

Mandodari : I will do even this for her! I do not know of another who would do this.

Chedi : Oh, Queen, look! With his palms all brought together in supplication, the king looks like an ocean with slightly open lotuses.

Mandodari : I hope that the king will not become angry with this chaste woman because his desire is frustrated.

Ravana : My lady, this is my humble supplication, my most humble entreaty.

Sita : Alas!

Mandodari : A resolute woman is she! She draws her feet away from the head of His Majesty as she would from dirt. The rumour that Sita is the daughter of Mother Earth and Rāma is Vishnu is now proved to be true.

Ravana : My lady, your feet are my only refuge.

Sita : Go and seek my husband's feet as refuge.

Ravana : What! Your seagirt Mother, Earth, is a common woman shared by all kings who enjoy a tribute of one-sixth given to them by their various subject peoples. Then what is the meaning of this chaste conduct of yours? [He asks] Where is my sword?

Mandodari : Alas! Has it come to this? She is a chaste wife. With my life I will save her from the danger from my king. Victory to your Majesty!

Ravana : What! My queen Mandodari, daughter of Maya!

Mandodari : Your Majesty, even Rama, her husband, is not the target of your sword any more than that this woman is your prisoner. If you ignore her, she will herself give up her life.

Ravana : What you say is correct.

[Off-stage]

Hail our Master! Hail His Majesty! Hail, Lord of Lanka! Hail our blessed Lord! Hail Lord of auspicious face! Ten 'Nadikas' have elapsed. The time for bathing is almost past. This way, Your Majesty.

Ravana : You have now become an impediment. Well, I shall see about this tomorrow morning.

[Ravana, Mandodari and Chedi exit]

Cast

Ravana : Guru Ammannur Madhava Chakyar

Mandodari : Usha Nangiar

Chedi : Kapila

Recitation of the text of Sita : Nirmala Paniker

Accompanists

Mizhavu : P.K. Narayanan Nambiar, C.K. Krishnan Nambiar, V.K. Hariharan, P.P. Rajeev.

Edakka : Kalnilayam Unnikrishnan

Kurumkuzhal : Sudhir Shankar

Troupe

Ammannur Chachu Chakyar Smaraka Gurukulam, Irinjalakuda

Udayana Pravesam in Kutiyattam form was presented on 14 January 1995 by the Ammannur Chachu Chakyar Smaraka Gurukulam with the help of the Sangeet Natak Akademi, New Delhi. The venue of the performance was Natana Kairali, Ammannur Chakyar Madhom, Irinjalakuda, Trichur Dist. Kerala. The dramatis personae were :-

Cast

Ravana	...	Guru Ammannur Madhava Chakyar
Mandodari	...	Usha Nangiar
Chedi	...	T.R. Saritha
Direction	...	Guru Ammannur Madhava Chakyar
Make-up	...	Kalanilayam Parameswaram

Accompanists

Mizhavu	...	V.K. Hariharan, C.K. Krishnan Nambiar, Kalamandalam Rajeev, Kalamandalam Narayanan, Ramesh.

Idakka	...	Kalanilayam Unnikrishnan
Talam	...	Subhadra Nangiar, Nirmala Paniker etc.

Achival Recording

Jatayuvadhankam (Act III) of *Ascharyachudamani* was performed by artists of Kerala Kalamandalam led by Painkulam Rama Chakyar on 26 June 1966 and is preserved in the archives of Sangeet Natak Akademi.

Audio ... Hrs. : Mts

00 : 50

DRAMATIC WORKS : A BIBLIOGRAPHY

Text

Aścarya - cūdāmani / by Śaktibhadra; ed. & tr. into English by C. Shankara Rama Sastri.- Madras : Balamanorama Press, 1926 (Śri Bālamanorama series; No. 10)

______ / by Śaktibhadra; ed. wth an English introd. by S.Kuppusvāmi Śāstri.- Madras: Śrī Bālamanoramā Press, 1926.

xxviii, 238, [3] p.; 21 cm.- (Śri Bālamanorama Series; no. 9)

The Wondrous crest - jewel in performance / by Śaktibhadra; ed. by Clifford Reis Jones; introd. & tr. by V. Raghavan.- Delhi; Oxford University Press, 1984.

Published in association with American Institute of Indian Studies.

Contains the production manual from the tradition of Kūṭiyāṭṭam Sanskrit drama, a glimpse into the dates, life and critical appreciation of the author through editorial foreword and introductory note.

Translations

Wonderful crest jewel / by Śaktibhadra; ed. & tr. into English by C. Śankarama Śastri.- Madras: Śrī Bālamanoramā Press, 1926.

(Śri Bālamanorama Series; No. 10)

Wondrous crest-jewel in performance / by Śaktibhadra; ed. by Clifford Reis Jones; introd. & tr. into English by V. Raghavan.- Delhi : Oxford University Press, 1984.

Published in association with American Institute of Indian Studies.

Kannada

Āścarya - cūḍāmaṇi / by Śaktibhadra; tr. into Kannada by K. Krishnamoorthy.- Bangalore : Rao & Sons, 1959.

______/ by Śaktibhadra; tr. into Kannada by M.B. Rāmakṛṣṇa Bhaṭṭa.- Bangalore: [s.n.], 1943.

iv, 90 p.; 18 cm.

Translated from Sanskrit original.

Malayalam

Āścaryacūḍāmaṇi / by Śaktibhadra; tr. by Koṭuṅṅallūr Kuññikkuṭṭan Tampurān- Trichur : Maṅgaḷodayam, [n.d.]

78 p.; 19 cm.

______/ by Saktibhadra; tr. into Malayalam by K.P. Narayana Pisharadi.- Trichur : Kerala Sangeeta Nataka Akademi, 1967.

Includes Malayalam stage manual.

Telugu

Aścarya - cūḍāmaṇi / by Śaktibhadra; tr. into Telugu by Bapatla Hanumantha Rao.

______/ by Śaktibhadra; tr. into Telugu by Kuppā Śrī Āñjanēya Śāstri.- Masulipatam : The translator, 1952.

xi, 122 p.; 18 cm.

______/ by Śaktibhadra; tr. into Telugu by Malladi Viswanatha Kavi.

______/ by Śaktibhadra; tr. into Telugu by Utukuru Anjaneya Sarma.

BIO - CRITICAL NOTICES

Āścaryacūḍāmaṇi / by comp. & ed. by K.P. Narayanna Pisharoti.- Trichur : Kerala Sangeeta Nataka Akademi, 1967.

In Malayalam

Contains brief information on playwrights life & works.

Aufrecht, Theodor. Catalogus catalogorum.- Weisbaden : Franz Steiner Verlag Gmb. H, 1962.

2 Vols.; 26 cm.

Banerji, Sures Chandra. A companion to Sanskrit literature. - Delhi : Motilal Banarsidass, 1971, Pp. 87-88.

Bhartiya, Kanti Kīshore. Sanskrit natakkar.- Uttar Pradesh : Prakashan Shakha, Suchana Vibhag, 1959.

(Hindi - Samiti granthamala; 25)

Contents : Shaktibhadra. Pp. 195-196.

Bhattacharya, Biswanath. Sanskrit drama and dramaturgy.- Delhi : Sharada Publishing House, 1994. Pp. 286-291.

Encyclopaedia of Indian literature .- New Delhi : Sahitya Akademi, 1987, Pp. 3570, 3963 - 3964.

Garg, Ganga Ram. An encyclopaedia of Indian literature.- Delhi : Mittal Publishers, 1982. Pp. 83, 364.

Gera, Vimla. Mind and art of Bhavabhut.- Delhi : Meharchand Lachhmandnans, 1973.

Contents : Saktibhadra Pp. 254-270. Govil, Suntosh. Study of the Ascarya Chudamani / by Santosh Govil. Ph.D. thesis approved by the University of Delhi in 1975.

Iyer, Ullur S. Keralasahityacharitam. (Vol. 1).- 4th ed.- Trivandrum : [s.n.], 1974.

Keith, A. Berriedale. The Sanskrit drama in its origin, development, theory and practice.- Oxford : OUP, 1924.

405 p.; 22 cm.

____________ Sanskrit - natak : Udbhav aur vikas : siddhanta aur prayog / tr. into Hindi by Udaybhanu Singh. - Delhi : Motilal Banarsidass, 1965.

Krishna Pisharoti, A. Bhasa's works.- Trivandrum : Sridhara Press.

Work also deals with Śaktiibhadra

Krishna Pisharoti, A and Rama Pisharoti, A. Bhasa's works : are they genuine? *Bull of London school of Oriental Studies*. Vol. III; Pp. 107-117.

Study on Śaktibhadra.

Krishnamachariar, M. History of classical Sanskrit literature.- Delhi : Motilal Banarsidass, 1989. Pp. 634- 636.

Pathak, M.C. Sanskrit nāṭaka men atiprākṛta tattva.- Jaīpur : Devanagar Prakashan, [n.d.] 18, 468 p.

Prasad, Ramadhar. Critical study of Ascaryachudamani of Shaktibhadra / by Ramadhar Prasad. Ph.D. thesis in Hindi approved by the Banaras Hindu University in 1982.

Raja Kunjunni, K. Contribution of Kerala to Sanskrit literature.- Madras : [s.n.], 1958.

Masterpieces of Indian literature (Vol. 3) / ed. by K.M. George.- New Delhi : National Book Trust, 1997. P. 1966.

Ramakrishna, G and others. An encyclopaedia of South Indian culture.- Calcutta : K.P. Bagchi & Co., 1983. P. 396.

Sahitya Akademi - New Delhi. The National bibliography of Indian literature.- New Delhi : The author, 1962-1990. 5 Vols.

Vatakkumar Raja. Keraliya - sanskṛta - sahitya charitram. Trichur : [s.n.], 1941.

Venkatasubramania Iyer, S. The Principal rasa in Saktibhadra's Ascaryacudamani' / by S. Venkata - subramania Iyer. *Vishveshvaranand Indological Journal* ; Sept. 1965; Vol. 3, No. 2; Pp. 249-254.

Winternitz, M. Śaktibhadra's place in the history of Sanskrit literature. In Kuppuswami Sastri Commemoration Volume.- Madras : [s.n.], 1937.

14

Śudraka

Śūdraka, the author of Mṛcchakaṭika occupies an important place in the domain of Sanskrit drama for portrayal of grim reality of life : The personal history and date of this playwright is subject to much speculation. The drama is assigned by different scholars to different dates ranging from the first century B.C. to the seventh century A.D.

On the likely date of the playwright, there is considerable difference of opinion among scholars Trend seems to be to assign it to the Gupta period, but some opts for a time before, some after and during that period. Even earlier dates have also been suggested as given in the following table.

Name of the Scholar		**Śudraka's date**
Paranjape and Reddi	....	1st Cent. B.C.
Horace Hayman Wilson	....	1st Cent B.C. or A.D.
Windisch	....	78 A.D. (During Kusāṇa period, when the influence of the Greek was the strongest)
Konow	....	3rd Cent. A.D. (Śūdraka is identical with the Ābhira prince Śivadatta (circa 250 A.D.) who overthrew the Andhra dynasty. [zeistschrift Kuhn,

		p. 108 f.). This view is refuted by J. Charpentier. *JRAS* 1923, p. 595 f.
M. Winternitz	...	3rd Cent. A.D. (After Bhāṣā)
Jacobi	...	4th Cent. A.D. (Based on the astronomical evidence in the Act IV of the Mṛchhakaṭikam which could not be written before the 4th cent. A.D. [*Bhavissa-athakahā*., Munich, 1918, P. 83)
Gawronśki	...	4th Cent. A.D. (On the basis of the language *Kuhn's Zeitschrift,* 44, 1911, P. 241 ff.]
Pischel	...	End of the 5th Cent. A.D.)
Mahendale	...	550-600 A.D. *The Date of Śūdraka,* Bhandarkar Commemoration Volume, Poona, 1917, P. 367 f.
Jolly	...	6th or 7th Cent. A.D. On the evidence of the legal procedure as found in Act IX [Hindu Law of Parition, Inheritance and Adoption, Calcutta, 1883, P. 68 f.
J. Charpentier.	...	Beginning of 7th Cent. A.D.
Nerurkar	...	First half of the 7th Cent. A.D.
Levi	...	7th Cent. A.D. [Later on abandoned this idea and fixed his date as 3rd Cent. A.D.]

In the prologue to *Mrcchakaṭikā*, it is given that he was a Brahmin of the Aśmaka country and was brought up along with a prince called Svāṭī. In boyhood, Svāṭī quarrelled with him and obviously the ill-feeling was nurtured as he grew up.

Among Śūḍrakas friends was one called Banḍhuḍatta. Once a Buddhist mendicant Sanghālikā inveigled Śūḍraka into a solitary cave annd tried to assassinate him, Śūḍraka overpowered the mendicant, killed him and escaped. Then he widely travelled cities like Ujjain, Maṭhurā, Viḍiśa and his adventures were many. He seized the kingdom of Ujjain and became its king, but in grateful recollection of youthful associations he sparely the life of the old king Svāṭī.

In the introductory portion of the drama we learn that the name of the author is Sūdraka, "first of warriors", with the walk of a noble elephant, the eye of a chakora bird, the face of a full moon, who, though a king, became a poet who is well versed in different branches of learning. He knows well the "Rig and Sama Vedas", mathematics, the art of singing, dancing, and wanton dalliance, and the management of elephants. The "Sūtradhāra" or stage manager also tells us that how this kingly dramatist lost his eyesight, had it restored to him by the favour of Śiva, then placed his son to the throne, performed the great horse sacrifice, and at the age of one hundred and ten years, immolated himself in fire.

It is true that with the discovery of the play *Caruḍaṭṭa*, and its attribution to Bhasa has led to very serious conjectures in literary history on the originality of this play, on the identity of Bhāsa and of Śūḍraka and of the condition of the classical literature before the Christian era.

While advocates of authorship of *Caruḍaṭṭa* say that *Mṛcchakatika* was a later enlargement of Caruḍaṭṭa, the opponents say that Caruḍaṭṭa was an abridgment of *Mṛcchakatika*. It is pertinent to note that *Caruḍaṭṭa* as extant, extends only to 4 acts and it is there incomplete and so far as these four acts go *Mṛcchakatika* is about a copy of it with very little difference. There are now springing up scholars who think Bhāsa was a poet of the Court of Śuḍraka.

A massive play comprising of ten elaborate acts and multituted of characters, to enact, *Mṛcchakatika* of Śudraka remain distinct and remarkable for many reasons such as its classical massiveness, multiple plots, delineation of almost all the major sentiments; for its language in both chaste Sanskrit and seven varieties of Prakrit; his depiction of social life spanning the plebian and the aristocratic, its dramatic synthesis of vast canvass of social life through his designing skill in a compact manner without structural looseness.

Though the subject matter of the play is an unconventional story of passion and love, but the play remains a major social document that at the same time furnishes broader public event of political upheaval as its sub-plot and superbly reveals the dualities and dichotomies which disturb and dislocate human life both at the individual and social levels.

It is not just a realistic play. Literary critic Dr. Madhusudan Pati feels it necessary to point out that Shudraka's realism is not confined to etching out life-like scenes and furnishing superb examples of dramatic conversion. More importantly, it involves the projection of a special aesthetic position and moral perspective. It is necessary, again, to emphasise that an urge for realism in the ordinary sense does not control the portrayal of life here. There might be a number of scenes which are preeminently realistic in treatment and inspiration. But scenes presenting life in an idealised, hightened style are still more numerous, and they constitute the heart of the play. What one actualy witnesses is an extended interplay between realism and idealism, both in termes of impulse and treatment running through the entire play.

The *Mṛcchakaṭika* is one of the few Sanskrit dramas which are not dramatic poems but possess distinctively dramatic qualities that should appeal to modern taste. Truly relevant to all times, it is in many respects the most human of all the Sanskrit plays. According to Wilson there is something strikingly Shakespearian in the skilful drawing of characters, the energy and the life of the large number of personages in the play, and in the directness and clearness of the plot itself… The chief value of the *Mṛcchakatika*, aside from its interest as a drama, lies in the graphic picture it presents of a very interesting phase of everyday life in ancient India…"

It gives a realistic view of life right from the gamblers and their quarrels, the burglar active in night, the theft of ornaments to the court and execution scenes.

Not only the plot is beautifully handled, but his delineation of varied characters are equally remarkable. Whether the female characters like Vasantasena and her maid Madanikā or the generous Carudatta, Bold and cultured Sharvilaka, wicked Sakara, all are portrayed with rare dramatic skill.

The language of the play is Sanskrit, but it is mingled with the variety of Prākrits. The Hero, the Viṭa, the royal claimant Āryaka, and the Brahmin their Śarvilaka speaks Sanskrit. Sauraseni is spoken by the Director after his Sanskrit exordium, the comedienne, Vasantasenā, Madanikā, her servant, Karṇapūraka, her slave, her mother, the wife of Cārudatta, the Sreṣṭhin or Guildsman, and the Officer of the Court, and Radanikā, Cārudatta's servant. Two policemen namely Vīraka and Candanaka speaks Avantikā. Prācyā is attributed to the Vidūṣaka. Six characters speaks Māgadhi. They are the Shampooer who turns Monk, Sthāvaraka, servant of the Sakāra Saṁsthānaka, Kumbhīlaka, Servant of Vasantasenā, Vardhamānaka, servant of Cārudatta, and the little Rohasena. The rest of the characters uses Apabramśa such as the The Sukāra speaks Sākārī, the low caste Chāndālas who act as headsmen speaks Cāṇḍāli and the Ḍhakkī ascribed to the chief gambler.

The favourite. metre of Śudraka in his *Mṛcchakaṭikā* is the Sloka that appears 83 times. Next favourite is the Prestty Vasantatilaka that occur 39 times and the Sārdūlavi-krīḍita 32 times. Other significant metres are the Indravajrā (26), with the Vansasthā (9), and the Upajāti combination of both (5). It can be noticed that there also occur other metres such as Praharṣini, Puṣpitāgrā, Mālinī, Vidyunmālā, Vaisvadevi, Sikhariṇī, Sragdharā and Hariṇī, and one irregular stanza. Of the Ārya there are 21 cases that include one Giti, with 30 moral in each half stanza, and Aupacchandasika is found in two instances. The Prākrit metres show considerable variety; of the Āryā type there are 53 as against 44 of other types.

S.K. De rightly says that each of the twenty - seven minor characters possesse an individuality which is rare in Sanskrit drama. But in the midst of this motley assemblage, the hero and the heroine stand out prominently.

Vasantasena, the heroine of his play is not just a harlot, she trade in love, but is a sophisticated ganika, an embodiment of beauty, good taste, elegance, artistic accomplishments. She is a cultured women who is revered by everyone and possess everything in life, but still a discontented soul in search of emotional fulfilment and love that ensure social and moral elevation and Vasantasena cherish a deep love for the noble soul with artistic temparament Charudatta of Ujjayani. For this generosity and other good qualities 'Charudatta', who once led a prosperous life is now in the state of penuary.

T.G. Mainkar righty notes that Humour is abundant in the play having both qualities, subtle and coarse. The action of the play is truly Shakespearian for the swiftness with which play progresses.

There are commentaries on the '*Mṛcchakaṭikā*' by Ganapti, by Pṛtvīḍhara, by Rāmamayaśarman, by Lallāḍīkṣita, by Śrīnivāsācārya, by Dharānanda.

'*Mṛcchakaṭika*' has widely been translated into foreign languages that includes Danish, Dutch, French, German, Italian, Russian, Swedish and many other languages.

It would not be out of context here to mention that to have a glimpse of what a classic is made of and how the definition of a classic is open to ever - expanding elaboration and mutation of meanings, a 'Classic Study Circle' of young Bengali novelists and poets was formed in 1996 by Sahitya Akademi, India's National Academy of Letters. This circle has planned a series of discussions of Indian and foreign classics. On 30 August 1996, Sri Kumar Ray, celebrated stage actor and director delivered lecture on Sudraka's *Mṛcchakatika*. He described the play as unique in the whole range of Sanskrit drama both for its thematic and formalistic novelties. Here one comes across an untold tale where the earthen carriage asserts itself against the royal chariot. A new social order, with the untouchables as the protagonists, voices its presence. This thematic compulsion made a number of reversions in the diction and folk voices emerged.

Apart from '*Mṛcchakaṭika*', the *Padmaprābhṛtaka*, literally the Present of a lotus is also attributed to Śūdraka. This dramatic monologue technically called Bhāna was first discovered and published in 1922 alongwith three other one-act plays ascribed to Vararuchi, Isvaradatta and Syamilaka. The single volume that comprises of all these four Bhāṇas is popularly known as the 'Caturbhānī'.

The play represent the true Bhāṇa tradition. Its language is lucid and its grace reminds us of Sudraka's most remarkable play *Mṛcchakaṭika*.

Padmaprābhṛtaka

Synopsis

In this Bhāṇa, Karṇīputra Mūladeva asks 'Viṭa' (libertine) to findout the mood of Devasenā, with whom he had quarrelled. The friend returns back from her place with a gift, ie, a lotus, the sign of reconciliation.

Śūndraka's *Padmaprabhartaka* or Lotus-gift is a mono - act in which an actor talks to others through the technique of ākāśabhāṣita. The whole play is a satire on contemporary society.

It is one of the four ancient bhavas. The similes and other figures are employed in Sanskrit in a humorous and satirical manner so as to produce laugher.

While commenting on Śūdraka's Bhāṇa '*Padmaprabhṛtaka*' [Gift of lotus], Prof. Biswanath Bhattacharya states that the characterisation is remarkable. The poet, the pedantic grammarian Dattakalasi and the other frequenters of the hetaera's quarters are all objectively reported in so masterly a manner that they appear life like. In point of diction also the play proves itself to belong to the vintage years of the dramtic art.

Mṛcchakatika

Synopsis

The main story is inspired from Bhasa's *Daridracārudatta*, the addition of the political intrigue in the play is Śūdraka's. Briefly, this ten acts drama is the saga of love of a high born merchant called Cārudatta in the town of Avanti who has become impoverished due to his excessive generiosity for Vasantasena, an accomplished and polished courtesan of Ujjayinī. A villain and fool, Sakara who is the brother-in-law of the wicked king Pālaka also seeks her hand, but she does not accept him. Unfortunately an exchange of vehicles lead to Vasantasena being carried away near Sakara in a garden. Here he strangles her and accuses Carudatta in the royal court. The latter is sentenced to death but is saved from execution by the appearance of his beloved Vasantasena, who is being rescued by a Buddhist monk formerly a gambler whom she had once helped.

Charudatta helps Āryaka, whom he had met in prison to escape. At last, Palaka is killed and Aryaka, now in power, allows Cārudatta to marry virtuous courtesan Vasantasena. The play that revolves around romantic theme contains dramatic developments involving a dynastic overthrow with host of characters and realistic portrayal of city - life.

Dramatic Personae

Āryaka	...	Prisoner (subsequently becomes King of Ujjain)
Chandanaka	...	Police Officer
Chārudatta	...	The hero, a dignified citizen of Ujjain who is reduced to poverty from his own generosity
Curṇavṛddha	...	A friend of Chārudatta
Darduraka	...	A gambler
Dhūtā	...	Wife of Chārudatta
Maitreya	...	Companion of Chārudatta, loyal to him to the end.
Madanikā	...	Maidservant of Vasantasenā
Māthura	...	Runs the gambling den
Pālaka	...	King of Ujjain who imprisoned Āryaka and was later killed and replaced by him.

Radanikā	...	Maidservant of Chārudatta
Rebhila	...	A merchant and friend of Cārudatta
Rohasena	...	Son of Chārudatta
Saṁsthānaka	...	The brother-in-law of the reigning king of Ujjain and the villain.
Saṁvāhaka	...	Professional masseur, also gambler, who becomes a Buddhist monk.
Śarvilaka	...	A Brahman in love with the maidserv--ant of Vasantasenā called Madanikā : commits larceny
Sthāvaraka	...	A servant of Saṁsthānaka
Vardhamānaka	...	A servant of Chārudatta
Vasantasenā	...	Heroine of the play who is in love with Chārudatta
Vīraka	...	Police Officer
Viṭa	...	A friend of Saṃsthānaka, the villain.

Plot :-

The following is a summary of the plot as it is developed in the course of the various Acts :-

Act One :- In the Prastavana (Prelude), after the Benedictory stanza (Nandi), the Sutradhara (Stage-manager) furnishes an interesting accounts of the playwright. A conversation between him and his wife (Nati), which follows, is intended primarily to lead up to the entrance of the Vidushaka (Maitreya). At this point, the proper play begins. Maitreya, is a poor but high born, honest and sincere friend of Charudatta who was once a wealthy citizen of Ujjayini, but no longer possesses his former wealth because of his generiosity and charitable deeds .

As per the instruction of Churnavriddha, who is Charudatta's friend, Maitreya has come to hand over a cloak to Charudatta. The latter enters and the cloak is given to him. From their conversation we learn about Charudatta's poverty. At this juncture, appears Vasantasena who is being pursued by Sakara (Samsthanaka), the villain and the brother-in-law of king Palaka of Ujjayini; he is accompanied by his two followers, Vita and Cheta. Inspite of repeated threatning from all, but with the same great indignation she rejects Sakara's suit. She takes refuge in Charudatta's mansion and her persuer light of a maid in Charudatta's employ named 'Radanika', and mistaking her as the object of their search. With the intervention of the Maitreya, they leaves the place.

Vasantasena is now being introduced to Charudatta. Though penniless man, still courtesan Vasantasena who had earlier heard of his virtues gets attracted to him. For further communation, she deliberately leaves her gems with Charudatta and obstensibly for safe keeping. Escorted by Charudatta, she departs, On returning he hands over the gems to Maitreya for safe custody.

Act Two :- This act focuses on Vasantasena, who has a confidential talk wih her maid Madanika. The former expresses the warmth of her feeling for Charudatta, and unfolds the reason of leaving those gems with her beloved.

After this, we are introduced to a scene where we find a number of gamblers; one of them 'Samvahaka' is seen running away as he cannot pay his debt. He is being chased by his creditor and the master of the gaming-house. However Samvahaka manager to escape with the assistance of another gambler and takes refuge in the house of Vasantasena, the latter pays his debt for him and rids him of his creditor.

The act thus, relates the generiosity of the courtesan to the gambler who decides to become a Buddhist monk (Bhikshu) and exits Karṇapūraka, one of Vasantasena's servants enters and narrates how an attack was made on a monk by a mad elephant; how he had just rescued him and eventually received as reward a cloak from Charudattta for his brave deed. Vasantasena recognize this as Charudatta's. She is deeply touched by his nobility and wears it herself.

Act Three :- In this act, Sarvilaka who is in love with Madanika, the slave-maid of Vasantasena is introduced. He was a poor Brahmin in Ujjayini who had turned a burglar because by any means he had to pay ransom in order to set her free from bondage and marry her. He breaks into Charudatta's house and steals the gems of Vasantasena from Maitreya's keeping. The alarm is raised and soon the theft is discovered. Charudatta is greatly distressed at the loss of the deposit, because he was bound in honour to return it to Vasantasena on demand. At this moment, his wife Duta dutifully hands over her own jewel-necklace to be given to the Courtesan in exchange for her ornaments. Charudatta, thereupon, instructs Maitreya to go to Vasantasena to deliver the replaced necklace and further, he was to state that her ornaments were lost by his master at gambling.

Act Four :- Sarvilaka who loves Madanika, the maid-servant of Vasantasena enters, he shows to her the jewels which he had stolen from Charudatta's house and now proposes to ransom her off from bondage. Seeing his sudden accession to wealth, that makes Madanika interrogates her and ultimately her lover confesses that they belonged to Charudatta. She asks Śārvilaka to restore the stolen jewels to Charudata, but Sarvilaka is not ready to face Charudatta and as no other option left, finally she suggest her to hand over the stolen properly to its rightful owner, Vasantasena by professing that Charudatta has sent them back by him, as his house was no more safe.

Therefore, Sarvilaka gives the jewels to Vasantasena, who though aware of his theft (as she listened to the previous conversation), sets his love, ie, Madanika free from slavery. At this moment, Śarvilaka has to leave suddenly leaving his lady love when he hears of the imprisonment of his friend Āryaka by order of the king Palaka. As the latters fear he might attain the kingship, as a seer had predicted so.

He proceeds to aid his friend who is reported to have escaped from his captivily. Maitreya then comes with the jewels, (it may be recalled that he was deputed by Charudatta) to offer her his wife's necklace to replace the lost ornaments. The courtesan is so pleased with his goodness of heart that she accepts the necklace simply to use it as a pretext to see Charudatta once more.

Act Five :- The hetaera pays the proposed visit to Charudatta inspite of untimely terrible rain, thunder and lightning in the month of phalguna that forces her to spend the night in his house. She returns those ornaments to him under the plea that she had lost his necklace, just as he had formerly lost her ornaments. Their longing for each other is unfolded in this act. Now both of them have come together and nothing can mar their happy union.

Act Six :- Vasantasena spends the night in her beloved house. In the morning Charudatta before learning his home instructs his servant to the neighbouring park 'Pushpaka randaka' in a carriage. Now appear Rohasena, Charudatta's son, who complains that he has only a little earth cart to play with, instead of a golden one desired by him (whence the title of the play 'Mṛcchakaṭika') Vasantasena gives him her jewels out of which the boy is to get one of gold. Now the servant 'Vardhamanaka' enters in and announces that the car is ready. The courtesan, however, asks him to wait so that she may finish her toilet.

Here we have an insteresting scene where Vardhamanaka suddenly realizes that he has forgotten the carriage cushion and thus goes back to bring them.

Just at this time, comes in Saraka's servant 'Sthavaraka' who is also driving his master's carriage in the same direction. But by error Vasantasena enters the car of Sthavaraka and is taken to the park. In the meantime, Aryaka whom Palaka had imprisoned, has escaped from the jail and is seeking a hiding place leaps into that of Cārudatta's carriage and is driven away by Vardhamanaka believing that it was Vasavadatta who had entered. However, the cart is shortly stopped by two policemen. One of them 'Chandanaka' looks into the carriage and recognizes the prisoner, but promises to protect him. He, therefore, deliberately contrives a quarrel with the other policeman, 'Viraka'. Whom he beats and leaves the place. The driver of the cart s still unaware of the fact that whom he was really driving. As the rorad is now clear, Aryaka escapes in safety.

Act Seven :- In this act, Chārudatta is seen conversing with the Vidūṣaka in the garden where he is to meet Vasantasena. He sees his cart drive up. Instead of Vasantasena, it is Aryaka who steps out of the carriage. The noble Chārudatta promises him safety and therefore, permits him to go off in it as that would allay suspicion. Aryaka departs in gratitude and Chārudatta no more stay there as has helped prisoner which was treason towards the king and himself goes out to find Vasantasena.

Act Eight :- In the Pushpakarandaka garden, Saṁsthānaka, Viṭa and a slave 'Cheta' meet the Bhikshu (Samvahaka), the shampooer turned monk who has come there to wash his robe in the tank. He is being insulted and beaten, and finally driven away by Samsthānakna. The cart with Vasantasenā then is driven up. He is surprised to find Vasantasena inside, but delighted as it gives him an opportunity to win her heart. He tries to renew his attentions to her by fair words. But this does not works. Vasantasena spurns him. To punish her, Saṁsthanaka orders Viṭa and Cheta to kill her. They indignantly refuse. He gets rid of them under one pretext and another, and then strangles her who falls down senseless but not dead. Saṁsthanaka boasts of his exploit. Both Vita and Cheta arrives on the spot. The former is digusted with his master's ways, decides to join the newly formed party of Aryaka and thus, leaves him. As 'Cheta' has witnessed crime, Saṁsthanaka intends to hold him a prisoner and orders Cheta to go to his place.

The rains blows on Vasantasenā; Saṁsthānaka buries the body under some leaves; an idea springs up in his mind.

As Cārudatta was his rival in her affections and it was for his sake that she insulted him as he believed, Saṁsthanaka decides to take revenge by proclaiming

Chārudatta as the murderer of Vasantasena. On his departure, the monk re-enters to dry his robe, discoveres Vasantasena. He restores her life by giving first aid and takes her to the monastry to be cared for.

Act Nine :- The venue of this act is the court of justice where Saṁsthānaka denounces Chārudatta as the murderer of Vasantasenā before the Judge who is presiding with two assessors. Saṁsthanaka alleges that Chārudatta had enticed Vasantasena to his Pushpakarandaka garden and then killed her for the sake of her gems. The Judge starts the proceeding by summoning Vasantasena's mother as a witness that establishes the existence of a love affair between her daughter and the citizen Chārudatta. She further tells the court that Vasantasena's was supposed to be in Chārudatta's house. Now Chārudatta himself is cited who denies any exact knowledge of Vasantasena's movements. Now appears the police officer, Viraka who complains before the jury that while he was trying to inspect a carriage which belonged to Chārudatta and in which the courtesan was supposed to be travelling in the direction of Pushpakaranda garden, he was being maulded and assaulted by his fellow guard 'Chandanak'.

Judge instructs Viraka to see if a woman's dead body is found in the park. He finds the signs of struggle in the park and also the dead body of a woman who was accidently killed there by the fall of tree. Viraka comes back and reports the matter to the court. Hearing the news of Vasantasena's death, Chārudatta makes no more serious effort to establish his innocence. Besides he was a poor citizen and was intelligent enough to realize that Judge would never give him a fair hearing. Finally Maitreya comes with Vasantasena's jewels which she had earlier given to Rohasena.

Saṁsthanaka tells that they belonged to Vasantasena and has come from Chārudatta's place and the ornaments must be the motive of the crime.

In the absence of any satisfactory explanation from Chārudatta and taking into consideration all the evidences, the judge declares him guilty and condemns Chārudatta to exile. But the king Palaka converts the sentence into one of death and now the Chārudatta is to be taken to the cemetery.

Act Ten :- In the final act, Chārudatta is being taken to the cemetery by two Caṇḍālas, who regret the duty they have to perform. On the way Chārudatta's guilt is proclaimed at each proclamation-station. His friend Maitreya (Vidusaka) brings in Rohasena so that his father can have a last look at his son's face. He entreats the executioners to release innocent Chārudatta.

Ceta, the servant of Saṁthānaka hears the proclamation and though chained at once jums into the street to reveal the truth. But Saṁsthānaka makes light of his words as a theif and a liar and convinces simple minded Caṇḍālas not to rely on his statement. Then they reach the place of execution and the headsmen decide to proceed with their work. When Chārudatta is about to be impaled, arrives Vasantasena accompanied by the monk. The innocence of Chārudatta is established and the lovers rejoice at their union. Sarvilaka then emerges to break the news that Āryaka has succeeded Pālaka whom he has slain and Chārudatta is being rewarded by him with the gift of the kingdom of Kusavati. The crowd shout in anger for Saṁsthānaka's death, but Chārudatta pardons him. Samvahaka, the monk becomes the head of the Buddhist monastries and similarly suitable honours are also conferred upon Sthavaraka, the Caṇḍalas, Candanaka etc. Above all, Vasantasena is made free of her profession and thus would be relieved of the stigma of being called a courtesan and now can become the lawful wife of noble Chārudatta.

Though the wicked king pershed at a distance from the scene, but at the end of the play every person on the stage is shown in a condition of happiness.

The usual '*Bharatavakya*' expresses good will towards all and unhappiness for none and with that the play terminates.

Mṛcchakaṭika in Performances

In Sanskrit

In the Second All - India Oriental Conference held at Calcutta in 1922, Sudraka's "Mṛcchakaṭika" was performed in Sanskrit.

Eminent scholar Prof. Suniti Kumar Chatterji reminiscenced.... I remember with pleasure several performances of this play by the members of the Sanskrit Sahitya Parishad of Calcutta, a learned body which aims at fostering the culture of Sanskrit and which with that end in view stages Sanskrit plays. Sanskrit scholars like the Late Pandit Gishpati Kāvyatīrtha and Kālipada Tarkāchārya, who were also fine historionic artists, made Maitreya and Saṃsthānaka and Chārudatta come to life once again, on the stage, before a Calcutta audience which did not feel the least bored in a long ten - act play. The play has thus a rare human interest. Many of the characters and the way in which they have been handled remind one of Shakespeare. All these go to make the work unique in literature, a re l "possession for ever."

Professor Dr. Asoke Chatterjee Sastri, (Formerly a Post - Graduate Teacher in the Deptt. of Sanskrit, the Calcutta University) in the role of Chārudatta in Śūdraka's' Mṛcchakaṭika performed in Sanskrit.

A scene from Mṛcchakatika

The Presidency College Sanskrit Association staged very successfully the Mṛcchakaṭika of Śūdraka in Sanskrit at the Third Oriental Conference, Madras in 1 December 1924.

The Madras Samskrita Academy also gave a fillip to Sanskrit dramatic activity. Amongst their successful productions, mention could be made, of Mṛcchakaṭika of Śudraka and for the effective portrayals of characters, the late S. Raghavachari as 'Śakāra' and S. Satyamurti, 'Maitrya' will be remembered.

'Mṛcchakatika' was staged in Sanskrit at the 'Kalidasa Festival, Ujjain in 1972.

Other versions

As regards to staging the play in other versions, we can start with the mentioning of Mery - Nerval's French production 'Chariot d' enfant' an adaptation of Śudraka's Mṛcchakatika. Legendary playwright Śūdraka's master piece 'Mṛcchakaṭika' has been successfully staged not only in India, but equally well received by the foreign audiences since long. On the 13th May 1850 Mery and Gerard de Nerval successfully staged this drama in five acts and seven tableaus, at the Odeon (Paris). Both of them had completely eliminated the political intrigue from the play. The ten acts of the original was condensed into five acts that led to the omission of many comic and descriptive scenes. Nevertheless, as a whole this French version succeeded in creating a novel unpression. The audience who were absolutely unfamiliar with India's theatrical tradition, art history, religion, philosophy etc. responded positively to the exotic atmosphere of the play.

On the 2nd January 1895 'Mṛcchakaṭika' of Śūdraka was put on the stage in the Nouvean Theatre (Paris) by the dramatic group 'L' Oeuvre'. The play was directed by Lugnē - Poe. Levi in his review of the play wrote : The director, Lugne - Poe, a man of intelligence and good taste, made the best of the modest resources at his disposal. Talented artists, de Toulouse Lautrec, Andrē and Valtat, painted beautiful sets which were both sober and full of light. Amateur actors full of good will spared on effort to lend authenticity to their characters. Ripert, one of them, succeeded through his noble demeanour and wise gravity to create almost instinctively a genuine oriental type..."

In the context of Indian versions, mention should be made of the actor Balgandharva who was noted for his female role 'Vasantasena' in Deval's Mṛcchakatika in Marathi. The first recipient of Sangeet Natak Akademi. Award, Shri Balgandharva emerged from the 'Kirloskar Natak Mandali' of Maharashtra.

Śudraka's 'Mṛcchakatika' was staged in Marathi by this Kirloskar Company in 1889. It was adapted by Govind Ballal Deval who once received a prize from the Maharaja of Indore for being an astute translator.

The drama became an instant success with packed theatre house. The leading roles were played by :-

Vasantasena	...	Krishnarao Gore
Charudatta	...	Bhaurao Kolhatkar
Shakara	...	Shankarrao Majumdar

Enlisted below is the recast of the play:

Vasantasena	...	Balgandharva
Carudatta	...	Pandarpurkar Bowa.
Shakāra	...	Bodas
Karnapuraka	...	Inamdar
Maitreya	...	Kashinath Vaman Parchure

Krishnaji Sakharam Gore

Kirloskar Natak Mandali's first Vasantasena

Balgandharva as Vasantasena in Mṛcchakatika (Act II)

Kirloskar Natak Mandali's Marathi version of Mṛcchakatika

Kashinath Vaman Parchure as Maitreya in the Marathi production of Mṛchhakatika (Act IV)

On 18 December 1891, Royal Bengal Theatre of Calcutta staged Śūdraka's classic 'Mṛcchakatika', in Bengali. The same day in 'Statesman' appeared the followed advertisement : *New Play ! New Play ! / First Performance of Vasantasena*

/ At the / Royal Bengal Theatre / On Saturday, The 19th Dec. At 9 P.M. / Vasantasena / A pure portrayal of mediaeval India / Sensational Scenes, Pathetic Passages ! / Sidesplitting Sentiments, / Seriousness and sorrow with levity and laughter / Under the distinguished Patronage / For details please read bills / Every effort has been made to render the play / Interesting ! Inviting ! Instructive ! / Kunja Bihary Bose / Manager, Advertising Deptt.

The play was repeated on 26 December 1891 and again on 2,9, and 17 January 1891.

Star Theatre [at 75-3 Cornwallis Street (Grey Street Crossing)], Calcutta first produced 'Mṛcchakatika' or the Toy Cart of Sudraka in Bengali version by Nritya Kabiraj on 26 August 1899. In this play, Vasantasena was superbly played by Tarasundari. Indian Daily News wrote on the same day in its advertisement column : *First Night ! First Night ! Star Theatre / To-day, At 9 P.M. Sharp / New Drama Mrich - Ha - Katika / or The Toy Cart*. The show was repeated on 2, 9, 16 and 24 September 1899.

This was an entirely different production from one staged at Bengal Theatre.

While commenting on the production, Statement in its 25 December 1891 issue wrote : For sometime past the management of this Theatre has devoted its efforts to reproducing Sanskrit dramas in Bengalee, and so for the atempt has been very successful... 'Basantasena', a reproduction in Bengalee from the Sanskrit of the well known drama "Mrich - Chhaketik"... the house was crowded in every part, the audience being most enthusiastic in its approval of the acting and fine scenery presented."

In Germany, one adaptaion of Mṛcchakaṭika had attracted large audience to the theatres about 1892-93 - another version was produced at Dresden and Leipzig. M. Winternitz documents in his book, 'Some problems of Indian literature' that he witnessed the play at the latter place in 1921.

Played at the Royal Court Theatre in Berlin, as well as at the Court Theatre at Munich, where it roused enthusiasm sufficient to recall the actors eight times before the curtain. The play as there acted was adapted for the stage from the well-known and accurate German translation of Bohtlingk.

In Poland, Helena Marcello - Palinska directed 'Clay Cart' of Śūdraka. The Play 'Wasantasena' [adaption of Emil Pohl]. It was performed at Warsaw, Variety Theatre, on May 8, 1898 (European Premiere - 1850 at Paris).

Critics declared the star of the evening to Marcello - Palinska who 'impressed as usual with its dramatic power and a marvellous play of features. She based her acting on the contrastive presentation of the feelings of Vasantasena - Courtesan. Rabski (The reviewer of Kurier Warszawski) highly wrote in praise of Frenkiel's acting - Frenkiel played in the Warsaw performances one of the best parts in Vasantasena - the part of the royal brother-in-law Samsthanaka. He created one of those characters that are included into an artist's unchangeable repertory. It was a psychological synthesis, glittering with a brilliant humour. The critics agree that Wojdalowicz's art, who presented an outstanding comical temperament acting the part of a Buddhist monk. Vasantasena's love - Charudatta "dressed by Ladnowski in a philosophical peace interrupted only with outbursts of love". The attempts to introduce a crows on to the stage failed entirely, as they looked as metal soldiers. Everything was forced, so drowsy and artificial. That it created the impression of marionettes and not alive people.

A Prisian production of Barrucand's adaptation of Śūdraka's Mṛchhakatika, with the title "Le Chariot d" enfant enjoyed a mediocre reception. The text was poorly translated and the play was significantly altered to fit his anarchistic politics, and the audience was shocked by the actor's nudity. It was performed at the Odean in 1895.

On 19 December 1899 'Basantasena', a Bengali version of Mṛcchakatika was performed at Bengal Theatre. History is silent about its translator.

'Seetharama Anjaneya Nataka' was established by Mote Narayana Rao Zamindar in 1921 at Eluru. Narayana Rao had a profound knowledge of western theatre performances. Popularly known as 'Mote-vari company', this company gained more popularity when all the major actors and technicians from 'Mylavaram Company', Bezwada joined this association. One of its major productions was a Telugu rendering of 'Mṛcchakaṭika of Śūdraka.

Neighborhood Playhouse was built on Grand Street in 1915 by Alice and Irene Lewisohn. It housed an amateur repertory company until 1920, when the ensemble turned professional.

This experimental group in New York offered 'The Toy Cart' in 1924, directed by Morgan and Irene Lewisohn. As critic says,. the production was marked for its non-realistic style, symbolic movements and hand gestures, and use of several conventions of Sanskrit theatre. The production was initially designed for a proscenium arch stage by Morgan and Lewisohn which is suitable as a playing space for Sanskrit drama. Ths was the maiden American production of the Little

Clay Cart was at the New York Neighbourhood play house by the National Theatre Conference in 1924. A Mughal - style latticed set was used, dividing the stage into two main acting areas - Charudatta's poor house and Vasantasena's mansion, with a path connecting the two. Instead of depicting the bullocks through mime, the director yoked two actors to create the four - footed animals.

'Shouvanik', a group theatre established by Biresh Mukherjee and Nibedita Das in 1957 stands out for opening the first open - air theatre in Calcutta, 'Mukta Angan', which is now the venue of many experimental productions by different dramatic groups. Shouvanik looked back to Śūdraka's Sanskrit classic 'Mṛcchakatika' for its second production. The Bengali adaptation by Jyotindranath Tagore was enacted in 1958.

Another group from South Calcutta named 'Theatre Unit' (founded on 6 February, 1958) by the famous actor, director and playwright Sekhar Chatterjee in association with Sadhana Roy Chowdhary and Dipten Roy staged this ancient classic.

Habib Tanvir while working with his Delhi based Naya Theatre had experimented with classical plays in lokdharmi style, often using folk artistes Mṛcchakatika (The Toy Cart) is regarded as one of his best-known productions.

Habib Tanvir reminicises : In 1958, before beginning Mṛcchakatika, I went home to Raipur to meet my family. It was summer. I heard that there was to be a nacha on the grounds of the high school where I was educated - nacha is a Chhattisgarhi form of secular drama : it was to start at 9 o'clock. I saw it all night through, which is the usual duration for a nacha. They presented three or four skits. There was Madan Lal, a great actor, Thakur Ram, another great actor, Babu Das, a very good actor too, Bulwa Ram, a glorious singer and what comedians, these fellows like music hall comedy. They were doing chaprasi nakal, sadhu nakal (take - offs). I was facinated. I went up to them and said - would you like to come to Delhi and join me in a production? they were happy to do so. So I enlisted Bulwa, Babu Das, Thakur Ram, Madan Lal, and Jagmohan, who was on clarinet. Then I was to go to Rajnandgaon to speak on Indo-Soviet friendship or something. There they wanted to know about my European tour. I described my Hungarian travels and sang a Chhattisgarhi song as an illustration. At the end a dark man with squint eyes and a short, grisly black beard, came up to me and said, 'come to my house'. This was Lalu Ram. He liked the folk songs. I went to his house. He offered me ganja, we shared ganja, and he heard many song from. He sang many, one of the best singers in Chhattisgarh, glorious voice. The session went on all night. So I enlisted Lalu Ram as the sixth member of the troupe. These six came to Delhi and participated in Mitti ki Gadi, with Bulwa and Lalu ram playing chandals and singing at the top of their voices, Jagmohan playing the clarinet, Madan Lal playing the gambler, Thakur Ram playing Sarvilak.

On his return to India in 1958 after three years in Europe, Habib Tanvir selected Sudraka's Sanskrit classic 'Mṛcchakatika' for his Hindustani Theatre, the first professional theatre of Delhi organised by him in 1954. For the Hindi version entitled 'Mitti ki Gāḍi' he brought six illiterate folk actors from Chhattisgarh. The play was a hit. Tanvir reminiscises : The late Begum Qudsia Zaidi was the driving spirit behind that venture. It was she who had collected the money and given it a practical shape. But when she saw these folk actors, she blew her top. "Are these the actors you are going to present to Zakir Saheb?" she asked. The *charas*-smoking Lalu Ram, now dead, was short, spindly-legged, squint-eyed and had a jet-black face, but he was the most melodious singer I have ever heard. Madan Lal was also extremely short, thin, with a drawn ebony-black face, but a live-wire as an actor. The late Thakur Ram, medium-sized, with a complexion the colour of dust and with *sharbati* eyes and a flat nose, had a wit as sharp as a razor. These two - Madan and Thakur Ram - were the best pair of comedians Chhattisgarh has ever produced. Yet another was Bhulwa Ram, also dark as mahogany and with a very flat nose and big dazzling white teeth which showed when he sang; and he sang gloriously. He is growing old with me and to this day remians in my theatre company, Naya Theatre, along with his son, who is now grown up. I do not know of another male singer in Chhattisgarh who could hold a candle to this unique singer.

A fifth was Shiv Dayal, with a weird long bony face, rather lanky, whom we later began to call Hanumanji. He was wizard of a tabla player in those days. He is still with me. The only man with an angelic appearance was the clarinet player, Jagmohan Kamle, but he was old. Bathed in white *khadi kurta, dhoti* and Gandhi cap, he had grey eyes, a complexion like a peach, and a long flowing milk - white beard. Given to opium, he had the energy of a man bursting with youth, and what music indeed did flow from his instrument! He too is gone now.

"Habib," said Qudsia *Apa,* "for God's sake, theatre demands young handsome faces, not these strange creatures." Dr. Zakir Hussain, at that time Governor of Bihar, was to come to see my rehearsal. He came and was pleased, but Qudsia *Apa* held her own, saying, "What else did you expect the poor man to say? He is a cultured, sophisticated man; of course he would praise them; that is just courtesy."

These actors obviously had subversive faces. But *Mitti ki Gadi* was a hit, although the production truly came into its own in its Naya Theatre incarnation 20 years later in 1978, by when I had de-colonised my actors and bestowed upon them the boon of autonomy of the mother tongue. This was yet another subversive element, for it scoffed at the so-called standard languages.

(Sudraka's Mṛcchakatika in Hindi 'Mitti Ki Gadi', directed by Habib Tanvir and produced by Naya Theatre, New Delhi).

Bhulwa Ram and Habib Tanvir in 'Mitti ki Gāḍi', The Hindi version of Śūdraka's 'Mṛcchakatika'.

Habib Tanvir called his production in Hindi as Nai Nautanki, ie, (New Nautanki). It was enacted without curtains, props, or sets. He was so interested in intermingling the folk and classical that he exploited six those tribal players in it. Balwant Garg writes 'In Sanskrit plays, scenic division is absent and action moves from one place to another in a continuous time sequence The living tradition of folk theatre has the same freedom of time and place. Tanvir used it effectively in staging the classical masterpiece.

'Mitti ki Gadi' Act I. Hindustani Theatre, New Delhi, 1958-59. Directed by Habib Tanvir. Maitreya, the jester, mimes holding a lamp in the palm of his upturned hand as he approaches. Vasantasenā "hides" by turning her back. Two servants watch their master. Saṁsthānaka, accost Radanikā, a maidservant. Performed on an open stage without scenery. Highly stylized costumes, by Shama zaidi were based on such regional theater models as Kathakali.

The Executioner in the Hindustani Theatre's production of Mitti ki Gāḍi.

Habib Tanvir

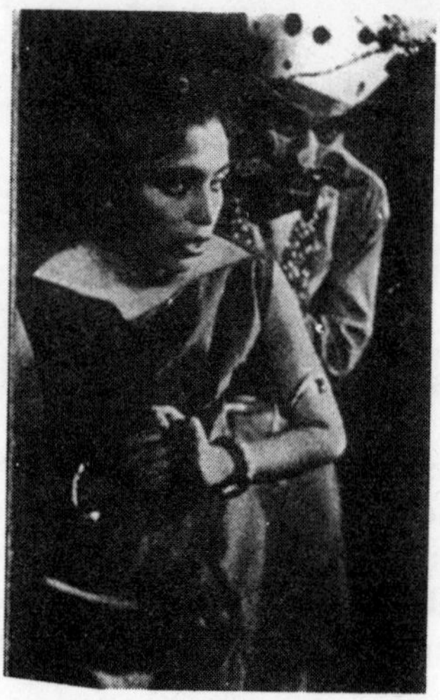

***The Hindustani Theatre's* production of Mitti ki Gāḍi.**

In 1959, Dr. Awasthi in 'Kalpana' (The Hindi Magazine), of April issue wrote on the Hindustani Theatres production of 'Mitti ki Gāḍi' (Mṛcchakaṭika) in Hindi. He complained that the director had not quite understood the entnire social and cultural implications of the play and the ways and means that he adopts to give it a modern look appear ludicrous'. Theatre is perhaps more conventional than other such art forms and can neither dispense with the old traditions and conventions, all at one go, nor absorb at once a lot of new elements and conventions.

'Mitti Kī Gāḍī' was also presented in Kalidasa festival at Ujjain.

A small group of committed theatre workers from Bangalore formed 'Bangalore Little Theatre' in the year 1959. The group included the talented expat couple Scott and Margaret Tod, and perhaps four foureigners with them. They had a vision of a Community Theatre with the motto "Think globally, act locally". They started with a reading of Wilde's 'The importance of being earnest in the last week of Sept. 1959 and their first production was in early 1960 with Moliere's The Prodigious Snob' original adaptation of the Sanskrit classic 'Mṛchhakaṭika' by one of its founder member, Prof. B. Chandrasekhara.

Sergei Esenin mentraons in our indigenous journal 'Natya' (Autumn International Number, 1958) that Pushkin Theatre in Moscow, had staged the play 'The White Lotus' (based on Mṛcchakatika of Śūdraka that kept the Soviet theatre - goers of the times spell bound.

An Andhra branch of the Bharatiya Natya Sangh, The *'Natya Sangham'* was established in 1954 with Hyderabad as its headquarter. Many eminent personalities such as Marri Chenna Reddy and M. Anandam were associated with it and it had illuminaries like A.R. Krishna or Abburi Ramakrishna Rao. Under latter's guidance, it founded a theatre institute called *'Natya Vidyalayam'* in 1959 and produced many plays of significance such as Śūdraka's 'Mṛcchakaṭika' in Telugu.

Contemporary theatre in Gujarat began wth Jashwant Thakar. A few year ago it was hard to find anyone, associated with the theatre in Ahmedabad, who had not trained under him. He started his career in the Gujarat division of the IPTA For years he headed the Drama Department of M.S. University, Vadodara and directed many student productions which were successful at the box office such as his five hour long, drama 'Sharvilak' based on Mṛcchakatika, without commercial considerations.

In Bombay, Vijaya Mehta directed Mṛcchakatika for German actors, employing Kathakali with the help of noted exponent Krishnan Kutty. No attempt was made to turn the actors into expert dancers, as the grammer of the hand gestures in Kathakali alongwith other aspects of its angikabhinaya demands rigorous training for several years. What Vijaya Mehta and Krishnan Kutty attempted was to give the flavour of Kathakali movements, and also of dance at the moments to enhance the impact.

Vijaya Mehta's production tried to associate itself with the classical traditions in Indian music. Here play made use of music as an inherent aspect. Such as in Mṛchhakatika one finds a wondering chorus with cymbals, a single daf and a lot of noises and humming.

In Andhra Pradesh as stated earlier in the field of theatre education on behalf of Natya Sangham, training classes for young workers were conducted at Ravindra Bharati Auditorium, Hyderabad in 1963. Natya Vidyalayam, starting a repertory, staged Mṛcchakatika and others dramas with the trainee students.

In 1964, The Little Clay Cart' was staged by the Hampstead Theatre Club, England, adapted for the stage by Reece Evans from the translation by Oliver. Mrs Namita C. Basham writes that this translation was subsequently published and obtained by Mrs Joyce (known as Jo) Gibson. Jo Gibson was active in repertory theatre in Canberra, had staged other classical works (Greek) and was on the look-out for likely plays to produce. Knowing Prof. Basham's skills in Sanskrit she took it to him. Prof. Basham, who was the then Professor and Head of the Department, Asian Civilization at the Australian National University at Canberra was critical of the translation and offered then and there to translate it. She said he did this very rapidly and improved on the translation immensely - making it less "flowery" and improving on the colloquial impact of the piece. They collaborated closely with the production, which was staged by the Arts Council of Australia in conjuction with the 'Kalidasa Society' - a society which originated at the Australian National University to study Indian culture.

Prof. Basham supplied most of the music - the Indian High Commission the rest. It was apparently cut down to 2 hrs. 30 mins. and was produced in a hall on campus on four nights, July 17-20, 1968.

In the year 1965, Balwant Gargi took his production 'Mṛcchakaṭika' to Washington and New York. The Little Clay Cart was staged at Penthouse Theatre, University of Washington, seattle. It was performed on an open stage without scenery. Costumes were based on North Indian dress. Action was deliberately stylized to create a vivid stage picture. The show was originally staged in an arena at the University, but redesigned for a proscenium arch stage when presented at the University Theatre, University of Minnesota in 1966. It is interesting to note that make up emphasized a single trait such as the Brahman's hooked nose, the villain's mustache or the maid's forehead marks. Balwant Gargi in his production used as a source of his inspiration, Nautanki, a North Indian village theatre form to which he had easy access.

The Little Clay Cart, **Act I. Penthouse Theatre, University of Washington, Seattle, 1965. Directed by Balwang Gargi. The jester Maitreya mimes raising a stick to threaten Saṁsthānaka's courtier. The frightened Saṁsthānaka uses a servant as a shield.**

The Little Clay Cart, **Act I. University Theatre, University of Minnesota, 1966. Directed by Balwant Gargi. The villain Saṁsthānaka theatens the jester Maitreya.**

Farley Richmond, a Fullnight scholar and the then Associate Professor of theater and director of Asian theater research at Michigan State University directed the Little Clay Cart. His version was designed by Jon Gillespie, a talented theatre student, who blended the four permanent pillars of their Arena Theatre into a simple architectural unit inspired by photographs of the interiors of the Jain temples at Mount Abu.

Śūdraka's 'Vasantasena' was directed by Krystynan Skuszanka in Polish at Wroclaw, The Polish Theatre on 24 September 1971 and again at Cracow, Slowacki Theatre on 31 March 1973. The translation of the original text was undertaken by Tadeusz Pobozniak.

Dramatis Personae

Vasantasena	:	Anna Lutoslawska
Charudatta	:	Janusz Peszek, Tadeusz Pokrzywko
Samsthanaka	:	Igor Przegrodzki

Off Stage

Scenography	:	Wojciech Krakowski
Music	:	Zbigniew Karnecki
Choreography	:	Leszek Czarnotax

Music played a prominent role in Skuszanka's production. In a conversation, she named the staging of Clay Cart, a musical performance.

The staging of 'Mṛcchakaṭika' by Krystyna Skuszanka is considered to be the premier of the play. The most attractive thing about the production is the possiblity of scening the "Indianism" of the staging the Polish Vasantasena and the model of the old-Indian theatre. The realization of the Natya-Sastra patterns in Skuszanka's staging. She excluded the tiresome parts and the parts that were not significant for the tempo ofthe stage action, she very often left the text fragments inessential for the plot development but faithful to the original text, and theatrically attractive that suited the tastes of the contemporary masses.

Balwant Gargi's production 'Mṛcchakaṭikam' Scene : Judge's court.

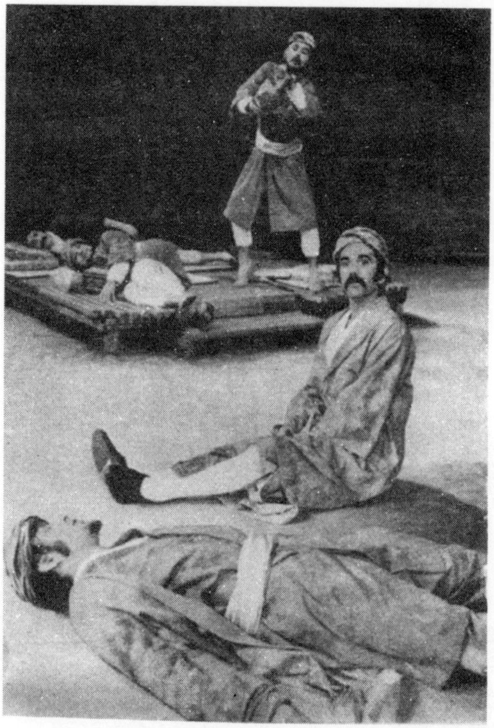

Three scenes from 'Vasantasena' (Mṛcchakaṭika) Polish Theatre, Wroclow. 1971.

Mohan Rakesh's Hindi version of Śūdraka's Mṛcchakaṭika was directed by E. Alkazi on 28 November 1974 for National School of Drama and there were three shows in the opening year.

National School of Drama's Hindi version of Mṛcchakatika under the direction of Ebrahim Alkazi was stated three times in Gandhi Memorial Hall and later in ten cities, it was staged thirteen times. For the first time, the National School of Drama, New Delhi participated in the Kalidasa Festival at Ujjain with their production 'Mṛcchakatika', directed by Ebrahim Alkazi. At Kalidasa Samaroha Ujjain over 15000 audience witnessed the production.

E. Alkazi's 'Mitti Ki Gaḍi' Hindi translation combined Rajasthani paintings and other elements of folk traditions in this Sanskrit classic. By incorporating the paintings of 'Chaurapancasika' illustration, he therefore, interpreted the design elements of classical Indian theatre like 'Mattabaruni', 'Gabaksha', 'Nepathaya' or 'Prekshagrha' which gave his students at National School of Drama, a complete understanding of the classical dictum.

Madhya Pradesh Kala Parishad organised a 'Festival of Plays' from the world classics in various Indian languages in the year 1977. Mṛcchakatika of Śudraka was one of the six classics that was chosen for this unique occasion. The celebrated director. Habib Tanvir directed the play for his group 'Naya Theatre' of Delhi and he employed Lok Dharmi style in a Chhattisgarhi translation. In this drama folk actors of the region participated and critics reckoned the production as of high merit.

Bohurupee, the most outstanding theatre group in Calcutta staged Sudraka's Mṛcchakatika in Bengali at the Academy of Fine Arts on 9 September 1979. The play was adapted by Kumar Ray from Jyotinrindranath Tagore's Bengali translation. The dramatis personae of this worthwhile production is as follows :-

Prastabak (Introduction)	:	Soumitra Basu
Sutradhar	:	Utpal Bhattacharya
Vasantasena	:	Anasuya Ghosh / Abheri Datta
Charudatta	:	Kumar Ray
Shakar (Sansthanak)	:	Arijit Guha / Kaliprasad Ghosh
Aryak	:	Shanti Das/Subir Guha/Mukunda Das
Nati	:	Bithi Mukherji
Maitreya	:	Tarapada Mukherji
Pandit (Biṭ)	:	Debtosh Ghosh

Mathur	:	Ashok Chatterji / Kali Mukherji
Jayaḍī	:	Sivaji Ray
Saṁvahak	:	Subrata Majumdar / Shyamalendu Majumdar
Darddurak	:	Samiran Mukherji / Partha Goswami
Madanika	:	Namita Majumdar
Sharvilak	:	Soumitra Basu
Dhuta Devi	:	Bithi Mukherji
(Maid of Vasantasena)	:	Madhuri Das/ Arunita Majumdar
Bardhamanak	:	Shymalendu Majumdar / Gautam Basu
Veerak	:	Partho Goswami
Chandanak	:	Balai Gupta / Dilip Ray
Dās (Sthabarak)	:	Shivaji Ray
Vicharak	:	Kaliprasad Ghosh / Utpal Bhattacharya
Shodhanak	:	Shyamjiban Ghosh
Chandal - 1	:	Atul Saha
Chandal - 2	:	Abhijit Nandi / Kali Mukherji / Prabir Biswas / Ranen Mitra.

Off Stage

Light	:	Dilip Ghosh
Stage	:	Utpal Nayek
Music	:	Dineshchandra Chandra
Costume	:	Suren Chakrabarti
Make up	:	Shakti Sen.

Acknowledgements :- Prahlad Das, Prasun Banerji, Mira Banerji, Argha Sen, Batu Pal, Kanchan Dasgupta, Shankha Ghosh, Sukumari Bhattacharya and Amiya Deb.

Scene from Bohurupee's Bengali production of Śūdraka's Sanskrit drama 'Mṛcchakatika' (*The Little Clay Cart*), directed by Kumar Ray in Calcutta in 1979.

Habib Tanvir directed 'Mitti kī gaḍi' in Lokdharmi style at the 25th Akhil Bharatiya Kalidas Samaroha that was held at Ujjain from 27th November to 5th December 1982.

Produced by the Theatre and Dance Department, Trinity College, Hartford, Connecticut and directed by Balwant Gargi, Director-in-Residence, the Little Clay Cart of Sudraka was staged at the Goodwin Theatre of Trinity College on April 24, 1985. The production was designed to be a visual experience. A team of twenty-eight actors, dancers and singers had rehearsed for six weeks. The director recalls 'The players move, gallop, dance, kick, they create palaces, temples, gardens, streets, gambling dens, towers, and the seven courtyards of the gilded mansion of the courtesan through stylized movements and sculptural freezes. A rangapatti (hand - held curtain), as used in folk dramas and dance forms, opens the play Two dancers, representing proscenium pillars, glide in rhythmic steps while holding the richly textured curtain. Some characters are introduced from behind this curtain to make their entry more effective. The musicians, drummers, and chanters sit in view on stage in the tradition of an Indian folk play. Many of the actors perform double and triple roles. Those playing the principal characters take on no other parts, but those playing subsidiary characters, with a change of costume and make-up, become totally different, sometime their opposites. For example, the two gamblers of Act Two change into cart drivers in Act Six, and become excutioners in Act Ten. A penniless derelict is transformed into a judge and the stage manager into a thief.

There is multiple action on the stage - inside the house and in the brightly lit "dark street" where the king's brother-in-law and his retainers chase Vasantasena. In white light, the actors create the illusion of pitch darkness by their groping actions and stretched-open eyes.

The geometrically and mathematically worked-out movements melt into logical rhythms and are believable, natural, and stunningly spectacular. It is a theater of wild movement, color, masks, ceremonials, music dance, flaming oil torches, fragrant flowers, incense fumes, and "close-up" action. Special costumes, maks, silks, jewelry, folk motifs, and instruments have been flown from India to provide an authentic atmosphere and color.

The American spectator, familiar with the use of half-masks, dummies, song, dance stylized, makeup, the double, will find all these elements and much more in this classical Sanskrit masterpiece. Contemporary Western master have borrowed from Asian techniques. It will be of some interest for the viewer to go to the roots and see these exciting forms from the other end of the telescope.

The ancient sage Bharata, in his two-thousand-year-old exhaustive treatise on dance and drama, *The Natyasastra,* says, "Drama gives wisdom to fools, courage to cowards, peace of ruffled minds, diversion to kings, and enetertainment to all." *"The Little Clay Cart* ideally stands this test."

In the rural area of north-west Karnataka, there is an unknwon village called Heggoddu in the Shimoga district of the state.

Here in the year 1949, Ninasam came into being as an amateur dramatic society and it was K.V. Subbanna, the modest visionary who has been the guiding spirit of the group that has grown into a full fledged theatre institute. Ninasam focuses on theatre work, implented through the training of fifteen students a year at the institute and concretized through the productions of Ninasam Tirugata, an itinerant Repertory Company that has performed in all nineteen districts f Karnataka. Between October 1985 to April 1988, Tirugata has performed 430 shows of eleven productions from Shakespear's Macbeth, Brecht's Three Penny Opera, Gorky's the Lower Depth to our indigenous classic Mṛcchakatika of Śūdraka.

From 24 March to 3 April 1990, Paschimbanga Natya Academy, Govt. of West Bengal organised a theatre festival called 'Rājyanātyotsava'. Śūdraka's

Mṛcchakatika was staged in Bengali by the drama group named 'Samikshan'.

To suppliment and enrich the teaching programme a number of play - reading enactment sessions were organised followed by discussion with experts by the National School of Drama in the year 1991-1992. Śūdraka's 'Mṛchhakatika' featured inthis programme.

Second year students performed Mṛcchakatika in Mohan Rakesh's Hindi adaptation from 19 to 22 November, 1993 at the Shri Ram Centre Auditorium, New Delhi. Sonal Mansingh was director of movement and choreography, B.V. Karanth scored the music and direction was by D.R. Ankur.

'Mṛcchakatika' in Hindi version, produced by the NSD under the direction of D.R. Ankur.

'Gara kī Gaḍi' in Malvī, presented by Rangmandal, Bhopal and directed by B.V. Karanth.

Third Year students of the National School of Drama presented "Mitti ki Gāḍi", Mohan Rakesh's Hindi translation of 'Mṛcchakatika' at Abhimanch, NSD's own theatre in the month of October 1998 making one more addition in the long list of successful productions by the country's apex theatre training school. Robin Das directed this ancient classic and made optimum use of the wealth of dramatic talent at his disposal which was bolstered by first year students in mute roles to recreate ancient Ujjain where the play is located. Ashok Sagar Bhagat's finely balanced lighting, excellent costumes by Sonalee Hardikar, the props by Satyabrat Rout, imaginative multi-level sets coalessced into strong production value. The music was rendered by Sunil Mishra, Balram Sharma, Gourang Choudhary, Dharmendra Pandey, Guru Kishore, Haridesh Kumar, Sudhir Gautam and Pt. Rajendra Prasanna.

Critic Smita Nirula writes that director Das designed the play beautifully, adding some touches of his own. For example, Charudatta's silent entry into scenes where Vasantasena is talking about him to her friends is lyrical. The use of a puppet as Vasantasena's mother overseeing and commenting on some of the action was very interestingly done. The larger - than - life and yet not-all-presence also commented on the age and illness of the character. The humour inherent in the script was stressed by the agility of the actors and their well defined movements (Chhau training by Guru Janmejay) The energy leapt across the stage and flowed into the auditorium... the storm scene where Vasantasena is finally accepted into Charudatta's household was imaginatively designed with Sharvilak showering the players with water and an actor portraying the rainclouds running through the action."

The tempo of the play was well maintained giving the play a professionally - manicured, all round glors. Those who stood out in the richly - talented cast are:-

Vasantasena	...	Heeba Manara Shah
Charudatta	...	Suresh Bhatia
Sakara	...	Noushad Mohammad
Maitreya	...	Mohammed Aashique Hussain

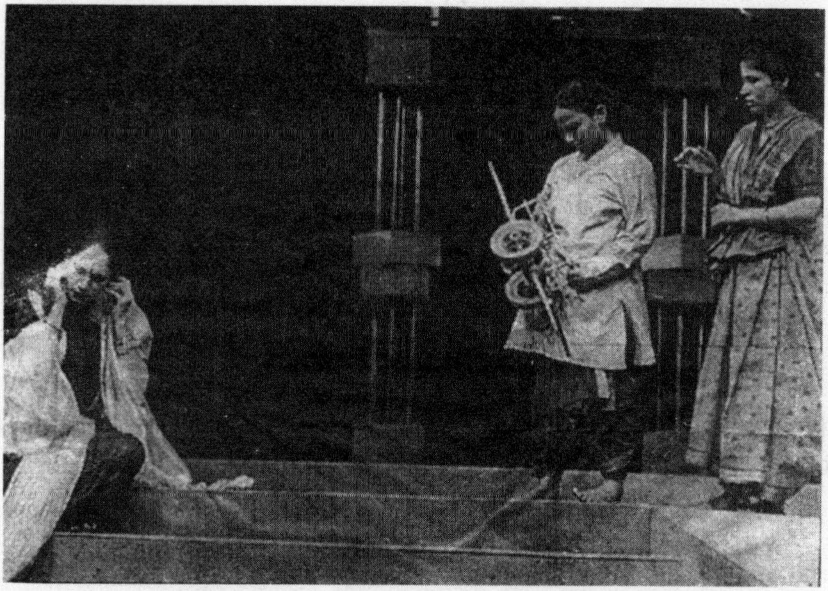

Scene from the NSD production 'Mitti ki Gāḍi'

Select Costume Designs of Mṛcchakatika

Candanaka

[Costume and sword adapted from the scene of a royal procession, Ajanta Cave No. 17] (*Courtesy : Dr. Tarla Mehta)*

Vīraka

[Costume and sword adapted from the scene of a royal procession, Ajanta, Cave No. 17]

Courtesy : Dr. Tarla Mehta.

Vardhamānaka

(Ceṭa)

[Manner of draping the dress adapted from Ajanta, Cave No. 17 scene of a royal procession]

Courtesy : Dr. Tarla Mehta

Sthāvaraka

(Ceṭa)

[Manner of draping the dress adapted from Dr. Motichandra's work., p. 117, fig. 327 (late sixth century)]

Vasantasenā

[Costume approximated on central figure in the toilet scene. Ajanta, Cave No. 17 (late sixth century) G. Yazdani's work., pt. III. p. 95, pl. LXIV. Her hair style from the same cave, Harringham, pl. xxv, 29. (*Courtesy : Dr. Tarla Mehta.)*

Ceṭī (Maid)

[Adapted from the costume of the female chawri bearer in the toilet scene, Ajanta, Cave No. 17 (late sixth century)]

Courtesy : Dr. Tarla Mehta.

Āryaka

[Costume approximated] (*Courtesy : Dr. Tarla Mehta)*

DRAMATIC WORKS : A BIBLIOGRAPHY

Text

Mṛcchakaṭika / by Sudraka.- Bombay : [s.n.], 1896.

______/ by Sudraka.- Bombay : Nirṇayasagar Press, 1900.

______/ by Sudraka.- Bonn : [s.n.], 1847.

(Edition of F. Stenzler Sanskrit Seires.)

______/ by Sudraka. 4th ed. Meerut : Sahitya Bhandar, 1976.

_____/ by Sudraka, comm. by Prthvidhara; ed. by Kasinatha Panduranga Paraba and Vasudeva Sarma.- Varanasi : Chaukhamba Orientalia, 1987.

9, 260, 6p.

______/ by Śudraka; comm. by Prthvidhara ed. by Narayan Ram Acharya.- 8th ed.- Bombay : Nirnayasagara Press, 1950.

8, 298 p.; 18 cm.

Includes index.

______/ by Śudraka, ed. by Adolf Friedrich Stenzler. 1847.

Adolf Friedrich Stenzler (1807-1887)

Adolf Friedrich Stenzler was born on 9-7-1807 in Wolgast. He is known for his careful editing of several Sanskrit texts. This indologist broughtout Śudraka's 'Mṛcchakatika' in 1847 which was considered a model for later scholars. This edition later served as the basis for R. Pischel's Prakrit Grammar, as Stenzler had given clear definitions of the various dialects used in the play. The scholar died in the year 1887.

______/ by Sudraka; ed. by J.V. Misra.- Benaras : Caukhamba Surabharati Prakasana, 1985.

(Caukhamba Surabharati Granthamala; 76)

______/ ed. by K.P. Parab.- Bombay : [s.n.], 1900

294 p. Includes commentary of Pṛthvidhara. 3rd ed. rev. by Mahādeo Gangādhar Sāstrī Barke; published in 1909. 5th ed. rev. by Wāsudev Laxman Śāstrī Paṇśikar.; published in 1926.

______/ by Sudraka; ed. by K.P. Parab and H.M.S. Śāstrī.- Bombay: [s.n.], 1902.

______/ by Sudraka; ed. by M.M. Haridāsa Siddhāntavāgīśa with comm. 'Vasantasuṣamā'.- Calcutta : [s.n.], 1922. 3rd ed. appeared in Śaka 1878.

______/ by Sudraka; ed. by M.R. Kale with the comm. of Pṛthvīdhara, various readings, a literal English tr., notes, and introd.- [s.l.] : [s.n.], 1924. 2nd ed. published in 1962. 3rd ed. published in 1972.

______Delhi : Motilal Banarsidass, 1972.

______/ by Śudraka; ed. by Mahaprabhulaha Goswami & .. etạl.. - Benaras : Chowkhamba Sanskrit Seires Office, 1954. (Haridas Sanskrit Granthamala; No. 252)

______/ by Sudraka; ed. by Narayana Rāma Ācārya with the commentay of 'Pṛthvīdhara. - 8th ed. - Bombay : Nirnaya Sagar Press, 1950.

______/ by Sudraka, ed. by Otto Von Boehtlingk. St. Petersburg: [s.n], 1877.

Otto Von Boehtlingk (1815-1904)

One of the greatest 19th century Indologist, Otto von Boehtlingk was born on 11 6-1815 in St. Petersburg. A member of the Imperial Academy of Sciences in St. Petersburg, he edited and translated Sanskrit classic Mṛcchakatika; d.i. das Irdene Waegelchen, from St. Petersburg in 1877. In 1885, he moved to Leipzig where he died on 1-4-1904.

______/ by Sudraka; ed. by R.D. Karmakar with text and English tr., introd., notes and appendices.- [s.l.] : [s.n.], 1937. 2nd ed. - Poona : [s.n.], 1950.

______/ by Sudraka; ed. by Ramāśaṅkar Tripāṭhi with an introd. in Hindi and a Hindi tr. alongwith a Sanskrit commentary.- Delhi : Motilal Banasidass, 1961, p. 778

______/ by Sudraka; ed. by T.E. Srīnivāsāchāri.- Madras : [s.n.], 1907.

______/ by Sudraka; ed. by V.G. Paranjape, text with commentary, notes and Eng. tr. in two parts.- Poona : [s.n.], 1937.

Contents : Part I : Text, and notes.

Part II : English translation.

______/ ed. with a comm. by J. Vidyāsāgara.- Calcutta : [s.n.], 1881

425 p.

2nd has 351 p.; published in 1891.

3rd ed. has 355 p.; published in 1898.

5th ed. has 582 p.; published in 1938.

______/ by Sudraka; ed. with a comm. by R.B Raddi.- Bombay : [s.n.], 1909.

______/ by Sudraka; ed. with a comm. by Rāmamayāsarman and a preface in Bengali by V. Majumdar.- Calcutta : [s.n.], 1870,

386 p.

______/ by Sudraka; ed. with English tr. by S.V. Karandikara.- Poona : [s.n.], 1919-20.

389 p.

______/ by Sudraka; ed. with introd. notes and English tr. by Vasanta Ramchandra Nerurkar.- 2nd ed. - [s.l.] : [s.n.], 1937.

____________ / by Sudraka; ed. with Sanskrit commentary by T.E. Śrīnivāsācārī.- Madras : Oriental Press, 1907.

488 p.; 21 cm.

____________ / by Sudraka; ed. with an English tr., intro., notes and append. by R.D. Karmārkar.- 2nd ed.- Poona : The editor, 1950.

xxxiii, 518 p.; 21 cm.

Play on the love of 'Cārudatta, an impoverished merchant for 'Vasantasenā', a hetaera.

____________ / by Sudraka; ed. with an introd., notes, English tr. & append. by Vasanta Rāmacandra Nerūrkar.- 2nd ed.- Bombay : Bombay Book Depot., 1937.

[493] p.; 22 cm.

Presented in two parts, the Pt. 1 contains introd., text and notes with five appendices and Pt. 2 comprises of the translation.

____________ / by Sudraka; ed. with Sanskrnit notes and Bengali translation by Haridās Bhaṭṭācārya.- Nakipur (Khulna) : The editor, 1922.

835 p.; 18 cm.

Play presented in ten acts of which the first four can be compared with Bhāsa's Cārudatta.

____________ / by Sudraka; comm. 'Jayanti' in Hindi and Sanskrit by Ramananda

Dvivedi and Jagadisaprasada Pandeya; ed. by Madanagopala Vajapeyi.- Varanasi : Bharatiya Vidya Prakashan, 1993.

85, 658 p.

____________ / curriculum Figlinum Śūdraka regis / Fabula Sanskrite edidit A.F. Stenzler.- Bonn : [s.n.], 1847.

8, 332 p.

______/ by Sudraka. Calcutta : [s.n.], 1829.

2, 343 p.

With a commentary explanatory of the Prākrit passages /

______/ by Sudraka; ed. by N.B. Godabole.- Bombay : [s.n.], 1896.

594 p.

With the commentaries of Lalladīkṣita and Pṛthvīdhara and various readings /

______/ by Sudraka; comm. by Prthvidhara; ed. with English tr. by M.R. Kale.- Delhi : Motilal Banarsidass, 1988

lxxii, 5, 600 p.; 22.5 cm.

Text with English tr., notes ec.

Translations

Bengali

______/ by Śudraka; tr. into Bengali by Aghornath Tattvanidhi, 1857.

First Bengali tr. of the Sanskrit play.

______/ by Śudraka; tr. into Bengali by Baikunthanath Basu.- 1899 [1306].

______/ by Śudraka; tr. into Bengali by Jyotirindranath Thakur.- Calcutta : [s.n.], 1901.

______/ by Śudraka; tr. into Bengali by Rammay Sharma Tarkaratna.- 1874.

______/ by Sudraka; tr. into Bengali by Sukumari Bhattacharya.- New Delhi : Sahitya Akademi, 1980.

10, 158 p.; 22 cm.

______/ ed. by M.M. Haridāsa Siddhāntavāgīśa with a comm. 'Vasantasuṣama.-

Calcutta : [s.n.], 1922.

3rd ed. appeared in Śaka 1878.

Sanskrita Sahitya Sambhar / ed. by Gaurinath Sastri & et al. [Vol. 7].- Calcutta : Navpatra Prakashan, [197-].

Includes Bengali rendering of Śūdraka's 'Mṛcchakatika'.

Danish

______: Lervognen Et indisk Skuespil / Oversat af E. Brandes.- Copenhagen : [s.n.], 1870.

In Danish.

Dogri

Mitti di gaddi / by Sudraka; tr. into Dogri by Ramnath Shastri.- Jammu : J & K Academy of Art, Culture & Literature, 1971.

179 p.; 22 cm.

Book received Sahitya Akademi Translation Prize of 1989.

Dutch

Het Leemen Wagentje / Indisch Tooneelspel, uit Sanskṛt en Prākṛt in het Nederlandsch vertaald door J-Ph. Vogel.- Amsterdam : [s.n.] 1897.

15, 216 p.

Tr. of 'Mṛcchakaṭikā' in Dutch.

English

Classical triptych : Sakuntala, the Little Clay Cart, Nagananda / tr. into English verse by H.W. Wells.- Mysore : University of Mysore, 1970.

The Little Clay Cart / by Sudraka; tr. from the original Sanskrit by Satyendra Kumar Basu; Foreword by Suniti Kumar Chatterji. - Calcutta : The University of Calcutta : 1939.

xxvi, 153 p.; 21 cm.

Tr. of ten acts play entitled 'Mṛcchakatika'.

______/ by Sudraka tr. from the Sanskrit with introd. and notes by Revilo Pendleton Oliver.- Urbana, Illinois : The University Illinois, 1939.

250 p.

______ *University of Illinois Bulletin*, May 27, 1938; Vol. xxxv, No. 78.

The Little Clay Cart : Mṛcchakatika / by Sudraka; tr. from the original Sanskrit and Prakrit into English prose and verse by Arthur William Ryder. - Combridge (Mass.) : Harvard University Press, 1905.

xxix, 176, [1] p.; 25.5 cm.- [Harvard Oriental Series ; 9]

The Little Clay Cart / by Sudraka; tr. by Arthur W. Ryder and adpat. by Agnes Morgan.- New York : Theatre Arts, 1934.

The Mrichchakati or the Toy Cart / by Śudraka; tr. into English by Horace Hayman Wilson. - U. Holcroft : Asiatic Press, 1826.

The Mrichchhakati or the toy-cart / tr. from the original Sanskrit by Horace Hayman Wilson.- Calcutta : Society for the Resuscitation of Indian Literature, 1901.

xiv, 200 p.; 15 cm.

Tr. of Mṛcchakaṭika.

Mṛcchakaṭika / by Sudraka; ed. by M.R. Kale with the comm. of Pṛthvīdhara, various readings, a literal English tr., notes and introd. - [s.l.] : [s.n.], 1924.

2nd ed. published in 1962.

3rd ed. published in 1972.

______Delhi : Motilal Banarsidass, 1972.

The Mrichchhakatika by Sudraka; comm. by Pṛthvidhara; ed. with English tr. by M.R. Kale.- Delhi : Motilal Banarsidass, 1988.

lxxii, 5, 600 p.; 22.5 cm.

Mṛcchakatika = The Little Clay Cart : a d rama in ten acts / by Śudraka; tr. into English by R.P Oliver.- Westport, CT : Greenwood Press, 1978. Also published in 1938.

Mṛcchakaṭika / by Sudraka; ed. by V.G. Paranjape, text with commentary, notes and Eng. tr. in two parts. - Poona : [s.n.], 1937

Contents : Part I : Text and notes.

Part II : English translation.

______/ by Sudraka; ed. by R.D. Karmakar with text and English tr., introd., notes and appendices. - [s.l.] : [s.n.], 1937.

______/ by Śudraka; ed. with English tr. by R.D. Karmakar.- 2nd ed.- Poona : The author, 1950.

33, 518 p.; 21 cm.

______/ by Sudraka; ed. with English tr. by S.V. Karandikara.- Poona : [s.n.], 1919-20.

389 p.

______/ by Sudraka, ed. with introd., notes and English tr. by Vasanta Ramchandra Nerurkar. - 2nd ed. Bombay : Bombay Book Depot, 1937.

[Mṛcchakatika] *In* Frazer, R.W. A Literary history of India. - London : T. Fisher Unwin, 1898. Pp. 272 - 283.

Contains excerpts in English from the play 'Mṛcchakatika'.

Plays of the year / ed. by J.C. Trewin. - London : Elek Books, 1965

Contains English rendering of Mṛcchakatika.

Select specimens of the theatre of the Hindoos / tr. by H.H. Wilson. - London : [s.n.], 1826.

Contents : 'The Mṛchhakaṭika or the Toy - Cart. Pp. 1-182.

Select specimens of the theatre of the Hindus / tr. into English by Horace Hayman Wilson.- 3rd ed.- New Delhi : Asian Educational Services, 1984.

Includes Mṛcchakatika.

Six Sanskrit plays / ed. by Henry W. Wells. - London : Asia Publishing House, 1964.

xxxi, 487 p.; plates; 21 cm.

Includes "The Little Clay Cart" of Sūdraka.

The Toy Cart / tr. into English by Arthur Symons. - Dublin : Maunsel & Co., 1919.

viii, 114 p.; 18.5 cm.

Tr. of 'Mṛcchakaṭika', a play in five acts.

______/ by Śudraka; tr. into English by N.B. Godabole.- Bombay : Govt. Central Press, 1896.

(Bombay Sanskrit and Prakrit Series; No. 52)

Two plays of ancient India / tr. into English by J.A.B. van Buitenen. - New York : Columbia University Press, 1968.

Contains 'Mṛcchakatika'.

______/ tr. into English by J.A.B. van Buitenen. - Delhi : Motilal Banarsidass, 1971.

Contents : 'The Little Clay Cart'. Pp. 1-180.

Adaptation

De, S.K. Tales from Sanskrit dramatists. - Madras : [s.n.], 1930. Pp. 62-96.

Contains the summary of the story of the Mṛcchakaṭika of Śūdraka.

French

Dondey - Duprē. [Mṛcchakaṭika] *Journal Asiatique;* 1827, Vol. X. Pp. 179 ff.

This is the first French rendering consisted of extracts translated from H.H. Wilson's English tr. of the Mṛcchakaṭika.

Le Chariot d' Enfant. Drameen vers, en cinq actes et sept tableaux / traduction par M.M. Mēry et G. de Nerval. - Paris : [s.n.], 1850.

French tr. of 'Mṛchhakaṭika'

Le chariot de terre cuite : drame sanscrit attribuē au roi Śūdraka, traduit et annotē des scolies de Lallā Dīkshita / tr. by Paul Regnaud.- Paris : [s.n.], 1876-77 4 Vols. - (Biblio. Orient. Elzēvir, Nos. 6-9)

This version was chosen for performance in Paris by Berrucand in 1895. cf. Levi, Revue de Paris, 1895, P. 818 f.

[Mṛcchakaṭika] / by Sudraka tr. into French by A. Langlois. - Paris : [s.n.], 1828. First complete French tr. from H.H. Wilson's English rendering of the play.

Mṛcchakatika : Le petit chariot d' argile, drame en dix actes / tr. by H. Fauche. - In Une tērade, ou drame hymne, roman et poeme, traduite pour la premiere fois du samscrit en francais (Vol. 1). - Paris : [s.n.], 1861.

"[The Toy Cart]" / by Śūdraka; tr. by Victor Barrucand. - Paris : [s.n.], 1895.

Tr. of 'Mṛcchakaṭika'.

2nd ed. - Paris : [s.n.], 1921

German

Mṛcchakaṭikā / metrisch ubersetzt von Ludwig Fritze. *In* Indisches Theater (Vol. 3). - Schloss - Chemnitz, 1879).

Mṛcchakaṭikā : das irdene Wagelchen, ein dem Konig Śūdraka zugeschriebenes Schauspiel ubersetzt von otto Bohtlingk. - St. Petersburg : [s.n.], 1877, 4,

213 p.

Vasantasena / by Sudraka, tr. into German by Lion Feuchtwanger. - Munich : [s.n.], 1916.

This translation was staged many times in Germany.

Vasantasenā : drama mit freier Benutzung der dichtung des altindischen Konig Śūdraka / von Emil Pohl. - Stuttgart : [s.n.], 1893.

128 p.

Vasantasenā oder das irdene Wagelchen / freie ubersetzung von Michael Haberlandt. - Leipzig : [s.n.], 1893,

20, 214 p.

Vasantasenā oder das irdene Wāgelchen : ein indisches Schauspiel in zehn Aufzūgen / von Konig Śūdraka; Deutsch von Hermann Camillo Kellner. - Leipzig : [s.n.], 1893.

200 p.

2nd ed. has 199 p.; published in 1894.

Gujarati

Mṛcchakatika / by Sudraka; tr. into Gujarati by Sundaram alias Tribhuvandas Purushottam Luhar. Bombay : Padma Prakāshan, 1944.

xiii, 144 p.; 18.5 cm.

Mruchchhakatik ane Bhagvadjjukiya / comp & tr. by Sundaram 2nd ed. - Ahmedabad : Ravani Prakashangruh, 1959.

xiv, 150 p.; 18.5 cm.

Gujarati rendering of Sudraka's Mṛcchakatika.

Adaptation

Sharvilak / by Rasiklal C. Parekh. - Ahmedabad : Gujar Grantharatna Karyalaya, 1957.

xx, 216 p.

The book received the prestigious 'Sahitya Akademi Award' of 1960 in Gujarati language.

The play in based on Sanskrit classics *'Darida Carudatta, of Bhasa and 'Mṛcchakatikam' of Sudraka* and even certain portions of this play is nothing but the direct translation of the above two plays. The playwright has also made use of certain materials from *'Pratijnayaugandharayana'* of *Bhasa*.

Hindi

Mitti ki gaḍi / by Śūdraka; tr. by Kadasiyā Zaidī. - New Delhi : [s.n.], [n.d.]

Tr. of 'Mṛcchakatika' in Hindi.

______/ by Śūdraka; tr. by Satyavrata Siṁha. - 2nd ed. - Allahabad : Parimal Prakahsan, 1964,.

______/ by Śūdraka; tr. into Hindi by Sudarshan Chopra. - Delhi : Sahitya Sahakar, 1981.

80 p.; 17.5 cm.

______/ by Śudraka; comm. by Brahmānanda Śukla. - Varanasī : Master Khelarilal & Sons, 1953.

______/ by Śudraka; comm. by Mahāprabhulāla Gosvāmī and Ramakanta Dvivedī; ed. by Rāmanuja Ojhā. - Varanasi : [s.n.], 1954.

______/ by Sudraka; ed. by Ramāśaṅkar Tripāṭhi with an intro. in Hindi and a Hindi tr. alongwith a Sanskrit commentary. - Delhi : Motilal Banarsidass, 1961.

778 p.

______/ by Śudraka; tr. into Hindi by Balkṛṣṇa Bhatt. [19th cent.]

______/ by Śudraka; tr. into Hindi by Damodar Śastrī. - [19th cent.]

______/ by Śudraka; tr. into Hindi by Dayal Singh [19th cent.]

______/ by Śudraka; tr. into Hindi by Gadadhar Bhatt. 1980.

______/ by Śudraka; tr. into Hindi by Lalita Sahagal and Ugrasena Nārang. - New Delhi : Delhi Press, [n.d.]

______/ by Sūdraka; tr. by Mohan Rākeś. - Delhi : Rajkamal Prakashan, 1962.

______/ by Śudraka; tr. by Rājendra Siṁha Gauḍ. - Allahabad : Sahitya Bhavan, [n.d.]

______/ by Śudraka; tr. into Hindi by Rangeya Raghav. - Delhi : Rajpal & Sons, 1957.

212 p.; 18.5 cm.

______/ by Sūdraka; tr. by Rājeśvaraprasāda Gupta. - Jabalpur : Sushma Sahitya Mandir, [n.d.]

______/ by Śudraka; tr. into Hindi by Sītaram 1899.

______/ by Sūdraka; tr. by Sītārāma Lālā. - Allahabad : National Press, 1917.

______/ tr. into Hindi prose and verse by Lālā Sītārām. - Allahabad : Pracin Natak Manimala, 1913.

v, 159 p.; 18.5 cm.

Sone kī gāḍī / by Śudraka; tr. by Rāmājñā Dvivedī. - Patna : Pustak Bhandar, 1869.

Vasantasenā / by Sūdraka; tr. by Thakuradatta Miśra. - Allahabad : Kitab Mahal, 1956.

Italian

Introduzione alla versione del Mṛcchakaṭikā [opera di Śūdraka] / da Michele Kerbaker. - Florence : [s.n.], 1872.

Includes Italian tr. of first act.

______/ versione italiana di Michele Kerbaker. *Rivista* Europea, Florence. Dec. 1869 and *the Giornale Napolitano* (New Series; No. 9); 1884. Pp. 1-83.

Published in parts.

In Italian.

Kannada

______/ by Śudraka; tr. into Kannada by D.N. Mulabagala. - Dharwad : S.S.

Kulkarni, 1951.

220 p.; 18 cm.

______/ by Śudraka kavi; tr. into Kannada by K.V. Iyer. - Mysore : Pustakalaya, 1978.

xvii, 94 p.; 18 cm.

Maithili

______/ tr. by Īśanāth Jhā. Darbhanga : Darbhanga Press, 1955.

xxiv, 232 p.; 18 cm.

Tr. from original Sanskrit into Maithili.

Malayalam

Mrichakatikam / by Śudraka; tr. into Malayalam by K. Kesavan Potti. - Kottayam : D.C. Books, 1985.

152 p.; 18 cm.

Mṛchhakaṭikam / tr. into Malayalam by Varavūr Śāmu Mēnōn. - Trichur : Vāṇīkaḷēbaram Press, [n.d.]

241 p.; 23 cm.

Manipuri

Mṛcchakaṭikam / by tr. from Sanskrit original by Aribam Brajabehārī Śarmā. - Imphal : Raj Store, 1972.

245 p.; 18 cm.

Marathi

Mrichchhakatik natak / by Śudraka; tr. into Marathi by Patshutam Tatya Godbole. - Pure : S.R. Godbole, 1935.

240 p.; 18 cm.

Saṅgit Mṛcchakaṭika / by Sudraka; tr. by Govinda Ballāḷ Deval; introd. by P.R. Lele. - 10th ed. - Bombay : Balvant Pustak Bhandar, 1953.

viii, 114 p.; plate; 18 cm.

First published in 1889.

Tr. of 'Mṛcchakaṭika', a play in seven acts.

Vasantasenā / by Sudraka; tr. by Pralhād Keśav Atre. - Bombay : Rāmkṛṣṇa Pakashan Mandal, 1943.

viii, 83 p.; plate; 18.5 cm.

Marathi rendering with 48 scenes with few changes.

Adaptation

Islāmpūrkar, Vāman Śāstrī. Cārudatta āṇi Vasantasenā / by Vaman Śastri Islāmpurkar. - Bombay : Vāsudev Moreśvar Potdār, 1889.

xvi, 279 p.

Novel based on Śūdraka's famous play 'Mṛcchakaṭika'.

Nepali

Maṭo ka gāḍha / tr. by Mallināth Pauḍyāl. - Varanasi : Babu Madhabprasad Sarma, 1971.

170 p.; 17 cm.

Tr. of Mṛcchakaṭika.

Russian

'Vasantasenā, : drevnaya in dēiskaya drama / Perevod s Sanskrits-kago C. Kossovica. *Moskvityanin,* 1849 (Moscow).

Russian tr. of 'Mṛcchakaṭika'.

Swedish

Mṛcchakaṭika : Den lilla lervagnen / Eff indiskt skādespel ofversatt av Hilding Andensson. - Lund : [s.n.], 1899.

133 p.

Swedish rendering of 'Mṛcchakaṭika'.

Vasantasena : Indiskt drama 5 akter / Fritt after Emil Pohls tyska bearbetning. - Stockholm : [s.n.], 1894.

119 p.

Tr. of 'Mṛcchakaṭika' in Swedish.

Tamil

Maṇṇiyal ciṛutēṇ / tr. by M. Katirēś Caṭṭiyār. - Melaccivapuri : Sanmarg Sabhai, 1933.

lxxxiv, 430, [2] p.; 18.5 cm.

Telugu

Mṛcchakaṭikamu / tr. by Tirupati Venkaṭēśvara Kavulu. - 6th ed. - Kadiyam : Cel̤lapil̤l̤a Vēṅkaṭśāstri & Sons, 1953.

203 p.; 21 cm.

Padmaprabhṛtaka

Text

[Padmaprabhrtaka] In Caturbhāṇī/ed. by M. Rāmakṛṣṇa Kavi and S.K. Rāmanātha Śāstrī. - Trichur : Maṅgalodayam, 1922.

x, [124] p.; 21 cm.

Book contains four one act monlogue plays (bhāṇas) somewhat closely connected with 'Mṛcchakaṭika', discovered in 1922; One of these play include Śūdraka's 'Padmaprābhṛtakam'.

Padmaprabhrtaka / by Sudraka; ed. by R.A. Loman. - Amsterdam : [s.n.], 1956.

'Bhāṇa ascribed to Śūdraka.

BIO - CRITICAL NOTICES

Acharya P.B. The Denouncement and its dramatic propriety in Abhijñanrasakuntala, Uttararamacarita and Mṛcchakatika / by P.B. Acharya. *Sanskrit Ranga* (Annual Number); 1976; Vol. 6; Pp. 38-58.

Adya Rangacharya. Drama in Sanskrit literature. - Bombay : Popular Prakshan, 1967.

Pp. 16, 44, 60, 91, 119-127, 140, 166, 205, 207.

Aggarwal, H.R. A short history of Sanskrit literature. - 2nd rev. ed. - Delhi : Munshiram Manoharlal, 1963 (Sudraka, P. 182).

Aufrecht, Theodor. Catalogus catalogorum. - Weisbaden : Franz Steiner Verlag Gmb. H, 1962.

2 Vols.; 26 cm.

Banerji, Biswanath. King Śūdraka and the role of Śakāra in the Mṛcchakaṭikam. In A corpus of Indian studies. - Calcutta : [s.n.], 1980. Pp. 281-294.

Banerji, Satya Ranjan. Mṛcchakatika or the toy-cart of King Sudraka; a study. - Calcutta : Sanskrit Book Depot, 1984.

xxiv, 103 p.; 22.5 cm.

______. Mṛcchakaṭike Sakarāsya vacanaviśesaḥ *Sanskrit Sāhitya Parishat Patrika;* Jan.-April 1976, Vol. L VIII, Nos. 9-12. Pp. 113-121.

Article deals with the interpretation of some of the verses of Śakāra in the 'Mṛcchakaṭika'.

Banhatti, Srinivas Narayan. Natyacharya Deval. - Pune : The author, 1967.

Book received Sahitya Akademi Award of 1969 in Marathi Language. It contains an article on Sudraka's classic Mṛcchakatika and its Marathi translation. Pp. 61-105.

Basak, R.G. Indian society as pictured in the Mṛcchakaṭika. *Indian Historical Quarterly*, 1929, Vol. V, Pp. 299-325.

Basham, A.L. The wonder that was India. New York : Grove Press, 1954.

Belvalkar, S.K. 'The Relation of Śūdraka's Mṛcchakaṭika to the Cārudatta of Bhāsa'

/ by S.K. Belvalkar. *Proceedings & Transactions of the First Oriental Conference,* at Poona, held on the 5th, 6th and 7th of Nov. 1919.

All India Oriental Conference I; Vol. 2, Pp. 189-204.

Bhartiya, Kanti Kishore. Sanskrit natakkar. - Uttar Pradesh : Prakashan Śakha, Suchana Vibhag, 1959.

(Hindi - Samiti granthamala; 25)

Contents : Śudraka. Pp. 63-79.

Bhat, G.K. Preface to Mṛcchakatika. - Allahabad : The New order Book Co., 1953.

vii, 254 p.; 19 cm.

_____. Sanskrit drama : problems and perspectives. - Delhi : Ajanta Publications, 1985.

Bhatt, S.C. Drama in ancient India. - New Delhi : Amrit Book Co. 1961.

Bhattacharya, Bhabatosh. Analytical study of Sudraka's Mricchakatika / by Bhabatosh Bhattacharya.

Ph.D. thesis approved by Viswa Bharati University in 1982.

Bhattacharya, Bimanchandra. Sanskrit Sahityer ruprekha. - 5th ed. - Calcutta : Vidyodaya Library Pvt. Ltd., 1972. In Bengali.

Bhattacharya, Biswanath. Sanskrit drama and dramaturgy. - Delhi : Sharada Publishing House, 1994.

Bhattacharya, Sukumari. Plot of the Mṛcchakaṭika. *Indian Historical Quarterly*; Dec. 1956, 32 (4); Pp. 412-416.

Boltz, A. Vasantasenā und die Hetaren in indischen Drama : Das Vedavolk in seinen Gesamtverhaltnissen : Zwei vortage. - Darmstadt : [s.n.], 1894.

56 p.

______Etta's, 5. Leiden : [s.n.], 1894. Pp. 279-305.

______['Bombay Branch Royal Asiatic Society'] *The Times of India;* 18th August 1895.

Report on Dr. Nishikanta Chattopadhyay's paper on 'Mricchakaṭikā', the Sanskrit drama by Śūdraka.

The Cambridge guide to Asian theatre / ed. by James R. Brandon. - Cambridge : Cambridge University Press, 1993.

The Cambridge guide to world theatre / ed. by Martin Banham. - Cambridge; Cambridge University Press, 1988.

Cappeller, C. Zur Mṛcchakaṭikā. *Festgruss an O. von Bohtlingk* (Stuttgart); 1888. Pp. 20-22.

Study of 'Mṛcchakaṭika'.

Chattopadhyay, Nishikanta.

Mṛcchakatika or the Toy-Cart of king Śūdraka : a study / ed. by Satya Ranjann Banerjee. - Calcutta : Sanskrit Book Depot (P) Ltd., 1984.

______Mṛcchakaṭika, or the Toy-Cart of king Śūdraka : a study. - Mysore : [s.n.], 1902.

10, 82 p.

______Three lectures : The reminiscences of the German University life, the true theosophist, and the Mricchakaṭikam or the Toy Cart. - Bombay : [s.n.], 89 p.

[Three lectures] / by Nishikanta Chattopadhyay. *The Bengal Times,* 18th May 1898 [Dacca].

'Three lectures : reniniscenes of German University life, The True Theosophist and the Mricchakaṭikā, or the Toy-Cart' / by Nishikanta Chattopadhyay. *The Indian Magazine and Review,* May 1896.

Review of Lectures delivered before different audience at Hyderabad.

Cīechowicz, Jan 'The Old - Indian theatre in Poland' / by Jan Ciechowicz. *Sangeet Natak Akademi Journal;* April - June 1976; Vol. 40; Pp. 23-40.

'Classics Study Circle'. *Sahitya Akademi Quarterly Newsletter*; July - Sept. 1996; Vol. IX, No. II. P. 8.

On Mṛcchakatika.

Comparative Indian literature / ed. by K.M. George. - Trichur : Kerala Sahitya Akademi, 1984.

Pp. 566-67.

The critique of Indian theatre / ed by M.L. Varadpande and Sunil Subhedar. -

Delhi : Unique Publications, 1981.

The Cultural heritages of India [Vol. V] / ed. by Suniti Kumar Chatterji. - rev. ed. - Calcutta : The Ramakrishna Mission Institute of Culture, 1978. P. 248.

Dalal, Minakshi L. Confiict in Sanskrit drama. - Bombay : Somaiya Publications Pvt. Ltd., 1973.

Contents : Śudraka. Pp. 236-247, 264-266.

Dange, Sadarshiv A 'The Mendicant of the Mṛcchakaṭika once again' / by Sadashiv A. Dange. *Journal of Asiatic Society (Bombay);* 1977-78; Vols. 52-53; Pp. 75-82.

Dange, Sadashiv A & Dange, Sindhu S. Critiques on Sanskrit dramas. - 2nd rev. ed. - New Delhi : Aryan Books International, 1994.

De, Sabitri. Sanskrit Sahityer anubad - dhara. - Calcutta : Chinmay Majumdar, [1983]

Contents : On Mṛchhakatika, Pp. 196-200.

De, Sushil Kumar. Aspects of Sanskrit literature. - Calcutta: Firma KLM, 1959
Contents : Mṛchhakaṭika. Pp. 16, 17, 19, 24, 268, 272.

'The Denoucement and its dramatic properties in Abhijñāna - Śākuntala, Uttararāmacarita and Mṛcchakaṭika'. *Saṁskṛta - Ranga Annaual;* 1972. Pp. 38-58.

Devasthali, G.V. Introduction to the study of Mṛchhakaṭika'. - Poona : Poona Oriental Book House, 1951.

184 p.

Includes notes and index

Chapters on (I) The Author (II) The Plot (III) A Critical appreciation (IV) Characters (V) Sources (VI) Śūdraka as a dramatist (VII) Society as depicted in the Mṛchhakaṭika.

Dictionary of oriental literatures (Vol. II) : South and South - East Asia. - Delhi : Vikas Publishing, 1975.

Dwivedi, Salagram. Literary cultural and political study of Mṛcchakatika / by Salagram Dwivedi.

Ph.D. thesis in Hindi, approved by Agra University in 1971.

______Mrichchhakatik : Śāstriya, sāmājik evam rajnitik adhyayan. - Varanansi :

Vishva Vidyalaya Prakashan, 1982.

349 p.; 22 cm.

Encyclopaedia of Indian literature. - New Delhi : Sahitya Akademi, 1987 - 1994.
Pp. 1102, 1103, 1108, 2434, 2765, 3639, 4661.

Frazer, R.W. A Literary history of India. London : T. Fisher Unwin, 1898. Pp. 270-281.

Gajendragadkar, S.N. Heroines in Sanskrit drama : Kālidāsa's plays and Mṛcchakatika. *Summary of Papers; All India Oriental Conference* : XXII [Gauhati]; 1965; Vol. 1.

Garg, Ganga Ram. An Encyclopaedia of Indian literature. - Delhi : Mittal Publishers, 1982.

Pp. 249-250, 417.

Gargi, Balwant. 'Production of "The Little Clay Cart"' / by Balwant Gargi. *Samskrita Ranga / Annual Number;* 1972; Vol. 6; Pp. 145-152.

______.'Production of the Little Clay Cart' / by Balwant Gargi *Sangeet Natak Akademi Journa;* July - Sept. 1967; Vol. 5; Pp. 37-44.

______.Theatre in India. - New York : Theatre Arts, 1962.

Contains an extremely useful general study in appreciation of The Toy Cart from the viewpoint of socilist realism.

Gawronski, A. Poczkathi dramatu indyjskeigo a Spraw Wplywow greckich / ed. by E. Sluszkiewicz. Uniejetnos'ci, Krakow : Polska Akad, 1946.

lxxii, 156 p.

In Polish with a preface in French.

On 'Mṛcchakaṭika'.

_____.Sprachliche untersuchungen ūber das Mṛcchakaṭika and das Daśakumāracarita. - Leipzig : [s.n.], 1907.

Study on the Mṛcchakaṭikā.

Ghatak, Jyotish Chandra. The Date of Mṛcchakaṭika from astrological data. *All India Oriental Conference* II; P. li.

______.*Journal of Dept. of Letters*. Calcutta University, XIV. p. 3.

Ghosh, Anjali. Critical study of the verse portions of Mricchakatika / by Anjali Ghosh.

Ph.D. thesis approved by the Gauhati University in 1983.

Glimpses of Sanskrit literature / ed. by A.N.D. Haksar. - New Delhi : Indian Council For Cultural Relations, 1995.

Contents : Śudraka Pp. 7, 108, 113-114, 116, 119, 132.

Goodwin, Robert E. Cārudatta in love, or How to appreciate *The Little Clay Cart*.

Paper presented at the 202nd Annual meeting of the American Oriental Society at Boston in April 1992.

Goswami, Satyan. Psychological study of the characters of Mricchakatika / by Satyan Goswami.

Ph.D. thesis in Hindi, approved by the Rajasthan University in 1987.

A History of Sanskrit literature [classical period, Vol. 1] / ed. by S.N. Dasgupta. - Calcutta : University of Calcutta; 1947. Pp. 239-248.

On Sudraka and his 'Mṛchhakaṭika'.

Horrowitz, E.P. The Indian theatre. - London : [s.n.], 1912.

Indian theatre : traditions of performance / ed. by Farley P. Richmond, Darius L. Swann and Phillip B. Zarill. - Delhi : Motilal Banarsidass, 1993.

Jain, Nemichandra. Indian theatre : tradition, continuity and change. - New Delhi : Vikas Publishing House, 1992.

Jhala, G.C. 'Cārudattam and Mṛchhakaṭikam' / by G.C. Jhala. *JBBRAS* Dec. 1952; Vol. 27 Suppl.

Keith, A.B. The Sanskrit drama : in its origin, development, theory and practices. - Oxford : [s.n.], 1924.

405 p.; 22 cm.

Reprinted lithographically in 1954, 1959 etc.

Contents : Pp. 127-142.

Authoritative study on Sudraka with chapters on

(1) The Precursors of Kālidāśa,

(2) The Authorship and age of the Mṛcchakaṭika.

(3) The Mṛcchakaṭika

(4) The Prakrits

(5) The Metres.

______Sanskrit-natak : udbhav aur vikas : Siddhanta aur prayog / tr. into Hindi by Udaybhanu Singh. - Delhi : Motilal Banarsidass, 1965.

Kellner, H.C. Einleitende Bemerkungen zu dem indischen Drama Mṛcchakaṭika. Zwickau, 1872. *In* Jahresb. d. Gymnasiums zu Zwickau.

Study of 'Mṛcchakaṭikā'.

Konow, Sten. Das indische drama. - Berlin : Watter de Gruyter & Co., 1920.

______tr. into English from original German by S.N. Ghosal. - Calcutta : General Printers & Publishers, 1969.

xcii, 213 p.

Krishnamachariar, M and Srinivasachariar. History of classical Sanskrit literature. - Delhi : Motilal Banarsidass, 1989.

Kulkarni, K.P. Drama and dramatists. - Satara : The author, 1927.

Kunhan Raja, C. Survey of Sanskrit literature. - Bombay : Bharatiya Vidya Bhavan, 1962.

Lēvi, Sylvain. Le Theatre indien. *Bibliotheque del' Ecolcdes Hautes Etudes* t 83 [Paris], 1890.

Analysis of the plot of 'Mṛcchakaṭikā'.

______'Le Theatre indein a Paris / by Sylvain Lēvi. *La Revue de Paris* ; 15 Feb. 1895; (Second Year, IV). Pp. 818-829.

In French.

Review of the play 'The Clay Cart' in French by 'L' Oeuvre theatre group.

______Le thēātre indien a Paris. *Revue de Paris;* 1895. Pp. 818-829.

Review on the production of Barrucand's French translation at Paris.

______The theatre of India / tr. from the French by Narayan Mukherji. - Calcutta: Writers Workshop, 1978.

Contents : *Sudraka* Pp. (Vol. I) 5, 8, 133, 173-187, 193, 240,274; (Vol. II) 30, 55, 69, 70, 128.

Mṛchhakaṭika. Pp. (Vol. I) 2, 133, 137, 175-187, 193, 204, 240, 241; (Vol. II) 55, 57, 59, 63, 66, 68, 69, 71, 84, 86, 87, 128.

Linguistic structure of Sanskrit drama : three - day seminar on Sanskrit drama held at Ranchi University from 24th to 26th March, 1982.

Papers presented on Rasa, Plot, Dialogue etc. with special reference to Śūdraka, Bhāsa, Kālidāsa.

Macdonell, A.A. India's past : a survey of her literatures, religions, languages and antiquities. - Varanasi : Motilal Banarsidass, 1956.

Mankad, D.R. The types of Sanskrit drama. - Karachi : Urmi Prakashan Mandir, 1936.

Marasinghe, E.W. The Sanskrit theatre and stagecraft. - Delhi : Sri Satguru Publications, 1989. - (Sri Garib Dass Oriental Series; No. 78).

Masterpieces of Indian literature (Vol. 3) / ed. by K.M. George. - New Delhi : National Book Trust, 1997.

Pp. 1967, 1195-1197.

McGraw - Hill encyclopaedia of world drama (Vol. 3) / ed. by Stanley Hochman. - 2nd ed. - New York : McGraw - Hill, Inc, 1984.

Mirashi, Vasudev Vishnu. Indological research papers (Vol.1). - Nagpur : Vidarbh Samshodhan Mandal, 1982.

xiv, 245 p.

Contains Article, on 'Mṛcchakaṭika' of Śūdraka.

_____ 'On the interpretation of a passage from the Mṛcchakatika' / by V.V. Mirashi. *Journal of Oriental Institute;* March - June 1965; Vol. 14, Nos. 3-4; Pp. 346-349.

Monier - Williams, Monier. Indian Wisdom. 4th ed. - London : [s.n.], 1893. Pp. 464, 471-74.

Study of 'Mṛcchakaṭikā'.

The Mrichchhakati (microform) : comedy with a commentary explaratory of Prakrit passages. - Calcutta : Education Press, 1829.

Mṛchhakatika : eka alocanatmak adhyayana. - Delhi : Eastern Book Linkers, 1985.

221 p.

Critical study of Śūdraka's Mṛcchakatika classical Sanskrit drama, fully bringing out the social conditions as found in the text.

Nyāyaratna, M. On the authorship of the 'Mṛcchakaṭikā'. *Proc. of the Asiatic Society of Bengal,* 1887. Pp. 193-200.

Pandey, Chandrabali. Śudrak : raja tathā kavi. - Varanasi : Motilal Banarsidas, 1953.

324 p.; 18.5 cm.

Pandey, Manju. Critical study of Mricchakatika / by Manju Pandey.

Ph.D. thesis in Hindi, approved by the Magadh University in 1986.

Parikh, J.T. Sanskrit comic characters. - Surat : Popular Book Depot, 1952.

Pathak, M.C. Sanskrit nāṭaka men atiprākṛta tattva. - Jaipur : Devanagar Prakashan, [n.d.],

18, 468 p.

Pati, Madhusudan. Sanskrit drama : essays in revaluation / by Madhusudan Pati. - Delhi : Amar Prakashan, [1991]

Contents : 'Mrichchhakatikam : thematic and tonal patterns' Pp. 27-46.

Pavolini, P.E. Il Carrcttod Arrgilla Conferenza. (Florence) *Rassengna Nazionale* Argilla, 1902, Vol. 24. Pp. 586-610.

On Mṛcchakaṭikā.

Poddar, Ram Prakash 'Date of Mṛcchakatika' / by Ram Prakash Poddar. *Journal of Gauhati University;* 1969; Vol. 20, No. 1, Pp. 25-31.

Pusalkar, A.D. Authorship and date of the Mṛcchakaṭika. *All India Oriental Conference* IX, Pp. 436-444.

______*Journal of the Andhra Historical Research Society, Rajamundry.* Vol. XI; Pp. 33-42.

Ryder, A.W. The Clay Cart. *Boston Transcript,* 1903, Nov. 21.

Contains selected passages in translation with study on The play 'Mṛchakaṭ ikā'.

Sahitya Akademi - New Delhi. The National bibliography of Indian literature. - New Delhi : The author, 1962-1990.

5 Vols.

Sarma, K.V. 'The Cārudatta and Mṛcchakaṭika : a reppraisal of their relationship' / by Satya Vrat *Visveshvaranand Indological Journal* / ed. by K.V. Sarma; Sept. 1976; Vol. xiv, No. II.

Sastri, Gaurinath. Sanskrit Sahityer itihas. - Calcutta : Sarasvata Library, 1969 ? [Aśvin 1376]

Satyavrat. 'The Carudatta and Mṛcchakaṭika' a reppraisal of their relationship' / by Satyavrat. *Vishveshvaranand Indological Journal;* Sept. 1976; Vol. 14, No. 2; Pp. 207-215.

Schuyler, Montgomery, *Jr.* A bibiliography of the Sanskrit drama. *Columbia University Indo - Iranian Series* (New York), 1906, Vol. 3.

Sethi, Atmaram. Anudit Hindi Sahitya : Vishishta grantha - suchi / by Atmaram Sethi. - Gurgaon : Indian Documentation Service, 1981.

Contents : Sanskrit (Pp. 1-624).

Sharma, Chitra. Sanskrit natakom mein samaj - chitran. - Delhi : Meherchand Lachhmandass, 1967.

Sharma, Viswanath. Critical study of Sudraka's Mricchakatika / by Viswanath Sharma.

Ph.D. thesis in Hindi, approved by the Rajasthan University in 1973.

Shekhar, I. Sanskrit drama : its origin and decline. - Leiden : E.J. Brill, 1960.

Pp. 26, 39, 64, 65, 106, 115, 117-21, 129, 135n 137-43, 148, 155, 156, 161, 172, 184, 185, 189.

Sundara Sastri, Panyam Śūdraka / by Panyam Sundara Sastri. - Mangalore : Bāla Sāhitya Maṇḍala, 1947.

ii, 191 p.; 18 cm.

Tirtha : the treasury of Indian expressions / ed. by Vijaya Ghose. - New Delhi : CMC Ltd. 1992.

Pp. 132, 207, 209.

Upadhyaya, Ramji. Sanskrit ke mahakavi aur kavya / by Ramji Upadhyay and Ram Gopal Misra. - Allahabad : Ramnarayan Lal Venimadhav, 1965.

Vardacharya, M.R. A study on Śūdraka's Mṛcchakaṭika [in Kannada]. *All India Oriental Conference VIII* (summaries); P. 37.

Verma, Jaynarayan and Gupta, Pushpa. Sanskrit Sahitya ka itihas. - Ghaziabad : Tarun Prakashan, 1991.

Verma, Mahendra Kumar. Critical and comparative study of Sudraka's Mricchakatika and Bhasa's Charudatta / by Mahendra Kumar Verma.

Ph.D. thesis approved by the Agra University in 1970.

Warder, A.K. Indian kāvya literature (Vol. 3). - Delhi : Motilal Bnarsidass, 1977. *Contains* : Śūdraka. Pp. 1-48.

Wells, Henry W. The classical drama of India. - Bombay : Asia Publishing House, 1963.

Wilson, H.H. Sur un drame indien : extrait du Calcutta Annual Register, et traduit par M. Dondey - Duprē fils. In *JA,* 1827, 1st Series, No. 10. Pp. 174-188, 193-209.

On Śudraka's 'Mṛcchakaṭikā'.

______. Select specimens of the theatre of the Hindoos / tr. by H.H. Wilson. - Calcutta : [s.n.], 1826-27,

3 Vols.

______. 3rd ed. - London : [s.n.], 1871.

2 Vols.

Treatment of love in Sanskrit literature. - Calcutta : [s.n.], 1929. Pp. 80-87.

Also contains critical study of Mṛcchakaṭikā.

Windisch, E. Uber das Drama Mṛcchakaṭikā and die Kṛṣṇalegende. *Bericht der phil-hist. Cl. der Kon. Sachs. Gesells, der* Wiss; 1885, [4]. Pp. 439-479.

Critical study of Mṛchhakaṭikā.

Winternitz, M. Geschisthe der Indischen literature (Vol. 3). - Praha, 1922.

______History of Indian literature (Vol. 3, Part - 1) / tr. into English by Subhadra Jha. - Delhi : Motilal Bnarsidass, 1963. Pp. 224-232.

Study of 'Mṛcchakaṭikā'.

15

Viśākhādatta

Visākhādatta is one of the most revered playwright of the classical Sanskrit thea tre. Flourished between 7th and 8th centuries, this ancient dramatist stood out above all for his purely political play '*Mudrā Rakṣasa*'.

From the prologue of this work, it could be known that he was son of the king Bhāskaradatta and grandson of Vateśvaradatta, a samanta or petty chief.

The dramatist himself is called 'Vishakhadatta' in six out of the nine manuscripts collated by K.T. Telang, but in the other three he is mentioned as Vishakhadeva and his father is called Prithu, the minister who was bestowed with the title of Maharaja.

On the strength of the variants that occured in the concluding verse of the play in the manuscripts, including Dantivarman, Rantivarman and (A) vantivarman.

The Avantivarman is employed to ascertain his date.

Some feels that Avantivarman might be the Maukhari king whose son married Harṣa's daughter, while other accepts him as the king of Kashmir (A.D. 855-83).

Scholar like Jacobi identifies the eclipse referred to in the play as that of December 2,860, when, he holds, Sura, the king's minister; had the play performed.

It has be added here that the author is referred to by Dhanañjaya in his '*Daśarūpaka*' and also by Abhinavagupta in his commentary on, Bharata's '*Nāṭya-śāstra*.

Therefore he can be placed probably between 750 and 850 A.D. As his exact date is controversial, but it is undisputable that he must have lived before 10th century.

Viśākhadatta remains immortal for his drama *Mudrarākṣasa*. His Mudrā - rākṣasa is a drama in 7 acts on the establishment of the Maurya dynasty in Magadha by Candragupta with the help of his minister Canakya by over throwing the Nandas and their minister Rākṣasa, who was finally won over by Cāṇakya for Candragupta. In this play, Nipunaka, the spy presents the signet - ring of Rakshasa to Chanakya. The ring is precious for Chanakya because with the aid of this ring he adopts a superb strategy to capture Rakshasa. That justifies the title of the play.

He excels in delineation of central character, ie, Chānakya. The play almost revoles around this historical figure and is rooted in one spot. Chanakya confine himself to his austere cottage. From here crafty Chanakya through his diplomatic skill, makes plans, devises, varied strategies, sends out spies, agents, provocateurs etc and subsequently achieves success. Throughout the length and breadth of the play he is shown as a ruthless minister-protagonist who has dedicated his life to the power-politics, but infact 'Chanakya' is in favour of the welfare of his kingdom, which he cannot be achieved until the Rakshasa is won over.

Vishakadatta again excels here in his rich poetic suggestion by introducing Lord Shiva's tāndava dance that infact reflects the fiery power, unhappiness, in one word, the inner state of Chanakya. He keeps his black tuft of hair united as a token of his vow of vengeance. He address to his audience in the second verse in his superb evocative style 'who wishes to keep uncoiled (ie keep his fury unsheathed') he further says 'The hair which was like a black cobra to the Nandas and which is like a line of black smoke rising from some hidden fire? But the same Chanakya in the concluding act of the play proclaims, he is actualy pinning for a life of quiet seclusion and selfless pieties.

In the words of modern scholar Abhiraj Rajendra Mishra '*Mudrārākṣasa*' is a marvellous play from the dramatic point of view. The dialogues are tremendously meaningful and the treatment of the rasas (sentiments) in superb. Chāṇakya, Chandragupta, Rākshasa and Malayaketu are the four mighty pillars of this drama. These characters, alongwith their peculiar individuality, seem to be alive and full of vitality. The playwright has achieved much success in popularizing even a difficult and complicated subject like politics. The absence of even a single female character makes this play distinctive. Another peculiarity lies in the absence of Vidūshaka or the traditional jester. The dramatic theme itself is so, convoluted and tricky and full of curiosity that the spectators never feel impatience. Every moment they remain alert, excited and eager to see the climax of the drama."

Regarding the language of the *Mudraraksasa*, the Sanskrit is classical, and the Prakrits number three, for, in addition to the normal Sauraseni and Maharastri, Magadhi is used by the Jain monk, by Siddhārthaka and Samiddharthaka as Candalas, by a servant and an envoy.

His poetry is precise, straight forward, written in lucid manner without any deeper poetic pursuits. With clarity and forcefulness he composed his verses keeping in mind the immediate dramatic purpose.

Chiefly used metres of this drama are Sardulavikridita (39), Sragdhara (24), Vasantatilaka (19), and Sikharini (18), the sloka occur 22 times. Other metres are sporadic, save Prakrit Āryas; they include Upajati, Aupacchandasika, Puspitagra, Praharsini, Malini, Mandakranta, Rucira, Vansastha, Suvadana (iv - 16), and Hariṇī.

It has rightly been observed by Prof. Biswanath Bhattacharya that nowhere the dramatist suffers from what is sarcastically called 'Kāvya-kaṇḍūḥ the vanity of parading one's poetic skill. ... He possesses the best of the qualities of a dramaturgist - the quality of complete self - effacement.

It has been acclaimed universally as a highly captivating play that was drawn out of a dry historical material. Besides it is devoid of the erotic sentiment, the Śringara rasa.

His all three dramas mentioned in the succeeding pages are historical which reflects his profound sense of history and intrinsive interest towards historical and traditional themes.

Mudra Rakṣasa is a verse drama, because the themes itself demands a poetry permeated with heroic (vira) rasa alongwith elements of terror (bhayānaka) and pīty (Karuna) etc. Thus, no particular sentiment is made here principal. Vira, Karuna, Raudra and Adbhuta, all these four sentiments are employed throughout the length and breadth of the play without clashing with one another.

According to Keith his diction is admirably forcible and direct; the martial character of his dramas reflect itself in the clearness and rapidity of his style, which eschews the deplorable compounds which disfigure Bhavabhuti's works. An artist in essentials, he uses images, metaphors, and similes with tasteful moderation; alone of the later dramatists, he realizes that he is writing a drama, not composing sets of elegant extracts.

Mudrārākṣasa is, however, objected to on the ground of its bad moral. It will be apt to quote H.H. Wilson who observes that its is a historical or political drama and represents a curious state of public morals, in which fraud and assassination are the simple means by which inconvenient obligations are acquitted, and trouble - some friends or open enemies removed. It is not, however, that such acts are not held in themselves as crimes, or that their perpetrators, if instigated by vulgar vice or ferocity, are not condimned as culprits; it is only when the commission of the crime proposes a political end that it is represented as venial, and is compatible with the possession of great virtues, and even with an amiable character."

Minakshi L. Dalal writes : *Mudrārākṣasa* is a drama mainly based on political conflict. In this matter, it differs from *Mṛcchakaṭika* for, the latter has also a political plot which only remains as a subordinate plot. It, therefore, provides good scope for the study of conflict in a theme which deals with something else than the usual theme of love. In a way, this play has a close resemblance to the theme of *Mahāvīracaritam* wiṭh political and strategic rivalry as its basic idea." The *History of Sanskrit Literature* by S.K. De and Dasgupta observes "There is enough martial spirit, but, there is no fondness for violent situations, no craving for fantastic adventures and no taste for indecorous afrightments. The action takes the form essentially of a conflict of wills, of game of skill, in which the interest is made to depend on the plots and the counter - plots of two rival politicians."

It is pertinent to mention here that alongwith the main conflict of in telligence, a great deal of psychological conflict is shown in case of Rākśasa and Candanadāsa.

On can find several cmmentaries of this finest nataka. Vateśvaramiśra, son of Gaurīpatimīsra of Miṭhila, attempted to give a double interpretation to this composition and to present it as a system of polity as well as a play. Dhundhirāja, son of Laksạmaṇa, wrote his commentary in the reign of King Sarabhoji of Tanjore in 1713 A.D. He furwishes a brief poetical introduction giving the story of the Nandas leading to the accession of Chandragupta and the events of the play. Other noteworthy commentaries are by Swāmi Saśtrī, a native of Ananṭasāgara or Solavandān, by T. Tarkavacaspaṭi, by Maheśvara, Vateśvara. Prakṛtācārya, Keśavaupadhyāya and Abhirāma, by Graheśvara, by J. Vidyāsagara, by Śarabhabhūpa. One can find a poetical epitome entitled 'Muḍrārākṣ asakathāsāra' by Ravikarṭana and a prose version of the story by Ananṭapandiṭā.

Though the subject matter is known to the audience, this political play does not looses its popular appeal. For its immense theatrical power, intellectual design and dramaic poetry, the play remains one of the masterpieces in the history of Indian drama.

Besides his only extant drama '*Mudrarakṣasa*', few scholars have even ascribed to him two more plays on the basis of literary evidences, namely '*Devi-Chandraguptam*' and '*Abhisarikavañchitakam*' (or - *bandhitaka*).

Abhisārikāvañchitakam

Synopsis

This sanskrit play is ascribed to Vīśākhadatta, quoted in the *Abhinavabhārati* of Acharya Abhinavagupta and the *Śṛngāraprakāśa'* of King Bhojadeva. In this drama, the heroine Padmāvatī by her clever impersonation of a huntress, ie, the role of an abhisārika, justifies the title of the play.

Based on the life - history of Vatsaraja Udayana of Kaushambi, ie, the popular Udayana - Vāsavadattā legend. The story revolves around Padmāvatī, who was charged with the killing of Udayana's son through Vāsavadatta. She assumes the role of a huntress to attract the attention of the king, Udayana and atlast regains her lost love by proving her innocence.

Devīchandraguptam

Synopsis

This was a historical drama that centred on Chandragupta, the son of Samudragupta and Devī Dhruvaswaminī.

Dhruvadevī, the heroine of the play was in her husband's camp with a small retinue where she was enjoying summer in the cool abodes of the Himalayan frontier. From here she is carried away by an unprincipled foreigner, a Śaka, by birth, and is much tormented to accept his hand.

Young Chandragupta, Dhruvadevi's husband forms a dramatic company and in the disguise of a courtesan approaches the licentious Śaka. By his political strategems, Chandragupta enables Dhruvadevī to escape and takes her place in a female garb. The Śaka prince is love-sick and becomes mad of his love to Dhruvadevī and complacency blinds him to the probable dangers from an offended enemy. Śaka prince allows himself to meet. The enemy in the disguise of Dhruvadevī in a secret chamber where he finally suffer for his follies.

The popularity of the theme is evident through its mention in the Banabhatta's *Harṣacharitam* and Rājaśekhara's *Kavyamimāmsā*.

No longer extant, the work is known only from citations in the *Nāṭyadarpana*.

Mudrā-rākṣasa

Synopsis

In this 7 acts drama, the crafty Chanakya, the minister of king Chandragupta of Pāṭaliputra, wins over Rākshasa the minister of the deposed Nandas to the side of the new king Chandragupta. I of the Maurya Dynasty. Thus the play is based on the revolution that placed Chandragupta, the Sandrakottos of Megasthenes on the throne in the early fourth century B.C.

Dramatis Personae

Chandragupta	...	The young king of Pāṭaliputra (Founder of the Maurya empire)
Chāṇakya	...	Chancellor of the Maurya empire (Pre ceptor of the King)
Rākshasa	...	Prime Minister of the former House of Nanda destroyed by Chāṇakya.
Malayaketu	...	A Prince; son of the King of the Mountains (Leading an army of invasion against Pātaliputra, in league with Rākshasa.)
Bhāgurāyaṇa	...	Supposed friend of Prince Malayaketu
Śārngarava	...	Chāṇakya's pupil.
Nipuṇaka	...	Emissary of Chāṇakya
Jīvasiddhi	...	Emissary of Chāṇakya
Siddhārthaka	...	Emissary of Chanakya
Samiddhārthaka	...	Emissary of Chāṇakya
Śakaṭa - dāsa	...	Friend of Rākshasa
Chandana - dāsa	...	Friend of Rākshasa
Viradhagupta	...	Emissary, Retainer, Courier of Rākshasa.

Priyamvadaka ... "

Karabhaka ... "

Vaihīnari ... Chandragupta's Chamberlain.

Jājali ... Malayaketu's Chamberlain

Śoṇottarā ... Maid - in - waiting of King Chandragupta

Vijaya ... Maid - in - waiting of Prince Malayaketu

Bhāsuraka ... Officer of Prince Malayaketu

Wife and Son of Chandana - dāsa, officers, Gendarmes, Retainers etc.

Plot :-

Act One :- In the first act, Chanakya, after having vanquished the Nanda dynasty tries to win over the Nanda Minister Rakshas in order to consolidate the newly founded Mauryan empire. As Rakshas is stubbornly loyal to his dead master's cause, Chanakya realizes that he has to win him over through guile. Therefore, he sent's henchmen, spies, and stooges to the court of Malayketu, the last of the allied Nanda princes, who with Rakshas' help make an effort to win back his father's kingdom.

A Tantric priest (actually a spy in disguise) comes to inform Chanakya that there remains three staunch friends of Rakshasa in the city - the Jain medicant Jivsiddhi who in reality is Chanakya's man, the scribe Shakatdas, and the jeweller Chandandas. One of them, Chandandas is still harbouring the banished Rakshas family, and to prove this he produces a signet ring of Rakshas which was found lying outside Chanandas's house.

Chanakya works out his plan of action on the basis of this ring. Eventually he sends his man Siddharthak to get Shakatdas to write unwittingly a letter that will incriminate Rakshas. He is to seal it with Rakshas' signet ring. Siddharthak is instructed to rescue Shakatdas from the gallow to which the latter is to be condemned shortly. Then he will present himself to Rakshas who is a certainly going to reward him and take him in his service. There after he is to make use of the sealed letter, and the reward which Rakshas shall give him. Consequently Shakatdas is publicly condemned to die, Jivsiddhi is thrown out of the city, and the third friend of Rakshas, Chandandas is summoned before Chanakya, who tries to force him to give up Rakshas's family. Chandandas being adamant, he is also condemned to death. If Rakshas' friends are willing to die for him reasons Chanakya, then Rakshas could do no less.

Act Two :- In the second act, Viradhgupta in disguise as the snakecharmer Jirnvish, returns from Kusumpur. Rakshas spy inform him that all of Rakshas' stratagems at killing Chandragupta have been foiled by Chanakya. Unfortunately the poison-maid has put an end to the Nanda King Parvateshvar instead of Chandragupta and other plans have also come to nought. He further adds the news of the capture of three friends of Rakshas who remained in Kusumpur. Suddenly one of them Shakatdas enters, followed by Siddharthak who has killed the executioners and rescued him from the gallows. Overwhelmed with joy Rakshas rewards Siddharthak by giving him some jewels which the Prince Malayketu had sent him earlier. He willingly takes Siddharthak into his service. Viradhgupta also breaks the news that tension has developed between Chanakya and Chandragupta. On hearing this, he instructs Viradhgupta to return to Kusumpur and tell the court singer Sthankalash Bhat to render inflammatory verses at the moment when Chandragupta and Chanakya openly disagree over an issue. Another spy Karbhak is also directed to bring back news of the cleavage. If Chanakya and Chandragupta quarrels among themselve then it will be much easier for Rakshas to overthrow the Mauryan dynasty and subsequently re-instate Malayketu.

Act Three :- (The Feigned Quarrel) In Chandragupta's court preparations are being made to celebrate the autumnal Kaumudi festival. But Chandragupta is perturbed because Chanakya has ordered him to stage a feigned quarrel in order to deceive Rakshas. Here comes the news that the festival has been curtailed by Chanakya. Chandragupta pretends to be annoyed and asks for explanation. Chanakya says that due to the warlike conditions prevailing in the country the festival has been cancelled. Sthankalash Bhat takes advantage of the situation and recites some sarcastic verses on kingship. These incite Chandragupta and he and Chanakya quarrel violently and Chanakya leaves in anger. Chandragupta having dismissed his guru, though polity and Chanakya demanded it, still feels guilty.

Act Four :- (Rakshas' Plans Mature) Karbhak returns from Kusumpur and reveals before Rakshas that Chanakya and Chandragupta have quarrelled. Rakshas suffers from a headache and Malayketu comes to visit him. After searing to avenge his family honour, he purposely overhears Rakshas's conversation, which is twisted to sinister proportions by his ever-ready companion Bhagurayana, actually a stooge of Chanakya. Suspicious of Rakshas Malayketu rushes in and demands why a war has not yet been declared. Surprisingly enough Rakshas supports the view because since Chanakya and Chandragupta have quarrelled, the time is favourable seeing opportunate moment. Malayketu excitedly gives orders for war to be declared and leaves. Now, Rakshas calls an astrologer to findout an auspicious hour for launching an attack. The only astrologer sitting outside is none other than Jivsiddhi, the Buddhist monk, who feigns a quarrel with Rakshas, and leaves in a huff telling Rakshas that he is traitor. Evening falls.

Act Five :- (The Forged Letter) Jivsiddhi and Siddharthak two of Chanakya's spies go on different missions to Malayketu's camp. In the camp Bhagurayana gives out passes to all who enter and leave, while rationalising on his need for money. Malayketu enters, puzzled over Rakshas' loyalty now that Chandragupta and Chanakya are estranged. He rides into the camp to find Jivsiddhi approaching Bhagurayana's tent - and he decides to hide and listen to the conversation. Jivsiddhi who knows that Malayketu is listening pretends to reveal that in reality it was Rakshas who had Malayketu's father Parvateshvar killed by the poison-maid and not Chanakya, and it was because of Rakshas who had wanted Jivsiddhi to further commit an even greater crime he had quarrelled with him. Malayketu is overwhelmed, and is willing to believe anything about Rakshas. At this juncture Sidharthak is led in to Bhagurayana because he tried to leave the camp without a pass. On being questioned about his errand he hands over the letter which Chanakya had entrusted to him earlier, and which had been written by Shakatdas. The letter is a message purportedly from Rakshas to Chandragupta promising the support of five of Malayketu's nearest allies to the Mauryan cause if they are hand somely rewarded. But on being given third - degree treatment, Siddharthak has purposely dropped a casket containing the jewels with which Rakshas had rewarded him for saving Shakatdas' life, and which Malayketu had originally given to Rakshas. Incensed Malayketu sends for Rakshas. Because of all this trumped-up evidence, and in particular with a letter written by his bosom friend Shakatdas, Rakshas can only blame fate and declare his innocence. He is denounced by Malayketu, who dismisses him and leaves to make immediate preparations for attack. Meanwhile he also orders that the five allied kings mentioned in the letter be tortured to death, thus defeating his own cause. Rakshas leaves the scene in grief and after pondering over his wretched fate, decides that the only honourable course open to him is to save his friend Chandradas from the gallows.

Act Six : - (The Mock Suicide) Generously rewarded by Chanakya Siddharthak enters and goes to meet his friend Samiddharthak. He tells Samiddharthak that after Malayketu had killed off his allies their armies fled, and then Bhagurayana and his friend took Malayketu prisoner. Soon after the imprisonment of Malayketu, Chanakya takes over the remnants of his army. News comes that Rakshas is on his way to Kusumpur to save his friend Chandandas. Siddharthak and Samiddharthak are to disguise themselves as Chandals and lead Chandandas to the execution grounds.

In the next scene Rakshas, to learn news of his friend Chandandas, goes to an abandoned garden outside Kusumpur. He comes upon a man about to hand himself, (actually Chanakya's another spy who is doing so under orders). When questioned, the man says he is taking his life because his friend. Vishnudas is going to burn himself to death on account of his friend Chandandas who has been codemned to the gallows. In anger, Rakshas unsheathes his sword and starts off to save his friend, but the man restrains him and advice him to leave his sword behind as the Chandals are heavily armed. He further suggests that if he is Rakshas, he only has to surrender himself in order to save his friend.

Act Seven :- Patliputra - Disguised as Chandals, Siddharthak and Samiddharthak lead Chandandas to the execution grounds. His weeping family follow behind. The moment he is about to be hanged Rakshas enters and restrains them, giving himself up as a hostage instead. Rakshas is led to Chandragupta's palace where a man with his face muffled confronts them. It is none other than Chanakya who explains to Rakshas that all the tactics used in defeating Rakshas were due to Chandragupta's desire to have him as his minister. Rakshas refuses the sword of office, but eventually (though reluctantly) he accepts when told that the life of his friend Chandandas depends on it. Thereafter, Chanakya orders that Malayketu be restored his hereditary kingdom, and that the war-elephants be set free. He ties up his loosened top-knot as his vow of defeating the Nandas fulfilled. Finally he leaves the palace for the penance grove, but their goes the people on the streets with their usual daily chores.

Mudrā - Rākṣasa in Performances

The Mudrā - Raksasa, literally the 'Signet of Rakshasa' is believed to have been first produced at Pāṭaliputra (Capital of India) at the Court of the Emperior Chandra - Gupta II (375 - 413 A.C.).

Some of the outstanding productions of this classic in recent times, in original Sanskrit and other languages, both Indian and foreign, are discussed briefly in the following pages.

One of the noteworthy presentation of the play in Sanskrit is of Sanskrit Ranga's production at Madras.

The Sanskrit Sahitya Parishad of Calcutta staged Visakhadatta's classic many a times. For the first time it was enacted by the members in (1919) [1327 (Bengali era)]. Then in 1930 [1338 (Bengali era)], the members of the Parishad were invited to Patna in the Six session of the All India Oriental Conference to stage the drama that was highly appreciated by the scholars and masses. The leading English daily '*Search light*' broughtout a review of this drama presented in its original form.

In 1340 (Bengali era), Sir Ashutosh Mukherjee, who was the President of the Seventh session of the All India Oriental Conference witnessed Parishad's production of '*Mudrarakṣasa*'. The play was a grand success.

The Assamese adaptation of the drama '*Mudrarakṣasa*' was written by Janardan Thakur in 1946. In this drama (appeared in print in the year 1953) Chanakya was depicted as a patriot and was highly inspired by Mura. Thakur's portrayal of Chanakya was quite different from the character of Chanakya of Visakhadatta *Mudrasakṣasa* or in D.L. Roy's play *Chandragupta*. Thakur followed the story of Roy's work. He however, wanted to show the patriotism of Chandragupta and to inspire the young generation against the British regime and was sucessful in this effort. The adaptation was staged many a time in Assam and was highly acclaimed.

The dramatis personae of the play were :-

Chanakya	...	Janardan Thakur / Anandachandra Barua.
Chandragupta	...	Dharanidhar Borgohain
Nanda	...	Nabin Chandra Barua
Madhavsena	...	Mukut Barua
Mura	...	Sivanath Goswami.

During the centenary celebration of the Calcutta University in 1957, the Post-graduate Department of Sanskrit presented the ancient classic that received wider acclamation from the distinguished scholars from all over India and abroad.

Mention should be made of Shastri Keshavram's Gujarati version of the ancient play '*Mudrarakṣasa*' in 1957 was staged more than once with grand success.

In Sanskrit, '*Chanakya - Vijayam*' was composed by Pandit Ramnath Mishra Sharma and the year of publication is not known. It contains five acts amongst which Act III comprises of three scenes and each of Act IV and V five scenes. There are nine male characters in it. This play was staged in Bhaubaneswar on the occasion of the All India Oriental Conference in October 1959.

Tirupati Venkata Kavulu (Divakain Tirupati Shastri) Chellapilla Venkata Sastry's Telugu rendering of '*Mudrarakṣasa*' was staged many a times in Andhra stage. This version contains seven acts, each comprising of seven scenes. Number of character is sixteen. Principal male characters numbering eleven and anxiliary one numbering five and is devoid of female characters.

An adaptation of *Mudrarakṣasa* was made into Punjabi by Sri Sukhraj Singh that focuses on the life of Chandragupta. This play in five acts and each act having five scenes was enacted more than once in Punjab and was well received.

Historical dramas are broadcasted from the All India Radio. Its Jaipur Centre produced the play that was directed by Prof. Hariram Acharya.

Thirty five years ago, ie, sometimes in 1963, Habib Tanvir directed '*Mudra Rakṣasa*' of Viśakhādatta in English and the version was rendered by P. Lal.

J.N. Kaushal wrote in 1975 issue of *Enact* that 'The political aspect of the play was boldly underlined in Habib Tanvir's production of this play in English a few years ago. Played against off-white wings and a back-drop designed by Alkazi. Tanvir created a live - wire atmosphere of political intrigues, spies, defectors and so on.

G.K. Bhat's Marathi translation of Vishakhadatta's '*Mudrarakṣasa*' was put on a stage based on the norms laid down by Bharata's *Natyaṣastra* by Vijaya Mehta.

For this play, the Sahitya Sangh was indebted to the famous choreographer Krishnan Kutty who adapted the mimetic repertoire of Kerala's Koodiyattam, the only surviving form of Sanskrit theatre in India. The music was composed by Bhaskar Chandravarkar who used a sizeable number of our indigenous instruments of the past. In this production, her use of the natyadharmi style was precise and well delineated. Though some stylized movements diminished the effect of the play, but her use of percussion music was very good and lightened the emotional tension of the scenes, wrote a drama critic. Those stoodout from the casts are

Chanakya	...	Chittaranjan Kolhatkar
Raksasa	...	Ravi Patwardhan
Chandandas	...	Ramachandra Kulkarni

It was at the instance of German theatre director Fritz Bennewitz that Vijaya Mehta directed 'Mudrarakṣasa' (1976) at Weimar with a German cast. In June 1976, a German production of 'Mudra Rakshasa' in the south of the GDR was given by the foreign audience a valid artistic status. It was a joint venture of Vijaya Mehta and East German director Fritz Bennewitz, the manager of the Weimar theatre presented at the German National Theatre.

Stage decorations were supplied by D.S. Godse from Mumbai; Franz Havemann and Ingrid Rahaus, Bhaskar Chandravarkar from the Poona Film Institute, and Konrad Aust were incharge of the music and the choric song suited with the milieu The great doyen of Maharashtrian set designers, D.G. Godse had a highly creative approach to set designing and lighting. He did a lot of work for the distinguished producer Vijaya Mehta. Dnyaneshwar Nadkarni observes : "It is enough to mention the sets and costumes he designed for her Natyasastra - inspired production of *Mudra raksasa and Sakuntala*. The entire setup conceived by Bharata as ideal for presenting a Sanskrit play was imaginatively duplicated on stage by the brilliant desiger. The forestage, the entrances and exits, the platforms all these were brought alive, as it were, after being in disuse for centuries.Godse and Mehta regularly went to the German Democratic Republic and played the same functions in German language productions of Mudraraksasa and Sakuntala as they did in the local pilot productions. We have, of course, no idea of how these productions were lit in the GDR but how fascinantnig those blonde actors and actresses look, made up and costumed as Raksasa or Sakuntala or Dushyanta. The indigenous character of the scenography here easily crosses the seas and reflects every detail of the original decor. It is the deep creative impulse in both versions which, I think, is responsible for this convincing demolition of national barriers".

Late Shri Dhirendra Kumar Parmar directed 'Mudraraksa' in Hindi version and was presented at the 'Kalidasa Festival' in 1978.

Mudraraksasa in performance

'Nandikar' the well known theare group from North Calcutta under thespian Ajitesh Bannerjee was founded on 29 June 1960. It presented Vishakhadatta's great classic Mudraraksa on 14 February, 1979 with veteran Sambhu Mitra as guest artiste in the role of Chanakya. The play was adapted and directed by Rudraprasad Sengupta.

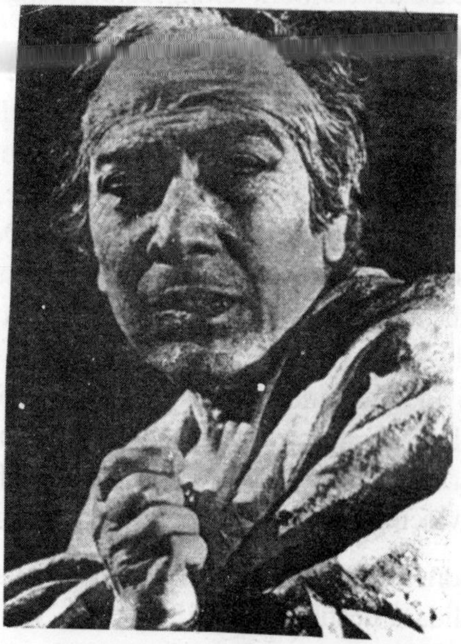

Shambhu Mitra as Chanakya in Bengali production of 'Mudraraksasa'

Nandikar's Bengali version of Viśakhadatta's 'Mudraraksasa'.

From left : Shambhu Mitra, Pilak Biswas, Nandita Ray Chaudhuri, Panchugopal De & Parimal Mukhopadhyay

To collect fund to establish a 'Bengali Natyamanch Samiti', two leading theatre groups of Calcutta namely Bohurupee and Souvanik staged the Bengali version of the Sanskrit classic. With an extraordinary skill, the doyen of Bengali theatre Shri Sombhu Mitra played the role of Chanakya. It is said that no other acting parallel to his excellent performance on the stage has been witnessed uptil now like him. Prof. Rudra Prasad Sengupta was the director of this venture.

In 1980, a Hindi version of Visakhadatta's *Mudraraksasa* was staged under the direction of B.V. Karanth for the National School of Drama. The play was also presented at the 'Kalidasa Festival'; Ujjain.

Scene from Vishakhadatta's Sanskrit drama Mudraraksasa ('The Signet Ring of Rakshasa') in Hindi, directed by B.V. Karanth in 1980.

Scene from Mudra Raksasa, Director B.V. Karanth

In collaboration with the Dept. of Public Relations and Cultural Affairs, Government of Haryana and Kurukshetra University, 'North Zone Theatre Festival' was organised from 1 - 7 Sept. 1986 in Kurukshetra. On 2nd September '*Mudraraksasa*' was staged in Hindi by the group 'Purvabhyas' of Lucknow under the direction of M. Salim Arif.

Inaugurated by K.S. Karanth, The 'South Zone Theatre Festival' was held in Mysore 14-20 Sept. 1986 in collaboration with the Directorate of Kannada and Culture, Government of Karnataka. On 17th Sept., '*Mudraraksasa*' was staged in Telugu under the direction of K.G.R. Gandhi and the troup was 'Kala Tarangini' of Vishkhapatnam.

At Delhi, the Malayalam version of *Mudraraksasa* was staged by the troupe the 'Root' of Trichur under the direction of Jos Chirmel on 25 November 1987 on the occasion of South Zone Theatre Festival at Madras in association with Tamil Nadu Eyal Isai Nataka Manaram. Madras. The same production was repeated on 16 January 1988 on the occasion of Natya Samaroha 87 (National Theatre Festival) sponsored by Sangeet Natak Akademi, New Delhi.

Mudraraksasa, directed by Jos Chirame (1987)

On 21 March1989, in the television serial 'Theatre through the ages', the drama *Mudraraksasa* was produced by the Calcutta T.V. Centre. Sri Sankha Ghosh was the tele-play director. This was an exciting exposition of Chanakya's political sagacity in the court of Chandragupta Maurya.

To suppliment and enrich the teaching programme a number of play - reading enactment sessions were organised followed by discussion with experts by the National School of Drama in the year 1991 - 1992. Vishakhadatta's '*Mudraraksasa*' featured in this programme.

As a part of theatre training in the National School of Drama, every year, the students in the second year, are introduced to Sanskrit classics - as text, and in performance. The various training inputs like study and analysis of a few selected Sanskrit plays, principles of Natyasastra, Indian aesthetics, understanding of Sanskrit theatre architecture, stylised acting, learning from witnessing traditional dance / theatre performances etc culminate in a public performance of a Sanskrit play production by students under the guidance of a teacher / director. In 1995, the second year students presented. 'Tridhara' : a performance of three Sanskrit plays - Kalidasa's *Abhijñanaśakuntalam* in Sanskrit, Bodhyana's *Bhagavadajjukiyam* and Vishakhadatta's *Mudraraksasa* in Hindi under the direction of Rita Ganguly, a senior faculty member of NSD and a well known classical singer who trained in several classical dance traditions. Held from 17-22 November, 1995, the five hour long performance in the specially erected Vikrisht Madhyam auditorium was aesthetically visualised and designed in corporating meticulously the various aspects of Sanskrit play production like stylised acting, music, spatial design etc.

Thus, an effort was made for the first time to capture the spirit and ambience of Sanskrit stage through a detailed study and research of various texts like Vastushastra, Shilpashastra and Manasara - shastra in consulatations with scholars, architects, designers and technicians.

Scenes from National School of Drama's production 'Mudraraksasa' in Hindi; Directed by Rita Ganguly (1995)

In 1996, '*Mudraraksasa*' was staged by Rangmandal from Bhopal under the able direction of Habib Tanvir at the National Theatre Festival in Calcutta, organised by Nandikar. The group handled this play of extreme linguistic sophistication with much ease. The two major casts of Chanakya and Raksasa sustained their intellectual vigour and the choric song suited witht he milieu.

Scene from 'Mudraraksasa' at the National Theatre Festival in Calcutta

The Manoj Joshi - Mihir Bhuta staged *Chanakya*, at the Kamani auditorium from June 19-21, 1998. The play, which has had over 119 shows in Gujarati and had also been staged in Calcutta too, has now been translated and produced in Hindi. The script took two years of intensive research before it took shape.

The two-and-a-half-hour play is being brought to Delhi by Hyphon Communications. Sunil Menon, organised the event, and Manoj Joshi played Chanakya and also directed the production.

With the shows in Delhi the group celebrated the silver jubilee of the Hindi version of the play.

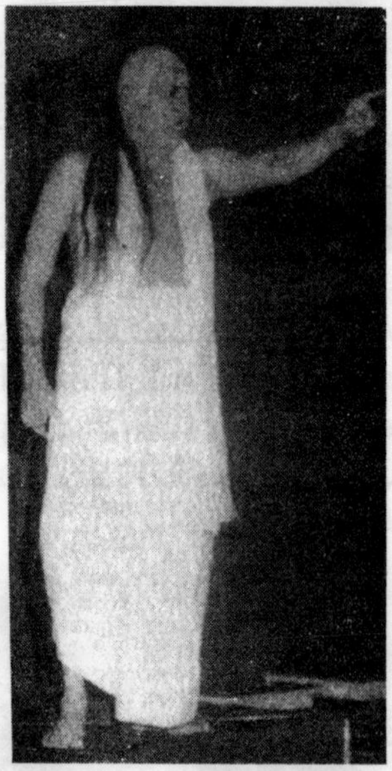

Supported by the Bharatiya Kala Kendra Trust, sponsored by the Bikalp drama group and Impressario - India, Naya Theatre of Habib Tanvir staged Vishakhadatta's fifth century Sanskrit classic in Hindi on 21 March 1998 at the Kamani Auditorium, New Delhi. A drama critic writes : The time tested Habib Tanvir formula of weaving Chattisgarhi folk dance, music and dialect into the play shows up to advantage in '*Mudra Raksas*' whose vast canvas is distilled down to a manageable scale by use of a "sutradhar" and a chorus to push the narrative along ... Tanvir's stragecraft is admirable. The entire cast moved like an well-oiled machine, entry and exit were splendidly calibrated to maintain a robust tempo, which for a play of this nature is quite an achievement. Ram Chandra Singh as Chanakya was outstandig. Endowed with a fine stage presence and powerful voice the handsome actor gained in stature as the play progressed, his trademark springy stride enabling him to criss - cross the stage. The major dramatis personae were :-

Chanakya	...	Ram Chandra Singh
Raksasa	...	Udai Ram
Mahananda	...	Yogesh Tiwari
The Jeweller	...	Chandan Das
Chandragupta	...	Anup Ranjan Pandey.

R.C. Singh (left) as Chanakya in Tanvir's 'Mudra Raksasa'

Costume Design of Mudra Raksasa

Cāṇakya

[Costume approximated from the painting depicting a minister, Ajanta Cave No. 17.]

[Two Executioners : The costumes visualised from the fresco of the royal procession, in Cave No. 17, Ajanta.

The Drummer : From another portion of a frieze procession in Ajanta Cave No. 17.]

Rākṣasa

[Costume visualised from Buddhist sculptures near Goli Village, Maharashtra]

[Candanadāsa : Costumes approximated from a citizen's dress, Ajanta Cave No. 17.

Candanadāsa's Wife : From Ajanta Cave No. 1

The son : From a painting in Cave No. 17 of a little boy.]

DRAMATIC WORKS : A BIBLIOGRAPHY

Text

Mudrārākṣasa. - Calcutta : [s.n.], 1831.

Mudraraksasa / comm. by Dhundhiraja; ed. by Kasinath Trimbak Telang. - Delhi : Nag Publishers, 1985.

375, 3 p.; 22 cm.

Mudraraksasa / commentaries 'Sudha' in Hindi and Sanskrit by Paramesvaradina Pandeya and Avanikumar Pandeya. - Varanasi : Chowkhamba Surabharati Prakahsan, 1991.

11, 406 p.

Mudrā rāksasa / ed. by Alfred Hillebrandt.- Breslau : Indische Forschungen 1912.

Mudraraksasa / ed. by D.V. Panta. -Calcutta, 1873. (Majumdar Series).

Includes the commentary of Dhundiraja.

Mudraraksasa / ed. by Jagadish Chandra Misra. - Varanasi : Chowkhamba Vidyabhavan, 1972.

Mudrārāksasa / ed. by K.H. Dhruva. - 3rd ed. - Poona : Oriental Book Agency, 1930.

Mudrārākṣasa / ed. by K.T. Telaṅga with Dhuṇḍhirājā's commentary. - 1884 (Bombay Sanskrit Series).

Mudraraksasa / ed. by M.R. Kale. - 6th ed. Delhi : Motilal Banarsidass, 1976.

various paginations; 21 cm.

-----. Delhi : Motilal Banarsidass, 1983

[394] p.; 22 cm.

Includes an English tr. by the editor & comm. of Dhundhiraja.

Mudraraksasa / ed. by Nirupama Vidyalankar. - 5th ed. - Meerut : Sahitya Bhandar, 1976.

Mudraraksasa / ed. by R.R. Deshpande. - Surat : Popular Book Store, 1948.

Mudraraksasa / ed. by Ramasankar Tripathi. - 2nd ed. - Varanasi : Visvavidyalaya Prakashan, 1971

391 p.; 21 cm.

Mudraraksasa / ed. by Satyavrata Singh. - Varanasi : Chowkhamba Sanskrit Series Office, 1973.

46, 350 p.; 18.5 cm.

Includes 'Sasikala' Sanskrit and Hindi commentaries.

-----. Banaras : Chowkhamba Sanskrit Series Office,

341 p.; 18.5 cm.

Mudraraksasa / ed. [with notes] by T. Tarkavachaspati. Calcutta, 1870 (Majumdar Series).

Mudraraksasa / ed. by Tarinish Jha. - 3rd ed. - Allahabad : Ramnarayanlal Veni Prasad, 1978.

Mudra-rāksasa / by Visakhadatta; ed. by Telang. - Bombay : Bombay Sanskrit series.

-----. 7th ed. - Bombay : Nirnaya Sagar Press, 1928.

Mudraraksasa/ ed. with a commentary and explanatory notes of the Prakrit passage. Calcutta : [s.n.] 1831.

157 p.

Mudrārākṣasa / ed. with a commentary 'Arthadyotanika' & a Bengali tr. by Aśvinīkumār Vidyābhūṣaṇ Bhaṭṭācārya. - Calcutta : Śāstra Pracār Press, 1917.

xxii, 295 p.; 21 cm.

Mudrārākṣasa / ed. with a commentary 'Cāṇakyacāturī' and a Bengali tr. by Haridās Siddhāntavāgiś Bhaṭṭācārya. - Nakipur, Khulna : The editor, 1928.

v, 471 p.; 19 cm.

Mudrārakṣasa / ed. with a commentary of Dhuṇḍhirāja. - Mysore : [s.n.], 1883.

Mudrārākṣasa / ed. with an introd., notes and English translation by Vāsudev Śāstrī Abhyaṅkar & Kāśīnāth Vāsudev Abhyaṅkar. - Ahmedabad : Nandlāl C. Bodivālā, 1916.

vi, [520] p.; 16 cm.

Mudrārākṣasa / ed. with an English translation, notes and various readings by

Moreśvar Rāmacandra Kāḷe. - 2nd ed. - Bombay : Sudhakar Press, 1911

[372] p.; 22 cm.

Includes a commentary by Dhuṇḍhirāja.

Mudrārākṣasa / ed. with Bengali & English translations, a Sanskrit commentary & Sanskrit by Śrīścandra Cakravartī. - Calcutta : Bhattacharya & Sons, 1908.

xxxvi, 508, [10] p.; 19 cm.

Includes appendices.

Mudraraksasa / ed. with commentary by J. Vidyasagar Calcutta, 1881.

Mudrārākṣasa / ed. with critical notes by Rāmacandra Bhaṭṭācārya. - Kalyanpur, Howrah : Pasupati Press, 1919.

viii, 187 p.; 21 cm.

Includes a commentary of Satīścandra Kāvyatirtha entitled 'Śīṣyabodhinī'.

Mudraraksasa / ed. with the 'Vimala' Sanskrit, Hindi and English commentaries and critical notes by Jagadisa Candra Misra. - Varanasi : Chowkhamba Vidyabhavan, 1985.

52, 508 p.; 22 cm.

'Mudrārakṣasa'. In Indische forschungen, no. 4 / ed. by A. Hillebrandt. - Breslau : [s.n.], 1912.

Mudraraksasa of Visakhadatta / comm. by Dhundhiraja; ed. with an English tr. by M.R. Kale. - Delhi : Motilal Banarsidass, 1983.

[394] p.; 22 cm.

Mudrārākṣasa or the signet ring / critically ed. with notes & translation by K.H. Dhruva. - 2nd ed. - Poona : Jagat Hitecchu Press, 1923.

xxiv, [304] p.; 21 cm.

Includes appendices and indexes.

Adaptations (Sanskrit)

Chanakya-katha / by Narayana Bhatta.

Chanakya-katha was composed by a Kerala scholar named Narayana Bhatta (A.D. 1559 - 1666) of Melaputtur. Most of his "prabandhas" or compositions was created for his Cakyar friend 'Ravi Nartake'. The latter produced a metrical version of the entire story of the drama.

Chanakya katha / by Ravinartake; commentary by Rajagopala of Madura (Madras - 1882). - Calcutta : Satis Charan Law, 1921. (Calcutta Oriental Series; 6).

One manuscript of 'Mudra raksasa' was found in Maharaja's palace library, Trivandrum that represents the work of Ravinartake who produced a metrical version of the entire story of the drama as well as the events that proceeded it. The version is 'Chanakya katha' and its manuscripts are obtainable in several manuscript libraries.

-----. Descriptive catalogue of the Maharajah's Palace Library Catalogue II.

p. 106.3 MSS. etc.

Ravi's work was published with a commentary by Rajagopala.

Chanakya-vijayam / by Pandit Ramnath Mishra Sharma.

5 Acts play in Sanskrit based on 'Mudraraksasa' of Visakhadatta' and was staged in 1959 at the All India Oriental Conference in Bhubaneswar.

Chanakya - vijayam / by Pandit Visweswara Vidyabhushan.

Pandit Visweswara Vidyābhushan's *Chanakya - vijayam* was composed in Sanskrit with the theme of intellectual victory of Chanakya against the powerful Nandas. He helped Chandragupta in acquiring the throne and overthrow the Nandas. It is a drama of national integrity composed in that dim past with a view to establishing a kingdom of joy and justice, peace and amity. Chanakya was depicted as indifferent to worldly prosperily was full of pity but of heroic nature and all the heroic qualities were found in him. The playwright was influenced by '*Mudraraksasa*' of Visakhadatta.

Mudraraksasa-natak-katha / by Mahadeva; ed. by V. Raghavan. - Madras : The University of Madras, 1946 (Saraswati Mahal Series, I).

'Maudraraksasa - nataka - katha' of Mahadeva is an excellent interpretation of the classical drama '*Mudraraksasa*'. For the common man, scholar presented the story of this complicated drama in a simple narrative form. In this prose version, he dealt with the story of the drama and incidents that paved the way for the main theme of the drama to take a precise shape.

Mudraraksasa - purvapithika or Mudraraksasa - purvasam - Kathanaka / by Ananta Bhatta.

In the middle of the 17th century A.D., Ananta Bhatta of Punyastambha on the Godavari and son of Tryambaka Pandita wrote '*Mudraraksasa - purvapithika or Mudrarakshasa - purvasam kathānaka*. A small work in prose that dealt with the introductory story leading up to the plot of Visakhadatta's drama.

Translations

Arabic

'Mudra raksasa' was translated by the Khalif of Bagdad into Arabic and the Arabs referred to its author Chanakya - as a 'Samaq of Indian [Source : Mudraraksasa / ed. by R.S. Pandit, Introd., p. 111.

Assamese

Mudraraksasa / tr. into Assamese by Rajnikanta Devasharma. Asam Sahitya Sabha, 1963.

Tr. mainly followed the edition of R.S. Walimbe, but at places, Telangs edition was also exploited.

Adaptation (Assamese)

Mudraraksasa-/ adapted into Assamese by Janardan Thakur. 1953.

Bengali

Mudrārākṣasa / ed. with a commentary 'Arthadyotanika' and a Bengali tr. by Aśvinīkumār Vidyābhūṣan Bhaṭṭācārya. - Calcutta : Śāstra Pracār Press, 1917.

xxii, 295.; 21 cm.

Mudraraksasa / tr. into Bengali by Hari Nath Sharma, 1860.

Not an absolute translation of the original classic, divided the drama in chapters and not in acts. The praise in glory of Lord Mahadeva is ignored and the kingdom Magadha has been thoroughly depicted in the purvapithika.

Mudraraksasa /tr. into Bengali by Jyotindra Nath Tagore. 1900 [1307 Bengali era]

A full-fledged literal rendering, highly influenced by Buddhist religion. He wrote this book in Champu style.

Mudrarakshasa / tr. into Bengali by Harishchandra Kaviratna. Calcutta, 1871 [1278 Bengali era].

In this authentic translation, a list of the kings and the kingdom was given in the introduction.

Mudrā-rākṣasa / ed. with Bengali and English translations, a Sanskrit commentary and annotations in English and Sanskrit by Sriscandra Cakravarti. - Calcutta: Bhattacarya & Sons, 1908.

508, x p.; 19 cm.

Includes appendices

Drama in seven acts.

Mudraraksasa / tr. into Bengali by Surendranath Deb. - Calcutta : Nabapata Prakashan, 1978.

This literal translation provides a short discussion of the drama, which acquaint us to the then prerailing social milieu and how the people of the remote past led their daily life.

Mudrarakshasa / tr. into Bengali by Utpal Bhattacharjee. - Calcutta : Modern Column, 1985.

Written in prose style.

[Mudrārākṣasa] In De, Sabitri. Sanskrit Sahityer anubad - dhara. - Calcutta : Chinmay Majumdar, [1983].

Contents : Mudraraksasa [Pp. 136-140].

Sanskrita Sahitya sambhar / ed. by Gaurinath Sastri & -- et.al. [Vol. 5]. - Calcutta : Navpatra Prakashan, [197-]

Includes Bengali rendering of Visakhadatta's '*Mudraraksasa*'.

Adaptation

Chandragupta / by Dwijendralal Ray. - Calcutta : Gurudas Chattopadhyay & Sons, [n.d.].

167 p.; 18 cm.

First published in 1911.

This famous drama of Dwijendra Lal Roy is an adaptation of the drama in Bengali. The subject matter of Visakhadatta was taken by Dwijendralal but he created some new characters in his drama. Rakshasa is absent here. The character of Katyana, the minister of Nandas is playwright's innovation. But there is a gulf of difference between Katyayana and Rakshasa. Chandragupta and Chanakya played important roles in Roy's work.

The latter also skillfully created many Greek characters such as of Helen, Selecus, Antigones etc.

English

Mudraraksasa / tr. into English by Aswini Kumar Bhattacharya. 1831.

Mudraraksasa / tr. into English by B.B. Goswami Calcutta, 1909.

Mudraraksasa / tr. into English by A. Hillebrandt. 1912.

Mudraraksasa / tr. into English by C.R. Devadhar and V.M. Bedekar. Bombay, 1948.

Includes Sanskrit commentary and explanatory notes.

Mudraraksasa / tr. into English by Deshpande. Surat : Popular Book Store, 1948.

Mudra - raksasa or the signet of the minister / tr. from the original Sanskrit by H.H. Wilson. - Calcutta : Society for the Resuscitation of Indian Literature, 1901.

xl, 137 p.; 15 cm.

Mudraraksasa / tr. into English by H.H. Wilson Oxford : Oxford University 1827.

First English rendering of the classic.

-----. *In*. Select specimens of the theatre of the Hindus / tr. into English by Horace Hayman Wilson. - 3rd ed. - New Delhi : Asian Educational Services, 1984.

Includes Mudra - Raksasam.

Mudraraksasa / ed. & tr. into English by Jivananda Bhattacharya and Ashutosh Vidyabhusasa. 1915.

Mudraraksasa / tr. into English by K.H. Dhruva. Baroda : Natun Vilas, 1900.

Mudraraksasa / tr. into English by K.T. Telang.

First published in 1884.

2nd ed. published in 1940.

Rakshasa's ring / by Visakhadatta; tr. into English. by M. Coulson. *In* Three Sanskrit play / tr. into English by Michael Coulson. - London : Penguin Books,

1981.

430 p.; 19 cm.

Includes Vishakhadatta's 'Rakshasa's ring'.

Mudraraksasa of Visakhadatta / ed. by M.R. Kale. - Delhi: Motilal Banarsidass 1976.

Text with English translation, notes etc.

Mudraraksasa / tr. into English with Dhundiraja's commentary by M.R. Kale.

First ed. is not available

2nd ed. published in 1911.

6th ed. published in 1976.

Mudrā - rāksasa or the signet ring / tr. into English from the original Sanskrit by Ranjit Sitaram Pandit. - Bombay : New Book Co., 1944.

xxvi, 227 p.; 21.5 cm.

Includes notes and index.

Mudraraksasa / ed. & tr. into English by R.S. Tripathy. - 2nd ed. Benaras : University Prakashan, 1971.

Mudraraksasa /tr. into English with Sanskrit commentary by R.S. Walimbe. Poona : [s.n.], 1960.

Mudraraksasa / tr. into English by S.C. Chakravarty. [s.l. : [s.n.], n.d.].

Mudraraksasa / by Visakhadatta, tr. into English with full annotation by S. Roy, 1918.

-----. enl. & rev. 3rd ed. by K. Roy, 1956.

Mudraraksasa / tr. into English by Van Buitenen.

Committee on Oriental Studies; Columbia University.

-----. New Delhi : Motilal Banarsidass, 1971.

First Indian Edition.

French

[Mudraraksasa] / tr. into French by V. Henry. - Paris : [s.n.], 1888.

German

Haag Friedrich - Beitrage Zum Verstandnis Von. Visakhadatta's Mudrarakshasa mit besondere Berilick Sichtigung des codex Perisinus Part I Burgdorf 186. pp. 12 & 19.

Mudraraksasa oder deskan zloos siegelring. Ausdem Sanskrit Zumersten Male and Mutrisch ins Deutsche libersct Zt. Von Ludwig Fritze, Leipzig, 1886.

133 p.

[Reclams Universal Bibliothek]

Gujarati

Mudraraksasa / tr. into Gujarati by K.H. Dhruva. Bombay : [s.n.], 1889.

240 p.

Published under the pseudonym 'Vanamali'.

[Meḷnī mudrikā athvā] Mudrārakṣasa / tr. by Kesavlal Haradas Dhruv. - 6th ed. - Ahmedabad : Vasant Mudraṇālay, 1925.

lxii, 140 p.; 18.5 cm.

First published in 1889.

Mudrā - rākṣasā / tr by Savāīlāl Chōṭālāl Vōrā. - Bombay : Oriental Printing Press, 1884.

xxiv, 151 p.; 21 cm.

Contains seven acts.

Mudraraksasa / tr. into Gujarati by Shastri Keshavram. Āhmedabad : Gurjar Grantha Ratna Karyalaya, 1957.

Hindi

Mudraraksasa / comm. by Brahmānanda Śukla. - Varanasi : Master Khilarilal, 1853.

Mudrārākśasa / comm. by Satyavratasiṃha. - Varanasi : Caukhamba Vidyabhavan, 1954.

Mudrārākśasa / comm. by Tariṇiś Jhā. - Allahabad : Ramnarayan Beniprasad, 1963.

Mudrārākśasa / tr. by Baladevaprasād Śāstrī. - Delhi : S. Chand & Co., 1950.

Mudraraksasa / tr. into Hindi by Bharatendu Harishchandra. 1875.

Mudraraksasa / tr. into Hindi by Bharatendu Harishchandra. - Varanasi : Nagari Pracharani Sabha, 1950.

The drama consists of seven acts, all the acts contains only one scene. Twenty male and three female characters dominate the drama. Such type of drama is not seen in Hindi literature. Bharatendu offered this drama to the king Sivaprakash, a great patron of literature & art.

Mudrārākśasa / tr. by Bharatendu Hariścandra. - Patna : Khadgavilāsa Press, 1893.

Mudrā - rākṣasa / tr. from Sanskrit by Bhāratendu Hariścandra. - Agra : Sāhitya Ratna Bhaṇḍar, 1925.

182 p.; 18.5 cm.

Mudrārākśasa / tr. by Bhāratendu Hariścandra. - Agra : Sahitya Ratna Bhandar, 1933.

Mudrārākśasa / tr. by Bharatendu Hariścandra; ed. by Sureścandra Gupta. - Delhi : Hindi Sahitya Sansar, 1963.

Mudrārākśasa / tr. by Bharatendu Hariścandra. - 4th ed. - Jullandhar : Hindi Bhawan, 1950.

Mudrārākśasa / tr. by Hardayālusiṃha. - New Delhi : Sāsta Sāhitya Mandal, 1955.

Mudraraksasa / tr. into Hindi by Jaikishan Prasad. - Allahabad : Bharati Bhandar, Leader Press, 1954.

This historical cum political drama depicts the struggle and victories of Chandragupta Maurya of Magadha empire. The translator composed the drama in just four acts, as against the original Sanskrit containing Seven acts. Jaikishan Prasad's first act has two scenes, the second act contains ten, the third comprises of nine scenes. The male characters are 21 in number and 18 female characters have been included in the drama.

Mudrārākśasa / tr. by Kanakalāla Śarmā. - Varanasi : [s.n.], 1936.

Mudraraksasa / ed. by Pushpa Gupta. - Delhi : Eastern Book Linkers, [n.d.]

xlviii, 414 p.; 22 cm.

Mudrārākśasa / tr. by Rāmaśankara Tripāthī. - Varanasi: Viswavidyalaya Prakashan, 1971.

Mudrārākśasa / tr. by Rāngeya Rāghava. - 2nd ed. - Delhi: Rajpal & Sons, 1960.

Mudraraksasa / tr. into Hindi by Rangeya Raghava. [Delhi ?] : Rajpal & Sons,

1957.

This is a seven act play and each act having only one scene. Eighteen male 13

Kannada rendering of the classic.

Maithili

Mudrārāksasa / tr. by Sudhākar Jhā. Śāstrī. - 2nd ed. - Darbhanga : Maithili Mandir, 1970.

xxvi, 144 p.; 18 cm.

Tr. from the original Sanskrit.

Malayalam

Mudrārākṣasa / tr. by Kaṇṇampuḷa K.S. Kṛṣṇa Vāriyar; foreword by R. Nārāyaṇa Paṇikkar. - Trivandrum : S.R. Press, 1949.

156 p.; 19 cm.

Mudrārākṣasa / tr. by M. Udaya Varma Rāja. - Trivandrum : N.S.S. Press, 1933.

114 p.; 23 cm.

Marathi

Kautilya / by Visakhadatta; tr. into Marathi by Narayan Kale. - Bombay : Popular Book Depot, 1961.

68 p.

Mudraraksasa / tr. into Marathi by K.S. Rajvade; rev. by K.S. Chiplonkar and ed. by S.P. Pandit. Bombay : [s.n.], 1947.

Adaptation (Marathi)

Islāmpūrkar, Vāman Śāstri. Arya Cāṇakya / by Vāman Śāstrī Islāmpūrkam. - Bombay : Vāsudev Moreśvar Potdar, 1890.

xlvi, 275 p.; 18 cm.

Novel based on Viśākhadatta's famous play 'Mudrārākśasa'.

Nepali

Mudrārāksasa / tr. into Nepali by Bhavānīdatta Pāṇḍe. 1833.

Oriya

Mudraraksasa / tr. by Bhagirathi Nepak. - Cuttack : Orissa Book Store, 1975.

Mudrārākṣasa / tr. by Mṛtyuñjaya Ratha. - Cuttuck : The translator, 1910.

120 p.; 17 cm.

Punjabi

Chandragupta / tr. of Mudraraksasa into Punjabi by Sukhraj Singh, 1942.

This contains five acts and each act comprises of five scenes. Staged more than once with success, the drama primarily depicts the life of Chandragupta.

Mudrārākśasa / tr. by Śamśer Singh 'Aśok'. - Lahore : Ātmā Rām & Sons, 1945.

xxii, 132 p.; 18.5 cm.

Russian

Mudraraksasa / tr. into Russian by I.D. Serebrykov. 1953 (Soviet Indology Series; No. 8).

Tamil

Mudrārākṣasa / tr. by E.K. Naṭēśa Śarma. - Madras : Pustak Nilayam, 1950.

xxxvi, 148, [9] p. : ill.; 21 cm.

Includes index.

Mudrārākṣasa / tr. by V. Śrīṇivāsa Śāstri & T. Śrīṇīvāsācāri. - Madras : Shakti Karyalayam, 1948.

135 p.; 18.5 cm.

Telugu

Mudrārākṣasa / tr. by Susarla Anantarāvu. - 2nd ed. - Madras: V. Ramaṇayya Bros., 1930.

116 p.; 18 cm.

Tr. from original Sanskrit.

Mudraraksasa / tr. into Telugu by Tirupati Venkata Kavulu (Divakain Tirupati Shastri) Chellapilla Venkata Sastry. East Godavari District : Venkateswara Publications Kadiyam, 1908.

Mudrārākṣasa / tr. by Tirupati Veṅkaṭēśvara Kavulu [i.e.] Divākarla Tirupatiśāstri. & Ceḷḷapiḷḷa Veṅkataśāstri.-Kadiyam: Ceḷḷapiḷḷa Veṅkaṭaśāstri & Sons, 1953.

122 p.; 22.5 cm., First appeared in 1908.

Urdu

Mudraraksasa / tr. into Urdu by Munavvar Lucknawi. - Aligarh: Anjuman Taraqqi Urdu (Hind), [n.d.]

264 p.; 17 cm.

BIO - CRITICAL NOTICES

Adya Rangacharya. Drama in Sanskrit literature. - Bombay : Popular Prakashan, 1967.

Pp. 60, 91, 165 - 172.

Aggarwal, H.R. A Shert history of Sanskrit literature. - 2nd rev. ed. - Delhi : Munshiram Manoharlal, 1963.

Contents :

(Visakhadatta. P. 182)

Antarkar, W.R. On the sources of the plot of the Mudra - Raksasa' / by W.R. Antarkar. *Journal of the University of Bombay* (New Series); Oct. 1969; Vol. 38, No. 74; Pp. 19 - 25.

Aufrecht, Theodor. Catalogus catalogorum. - Weisbaden : Franz Steiner Verlag Gmb. H, 1962.

2 Vols.; 26 cm.

Banerji, Sures Chandra. A Companion to Sanskrit literature . - Delhi : Motilal Banarsidass, 1971.

Sanskrit Sahityer itihas. - Calcutta : The Dacca Students Library, [1970 ?]

In Bengali.

Bansal, Santosh. Mudraraksasa : a historical and critical study / by Santosh Bansal.

Ph.D. thesis in Hindi, approved by the Agra University in 1968.

Bhat, G.K. Sanskrit drama :problems and puspectives. - Delhi : Ajanta Publications, 1985.

Bhatt, S.C. Drama in ancient India. - New Delhi :Amrit Book Co., 1961.

Bhattacharya,Bimanchandra. Sanskrit Sahityer ruprekha. - 5th ed. - Calcutta : Vidyodaya Library Pvt. Ltd., 1972.

Bhattacharya, Biswanath. Sanskrit drama and dramaturgy. - Delhi :Sharada Publishing House, 1994.

Chakravarti, Chintaharan. [Mudraraksasapurvasamkathanaka] *Indian Historical Quarterly*; Dec. 1946; Vol. 22, No. 4; Pp. 320-322.

Review of book published by the Deptt. of Sanskrit University of Madras in 1945. (Ganga Oriental Series; 3)

Chandra Prakash. Study of Mudraraksasa according to Natyasastra /by Chandra Prakash.

Ph.D. thesis in Hindi, approved by the Avadh University in 1984

Comparative Indian literature / ed. by K.M. George. - Trichur : Kerala Sahitya Akademi, 1984.

Pp. 565 - 566.

The Cultural heritages of India [Vol. V] / ed. by Suniti Kumar Chatterji. - rev. ed. - Calcutta : The Ramakrishna Mission Institute of Culture, 1978.

P. 241, 251.

Dalal, Minakshi L. Conflict in Sanskrit drama. - Bombay : Somaiya Publications Pvt. Ltd., 1973.

Contents : Vishakhadatta. Pp. 211 - 220.

Dange, Sadashiv A & Dange, Sindhu S. Critiques on Sanskrit dramas. 2nd rev. ed. New Delhi : Aryan Books International, 1994.

Deshpande, R.R. Who is the hero of Mudrārākṣasa ? *All India Oriental Conference XV;* P. 31.

Devasthali, G.V. Introduction to the study of Mudraraksasa / by G.V. Devasthali. - Bombay : Keshav Bhikaji Dhavale, 1948.

Dictionary of oriental literatures (Vol. II) : South and South - East Asia. Delhi: Vikas Publishing, 1975.

Encyclopaedia of Indian literature. - New Delhi : Sahitya Akademi, 1987 - 1994.

Pp. 828, 1102, 1106, 1108, 2434, 2771, 4586 - 87.

Gaidhani, M.G. Mudrārākṣasa and Arthaśāstra. *All India Oriental Conference XV*; P. 31.

Ganapathi Rao, S. 'Mudraraksasa nataka' /by S. Ganapathi Rao. *Journal of Tanjore Saraswathi Mahal Library;* 1963; Vol. 17, No. 1;

Pp. 37-47 & 1963; Vol. 17 No. 2; Pp. 1-4.

Garg, Ganga Ram. An Encyclopaedia of Indian literature. - Delhi : Motilal Publishers, 1982.

Pp. 250 - 252, 496 - 497.

Glimpses of Sanskrit literature / ed. by A.N.D. Haksar. - New Delhi: Indian Council for Cultural Relations, 1995.

Contents : Viśakhadatta Pp. 8, 61, 108, 109, 115, 116.

Gothawal, Santosh. Mudraraksasa : a study / by Santosh Gothawal.

Ph.D. thesis in Hindi, approved by the Rajasthan University in 1976.

Jain, Nemichandra. Indian Theatre : tradition, continuity and change. - New Delhi : Vikas Publishing House, 1992.

Joshi, Kunj Vihari. Mudraraksasa : a critical study / by Kunj Vihari Joshi.

Ph.D. thesis approved by the Kurukshetra University in 1984.

Kaushal, J.N. 'Last month in Delhi' / by J.N. Kaushal *Enact* Nov. - Dec. 1975, No. 107 - 108; Contains brief synopsis of 'Mudrar Raksasa' in English.

Keith, A. Berriedale. [About the date of Mudraraksasa] *JRAS* 1909. Pp. 145 f.

Keith, A. Berriedale. The Sanskrit drama in its origin, development, theory and practice. - Oxford : OUP, 1924.
405 p.; 22 cm.

-----. The Sanskrit drama in its origin, development, theory and practice. London :Oxford University Press, 1954.
Contents 'Viśakhādatta'. Pp. 204 - 212.

Keith, A. Berriedale Sanskrit - natak : udbhav aur vikas : siddhanta aur prayog / tr. into Hindi by Udaybhanu Singh. - Delhi : Motilal Banarsidass, 1965.

Krishnamachariar, M. and Srinivasachariar. History of classical Sanskrit literature. - Delhi : Motilal Banarsidass, 1989.

Lal, P. 'The Signet ring of Raksasa' /by P. Lal. *Illustrated Weekly India* ; 9 July 1967; Vol. 88, No. 23; P. 29.

Lēvi, Sylvain. The theatre of India / tr. from the French by Narayan Mukherji. - Calcutta :Writers Workshop,1978.
Contents : Viśākhadatta Pp. (Vol. I) 133, 203 - 206, 241.

Mudrārākṣasa. Pp. (Vol. I) 2, 114, 119, 203 - 206, 241; (Vol. II) 62, 66, 68, 84.

Macdonell, A.A. India's past :a survey of her literatures, religions, languages and antiquities. - Varanasi : Motilal Banarsidass, 1956.

Madan, A.P. 'Was the dramatist Viśākhadatta, a contemporary of Dantidurga' / by A.P. Madan. *Vishveshvarananda Indological Journal / ed. by S. Bhaskaran Nair; June - Dec., 1982;* Vol. XX, Nos I-II. Pp. 81 - 90.

Marasinghe, E.W. The Sanskrit theatre and stagecraft. - Delhi : Sri Satguru Publications, 1989. - (Sri Garib Dass Oriental Series; No. 78).

Master pieces of Indian literature [Vol. 2]. - New Delhi : National Book Trust, 1997.

Contents : Mudraraksasa - Vishakhadatta / Vishakhadeva. Pp. 1198 - 1200.

McGraw - Hill encyclopaedia of world drama (Vol. 3) / ed. by Stanley Hochman. - 2nd ed. - New York : McGraw - Hill, Inc., 1984.

Paradkar, M.D. 'Dhundhiraja : the commentation of the Mudraraksasam' / by M.D. Paradkar. *Journal of the Ganganath Jha Kendriya Sanskrit Vidyapeeth;* 1973; Vol. 29, Nos. 1 - 4 ; Pp. 384 - 394.

Pati, Madhusudan. Sanskrit drama : essays in revaluation / by Madhusudan Pati. - Delhi : Amar Prakashan, [1991]

Contents : 'Mudrārāksasam : poetry and characterisation'. Pp. 67 - 86.

Pathak, M.C. Sanskrit nāṭaka meṅ atiprākṛta tattva. - Jaipur : Devanagar Prakashan, [n.d.].

18, 468 p.

Prasad, Indu Bala. Critical study of Mudraraksasa / by Indu Bala Prasad.

Ph.D. thesis in Hindi, approved by the Magadh University in 1975.

Rangachar, S. On a stanza of The Mudrarakṣasa : miscellany. *Indian Historical Quarterly* June 1941; Vol. 17, No. 2; Pp. 255 - 257.

Rapson, E. [On Viśakhadatta]. *JRAS,* 1900.

Ruben, Walter. Der Sinn des Dramas 'Das Siegel und Rakshasa'. - Berlin, 1956.

Walter Ruben (1899-1982)

Walter Ruben was born in Hamburg on 26-12-1899. Already as a student he was interested in ancient history, and in 1915 he started taking private Sanskrit lessons from the Norwegian Indologist Sten Konow. Konow also advised him to study Indology after his return from the First World War. In 1919 Ruben went to Bonn, and later to Berlin, to study Indology under H. Jacobi and H. Luders. He obtained his doctorate in 1924. He was the Director of the Institute of Indian Studies at the Humboldt University. He worked extensively on Indian drama. Der Sinn des Dramas 'Das Siegel und Rakshasa' ("The meaning of the drama Mudrarakshasa"), Berlin 1956 is an important work of this period.

Sahitya Akademi - New Delhi : The National bibliography of Indian literature. - New Delhi : Theauthor, 1962 - 1990.

5 Vols.

Sastri, Gaurinath. Sanskrit sahityer itihas. - Calcutta :Sarasvata Library, 1969? [Aśvin 1376]

Satyavrat. A Note on the date of Mudrārākṣasa / by Satyavrat *Vishveshvaranand Indological Journal* / ed. by Virendra Sharma.; June - Dec. 1984; Vol. XXII; Nos. I - II, Pp. 214-217.

Sethi, Atmaram. Anudit Hindi Sahitya : Vishishta granthasuchi / by Atmaram Sethi. - Gurgaon : Indian Documentation Service, 1981.

Contents : Sanskrit (Pp. 1 - 624).

Shekhar, I. Sanskrit drama : its origin and decline. - Leiden : E.J. Brill, 1960.

Pp. 138, 142, 143, 148, 156, 162, 171, 189.

Shukla, Chandrakant. Literary study of Mudrarakṣasa /by Chandrakant Shukla.

Ph.D. thesis in Sanskrit approved by the K.S. Darbhanga University in 1972.

Shukla, Chandrakant. Viśākhadatta and his Mudrārākṣasa. 1982.

Sohoni, S.V. 'On Viśākhadatta's Devīcandragupta' /by S.V. Sohoni. *Annals of the Bhandarkar Oriental Research Institute, 1981;* Vol. LXII, Nos. I-IV.

Pp. 157 - 168.

Tirtha : the treasury of Indian expressions / ed. by Vijaya Ghose. - New Delhi :CMC Ltd., 1992. Pp. 132, 208.

Treatment of pathos in Sanskrit drama / ed. by Pushpendra Kumar. - Delhi : Nag Publishers, 1981.

Verma, Jaynarayan and Gupta, Pushpa. Sanskrit sahitya ka itihas. - Ghaziabad : Tarun Prakashan, 1991.

'Viśākha - Dattā's Mudrā - Rākṣasa. *Annals of the Bhandarkar Oriental Research Institute;* 1944, Vol. XXV, P. 260.

Review of English tr.by R.S. Pandit from the original Sanskrit.

Warder, A.K. Indian kāvya literature (Vol. 3). - Delhi : Motilal Banarsidass, 1977.
Contents : Viśākhadatta. Pp. 257 - 278.

Wilson. Theatre of the Hindus. Vol. II. P. 159.

Winternitz, M. History of Indian literature (Vol. 3) / tr. from German into English by Subhadra Jha. - Delhi : Motilal Banarsidass, 1985.

❑❑❑

